REVISED

Month-By-Month

WHAT TO DO EACH MONTH TO HAVE A BEAUTIFUL GARDEN ALL YEAR

GARDENING
IN OHIO

Published by Cool Springs Press, a Division of Thomas Nelson, Inc.,
P. O. Box 141000, Nashville, Tennessee, 37214.

McKeown, Denny.
      Month-by-month gardening in Ohio : what to do each month to have a
      beautiful garden all year / Denny McKeown and Thomas L. Smith—Rev. ed.
            p. cm.
      Includes bibliographical references and index.
      ISBN 1-59186-244-2 (pbk.)
      1. Gardening—Ohio. I. Smith, Thomas L. II. Title.
SB453.2.O3M386 2005
635'.09771–dc22

                              2005025225

First Printing Revised Edition 2006

Printed in Singapore
10 9 8 7 6 5 4 3 2 1

Managing Editor: Billie Brownell
Horticultural Editor: Dr. Ken Tilt; Jenny Andrews; Troy Marden
Designer: James Duncan, James Duncan Creative
Production Artist: S.E. Anderson

On the cover: Chrysanthemum 'Pink Procession', photographed by Liz Ball

Visit the Cool Springs Press website at www.coolspringspress.net

PHOTOGRAPHY AND ILLUSTRATION CREDITS

ILLUSTRATIONS
Bill Kersey, Kersey Design

PHOTOGRAPHY
Thomas Eltzroth: pages 7 (yarrow, top of page); 13 (gerbera daisy, top of page, and primrose, bottom of page); 28; 30; 35; 44; 47; 55; 65 (tomato collection, top of page); 67; 79; 84; 91 (grass close-up, top of page, and perennial rye landscape, bottom of page); 102; 112; 114; 117 (aster, top of page); 119; 133; 137; 143 (hybrid tea 'Peace', top of page); 146; 154; 157; 169 (hypericum, top of page); 171; 172; 182; 195 (trees underplanted with annuals landscape, bottom of page); 197; 204; 209; 218; 221(morning glory, top of page, and impatiens border, bottom of page); 225; 228; 239; 240; 242; 247 (Japanese iris landscape, bottom of page); 251; 260; 263; 267
Neil Soderstrom: pages 18; 24; 48; 57; 72; 74; 86; 122; 126; 130; 134; 140; 148; 150; 153; 166; 184; 187; 188; 193; 198; 226; 245; 264
Jerry Pavia: pages 22; 27; 37; 39 (dahlia, top of page, and iris landscape, bottom of page); 42 (tulips, muscari, and birch); 117 (perennial bed, bottom of page); 139; 145; 158; 164; 180; 192; 210; 223
Liz Ball and Rick Ray: pages 32; 59; 63; 65 (harvest bench, bottom of page); 121; 143 (rose courtyard, bottom of page); 160; 169 (spring azalea landscape, bottom of page); 195 (ginkgo, top of page); 213; 214; 216; 232; 237; 247 (water lily, top of page); 256; 259
Dency Kane: page 7 (pansy, middle of page)
Andre Viette: page 235
Netherlands Bulb Association: page 52

REVISED EDITION

Month-By-Month™

WHAT TO DO EACH MONTH TO HAVE A BEAUTIFUL GARDEN ALL YEAR

GARDENING IN OHIO

DENNY McKEOWN &
THOMAS L. SMITH

COOL
SPRINGS
PRESS

Nashville, Tennessee
A Division of Thomas Nelson, Inc.
www.ThomasNelson.com

DEDICATION

I would like to dedicate this book to my three children—Molly, Christopher, and Jenny—for making me very proud to be their father and for providing Grandpa Denny with fantastic grandkids. I would also like to dedicate this book to Pat and the positive effect she has had on my life. Many, many thanks and lots of love to all of you.

—Denny

This book is dedicated to all those people who have allowed me the privilege of sharing my passion and knowledge of gardening over the past four decades. I am particularly honored to have worked with thousands of students through the Horticulture and Communiversity Programs (a continuing education program) of The University of Cincinnati. Exposing people to the joys and excitement of discovery is as spine-tingling and rewarding today as it was when I first started. Nature is full of surprises....

—Tom

ACKNOWLEDGEMENTS

I would like to thank all of my industry peers, both past and present, who have shared and continue to share their knowledge and expertise. A thank you goes out to Infinity Broadcasting Company for affording me the opportunity to spread the gardening word via the radio.

—Denny

I extend a special thanks to the current horticulture team and grounds management at Spring Grove Cemetery and Arboretum in Cincinnati, Ohio, and to the teams over the past four decades. The horticultural knowledge gained from a one hundred and fifty year old garden is a horticulturist's dream. I would like to thank Denny and Cool Springs Press for the opportunity to work with them and to share my horticulture knowledge.

—Tom

CONTENTS

INTRODUCTION

In Ohio, like the rest of the Midwest, gardening can be very challenging on a monthly calendar. We've seen spring arrive as early as mid-February and as late as mid-April. This book gives advice and dos and don'ts based on the average. Always let the weather dictate what to do and what needs to be done each month.

This revised edition continues to use some of the information from another great author, Liz Ball. Liz is a horticultural writer, photographer, researcher, and teacher who has written and contributed to many gardening books. With all these qualifications, we felt it would be a natural fit to incorporate Liz's knowledge with our combined efforts and experience.

THE BENEFITS OF A GARDENING SCHEDULE

Successful gardening involves being willing to make time when it is time to do certain tasks in the garden. Caring for plants is a team effort, and the other member of the team, Mother Nature, is extremely organized. If we are to have success, we must cooperate with her schedule, although experience teaches that it is not as rigid a schedule as it may seem.

Over time, gardeners learn where there is flexibility and forgiveness in the rapid progression of the

days that become weeks, months, and then seasons. There is some adaptability in the seemingly relentless parade of responsibilities and tasks. In the effort to keep up, we can learn a lot about our own ability to be flexible and forgiving.

Caring for plants is not rocket science. Most of the tasks are not difficult at all. The difficult part is the timing—knowing when to do them. It helps to understand how plants grow and how weather and soil work, to know how plants and animals interact, to learn how light and moisture affect everything. It helps to consult a book such as this one that outlines the main tasks involved in raising and growing all kinds of plants through the year. Consider this book a basic calendar, a playbook that will make you a better member of the gardening team.

Eventually you will write a garden calendar of your own. You will read many reminders in this book about the value of keeping a garden notebook or journal. Not only will recording information about your previous years' gardens help keep you organized, it will also save you time and energy by reminding you of past mistakes. Recalling through your notes both the great successes and the notable failures will help you learn and understand the dynamics of weather, soil, light, moisture, and plant behavior on your own property. The calendar of tasks that evolves from your experiences in your own garden will

INTRODUCTION

ultimately make your own personal book much more useful than this one could ever be.

How to Use This Book

This volume is intended to be a practical reference. If you have only a couple of houseplants, or just grow some tomatoes during the summer, it will help. If you are a non-gardening homeowner and your landscape consists of only some spring bulbs, a lawn, and a few trees and shrubs, it will help. If you are a beginning gardener, it will give you the confidence to try a variety of plants. If you are an experienced gardener, it will inspire you to expand your gardening skills even further. It will help you anticipate and avoid problems and plan your work so you are not overwhelmed during the busy garden and yard care months.

• Look at it when you are planning a new garden or acquiring a new plant.

• Consult it when you are considering changes to your existing landscape.

• Use it as a guide for caring effectively for all the plants you grow, including proper times to prune.

Other Resources

To get a fuller perspective on growing the groups of plants included in this book, consult the resource material in the back. There is a glossary of terms used in the text. Planting charts have been included to provide additional information on our favorite plant species. There is a list of award-winning trees and shrubs that are especially appropriate for Ohio. There are lists of county extension agents, plant societies, horticultural organizations, and other information resources. This book is about time, about when to perform certain tasks in the yard and garden. For more detailed information on how to perform the specific tasks, consult books devoted to pruning, seed-starting, fertilizers, individual plant families, and design principles.

Gardening in Ohio

GROWING PLANTS IN THE HOME LANDSCAPE

State or regional climate is only one factor that influences gardening success; in many cases it is not even the most important one. All gardening is local, quite local. The conditions that prevail on your particular property have the most impact on plants. Specific elements such as the type of soil, the amount of light, the presence of wind, the frequency of rainfall, and even the incidence of visits by deer are most important. It is your job to choose plants that are suitable for these conditions. The more plants adapt to their environment, the healthier they will be. It is a rare property where the soil, light, and moisture conditions are uniform throughout. In every yard there are microclimates—small areas where conditions are modified by the presence of buildings, walls, drainage patterns, large trees, or rows of shrubs.

Second-story balconies, roof-overhang environments, and beds growing near pavement are different from open lawn areas. These special areas offer opportunities for fine-tuning plant choices so that an even wider palette of plants can be used. Get to know them by reading, asking experts, visiting gardens, joining plant societies, and mostly by experience and experimentation. All great gardeners will tell you about the huge number of plants they have inadvertently killed over the years as they learned which ones suited their yards.

Your plants are part of a unique ecosystem, a community of living things both animal and vegetable that interact in a mutual effort to survive and be healthy. Whether you are installing an entirely new landscape on an undeveloped property or maintaining and enhancing an existing garden, it is useful to consider the entire yard when planning and planting. Consider the variations and take advantage of them.

INTRODUCTION

We are always impressed by the organizational skills of the wonderful gardeners we know. At least in the gardening part of their lives, they are very focused and aware of tasks that need to be done. More importantly, they get them done. Even the busiest gardeners make caring for their plants a priority. We suspect this is why they are so successful. A sense of what needs to be done for plants over the months of the year is fundamental to being organized.

Familiarity with the rhythms of the seasons, and the concomitant needs of plants, both indoors and outdoors, helps gardeners anticipate their needs. For seasoned gardeners, this sense comes from years of experience and observation of plant and weather behavior in their yards and gardens.

For others, it can come from a book such as this one. Plants that have their needs met grow well and have relatively little stress. Plants without stress are vigorous and healthy. If they are not affected by the effort of coping with drought, poor soil, or insufficient light, their natural defense systems are at peak performance, and they are able to fend off pest and disease problems. The savvy gardener knows that healthy plants can largely take care of themselves. It is easier in the long run to learn what each plant prefers for soil, light, moisture, nutrients, and protection, and then provide it. A proactive approach, working with plants, is far easier than a reactive one, working against pest, disease, and environmental assaults later in the game.

PLANT NAMES

Most plants are referred to in this book by their common names, with their botanical names appearing in parentheses for accurate identification. Like people, plants have two names—a formal one and an informal one. Because the formal name is scientific, it is in Latin—that way, botanists and horticulturists anywhere in the world can be sure they are all talking about the same plant. The formal name has two parts: the first is the genus, which indicates the group of related plants it belongs to; the second is the species, the word often describing a particular feature the plant shares with other members of the group. For example, *Hydrangea macrophylla* is a member of the *Hydrangea* group of shrubs, and it is one of the large-leaved ones (*macrophylla* means "large leaves").

A plant usually has only one formal, scientific name, but it may have several common names. Like people's nicknames, plant common names vary depending on their source. Often limited to a specific region, these colorful, descriptive names may be deeply rooted in the history and experience of local gardeners. In some areas of Ohio, our native *Amelanchier laevis* is called juneberry or serviceberry. Common names remain in our memories better than Latin ones, because they reflect the regional and local culture which we share. For that reason we tolerate the confusion that sometimes arises when two different plants have the same common name. While they are not normally identified by "bold type," in this book we have used "bold type" for common names in order to make them stand out in the text.

GENERAL GARDENING TECHNIQUES

MAKE A PLAN

Just as in real estate, location is (almost) everything. The first step in plant care is to plan an appropriate place for each plant in its new environment. To maintain successful growth, provide a situation that emulates its natural environment as closely as possible. For example, most flowering bulbs prefer sun and well-drained soil.

1. Make a sketch showing existing plants.
2. Identify areas of best sun and shade.
3. Identify potential or actual microclimates.
4. Locate existing drainage patterns and utilities.
5. Note which areas are convenient to the water source.

INTRODUCTION

6. Designate an area for a compost pile.

7. Consider fencing needs.

CHOOSE GOOD PLANTS

Choose plants that are appropriate for the sites. Do not select a plant simply because it is trendy, on sale, or gorgeous. It is easier to choose plants to fit the conditions on the property than to try to change conditions to suit the plant. Plan for different types of plants—trees, shrubs, bulbs, herbs—and lots of varieties of each. The more diverse the plants on your property, the more hosts there will be for the beneficial organisms and insects that will help protect plants from predators.

• Choose perennials appropriate for your hardiness zone.

• Choose disease-resistant plant varieties.

• Buy many diverse kinds of plants.

• Select varieties for your preferences in color, height, texture, and other qualities.

• Choose plants to solve landscape problems.

VALUE THE SOIL

Before planting, consider the value of the soil. Taking or sending soil samples to a laboratory for analysis is important. Separate tests for lawn areas, vegetable garden areas, and landscape planting areas are advised. In many areas of Ohio the soil has historically been rich and arable; strive to maintain it. Good soil reduces garden work because it provides plant nutrients and holds moisture. The cliché is true: Take care of the soil and it will take care of the plants. The following are important concepts of soil management which should be considered:

• Maintain soil acidity. Test for pH.

• Do not dig or cultivate soil that is very wet or extremely dry.

• Avoid compacting the soil.

• Add organic matter to the soil when needed.

• Reduce the use of pesticides that kill beneficial organisms in the soil.

• Use slow-acting fertilizers that work with microbial life to help the soil provide nutrients to plants.

• Protect the soil and reduce erosion with a layer of organic mulch or a cover crop.

PLANT PROPERLY

In recent years we have learned a lot more about plants. New technology has promoted an understanding of how roots work at the molecular level, and this has changed planting practices for some groups of plants, especially trees and shrubs.

1. Plant at the correct depth.

2. Plant at the correct time of year.

3. Choose the correct planting method for bare-root, container, or balled-and-burlapped plants.

4. Allow enough space for the mature size of the plant.

5. Provide follow-up care until the plant is established.

WATER THOUGHTFULLY

Even though Ohio usually receives adequate rainfall over the year, the rain does not always fall at regular intervals, and supplemental watering is often necessary. This is especially true for lawns and vegetable crops in summer. Plants vary in their need for moisture, and soils vary in their ability to hold the moisture and make it available to plants. Water by hose, sprinkler, or drip irrigation.

• Water newly planted plants generously.

• Water established plants only when insufficient rainfall makes watering necessary.

• Water the soil rather than the plant.

• Water plants according to individual needs.

• Water according to soil quality—the better the soil, the less often watering will be needed.

• Water lawns deeply but not often.

• Conserve water by mulching to reduce runoff and loss through evaporation.

INTRODUCTION

FERTILIZE JUDICIOUSLY

How and when to fertilize plants is easy to determine. Why we fertilize is a little more complicated to explain. In situations where the soil has been depleted of certain nutrients—primarily nitrogen, potassium, phosphorus—and they have not been replaced naturally by the annual cycle of decay of organic debris, the gardener must add them to the soil in the form of fertilizer. The action of microbial life in the soil along with soil temperature and moisture helps convert the nutrients in the fertilizer into a form that can be taken up by plant roots. Whether that happens rapidly or slowly depends on whether or not the fertilizer, especially its nitrogen, is soluble in water. Depending on what the soil test reveals, you may need fertilizer that is complete (has all three major nutrients). Sometimes the soil test will show that all nutrients are present, but they are not in balance. Then you must use a special fertilizer that features a greater proportion of one or more nutrients.

- Maintain the correct soil pH to assure optimum effectiveness of fertilizer.
- In many situations, use slow-acting fertilizers for long-term, consistent nutrition over many weeks.
- Water soluble fertilizers can help plants that need a quick source of nutrition.
- Fertilize just before or near the end of the active growing season, not when plants are dormant.
- Fertilize the soil in situations where plants utilize lots of nutrients.

PRUNE PURPOSEFULLY

Pruning is a very important part of landscape management. When done properly at the correct time, it can encourage growth, prolific blooming, and fruiting. It can rejuvenate a plant, reduce disease, or create a hedge or an espalier work of art. When done improperly or at the wrong time, it can ruin the next bloom season or even kill a plant. Woody plants such as trees, shrubs, and vines are most often pruned to control their size, but pruning at the wrong time can actually stimulate plant growth.

- Always have a pruning goal, and time the procedure correctly.
- Keep pruner, lopper, saw, and mower blades sharp.
- Prune dead, diseased, or damaged plant parts promptly.
- Move plants that need constant pruning (to control size) to a larger space.
- Prune to maintain the natural shape of the plant. Reserve shearing for plants that will be trained to be formal hedges or topiary.

PROTECT VULNERABLE PLANTS

If plants are chosen, sited, and cared for correctly, most of the time they will be able to cope with environmental and pest problems—but because cultivated plants in a residential landscape are in an essentially contrived environment, they sometimes need some protection from the elements and natural enemies.

- Stake plants that are vulnerable to injury by wind, rain, and people.
- Know which potential pest problems affect your plants.
- Observe and inspect plants regularly for pest problems.
- Treat serious plant problems as quickly as possible.
- Shelter or spray foliage of plants exposed to harsh winter wind and sun.
- Fence out undesirable wildlife.
- Mulch plants to buffer soil-temperature extremes around their roots.
- Overwinter tender plants in frost-free areas.
- Acclimate plants gradually to indoor or outdoor sites.

USDA Cold Hardiness Zones

ZONE	Average Annual Min. Temperature (°F)
5A	-15 to -20
5B	-10 to -15
6A	-5 to -10
6B	0 to -5

ANNUALS & BIENNIALS

Everyone loves annuals because they are reliable. It is no wonder that annuals are the type of flowering plant most commonly planted by non-gardeners and beginners who want to decorate their home landscapes, apartment balconies, and sunny windows; they are also found in the most elegant gardens of the most experienced gardeners. They offer so many months of nonstop blooming for such a small investment.

DEPENDABLE ANNUALS

Count on annuals to bloom with extreme vigor. Once the weather warms up, there is no holding them back. In no time at all they will be spilling onto the walks, punctuating the border, climbing arbors, carpeting beds, hanging from the porch roof in baskets and windowboxes, and overflowing containers of all kinds in and around the yard. They are perfect for sustaining color in the yard during the pauses between the various bloom times of both woody and herbaceous perennials.

Count on annuals for color, just about any color imaginable. With the exception of true black, there is probably an annual out there with the exact color you want. Petunias, geraniums, salvias, marigolds, zinnias, impatiens—the list goes on

and on. Reliable color means the yard has a consistent look all season long. It means it is even possible to match color trim on shutters, lamp posts, and windowboxes!

Count on annuals to keep producing blooms all season long. They live only one season, and they make the most of that time. Under a biological imperative to produce as much seed as possible to assure future generations, annuals direct their energy to producing flowers. This means a steady supply of blooms for indoor arrangements and outdoor beauty. By the time frost arrives to end their lives, they have given their all.

Count on annuals for versatility. Whatever the landscape situation, there is probably an annual that will suit it. Need a ground cover planting? There are annuals that creep. Need a screen to block a view? Many annuals are vines and will climb rambunctiously over a fence or trellis. There are trailing annual plants for hang-ing from baskets or for scrambling over an eyesore to hide it. Others provide fragrance, attract butterflies or hummingbirds, edge a bed, lighten a shady area, or provide interesting, colorful foliage.

Count on annuals to be easy to care for. Most are quite self-reliant, requiring very little care once established. If they are planted correctly in an appropriate place, they manage just fine with only some extra water during drought conditions, a liquid fertilizer nutrient boost every so often, and perhaps pinching back for renewal during the dog days of summer. Annuals rarely have serious disease or insect problems. In the event that serious insect or disease problems occur, annuals are inexpensive enough that it is a simple matter to pull them up and replace them with new transplants.

Count on most annuals to grow easily from seed. If planted indoors under lights ahead of the season, most types of annuals quickly germinate from seed in their effort to start pleasing, and most are very easy to grow from seed right in the garden. If sown in early or mid-May, they will have time to sprout and mature into flowering plants for the season; they are never very far behind the homegrown or store-bought transplants that are put into the garden slightly later in May.

PLANTING ANNUALS

Annuals, by definition, live their entire lives from seed through youth to mature flowering and seed formation over the course of a single season. Inevitably, they die with the onset of cold and frost. Each spring brings new opportunities to try annuals of different types and new colors, as soon as they are available at the garden center as young plants for transplanting into garden beds and containers. Purchasing started plants makes it possible to acquire exactly the color and number of plants you need. For many, this is the easiest, most efficient way to grow annuals.

HELPFUL HINTS

All-America Selections (AAS) is an independent, nonprofit organization that tests promising new varieties of annual flower and vegetable plants. Each year plants that show outstanding performance in approximately 200 trial gardens across the country are selected as winners. They must demonstrate superior home-garden qualities when compared to existing varieties already on the market in North America. They must also meet criteria for introductions such as laboratory germination tests. Look for the AAS emblem on plant labels, seed packets, and catalog descriptions to ensure that you will be growing winning varieties. For more information, visit the AAS website: **www.all-americaselections.org**.

Among last year's annuals, however, there may have been some "hardy" types that can handle some chill. Tougher than the average annual, these plants release copious numbers of seeds as they die and dry up. Since these seeds are able to withstand winter weather and germinate on their own in the spring, a new crop is virtually assured. Leave these bonus plants in place and thin them as they grow, or transplant them to other places in the yard. Some examples of hardy annuals are spider flower, snapdragon, four-o'-clock, cosmos, love-in-a-mist, and pot marigold.

SOWING SEED

Growing annuals from seed is less expensive than buying transplants. If you do not want to invest in and master the equipment for indoor seed-starting (or simply cannot get your act together to start seeds when it is still winter outside), wait to sow seed directly into the garden. This is the preferred method for those annuals that do not transplant well because they have taproots, or because they grow too fast after germinating indoors while spring

---

HELPFUL HINTS

There is time now to do things you will not have time for once the gardening season begins.
- Clean and sharpen tools.
- Paint the wooden handles of tools with a bright color so they are easily found in the garden.
- Check **geraniums** that are overwintering bare-root in the dry basement.
- Catch up on journal entries.
- Read gardening books, magazines, and catalogs.
- Clean up empty containers stored indoors.
- Commit to trying at least three new annuals in your garden.

---

makes up its mind to arrive. Young seedlings grown outdoors in the garden are immediately acclimated; they do not need hardening off.

Broadcasting the seeds creates an informal, natural look in a bed or border, along a wall or fence, or in a mini-meadow. Simply take a handful of seeds, and gently sprinkle them randomly over the prepared soil. If the seeds are particularly tiny, such as those of portulaca or petunia, mix them with a bit of coarse sand or vermiculite so they are easier to cast evenly over the area. Toss larger seeds such as nasturtium freestyle then poke them gently into the soil where they fall. Check to see if the package label says seeds

must be covered with soil or left exposed to light.

Alternatively, you may choose to sow annual seeds in more formal rows. This is the most efficient way to plant if you are growing them for cutting, or if you want to fit them into a designed bed where several plants are in front of or behind them. Follow the directions on the seed packet.

JANUARY

ANNUALS & BIENNIALS

PLANNING

It's never too soon to begin planning this year's garden. The colorful seed and plant catalogs are piling up, begging for attention, and January is the perfect time to consult them. Most mail-order companies have websites that offer help for gardeners. Even if you do not buy your plants or seeds by mail, catalogs provide a wealth of information. They:

- highlight new varieties.
- provide cultural information.
- help you learn the names of plants—common and botanical.
- help you compare prices.
- provide cooking and storing information for vegetables, fruits, and herbs.
- suggest ways to use plants in your landscape.

Think about whether you will raise your own seedlings indoors or wait and buy transplants from the garden center. While it is a bit early to start seeds, it is not too early to select and order them.

Order seed-starting supplies as well. Commercially designed equipment such as adjustable fluorescent lights and a heat mat will produce sturdy, vigorous seedlings. Study the catalogs for various seed-starting systems that can make it much easier to produce young plants than make-shift windowsill arrangements.

Consult past garden journals or calendars to refresh your memory of the annuals that did best and looked best in your garden last year. Labels that you have (hopefully!) kept will remind you of the specific varieties you chose.

In anticipation of planting seeds to raise your own seed-lings, buy or build a sturdy, free-standing light table for seedlings. This can be put out of the way in a basement or unused room and will free up valuable counter space elsewhere.

1. Securely fasten a board onto already-assembled saw-horses, or convert an existing

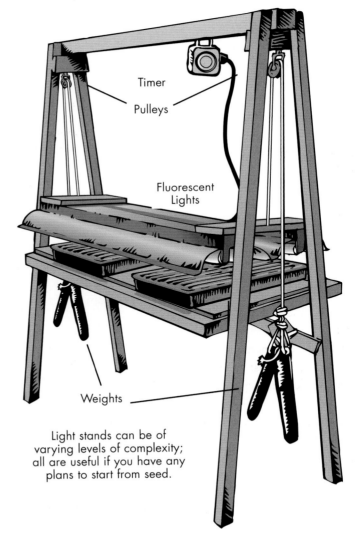

Timer

Pulleys

Fluorescent Lights

Weights

Light stands can be of varying levels of complexity; all are useful if you have any plans to start from seed.

workbench to use as a shelf to hold trays (flats) of sown seeds. Surfaces that measure 4 feet long and 20 inches wide are roomy enough for several flats or small pots.

2. Erect lights over the shelf—install a frame to support one or two inexpensive shop lights that hold at least two 40-watt ordinary fluorescent tubes. If you suspend them on chains from hooks in the ceiling over a shelf or bench, they can be easily adjusted for height.

3. Arrange the light setup so that the lamps can be raised so they are always 4 to 6 inches above the stem tips of young seedlings as they grow.

PLANTING

If you are propagating some annuals from last year by rooting stem cuttings taken in the fall, they should be well rooted by now. Pot up **coleus**, **geranium**, **wax begonia**, **impatiens**, and others in a soilless mix with granular slow-acting fertilizer added. You can tell they are established when they begin to develop new leaves.

Seeds of cool-season annuals that need a long head-start may need sowing indoors by the end of this month. Read the instructions on the seed packets. Most warm-season annuals will not go

out into the garden until May, so wait awhile before sowing their seed indoors.

CARE

Planted rooted cuttings need lots of bright light in winter when daylight hours are limited. Put them in a south or west window or under some fluorescent lights in the kitchen.

WATERING

Periodically check newly potted rooted cuttings for moisture. If the house is warm and/or they are in clay pots, they may dry out quickly.

FERTILIZING

If you added granular slow-acting fertilizer to the planting medium when you potted up the cuttings, there is no need to fertilize any more. If not, add some very dilute water-soluble (fast-acting) fertilizer to their water every two weeks or so. Plants that are not blooming do not need much fertilizer.

PRUNING

As they stretch to reach the limited light from the window, indoor

annuals develop leggy stems. Pinch them back to keep the plants compact. Put them under fluorescent lights if necessary.

PROBLEMS

Indoor plants of all kinds are bothered by pest insects because the plants are under stress. New seedlings and young plants are extremely vulnerable. Typically the air is too dry from hot-air heat, there are drafts, and the light is insufficient because of the reduced number of daylight hours in early winter.

Whiteflies, aphids, scale, and mites—the big four—plague potted annual cuttings and annual plants brought indoors just as they do regular houseplants and outdoor plants.

• Rinse infested foliage and stems under the faucet to interrupt the insects' life cycle.

• Spray persistent pests on plant foliage with commercial insecticidal soap.

• Pinch off leaves that have scale if the plant can spare them; otherwise, scrape off the crusty bumps with a fingernail.

• Spray the plant thoroughly with light (superior) horticultural oil to handle major scale infestations.

FEBRUARY
ANNUALS & BIENNIALS

 PLANNING

Finalize your decisions about which annuals to start as seeds. Some are best started indoors several weeks before last frost is expected. Some seeds you will sow directly into the garden when the soil warms and dries. If you prefer to purchase annuals at the store, look for them in garden and home centers soon.

Many mail-order seed catalogs advertise commercially raised young annual or biennial plants. If you plan to use them, get your order in early to be sure that the company will have your first choice. The young plants will be delivered at the appropriate planting time for your part of Ohio.

Seeds of plants that do not mind cool weather, such as **pansy** and **calendula**, should be started indoors this month. To determine when to sow the seeds, first check the individual seed packets for the germination time, then count backwards on the calendar from the last frost date in your region of Ohio.

 PLANTING

Look for young **pansy** transplants now at your local garden or home center. If they have been kept in cool conditions at the store, they will be hardened off enough to go right into the ground as soon as it thaws and are hardy enough to survive a late snow.

Some biennials—plants that sprouted and developed leaves last season and will be flowering this season—may be visible in the garden now. Look for clumps of **forget-me-not** and **money plant**. You may want to transplant some plants from the larger clumps to other locations when the soil thaws and becomes workable.

Sprouts from seeds sown indoors at the end of last month will need transplanting into larger pots by mid-month. Use regular soilless planting mix with slow-acting fertilizer, and repot.

Moisten soilless mix and fill seed starter trays or peat pots with the mix.

It's time to set up a light stand if you are starting seeds indoors now. Follow these steps to start seeds indoors under lights:

1. Fill your flats or peat pots with moistened soilless mix. Fine-grained soilless mixes labeled specifically for seed-starting are ideal, but not essential.

2. Sow the seeds in the flats according to the seed packet instructions. Some seeds must be covered with mix; others require exposure to light.

3. Label each flat or pot to keep track of what you are growing, as new sprouts look amazingly similar.

4. Cover the flats or pots with plastic wrap until seeds sprout, or slip them into plastic bags to prevent the potting mix from drying out.

5. Attach the lights to a timer and set it so the plants receive 10 to 12 hours of bright light per day.

6. Optional: Set the flats or pots on a warming mat (72° F) to promote faster germination.

CARE

Pot the rooted cuttings you took in the fall as soon as substantial roots develop. To promote sturdy stems and a compact habit, pinch leggy stems back. (These pinchings might be rooted for even more plants!)

To care for indoor seedlings:

1. Remove any plastic covers from the new sprouts to avoid damping off. Moisten planting medium when it begins to dry out.

2. Adjust the lights periodically so that they are always about 4 to 6 inches above the growing plants.

3. To avoid a hopeless tangle of roots, transplant seedlings from the seed flats as soon as they develop true leaves (their second set). Plant them in individual pots in soilless medium.

WATERING

Water young plants from rooted cuttings when the soil feels dry about 1 inch down. Caution, do not overwater.

Keep seedlings moist, but not wet. Water from below, if possible.

FERTILIZING

If you did not add slow-acting fertilizer to the potting medium of rooted cuttings, add some water-soluble fertilizer to the water every two weeks when you water them.

Seeds carry their own energy for early development. Delay fertilizing until you transplant the seedlings into individual containers. Add a granular,

slow-acting fertilizer to the planting medium, or water gently with a very dilute liquid fertilizer every week or two.

PRUNING

No pruning is necessary this month.

PROBLEMS

Aphids and whiteflies can annoy young indoor annuals. They seem to come out of nowhere, but they are probably on nearby houseplants. Spray persistent pests on plant foliage with commercial insecticidal soap.

Damping off is the bane of seedlings. It is caused by a pathogen in the real soil base and is aggravated by overwet medium. Young seedlings will seem to be progressing well then suddenly their stems darken near the surface of the planting medium and they topple over. To prevent damping off:

• Use a soilless planting medium. (It is sterile.)

• Water sprouts from below.

• Maintain light and humidity to avoid stressing new sprouts.

MARCH

ANNUALS & BIENNIALS

PLANNING

This is the month to start thinking seriously about beginning outdoor work in the yard and garden. While it is still too early to transplant most plants into cold, wet garden soil, some cold-loving annuals will start to appear at garden centers. **Pansies** and their **Johnny-jump-up** and **viola** cousins can handle chill, and you can try planting them in windowboxes and containers filled with soilless mix.

Some of the seedlings you have raised may be outgrowing their indoor space, but it is too soon to transplant them directly into the garden. Consider setting up a "halfway house" or cold frame outdoors to help the young plants begin their transition to the cooler yard. Spending some time in this sort of sheltered nursery is a good way for them to "harden off"—to adjust to cool, outdoor conditions before they go into the ground.

PLANTING

Certain annuals can be sown directly into the garden this month even though it is still cold. **Sweet peas** and **corn poppies** are good examples. Their seeds need chilly conditions for germination. Check seed packets for exact timing.

Sometime this month you can sow seeds indoors for those warm-weather-loving annuals that need six to eight weeks lead time before they are old enough to go into the soil. Determine the date for the expected last frost in your area in Ohio, and count back the number of weeks indicated on the seed packet. Consult your garden notebook or journal for previous years' dates.

CARE

Annuals established from rooted cuttings probably have been enjoying the increased daylight hours as spring approaches. They may need repotting into larger containers before it is safe to finally plant them outdoors.

Adjust fluorescent lights over young annuals grown indoors from seed to within 4 to 6 inches of the tops of the plants as they grow. This will keep the stems sturdy. You can tell the days are getting longer—there are more daylight hours—when you have to adjust the timer. If seedlings are growing on a windowsill, rotate them periodically so that light falls on every side. This will keep them from bending too much.

Research suggests that gently brushing tender tops of seedlings a couple of times a day with your fingertips or open hand helps them develop sturdy stems.

WATERING

Use a houseplant water meter to be sure annuals grown from rooted cuttings do not dry out. While the central heating is still on, the potting medium will dry out faster—especially in clay (terra cotta) pots. Stick the probe down into the soil to where the roots are growing, and water if the meter indicates dry.

Keep seedlings moist, but do not soak the soil; it is okay if they dry out slightly between waterings. In fact, many annuals like to have a wet/dry cycle. If seedlings dry out very quickly, this signals that they need repotting into a larger pot. A larger volume of planting medium will hold more moisture. Always use tepid water, not water directly from the cold-water faucet.

FERTILIZING

In milder parts of the state, it is often possible to start working the soil by the end of this month. If the soil has dried out enough so it does not turn into a sticky ball when you grab a handful and squeeze, begin to dig the beds to loosen and aerate the soil in your annual beds. To provide transplants with long-term, consistent nutrition, add granular slow-acting fertilizer to the soil as you work.

PRUNING

The key to full, compact, bushy annuals is pinching the tips of their stems periodically as they mature from seedlings to young transplants. The plants will generate more stems and foliage. Do this with plants purchased at the garden center as well, if they show a tendency to grow too lanky.

HELPFUL HINTS

These are the advantages to growing annuals from seed indoors:
- It is less expensive.
- There is no need to wait until spring to garden, and you can enjoy indoor gardening.
- There are more varieties to choose from.

These are the advantages to buying annuals as transplants:
- It saves time and energy.
- Professionally raised plants are dependably sturdy.
- You are able to choose just the number of plants you want.
- It is easier to select for color.

PROBLEMS

Spider mites are often a problem on plants that have been under the stress of indoor living for months. If indoor annuals look a little "off," their foliage slightly mottled or speckled with yellow dots, inspect them. Spider mites are almost too small to see without a magnifying glass, but they cause pale stippling on the leaves, and sometimes they make a fine webbing on stems and leaves. Wash the plant foliage in tepid water from the faucet several times a week to remove and disrupt the mites. Use insecticidal soap or consider a miticide for stubborn infestations. Always follow label directions.

Damping off remains a threat to new homegrown seedlings (see February).

Leggy stems on seedlings are a condition usually caused by insufficient light. Lower the fluorescent lights to within 4 to 6 inches of the plant tops.

Pale, yellowed foliage indicates that seedlings or young potted annuals need some fertilizer.

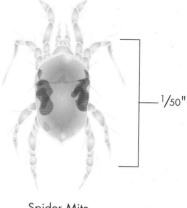

1/50"

Spider Mite

APRIL

ANNUALS & BIENNIALS

PLANNING

Finally! Annual gardening goes outdoors by the end of this month. Spring is on the calendar, if not on the thermometer, and the switch to Eastern Daylight Saving Time shifts the increasing number of daylight hours to later in the day so there will be more time to garden after work.

Young annual plants are arriving daily at the garden center in a swirl of bright color. Think about trying an annual you have never grown before. Notice which plants prefer sun and which do well in part shade so you will have the right plant for the right place in your landscape. While you are at the garden center, buy bags of soilless potting mix and granular, slow-acting fertilizer labeled for flowers. Other things on the shopping list: stakes, string, plant labels, journal or notebook for garden records, insecticidal soap, and light horticultural oil.

If you need an excuse to get outdoors, there's lots of work to be done:

- Clean up hanging containers, garden ornaments, and flower pots.
- Clean, repair, and refurbish birdhouses and feeders.
- Pick up sticks and other debris on planted beds.
- Reset and secure stones in walls and terraces that may have been moved by freeze-and-thaw cycles in the soil over the winter.

PLANTING

If you are not already enjoying them in the garden, put out some **pansies**. They are ideal for a ground cover planting among **daffodils**, **tulips**, and other bulbs. They also brighten windowboxes and planters.

Young plants that are waiting in a cold frame can come out to enjoy milder days. Be sure to vent the cold frame on days when there is strong sunshine so that plants do not cook while they wait their turn for planting in the garden. Prop open glass covers, or cut slits in plastic tunnels or covers.

Sow seeds of hardy annuals such as **cleome**, **cosmos**, **four-o'-clock**, **portulaca**, and **sweet alyssum** directly on the soil in the area of the garden you want them to grow.

CARE

When the soil dries out a bit from spring rains, get outdoors and clean up any planting areas that were overlooked last fall. Pull out weeds and dead plants, and pick up winter debris. Do not disturb the soil in areas where you encouraged plants like **cleome** and **love-in-a-mist** to self-sow last fall; there will be new sprouts there soon.

By the end of the month, most seedlings raised indoors can be set outdoors daily for increas-

Pansy 'Melody Purple'

ingly longer times to adjust to the weather. Bring them in at night until it is mild enough for planting. This "hardening off" process gets them used to the outdoors so they will experience less transplant stress when they are finally planted in the garden or in a decorative outdoor container. While they wait (a cold snap may delay planting for a week or two), some young plants may grow so large that they need repotting into larger pots.

WATERING

April showers should keep **pansies** and new seedlings outdoors moist and perky. If rain is not reliable, water areas where seeds are due to sprout or young sprouts have recently appeared. There is no need to water deeply; just moisten the soil down an inch or so. Water biennial plants such as **money plant** and **forget-me-not** more deeply, since their root systems will have grown deeper. Plants in mulched beds will not dry out as fast as seedlings and newly sprouted seeds.

FERTILIZING

When the soil is dry enough to work easily, prepare annual beds. Dig and turn over shovels-

ful of soil to aerate it. Mix in some granular, slow-acting fertilizer while you're at it. This is also a good time to incorporate some organic material such as compost, chopped leaves, or mushroom compost into the beds if the soil is sandy or has a lot of clay; these amendments also improve soil fertility to some degree.

PRUNING

Pinch back leggy stems of maturing seedlings and plants grown from potted rooted cuttings if necessary. This will make their stems more sturdy and their foliage denser. Pick **pansies** to enjoy indoors. This practice will encourage many additional blossoms.

PROBLEMS

Weeds are responding to spring weather, too. Cultivating the soil brings many weed seeds to the soil surface where they are exposed to the sun and begin to sprout. Watch for young sprouts, and pull them as soon as they are large enough to grasp between thumb and forefinger. They pull up easily if the soil is moist.

Deer love to nibble on tender annuals. Protect planted beds and containers with spray repellent, or erect a barrier such as wire fencing.

MAY

ANNUALS & BIENNIALS

PLANNING

Young annuals are available at the garden center in riotous abundance this month. Think about what you want to achieve with your plantings.

1. Choose tall varieties to screen unpleasant views or for privacy, to make a backdrop for other flowers, or for cutting.

2. Medium-height annuals anchor container plantings and fill in mixed borders.

3. Low-growers are ideal for ground covers, hanging baskets, and edges of planted beds.

Perhaps you would like to attract butterflies, hummingbirds, and/or beneficial insects to your garden. Or, this might be the year to try a fragrance garden or to grow annuals for drying or floral crafts. Study displays, and read plant labels and materials available at the garden center to learn which plants attract wildlife or fulfill your other design needs.

PLANTING

Prepare planting beds and containers for transplants. In all but the coldest areas of the state (where frost is still a possibility as late as the third week of May), young plants that were displayed outdoors at the garden center probably can go right into the garden or hanging basket. Those that were grown indoors will need a few days of gradual exposure to the outdoors to adjust to the weather before you plant them permanently.

1. Dig a hole in prepared soil about the size of the container that the young transplant is in.

2. Slip the plant from its pot. If it sticks, tap the bottom of the pot with a trowel. (Sometimes young plants are potbound, their roots crowding the pot and protruding from the bottom. With your fingers or a small stick, gently tease tangled roots apart so they hang freely.) Slide the pot off the rootball.

3. Set the plant in its hole, making sure it is at the same depth it was in the pot.

4. Gently firm the soil over the roots and around the stem, and water well.

5 If there is no slow-acting, granular fertilizer in the soil, add water-soluble fertilizer to waterings after a few days, and afterward according to package label instructions.

Remember to space plants correctly so they will have enough room when they are mature. They will be growing all summer and may become too crowded. Most plant labels provide spacing information.

Check the condition of the roots of potted transplants before you plant them; if they are rootbound, gently separate the roots.

Sow seeds for other annuals outdoors as soon as your area is safe from frost.

1. Dig the soil to loosen it, and remove lumps and debris to make a smooth seedbed.

2. Trace a shallow indentation in the soil with a pencil or your finger in a pattern that you prefer.

3. Dribble the seeds into the indentation, and cover with soil. (Some seeds need light to germinate, so read the seed packet carefully.) Pat the soil gently to encourage contact between soil and seed, then water.

CARE

Plant on a cloudy day or late in the day so new transplants will not suffer added stress from the sun while they cope with transplant shock. If it is unseasonably warm, erect some temporary shade for them for a few days.

An inch or two of organic mulching material or fine bark mulch such as chopped leaves over the bare soil around transplants will discourage weeds and help keep the soil moist and cool. Keep the seedbed where you have planted annual seeds moist and free of debris.

WATERING

Water new transplants immediately to settle the soil comfortably around their roots. If it does not rain for more than five days, check the soil moisture. Annuals in containers in the sun will need watering more often, especially when it gets hotter. This is especially true if the containers are clay or terra cotta.

FERTILIZING

If you have already added granular slow-acting fertilizer to the soil when preparing the bed, do not fertilize again now. If you have not added fertilizer, add it to the soil as you plant each seedling according to the directions on the package label. If you plan to water-in fast-acting fertilizer, be conservative. Too much nitrogen too soon or too often promotes excessive tender growth and very few blossoms.

PRUNING

Snip off any broken stems or crushed leaves from store-bought transplants before you plant them out in the garden.

Sprouts of self-sown seeds from last season's **cleome** or other notorious self-seeders will thickly carpet a bed. Thin them by pulling up most of the spindly seedlings, leaving a potentially sturdy seedling every few inches where you want them to grow.

An alternative is to treat the site as a nursery bed. Thin to encourage strong remaining seedlings, and then transplant them to other areas of the garden.

PROBLEMS

Weed problems will continue, because new weed seeds come to the surface and find light to germinate when the soil is disturbed by planting. Pull them as soon as they appear. Mulching the soil when young annual transplants are 4 inches tall will cover weed seeds.

Deer and rabbits like tender new growth on young plants. Spray threatened annuals with repellent products as directed on the label until plants are older and tougher. Fences or wire barriers are the best deterrents.

Slugs show up very early in the season and can be treated in a number of reliable ways. Check your local garden center for slug baits.

JUNE
ANNUALS & BIENNIALS

PLANNING

Annuals really start to "show their stuff" this month as warm weather settles in. Take time to record in a journal or notebook information on which plants do best and look best as the season unfolds. Have a few transplants on hand to replace **pansies** if hot weather causes them to peter out. Certain ephemeral perennial plants such as **bleeding heart**, **Virginia bluebells**, and **poppies** will die back and leave empty spaces in the garden that can be quickly filled with pots and baskets of annuals.

Decide if you want to encourage the resident biennials on your property. Those that are in their second season will be flowering and then forming seeds. If you want to limit the abundance and spread of **forget-me-nots**, **money plant** (also called **honesty**), **hollyhocks**, **sweet William**, and others, pull up the plants after they bloom and before they sow their seed.

PLANTING

In the coldest areas of the state it is now probably safe to plant warm-weather annuals outdoors in the ground or in containers. Elsewhere in Ohio, it is warm enough for even the tropical plants to go out on the patio or into the garden. Although plants such as **mandevilla**, certain **hibiscus**, **plumbago**, **bougainvillea**, and others are perennials by nature, they are not hardy enough to survive winter months in regions where it actually gets cold. Treat them as you would annuals in containers or in the ground.

Seedlings from last year's self-sowers are probably large enough to transplant. You can leave some in place to mature, transplant others to a new location and provide "extras" to friends and neighbors.

CARE

When young transplants or direct-sown seedlings reach about 4 inches tall and produce a second set of leaves (their true leaves), spread some organic material as a mulch over the bare soil between and around them. This will discourage weeds from competing with the young plants for soil moisture and nutrients. It will also prevent the soil from drying out too quickly.

By the end of the month, some tall annuals will need staking to prevent their collapse from wind or heavy rain. It is best to stake plants like **zinnias**, **American marigolds**, **cosmos**, and **larkspur** before they are at full height, when there is less risk of disturbing their roots. Tie plant stems loosely so there is room for them to grow thicker over the season.

Start picking flowers as they develop to enjoy indoors. This practice will also encourage sturdier stems and stimulate the production of more blooms.

WATERING

Most annuals are shallow-rooted, spending their energy blooming rather than developing deep root systems. This means they experience dryness fairly quickly when rainfall is limited. The soil dries out even faster when it's hot. Watch for wilt that does not go away when the sun and heat abate. If annuals are not mulched, check their soil more often than you check mulched plants. Insert the probe of a houseplant water meter into the soil about 2 or 3 inches, and water if the meter registers toward the dry reading.

Water the soil, not the plants, if possible, to help discourage mildew on plant foliage.

FERTILIZING

If there is no granular, slow-acting fertilizer in the soil, water-in dilute fertilizer at intervals indicated on the package label.

Remember, annuals in containers depend entirely on slow-acting complete fertilizer in the potting mix or periodic fertilizer watering for their nutrition. A good way to deliver a quick boost of nutrition to annuals is to spray their foliage with a dilute soluble fertilizer.

 ## PRUNING

Some plants drop their dead blossoms, while others hold on to them. Decaying flower heads can promote fungal infections and are unsightly. Pinch off faded blooms from large-flowered annuals such as **petunia**, **annual phlox**, and **marigold** to keep them looking attractive and to forestall possible mildew problems.

No matter how carefully you sow seeds directly into the garden, there are always more new sprouts than are desirable, and they are never spaced far enough apart. Thin seedlings to ensure the remaining ones will have sufficient light and air to grow into healthy plants.

HELPFUL HINTS

While annuals are famous for their nonstop, richly colored blooms, some are most valuable in the garden for their foliage. Brightly colored, interestingly variegated, or unusually shaped foliage works wonders in planted beds and decorative containers. It is a simple matter to pinch off insignificant or inconspicuous flowers. Use them as fillers, color accents, or texture contrasts along with flowering annuals. Some examples of annual or tropical plants that feature foliage are:

- **Coleus**
- **Croton**
- **Dusty Miller**
- **Orach**
- **Ornamental Cabbage and Kale**
- **Perilla**
- **Persian Shield**
- **Polka-Dot Plant**
- **Taro**

 ## PROBLEMS

Since pest insects arrive in the garden before beneficial ones do, expect pest problems early in the season.

Aphids are the most common early arrivals, as they love tender, juicy young plants. These soft-bodied, pear-shaped insects cluster at the new tips of stems and foliage and suck their juices. Handle them in one of the following ways:

- Pinch off infested stem tips and discard them in the trash.
- Wash aphids off stems and foliage with a forceful water spray from the hose.
- Spray insecticidal soap or fine horticultural oil on the offenders according to label directions.

Coleus 'Japanese Giant'

JULY
ANNUALS & BIENNIALS

PLANNING

If you are growing certain annual flowers to be dried for floral crafts, plan to begin harvesting later this month, and then continue into fall as the various plants mature and produce perfect blooms. While many flowers are easily air-dried, some dry best in silica gel and/or borax and sand. Have these materials and appropriate equipment on hand to use the minute you can pick blemish-free, fresh blossoms.

Plan for the maintenance of the garden and planted containers while you are away on vacation. Arrange for someone to water container plants daily if it is very hot and dry. Gather the plants into one or two locations near the hose or water faucet to facilitate the job.

PLANTING

Get all remaining warm-season annuals out of their little market packs (which dry out so quickly) and in the ground as soon as possible. They are likely to be potbound, so take time to gently loosen their matted roots. Plant in the evening or on an overcast day to minimize stress from heat and sun while the young plants cope with transplant shock. Water, then mulch them well.

If you have not already done so, plant some **sunflower** seeds, which will produce wonderful golden flowers in the fall. These days **sunflowers** come in all kinds of colors and different heights, and some are pollenless and do not produce seeds. Check to make sure you are planting varieties that have the characteristics you desire.

CARE

Mulch the soil around transplants that are over 4 inches tall with an inch or so of some organic material such as chopped leaves or shredded bark. This will discourage weeds, block evaporation of moisture from the soil, reduce wasteful runoff from rain or watering, and cool the soil.

Stake tall plants such as **sunflower**, **larkspur**, **hollyhock**, or **spider flower** to prevent their collapse from wind or heavy rain. Use sturdy, unobtrusive green or brown stakes that are a foot

Tall plants, such as hollyhock, will benefit from staking.

taller than the expected height of the plant. Insert them a foot into the soil next to the plants while they are still young, and tie plant stems with twine or other soft material—loop the tie around the plant stem, then loop it around the stake, tying it loosely so there is room for stem growth. Pick more flowers to enjoy indoors. This practice stimulates plants to produce even more blooms.

WATERING

Check the soil around annuals if there has been no rain for several days, or if the plants are wilting. Insert your finger or the probe of a houseplant water meter through the mulch and into the soil about 2 inches. If the soil is dry, water gently for several minutes so the water can penetrate to the shallow roots. If the soil is already wet, the wilting may be due to heat, in which case the leaves will perk up by evening. Overwatering is the problem if the leaves do not perk up in a few hours.

FERTILIZING

The slow-acting fertilizer mixed into the soil at planting time is sufficient for most plants for six to ten weeks or more, depending on the product. Some prodigious

bloomers might also appreciate a boost from a foliar spray of a kelp-based or other soluble liquid product. Spraying it directly on the foliage provides the nutrition quickly and does not affect the soil. Do not overdo.

Too much nitrogen stimulates plants to produce lots of excess foliage, which reduces the amount of bloom. Also, excess nitrogen distracts the plants from producing flowers. Never fertilize a plant that is under stress from drought or extreme heat.

PRUNING

By the end of the month, some annuals such as **petunias** and **impatiens** may develop thin, leggy stems. Pinch back each stem a few inches; this will promote bushiness by stimulating the development of fresh foliage and new flower buds. Plants in containers may need to be cut back, too. Do this before going on vacation and the plants will be blooming again with their new flush of growth when you return.

Spider flowers (cleome) will be stretching upward and developing seedpods along their elongating upper stems. If it is important to you to minimize reseeding, pinch or snip off these pods as they are ripening, before they

dry, burst, and scatter their seeds. Cutting back the main stem encourages branching.

Leave the attractive seedpods on **love-in-a-mist (nigella)**, as they add to the ornamental appearance of the plant. Cut them off when the plants finally finish flowering and the pods have dried to crispy capsules. The black seeds in the chambers of the capsule are easy to harvest and save, or to scatter for a repeat crop.

PROBLEMS

Japanese beetles appear this month. Check the plants in your yard that they traditionally prefer (some Japanese beetle favorites are **four-o'-clocks**, **hollyhocks**, **roses**, and **zinnias**), and try to catch the earliest arrivals. If possible, handpick them or knock them off leaves into a jar of soapy water. Use Neem or a pyrethrum-based insecticide according to label directions if infestations are overwhelming.

Infestations of aphids and mites can seriously damage plants in a few days. If the infestation is light, insecticidal soap works well. The soap also controls thrips, whiteflies, plant bugs and lacebugs.

AUGUST

ANNUALS & BIENNIALS

 PLANNING

While many favorite annuals are capable of blooming with gusto until frost, others tend to peter out by late August. Sometimes they just run out of steam; other times it is just the colors that seem tired. With the onset of fall, with its shorter days and golden light, it is time to replace them with plants that have a richer color palette. Sow seeds for seedlings early in this month, or plan to purchase young transplants as Labor Day approaches for fall replacements in beds and containers. Some possibilities are **celosia**, **marigolds**, **red salvia**, and others that feature rich golden, orange, and red harvest colors.

Plan to visit gardens while on vacation. Public gardens and arboreta in New England, the Midwest, and the South feature many familiar annuals that grow well in Ohio, as well as many you may not be familiar with. Enjoy beauty, inspiration, and educational experiences at public gardens that will benefit the garden at home.

 PLANTING

This month is really too hot and droughty to plant or transplant significant numbers of annual plants, so it is best to wait until after Labor Day. However, it is not a problem to replace the occasional dead or damaged annual in container arrangements. Sometimes a group of annuals in a bed dies out for some reason and needs replacing. Do this on an overcast day, or provide shade for new transplants. Water them well.

By mid-month, seeds planted to start young annual plants for the fall flower garden will be sprouting, if they have not already done so. When they are about 2 or 3 inches tall, thin them to the correct spacing, indicated on the seed packet.

 CARE

Continue to protect plants from the elements. Heat stimulates the activity of the microbial life in organic mulch, which causes it to decompose faster than normal. Add material to the thinning mulch layer to maintain one inch of mulch over bare soil around annuals in the garden. The mulch will conserve water and cool the soil. As it decomposes, it enriches the soil.

If you intend to harvest their seeds for use as birdseed or food, cover the maturing heads of **sunflowers** with garden fleece or cheesecloth to prevent the squirrels and finches from taking them. If they are too tall to reach, cut off the seedheads as soon as they start to mature, and put them in a dry space indoors for the seeds to ripen and dry. If you do not mind if the animals get the seeds, allow

Celosia 'Toreador'

them to dry on the plant, or pick the heads and let them dry on the ground in the sun.

WATERING

Watering is critical to getting plants through the heat and possible drought that is typical of this month. Most annuals positively love the sun and heat and can be counted on to soldier on during this stressful weather as long as they receive sufficient moisture. Those in containers need watering once or twice daily, especially if they are in the sun most of the time. Those in clay (terra cotta) containers dry out fastest. Beds of annuals that are not mulched will need watering more often than those that have a protective layer of mulch.

FERTILIZING

Do not fertilize plants that are coping with harsh heat and drought. Water them and help them through the stress first. As it decomposes, the protective mulch will provide some nutrition, as will the slow-acting fertilizer that was incorporated into the soil at planting time. Wait until the weather breaks, then spray their foliage with a diluted liquid fertilizer to give plants a nutritional boost.

HELPFUL HINTS

The All-America Selections (AAS) organization sponsors display gardens and trial gardens filled with annual flowers and vegetables at many locations throughout the country.

Some of the display gardens in Ohio are:

Cincinnati	Spring Grove Cemetery and Aboretum
Cincinnati	Krohn Conservatory-Hinkle Gardens
Cleveland	Rockefeller Park Greenhouse Gardens
Mansfield	Kingwood Center
Newark	Wilson's Hillview Display Garden
Oxford	Miami University
Strongsville	Gardenview Horticultural Park
Wooster	Ohio State University
Youngstown	Fellows Riverside Gardens

PRUNING

Pick flowers to enjoy as bouquets indoors or to dry for floral crafts. Groom plants by deadheading faded flowers, snipping off dead or injured stems and leaves. Do not allow dried or rotted plant debris to lie in planting beds; this fosters disease problems.

Remember to allow some flowers to ripen and produce seeds to attract birds. Finches of all kinds love the seedheads of **gloriosa daisies** and many other annuals.

PROBLEMS

Mildew can be a problem during August. Some plants seem to be prone to developing the telltale gray coating on their foliage.

- Choose varieties of **zinnia**, **annual phlox**, and **garden verbena** that are listed as mildew-resistant.
- Make sure plants are far enough apart so they can receive good air circulation.
- When you water, water the soil, not the foliage.

Mildew is unsightly but not life-threatening. It is best ignored on annual plants, which will be pulled up in a few weeks anyway.

Winds and heavy rains from August storms can be fierce, and sometimes there are brief hailstorms at this time of year. If you have not had a chance to do it so far, stake plants that have grown very large such as **zinnias**, **spider flower**, and **phlox**.

September

ANNUALS & BIENNIALS

PLANNING

Contrary to popular belief, in much of Ohio the end of the gardening season does not arrive this month. There are a few wonderful weeks of gardening weather ahead. In the warmer areas, there may be many weeks to enjoy gardening. As temperatures moderate from summer heat, get back out in the yard and enjoy the fresh flush of flowers. This is when annuals are much appreciated, because most are still going strong. Those in warm fall harvest colors of orange, yellow, and gold will light up the landscape for another month or six weeks.

Some "annual" plants that will need some attention soon are the tropical plants on the deck or patio. Although **brugmansia**, **mandevilla**, **taro**, **abutilon**, **bougainvillea**, and others are actually perennial by nature, they are too tender to withstand Ohio winters. Consider them annuals, and decide whether to allow the frost to kill them outdoors or to bring them indoors in pots and try to winter them over, either displayed as houseplants or stored in a cool, dark place.

While the impressions of your garden are fresh in your mind, make some notes in your garden journal or notebook.

- What annuals were most successful this summer?
- Are there areas where you did not plant annuals that you would like to plant with annuals next season?
- What problems did annual plants encounter this year, and how did you solve them?
- What changed in the yard over the season?

A gardener's landscape is very much like an artist's painting: it is never finished. You will always find places that can be improved with a little dab of color or a broad stroke of texture. Fortunately, there is always another season ahead, and there will always be another opportunity to improve the picture.

PLANTING

Replace tired summer annuals, and fill in bare spots that have developed in containers and garden beds over the season with fall-colored plants. Plant **ornamental cabbage** and **kale** that are guaranteed to withstand light frost and increasingly chilly weather.

Richly hued **marigolds** that have been growing on the property should continue to be fine for another month. Other annuals with warm seasonal colors will also make the transition. Some suggestions:

- **Impatiens** 'African Queen'
- **Cosmos** 'Bright Lights'
- **Celosia**
- **Gazania**
- **Snapdragon**
- **New Guinea Impatiens** 'Macarena'

CARE

As soon as nighttime temperatures drop to about 55 degrees Fahrenheit, bring in those tropi-

If your brugmansia is too beautiful to be allowed to die, you can overwinter it.

cal plants that you intend to try to winter over as houseplants.

There are three ways to overwinter favorite **geraniums**:

1. Treat them as houseplants. Cut back their leggy stems, dig them up, pot them up in soilless mix with granular, slow-acting fertilizer mixed in, and bring them indoors.

2. Propagate new plants. Take stem cuttings to root in damp perlite or sand. Plant the rooted cuttings in pots later in the fall or early winter, keeping them under bright lights to encourage sturdy stems and foliage. (**Impatiens**, **coleus**, and **begonia** also root easily in a container of damp sand on the windowsill.)

3. Store them as dormant plants. Dig up plants, remove soil from the roots, and hang them in a cool dry storage area.

WATERING

Continue to water annuals in containers and garden beds if rainfall is scarce. Annuals need less water as temperatures cool.

FERTILIZING

There is no need to fertilize annual plants in garden beds at this time of year since the frost will soon kill them. Those brought in to overwinter as houseplants will need some granular, slow-acting fertilizer mixed into their soilless potting medium to give them consistent nutrition over the winter months.

PRUNING

Pull up any annuals that are obviously exhausted or dead, and smooth mulch over the area for a neat appearance. Cut off any seedpods or capsules that develop on those annuals you do not want to self-sow seeds for next year. When the first frost blackens the most tender annuals, pull them immediately.

Clip off broken or diseased stems from annuals promptly. Pinch off unsightly dead flowers or discolored leaves to keep them looking fresh and perky.

PROBLEMS

Insect eggs, disease pathogens, and fungal spores nestle in the crevices of plant leaves and stems. They overwinter there, conveniently situated for next season. Pull up dead, decaying plants promptly, and discard them in the trash to prevent future pest and disease problems. (Healthy plants can go into the compost pile.)

Deer in the area will make an appearance. Spray a repellent product on the remaining flowering annuals to prevent damage. Those in hanging baskets are usually safely out of reach.

Many weeds develop seed this time of year. Continue to pull them wherever they appear—hopefully before their seeds dry and disperse. It is important to prevent them from going to seed so they do not come back to haunt next season.

HELPFUL HINTS

Many Ohio gardens are shaded by large trees that grow so well in our state. Here are some annual flowers that tolerate some shade:

- **Beefsteak Plant** (*Perilla frutescens* 'Atropurpurea')
- **Browallia** (*Browallia* sp.)
- **Coleus** (*Solenostemon scutellarioides*)
- **Impatiens** (*Impatiens walleriana*)
- **Nicotiana** (*Nicotiana alata*)
- **Periwinkle** (*Vinca major* 'Variegata')
- **Polka-Dot Plant** (*Hypoestes phyllostachya*)
- **Wax Begonia** (*Begonia semperflorens*)
- **Wishbone Flower** (*Torenia fournieri*)

OCTOBER

ANNUALS & BIENNIALS

PLANNING

In anticipation of the first light frost this month, bring in any particular annuals that you want to keep over the winter.

Make a note of when first frost arrives. In most regions it is about the same time every year, give or take a week or two. In the coldest parts of the state it may arrive anytime after mid-September, although the benchmark date is between October 1 and October 15. In the warmer areas, the first light frost may not arrive until the third week of October. Conditions vary within your own yard, too. The best way to determine if a light frost has occurred during the night is to check indicator plants. These are the tenderest annuals that are quite susceptible to even the lightest frost. **Impatiens** and **nasturtiums** are two examples.

Some summer annuals that can handle light frost are **marigolds**, **snapdragons**, **petunias**, **portulaca**, and **verbena**.

PLANTING

Put in fall plantings of **ornamental cabbage** and **kale** to fill bare spots. These plants will withstand frosts until early winter when a hard frost comes along. (Do not leave them in the ground once they have been frozen, because they will smell just like rotten cabbage when they thaw!)

If you have not already done so, take stem cuttings from any favorite annuals that you wish to keep going indoors over the winter.

- Remove any flowers or buds and foliage that are within an inch of the cut ends.
- Dip the cut ends in powdered rooting hormone from the garden center and insert them in a pot of moist perlite, sand, or seed starting medium.
- Cover the container with a clear plastic bag to maintain humidity.
- When the stems in water develop tiny root fibers about an inch long, pot them up.
- In a couple of weeks, gently tug on the stems of those plants in the growing medium to ascertain whether they have roots. Then pot them up.

Any cuttings that you took last month will probably have developed roots by now. Pot them up in small containers filled with soil-less medium and granular slow-acting fertilizer. Water well. After they adjust to the transplanting, set them where they can get maximum bright light.

CARE

Pull out annuals when they succumb to frost. Clean up rotting organic debris, and cover the bare soil with a one or two inch mulch of compost, chopped leaves, or pine needles to pro-tect the soil over the winter. Some self-sowers—**cleome**, **four-o'-clock**, **love-in-a-mist**—will leave lots of seeds behind on the soil.

- To encourage copious numbers of free seedlings next spring, disturb the soil as little as possible while removing the dead and dying plants.
- To discourage hosts of seedlings, rake up the remaining summer mulch and replace it with a fresh layer of chopped leaves or other material.

WATERING

Water any annuals that are still going strong if rainfall is scarce. In cooler weather they do not require as much moisture as they did during the hot summer. If they are well mulched, they should be fine.

FERTILIZING

No fertilizing is necessary this month.

PRUNING

Remember to collect seeds from any annuals you think you would like to grow again next year. Cut off the ripening seedheads prior to throwing the spent plants onto the compost pile. Store the seeds tightly wrapped in a cool place, such as the back of the refrigerator or an unheated garage.

Reminder: Flowers and fruit grown from seeds can be very variable in color and size.

Clean up the annual beds. For a head start on next year, dig in some chopped leaves left by the mulching lawn mower during the last few mowings. The leaves will provide organic matter and condition the soil as they decompose. Then mulch the cultivated bed with more leaves, pine needles,

HELPFUL HINTS

It has long been the routine in the South to plant **pansies** in the fall. Only recently have **pansies** become available farther north for fall planting. What a great idea! They have an opportunity to grow strong root systems during the mild fall days when the weather suits them perfectly, and they are able to become well enough established to withstand cold and snow over the winter months. When winter wanes and hardy bulbs begin to bloom, the **pansies** are ready to bloom, too. They are wonderful in beds of their own or interplanted with **tulips**, **daffodils**, or **hyacinths**.

straw, or other organic material to protect it over the winter.

PROBLEMS

Aphids, whiteflies, and spider mites manage to plague annuals that have been potted up and brought indoors to overwinter (**coleus**, **geranium**, **impatiens**,

and **wax begonias**). To avoid bringing indoors any eggs and larvae with the plants, wash foliage with a forceful spray of tepid water to dislodge the pests while still outside. Then spray thoroughly with insecticidal soap. Plan to do this every month or so while the plants are indoors.

Insufficient light is a fact of life for summer annuals that are overwintering indoors. Place them in the brightest window or set up fluorescent lights for them. If you have a seed-starting table (see January or February), they can spend the darkest early winter days there until you need it for seed-starting early next year.

Ornamental cabbage and kale

NOVEMBER

ANNUALS & BIENNIALS

PLANNING

With the advent of the first hard frost, the main season for growing annuals outdoors is over. It is a good time to rethink the garden. If you have really enjoyed this year's annuals, you may want to try more next year.

Think about a cutting garden as a possibility for next year. More a production garden than a display bed, the garden plot can be tucked in an out-of-the-way place and does not require the maintenance that a display garden does. Plant lots of annuals to display indoors or for gift giving in easy-to-access rows for harvest. Grow some plants with interesting foliage, pods, or flowers that dry easily for floral crafts and dried arrangements.

Gather together all the paperwork that has accumulated from your gardening activities this past season. It is helpful to develop the habit of saving the labels from plants that you buy and grow each season. Try to find the seed packets and labels that came with your annuals, and store them with your garden notes. It's worth keeping the label information, which includes the name of the plant, a color picture, and information about its cultural requirements. The labels are a good place to start when planning and ordering next season's annual flowers.

PLANTING

As long as the ground remains unfrozen, it is still okay to plant **pansies**. They will handle cold and snow just fine with a little protective mulch on their soil to buffer temperature extremes that might otherwise disturb the soil and heave them out of the ground.

CARE

Pull out the hardier annuals—including **ornamental kale** and **cabbage**—that have finally succumbed to hard frost. Mulch all bare soil and any young **pansy** plants with a two-inch layer of chopped leaves for winter protection.

WATERING

Watch the soil of annuals that have been potted for indoor overwintering; it will dry out quickly if the heating system runs most of the time. On the other hand, beware of overwatering and causing plants to rot. Use a houseplant water meter to determine whether the soil has actually begun to dry out before automatically pouring more water on plants. Until they resume blooming, they will not need as much water each time as they did outdoors.

FERTILIZING

Annuals will stall when they are brought indoors. So will newly rooted and potted stem cuttings. They need a period of adjustment to the new, less-than-ideal conditions. Light deprivation due to shortened winter daylight hours will slow their growth, too. While they adjust, they can manage on the slow-acting granular fertilizer added to their soilless potting mix; they will begin to bloom freely again in a few weeks.

PRUNING

No pruning is necessary this month.

PROBLEMS

Aphid, mite, whitefly, and scale problems are likely to develop on indoor annuals because the plants are under stress. Daylight hours are reduced dramatically, heating systems dry out the air and cause hot blasts, and opening doors causes cold drafts. Under these circumstances, pest eggs hidden on the plant may hatch. To prevent problems, try to keep your plants as stress-free as possible by giving them strong light, adequate moisture, and even air temperatures. Rinse their foliage with tepid running water every so often, and follow up with a foliage spray of insecticidal soap, hot pepper wax, or similar repellent to stop problems before they develop.

HELPFUL HINTS

While some gardeners avoid annuals that tend to self-sow, many welcome them to their gardens. Here are some that may appear year after year:

- **Snapdragon** (*Antirrhinum majus*)
- **Browallia** (*Browallia speciosa*)
- **Calendula** (*Calendula officinalis*)
- **Bachelor's Button** (*Centaurea officinalis*)
- **Cleome** (*Cleome hassleriana*)
- **Rocket Larkspur** (*Consolida ambigua*)
- **Cosmos** (*Cosmos bipinnatus*)
- **California Poppy** (*Eschscholzia californica*)
- **Impatiens** (*Impatiens wallerana*)
- **Morning Glory** (*Ipomoea sp.*)
- **Toadflax** (*Linaria maroccana*)
- **Sweet Alyssum** (*Lobularia maritima*)
- **Money Plant** (*Lunaria annua*)
- **Four-o'-Clock** (*Mirabilis jalapa*)
- **Bells of Ireland** (*Moluccella laevis*)
- **Forget-Me-Not** (*Myosotis sylvatica*)
- **Baby Blue Eyes** (*Nemphila menziesii*)
- **Corn Poppy** (*Papaver rhoeas*)
- **Love-in-a-Mist** (*Nigella damascena*)
- **Moss Rose** (*Portulaca grandiflora*)
- **Wishbone Flower** (*Torenia fournieri*)
- **Johnny-Jump-Up** (*Viola tricolor*)

Toadflax

December

ANNUALS & BIENNIALS

 PLANNING

In the warmest parts of Ohio the ground may not yet be frozen. Continue to enjoy **ornamental cabbage** and **kale** until severe cold turns them mushy, then dig them up and discard them.

Make the final entries for the year in your garden notebook or journal. Record the dates of the arrival of the first frost and then the hard frost. This will be a useful reference for next year. When the new seed and plant catalogs begin to arrive in the mail this month, put them aside until holiday festivities are over and you can give them your full attention. Clean up and inventory seed-starting supplies so you can order additional pots or soilless mix right after the new year.

 PLANTING

To grow your own **pansy** seedlings, sow seeds this month, and prepare to put the sprouts under lights when they appear (see January or February on growing seedlings indoors). Pot seedlings individually when they grow large enough to handle.

Check stem cuttings that are in water or flats of moist vermiculite or perlite to see if rooting has started. Pot up those that have developed good root systems. Use soilless medium with some granular, slow-acting fertilizer mixed in. Set them under lights.

 CARE

No care is necessary this month.

 WATERING

Water new sprouts and previously potted rooted cuttings when the soil feels dry.

 FERTILIZING

Add granular, slow-acting fertilizer to the potting mix for rooted stem cuttings and new seedlings. Hold off on other fertilizer until annuals begin to bloom well. Then water-in some very dilute fast-acting fertilizer every few weeks or as the label directs.

 PRUNING

When annual plants adjust to indoor life and begin to grow, they may stretch to get more light. Pinch back stems of **begonia**, **impatiens**, **geranium**, and others to make more compact plants. Set them under artificial lights if necessary.

Pick up fallen leaves and other debris around plants to avoid disease problems.

 PROBLEMS

The trick to preventing serious pest and disease problems is to examine your annuals and other nearby plants frequently for signs that something is amiss. The sooner you notice and diagnose a problem, the easier it is to deal with. Things to look for:

- Ants crawling on stems and foliage
- Shiny, sticky coating on the leaves and pot rim
- Tender growing tips and new foliage that is twisted, discolored
- Fine webbing near the main stems and leaf stems
- Leaves pale or speckled
- Lower leaves turning yellow and dropping
- Stems discolored near the soil line
- Leaves yellowed except for dark-green veins
- Gray or white coating on the foliage

BULBS, CORMS, RHIZOMES, & TUBERS

It is likely that some variety of flowering bulb appears on almost everyone's list of top ten flower favorites, and tulips and daffodils rank highly among the public's all-time sentimental favorites. They are right up there with daisies as the flowers most easily recognized by children and youth who have virtually no gardening experience or special knowledge of plants.

This familiarity suggests how thoroughly daffodils and tulips in particular and spring-flowering bulbs in general have pervaded our popular culture. And it's no wonder! Indoors in the winter, pots of forced tulips or bouquets of cut daffodils and tulips anticipate the arrival of warm weather, promising yet another spring of beauty. Then these flowers bloom outdoors, appearing on the scene to a grateful world weary of winter. Their rich, cheery colors and distinctive shapes decorate the outdoor landscape.

BULBS FOR THE GARDEN

It is no coincidence that many other varieties of flowering bulbs appear on home gardeners' lists of flower favorites as well. What else is easier to

grow and care for? Stick them in the ground and they will do the rest. Bulbs offer enormous returns on a very small investment of time and effort. They also provide an opportunity to get double duty from planting areas, because they die back after blooming to make way for another wave of plants that can show off during a subsequent season.

Most new home gardeners' first bulb-growing experiences are with a few hardy spring-flowering bulbs such as tulips, daffodils, and hyacinths. Success is virtually guaranteed because these bulbs are so self-reliant. Success often leads to experimentation with other hardy bulbs, including the wonderful minor bulbs such as crocus, snowdrop, and glory of the snow. In no time at all, a gardener will be eyeing the later-flowering bulbs such as lilies and ornamental onions (alliums), which beckon from garden center shelves. It is only a matter of time before the lure of growing fall-blooming sternbergia and autumn crocus becomes irresistible.

You can always find interesting and unusual bulbs to grow. Choose fritillaria or dogtooth violets, and tiny squill or winter aconites. Go beyond traditional spring bloomers and try summer-blooming crocosmia and fall-blooming Italian arum. Then try those such as colchicum that have two seasons—one to show off foliage, another to flower. Take advantage of the versatility of bulbs, and use them many different ways in the landscape. Naturalize snowdrops or crocus in the late-winter lawn. Plant anemones and daffodils as ground covers in woodland areas. Mix and match tulips and grape hyacinths in beds or borders. Combine iris and ornamental onions. Use dahlias and lilies in the summer flower border. And don't forget that many bulbs will grow in containers and, surprisingly, some will grow in water.

TYPES OF BULBS

The term "bulb" has both a general and a specific meaning. For gardening purposes (and this chapter), it describes any plant that has special fleshy organs formed from underground modified stems that store energy in the form of carbohydrates. These organs come in several different forms.

A true bulb is a distinctive kind of storage organ, one that has compressed within it a short stem, an already formed flower bud, and rings or layers of foliage around the bud that appear as scales on its outer surface. One way to see this kind of structure is to slice a cooking onion in half. Some true bulb examples are:

- amaryllis
- hyacinth
- lily
- narcissus
- tulip

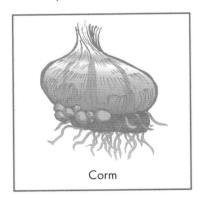

Corm

Another type of energy-storage organ is a corm. Resembling a thick, flat, brownish disk, it too is a compressed stem. A close look reveals a growing tip on one side; the other, even flatter side is where roots emerge after the corm is planted. There are no scales on

True Bulb

the outer surface. Some examples of plants that grow from corms are:

- crocosmia
- crocus
- freesia
- gladiolus

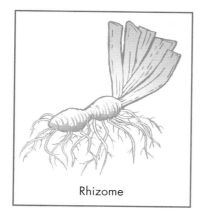

Rhizome

Yet another form of energy-storage bulb is a rhizome, a swollen, fleshy length of modified stem that likes to lie horizontally in the soil. The roots grow along the bottom of its length, and shoots grow from the top, usually at one end. Some plants that grow from rhizomes are:

- bearded iris
- canna
- waterlily

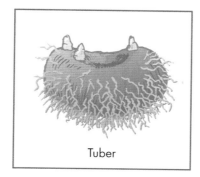

Tuber

Tubers are energy-storing mechanisms for some of the plants included in the general category of bulbs. They are essentially swollen, rounded stems covered with scalelike leaves and eyes, or growth buds. Stems and buds may grow from all sides of a tuber. Examples:

- caladium
- jack-in-the-pulpit
- lotus
- orchid
- potato, ornamental or edible

GROWING BULBS

You can see that the world of bulbs extends far beyond the traditional spring crocus, daffodils, and tulips. In fact, there can be bulbs blooming in the garden through nine or ten months of the year. For the most part, these successive waves of colorful flowers and handsome foliage take very little care beyond routine watering, some fertilizer, and cleanup.

After the hardy bulbs bloom, die back, and then go dormant to ride out the hot season, tender summer bloomers sustain the colorful parade. Growing tender bulbs in the garden requires a bit more work because some of them need staking and deadheading as they grow and bloom over the long summer season. It also requires a bit more skill and knowledge if the intention is to keep them for the following summer. Because they cannot withstand winter weather in Ohio, tender bulbs must be dug up to be stored over the winter. Another option is to leave them in the soil to freeze and die, then replace them the following spring.

Fall-blooming bulbs take over soon after Labor Day when the daylight hours begin to fade and the evening temperatures begin to drop. Their flowers brighten the fading fall garden as they bloom among the falling leaves. As carefree as their spring counterparts, these hardy bulbs die back and go dormant again as temperatures fall and winter arrives.

JANUARY
BULBS, CORMS, RHIZOMES, & TUBERS

PLANNING

The wonderful thing about bulbs, especially the hardy types, is that they are basically carefree: once you get them in the ground, they take care of themselves. Under cover of snow or winter mulch the hardy, spring-blooming ones are already stirring, preparing to emerge from dormancy. Those that are "true" bulbs, such as **tulips**, have their entire flower

Tulips have their entire flower structure fully formed in miniature, deep within each bulb.

structure fully formed in miniature, deep within each bulb. Because bulbs store the food the plant will need, (manufactured last spring as their foliage soaked up the sun's energy), they are virtually self-reliant. Last fall they developed root systems to sustain them, and shortly their internal calendars will signal the time for each type to begin to grow toward the soil surface.

Tender, summer-flowering bulbs have a different schedule because winter weather kills them in the soil. They are typically grown as annuals in Ohio, planted when the soil is warm, then pulled from the ground—for potting, storing, or discarding—when frost threatens in the fall. This month is a good time to study the colorful mail-order catalogs and select the bulbs you want to grow this summer.

PLANTING

No planting is necessary this month.

CARE

If you notice **crocus** and **daffodil** foliage emerging already, don't panic. In fact, don't do anything.

There's no need to pile more mulch on the foliage for protection—just leave it alone. Frost and snow might brown the tips a bit, but the bulbs will develop more foliage and will be fine (hardy bulbs have a lot of experience with winter weather)!

What to do with a gift-planted **amaryllis** bulb that has finished blooming? There are two choices—treat it as an annual plant and throw it away, or keep it for next year. To keep it for next year:

1 Cut off faded flowers and stems.

2 Allow the big straplike leaves to develop and soak up the sun in a bright window.

3 Water it as you would a houseplant to keep the soil moist, not overly wet.

4 Fertilize it with houseplant fertilizer if there is no apparent granular, slow-acting fertilizer in its planting mix.

5 When nice weather arrives in spring, put it outdoors in the light. Protect the drooping foliage from slug attack.

6 In the fall, bring it in, stop watering, and let the leaves die back so it can have a dormant period. Then water it to begin the bloom cycle once again.

If bulbs planted in pots last fall for forcing indoors have had a long enough chill period, you will notice that green shoots are starting to emerge. Each bulb will have developed lots of roots, which may be nudging the crowded bulbs up out of the soil or gravel a bit.

1. Move the pots into warmth gradually, beginning by putting them in an area that is about 45 degrees F. for a few days, then into one that is closer to 60 degrees F. Water the bulbs when the planting mix is dry.

2. Place the bulb pots in a bright, sunny window as the buds swell. Avoid overheated rooms, which will cause the buds to bloom and fade very quickly.

 WATERING

If their soil dries out, keep watering pans of bulbs that need longer cool storage for forcing. Make sure the soil or gravel has good drainage.

 FERTILIZING

Bulbs come packaged with fertilizer in the form of stored energy. Those that are potted for forced bloom have enough to produce lovely blooms. If you later plant them in the ground, add granular, slow-acting fertilizer or bulb fertilizer to the soil at planting time.

 PRUNING

Improve the appearance of blooming potted bulbs by mulching their soil surface lightly with decorative gravel, colorful pebbles, sphagnum moss, or some other attractive material. Trim off any withered foliage tips or blooms.

 PROBLEMS

Rot is sometimes a problem with bulbs potted for forcing. It destroys bulb roots in poorly drained soil. Always examine bulbs carefully for discolored, soft spots before planting them, and do not overwater.

Aphids and fungus gnats sometimes attack hardy bulbs blooming indoors. Wash off the aphids, or spray affected plants with commercial insecticidal soap. Flying gnats are more nuisance than danger. Their larvae in the soil go after plant roots, so discard the soil in the trash after the bulbs are finished blooming. Discard heavily infested bulbs as well.

HELPFUL HINTS

Since January is the month of new beginnings, it is an appropriate time to begin a garden journal. Journaling is one of the easiest, fastest ways to become a better gardener. While it may seem as though jotting down notes every week or so takes extra time, it in fact saves time. A journal reminds us of our successes and failures. Knowing what did not work helps prevent wasting more time, energy, and money trying it again. Recording the weather, noting what is blooming, listing new plants and their names, and making sketches of where plants are located give gardeners a new perspective on their efforts.

A journal can be a bunch of notecards, a lined legal pad, a calendar, a computer file, or a lovely bound book—there are no rules. Keep it nearby—perhaps on top of the refrigerator, in the tool shed, or beside the bed—so you can make notes when you think of them.

FEBRUARY
BULBS, CORMS, RHIZOMES, & TUBERS

 PLANNING

Look for **snowdrops** and **winter aconite** anytime now; note when you see the first flower. If you do not have any of these stalwart early bloomers, plan to purchase some late next summer to plant in the fall. When winter becomes tiresome, the appearance of these flowering bulbs is great encouragement.

Snowflake

If you have not already made a sketch of where hardy bulbs are planted in the yard, get ready to make one this spring as their bloom season unfolds. It will be useful for planting bulbs next fall and will also help with locating spots for tender bulbs later this spring. Think about planting foliage ground covers over bulb beds. **Ivy, pachysandra, liriope, sweet woodruff,** and others will help to cover unsightly ripening bulb foliage later this spring.

Plan where you will site tender, summer-blooming bulbs later this spring. (Don't forget that many also do well in containers.) You can order bulbs by mail any time now.

Shopping List: containers for summer bulbs, soilless potting mix

 PLANTING

As soon as **pansies** become available at the garden center, they can be planted in and amongst where you have planted bulbs such as **tulips, hyacinths,** and **daffodils. Calendulas, forget-me-nots,** and **primulas** are also cool-weather annuals that look really lovely when interplanted with hardy bulbs in special beds, in the garden, or in containers.

When **snowdrops** are finished blooming and only their green foliage remains, they can be moved or thinned. If the ground is workable, take this opportunity before the season begins full force to transplant the little bulbs to new sites for next year. They are ideal for edging beds or naturalizing in woodland settings. Using a trowel, plant them an inch or two into the soil. If you choose to plant them in the lawn, you will have to delay mowing that area until the foliage ripens and dies down six to eight weeks after bloom.

 CARE

The earliest bloomers of the hardy bulbs will be showing up anytime now. In fact, if it has been a mild winter and they are planted near heat-retaining masonry walls, **snowdrops, crocus,** and even certain types of **daffodils** may have already started to emerge through the mulch. Do not be concerned if a sudden freeze or snowstorm comes along; the bulbs will be fine. The mulch covering on the soil will help it stay chilly, which will slow the bulbs until it is late enough in the winter for them to emerge safely.

Check stored tender bulbs such as **cannas**, **dahlias**, and **glads** from last year. Discard any that are mushy or dried out. Make sure the temperature in the room doesn't freeze. In another month or two it will be time to bring them out of storage to plant in pots for an early indoor start prior to planting out. It is not safe to put tender bulbs into the ground until late May or early June.

WATERING

Hardy bulbs planted out in the yard in mulched beds will not need watering even if winter rain and snow is limited. Those planted in windowboxes and planters outdoors aboveground may need watering. Make sure containers have drainage holes so excess water or melting snow can drain away.

FERTILIZING

Sprinkle granular bulb fertilizer over the soil of beds of hardy bulbs now, so there will be time for the nutrients to soak down to the roots before bloom time. Broadcast it over the soil, then scratch it into the surface a bit.

HELPFUL HINTS

There are lots of small bulbs that bloom literally and figuratively in the shadow of the more familiar, high-profile **Dutch crocus**, common **tulips**, and **daffodils**. Many of these are resistant to squirrels in areas of Ohio. Some small bulbs:

- **Checkered Lily** (*Fritillaria meleagris*)
- **Dogtooth Violet** (*Erythronium* 'Pagoda')
- **Glory of the Snow** (*Chionodoxa sp.*)
- **Snow Crocus** (*Crocus tomasinianus*)
- **Snowdrop** (*Galanthus nivalis*)
- **Snowflake** (*Leucojum aestivum*)
- **Squill** (*Scilla sibirica*)
- **Striped Squill** (*Pushkinia scilloides*)
- **Winter Aconite** (*Eranthis hymenalis*)
- **Wood Hyacinth** (*Hyacinthoides* sp.)

PRUNING

After hardy bulbs have bloomed out in the yard, it is important to allow their foliage to continue to grow. (Clip off the faded flowers of the larger types—**tulips**, **hyacinths**, and **daffodils**—to direct their energy into manufacturing carbohydrates for energy rather than producing seeds.) Resist the temptation to neaten the foliage, even though it gets pretty unsightly as it ages and flops. Clean it up only after it is so limp it pulls away easily.

PROBLEMS

Squirrels just love early **crocuses**—probably because there are few fresh food alternatives, and **crocuses** are fresh and tender. Fashion low covers from wire hardware cloth to lay over threatened **crocus** beds to deter the critters. Soon squirrels will find other food, and later-blooming **crocuses** are not as bothered by them.

Deer, if they are in the area, will be a problem for spring bulbs. They love **crocus** and **tulips**. Use the squirrel preventative mentioned above, or spray plants with repellent as directed on the product label.

MARCH
BULBS, CORMS, RHIZOMES, & TUBERS

 PLANNING

Spring-blooming bulbs begin their main show this month, and often the show coincides with Easter and other religious holidays. It is not surprising that the seasonal display in the yard is echoed or anticipated by the array of gift plants in florist and garden center windows.

Tulips and **daffodils** are available in a dizzying array of types and varieties, and they also have varying bloom times. As you enjoy spring-blooming bulbs in your garden and elsewhere, think about planting more next fall. Plan for continuing bloom from March through May by selecting and planting early-, mid-, and late-flowering varieties of your favorites. Even though you will not receive the bulbs until fall when it is planting time, the best time to choose is now when the flowers are on display in public and residential landscapes. Ordering bulbs ahead of time often saves money, too.

The long, wide, straplike leaves you may notice in gardens this time of year belong to **summer amaryllis**, also called **resurrection lily**. They will die back and disappear soon. Look for amaryllis-like flowers without foliage in the same places next August.

Shopping List: stakes, bulb fertilizer

 PLANTING

Snowdrop blossoms have faded by now, and only the foliage persists. During the next month or so while the leaves are still green, divide overcrowded clumps of **snowdrops** if the ground has thawed sufficiently.

Plant cool-season annuals—**forget-me-nots**, **pansies**, **English daisies**—as companion plants for spring-flowering hardy bulbs. They will soon appear at the garden center.

If you did not plant hardy bulbs last fall but would love to have some **tulips** or **daffodils** now, purchase some potted ones that are just starting to show new foliage. Set each pot outdoors in the garden bed, either placing it on the soil or sinking it into the soil. An alternative is to remove the bulbs from the pot, taking care to keep the soil intact around the roots, and plant the entire clump in the garden bed.

 CARE

The earliest **crocuses**, tiny **snow crocuses**, and **aconite** naturalize easily, often spreading into lawns. After they bloom, delay mowing the lawn to allow their foliage to ripen. Pots of **tulips**, **daffodils**, **hyacinths**, **lilies**, and other forced bulbs may be planted outdoors after the foliage has ripened. They will adjust to the outdoor schedule and bloom next year in the yard. In the case of **amaryllis**, which is tender and will not winter over in the soil, set the pot of foliage outdoors for the summer. (See October for instructions for forcing blooms indoors.)

In a few weeks it will be time to take the tender bulbs out of winter storage. Check them this month to be sure they have not dried out.

 WATERING

Normal spring rainfall or melting snow should provide sufficient moisture for bulbs. If it has been a dry winter, water bulb beds after the ground has thawed.

 FERTILIZING

Bulbs, corms, rhizomes, and tubers are special structures in which plants store energy from the previous season, so these plants do not require spring fertilizing.

Common **tulips**, including **Darwin hybrids** or **Cottage types**, are not always reliably perennial. They are not as strong

HELPFUL HINTS

There are all kinds of **daffodils**, also called **narcissus**, and the various types bloom at different times throughout spring. It is possible with a little forethought to have some blooming continuously in the yard for up to three months.

• Small **daffodils** that have reflexed petals (such as 'Peeping Tom') appear in March and April.

• The familiar large-cup and "trumpet" types such as 'King Alfred' start the main April bloom time. They are followed by small-cup, double **daffodils**. Some have fancy, split, frilly trumpets.

• Dainty nodding types that bear several flowers per stem are often fragrant; **jonquils** and **tazetta** varieties bloom in mid- to late April.

• **Poet's narcissus** (*Narcissus poeticus* 'Actea'), with tiny cups edged with red or orange, are among the latest to bloom. They appear in May.

Daffodil (tazetta type)

their second year of bloom and weaken even more after that. Fertilizing them twice a year, in early spring and fall, helps to keep them stronger.

PRUNING

Pinching off the faded flowers of minor bulbs such as **squill**, **anemone**, and **snowdrops** is not necessary because they are fairly unobtrusive. Snip or pinch off faded **narcissus**, **tulip**, and **hyacinth** flowers to improve the appearance of the plants while

their leaves continue to grow. This also prevents their wasting energy on developing unnecessary seedpods. Do not cut back, tie, or otherwise disturb the foliage while it is still green; this interferes with collecting sun for next year's energy.

PROBLEMS

Deer are quite fond of hybrid **tulips** and will nibble the blossoms from the tops of their stems. An entire bed of **tulips** may disappear overnight. If deer are just

occasional visitors to the yard, try spraying the **tulips** with repellent, or protect them with cages of chicken wire while they are in bloom. If deer are a regular nuisance, either fence the property or grow **narcissus** instead of **tulips**.

Mice will nest in the same kinds of dark, cool places where tender bulbs are stored indoors over the winter. Keep an eye out for signs of their activity when you check the bulbs, and set traps if necessary. Take pains to block holes and cracks around doors, utility wires, and pipes.

APRIL
BULBS, CORMS, RHIZOMES, & TUBERS

PLANNING

Garden beds and borders that were brown and empty just a month ago are alive with colorful flowering bulbs this month. To maintain the long-term health of hardy bulbs, allow the foliage to collect energy from the sun until it matures and dies back. The appearance of these beds is always a concern. Take some time to evaluate the location of your plantings of **narcissus**, **tulips**, **hyacinths**, **ornamental onions**, and others. If their foliage looks unsightly or obscures the developing perennial flowers

Dividing bulbs follows the same process; in this example, a daylily is being divided.

that are currently emerging, you may want to transplant the bulbs to areas where the dying foliage will be less obtrusive:

- Plant bulbs in beds of evergreen ground covers such as **ivy**, **pachysandra**, and **vinca**.
- Plant bulbs among perennials that will emerge and leaf out just in time to mask ripening bulb foliage (examples: **daylily**, **hosta**, **liriope**, and **colchicum**).

Soon it will be time to plant tender bulbs. Check your garden journal to identify places that will be empty after spring bulb foliage dies back. These spots and those left by ephemeral spring perennial plants such as **bleeding heart** and **Virginia bluebells** are perfect sites for pots and planters filled with summer-blooming bulbs.

Visit a public garden or arboretum where spring bulbs are in full display. This is a good way to enjoy and learn about new or unusual varieties.

Shopping List: potting mix, bulb fertilizer, watering can

PLANTING

Like **snowdrops**, **daffodils** can be divided while "green." Although they can go indefinitely without thinning, as they do when naturalized in a meadow or woodland, sometimes clumps become disproportionately large for a garden bed or border. Crowding may decrease the number of blooms. Rather than wait until fall when you may forget or cannot find them, do the job as soon as they finish blooming.

1. Carefully dig the clump of bulbs out of the ground so it is free of soil. Take care not to damage or break the foliage.

2. Gently brush excess soil from the bulbs, and separate them, teasing apart the tangled roots at the base of each large knobby bulb.

3. If a large bulb has developed several good-sized subsidiary bulbs with roots, you may choose to separate them from the mother bulb by breaking them apart, or you can plant them intact.

4. Replant some of the bulbs in the former location, 4 to 6 inches apart and about 6 inches deep. Water well.

5. Plant the remaining divisions elsewhere, or give them away. Smaller ones may not bloom for a year or two. They are perfect for naturalizing.

If you have stored **tuberous begonias** in pots, you can begin to nudge them out of dormancy by watering them and bringing them gradually into the warmth of the house. It is still too early for them to go outdoors.

Rather than wait until next month when the weather has warmed up, start tender bulbs indoors now. Bring them out of winter storage, cull any injured or diseased, and divide those overgrown. Plant **canna**, **caladium**, **dahlias**, and others in soilless potting medium with a bit of granular, slow-acting fertilizer mixed in. Water them, and set the pots in a bright room for a few weeks. They will be well sprouted when it is warm enough to plant them outdoors.

This is a good time to plant outdoors the hardy bulbs that you forced indoors back in January and February. Keep any remaining foliage intact, and plant as you would in the fall (see October for planting instructions).

CARE

Later this month, check stored tender bulbs that you intend to plant outdoors next month. Go through the bulbs now and discard any that look bad. Clean the soil off them, and remove desiccated pieces of root or sections of rhizome. Divide **dahlia** tubers where they are linked, making sure each separate tuber for planting has an "eye," or growing tip. Break off bulblets or cormlets from **begonias** and **glads** to plant separately. They are too young to bloom this year; wait until late May to plant them outdoors.

WATERING

If the April showers live up to their reputation, there will be no need to water bulb beds this month. Make sure the potted medium of tender bulbs is moist, but never soaking wet.

FERTILIZING

If you want to fertilize hardy spring bulbs to help them develop good foliage, wait until after they bloom and you have clipped off the faded flowers. If you can't get to it now, plan to fertilize in the early fall when you plant new bulbs—that is the most important time to fertilize.

PRUNING

Cut off faded **tulip** and **daffodil** flowers as soon as they finish blooming and their petals drop. Cut back the stems to where the leaves begin, leaving as much foliage as possible.

PROBLEMS

Rabbits as well as deer may be damaging your blooming **tulips**. Spray vulnerable **tulips** with repellent, or put up a temporary barrier such as a wire cage to protect them.

Tulip fire (*Botrytis tulipae*) is a serious disease which attacks **tulips** that have been growing in the same place for several years and deforms their flowers and bulbs. Dig up and discard affected bulbs, and do not plant **tulips** in that soil for at least four years. The disease will die out on its own.

MAY

BULBS, CORMS, RHIZOMES, & TUBERS

PLANNING

Danger of frost should be past in Ohio this month—early May in the Cincinnati area, late May in the Cleveland area. Finally the soil has dried out from April rains and is warm enough for planting tender, summer-blooming bulbs. When planting **dahlias**, **cannas**, and others in containers, remember that they will grow larger over the summer, and factor that into the design.

Not all summer-blooming bulbs are tender, requiring special winter storage; some types will overwinter in the soil in Ohio. **Ornamental onions** of various kinds will bloom this month along with the **rhododendrons** and **mountain laurel**. **Hybrid lilies** and **crocosmia** foliage will appear as the weather becomes increasingly warm, and they will bloom in summer. Plan to plant more of these types if you feel you do not have time to plant tender summer bulbs every year.

Shopping List: potted tender bulbs, ground cover plants

PLANTING

This is a busy planting month.

• **Tuberous begonias** overwintered in pots as houseplants may need repotting into larger containers. They can go outdoors into the garden in their pots or directly into the soil. Choose a shady spot that receives good air circulation, indirect or filtered light, and good soil that drains well.

• Finish planting out in the yard those gift plant bulbs from Easter that you do not intend to throw away (see August and September for planting instructions for hardy bulbs). The **amaryllis** bulb should stay in its pot; set it in a bed or on the deck outdoors so its great foliage can enjoy the sun.

• Plant all your tender bulbs by the end of the month. If they have been started in pots and are already sprouted, transplant them into the garden or into decorative containers with other plants when the weather is dependably warm.

• Plant the first wave of **gladiolus** corms mid-month. To enjoy continuous blooms over the season, plant more corms every two weeks until July.

CARE

Certain summer-blooming bulbs need support to prevent their collapse in heavy rain or wind. Support **lilies** that will grow over 3 feet tall when they begin to gain some height. Insert a stake into the soil near each stem gently so it does not damage the bulb. Use green twine to loosely tie the stem to the stake. Do the same with **dahlias** and **glads**. Make sure the stakes are shorter than the ultimate height of the plant so they are unobtrusive. Clumps of narrow **crocosmia** foliage may need support. Set up stakes around the perimeter of the planting then tie twine to them in a circle to hold them upright.

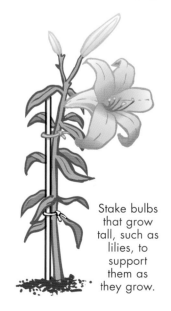

Stake bulbs that grow tall, such as lilies, to support them as they grow.

WATERING

Water the soil where newly planted summer bulbs are located to make sure the soil settles around them properly. Those in pots will need closer attention for watering, because soilless potting medium tends to dry out faster than garden soil, especially when the weather gets hotter.

FERTILIZING

Although bulbs, corms, rhizomes, and tubers store energy for the plant to use, plants benefit from nutrients in the soil as well. Some, such as **dahlias** and **begonias**, produce flowers all summer and welcome an extra ration of fertilizer to sustain strong growth. To enhance the fertility of your soil, sprinkle some slow-acting, granular, all-purpose fertilizer over the soil of bulb beds so the rain can soak it in. Mix it into the potting medium when planting or transplanting bulbs in containers. If the bulbs are already in containers, sprinkle the complete, slow-acting granular fertilizer over the surface of the planting mix.

PRUNING

By month's end, the foliage of the earlier hardy bulbs will be yellowing and collapsing. Clean it up when it has ripened to the point that it easily detaches from the underground bulb when you tug on it.

PROBLEMS

Insects crawling all over round, lilac-blue **ornamental onion** blossoms are beneficial! **Ornamental onion** flowers are valuable allies in pest control because they support the tiny predator wasps, lacewings, and other insects that attack pest insects and their larvae throughout the garden.

Aphids and mites are potential problems for blooming bulbs, just as they are for other plants. Try washing off the clusters of insects at tender foliage tips and buds. If that doesn't work, spray them directly with insecticidal soap.

Fungal diseases may mar the foliage of certain bulbs. **Tuberous begonias** sometimes develop mildew and leaf spot infections. The best defense is a good offense. Make sure they have good air circulation, and keep foliage dry. Pinch off infected leaves, and clean up fallen leaves promptly to arrest the spread of the fungus.

Weeds are easily controlled if you deal with them early before they get entrenched. Pull or spot-treat stubborn weeds with herbicide before the bulbs emerge from the soil. Mulch bare soil to discourage the growth of weeds.

HELPFUL HINTS

Many summer bulbs are magnets for hummingbirds and butterflies. Their richly colored, often fragrant, blossoms entice visitors on the lookout for nectar and pollen. Watch your **cannas**, **crocosmias**, **lilies**, and **glads** for hummingbirds. The trumpet shapes of these flowers are just what hummers like. The brilliant colors of **dahlias** make them a favorite of butterflies, which also visit **lilies**, **crocosmia**, and **gladiolus**.

JUNE

BULBS, CORMS, RHIZOMES, & TUBERS

 PLANNING

As spring turns into summer, you may find more bulb catalogs in your mailbox. This will give you an opportunity to order hardy bulbs for fall planting ahead of time, if you have not already done so. There are many advantages to pre-ordering fall bulbs in late spring:

• The bulbs you need are fresh in your mind from the bloom season just past.

• You can find and have first choice of the less common bulbs that are in limited supply.

• Mail-order firms often offer smaller-sized bulbs in bulk for naturalizing at an economical price.

• Pre-ordering usually earns a discount.

• Bulbs will be shipped at the end of the season when it is appropriate to plant them.

Remember the New Year's resolution about trying at least one new bulb this year? Study the photographs and information in the catalogs and choose something that looks interesting. Some suggestions: **fritillaria**, **colchicum**, **dwarf iris**, **hardy cyclamen**, and **snowflake**.

Shopping List: pre-ordered fall bulbs, garden stakes

 PLANTING

Last call for transplanting into the ground those tender summer bulbs that were started in pots. Soon they will outgrow their pots and need larger ones if they are not planted. Time is also running out for thinning clumps of **daffodils** and replanting the bulbs while their foliage is still attached to make it easier. You can dry and store the extra bulbs from the clumps until fall planting time, but why go to the trouble? Plant them in a new bed, under trees and shrubs, or naturalize in a woodland setting now, and the job is done.

Remember to put in another planting of **gladiolus** corms so there will be **glads** in bloom when the first batch fades.

 CARE

Continue staking plants that need support. Some **dahlias** grow very tall by midseason, and their brittle stems break quite easily. Stake **glad** stems individually to prevent

It's time to transplant any tender bulbs that you started in pots.

their heavy blossoms from flopping in heavy rains.

WATERING

A sudden onset of heat and/or lack of rain later this month may require getting out the garden hose. Summer-blooming bulbs appreciate the water because they are in their major growth period. Those planted under trees may miss out on light rainfall because the canopy of new leaves blocks it. Those planted in pots and ornamental containers dry out quickly in the heat.

Hardy spring-blooming bulbs have finished their season and are going dormant to wait out the coming weeks of heat. Most prefer dry conditions during this time and do not need supplemental watering.

FERTILIZING

The slow-acting granular fertilizer incorporated into bulb soil or potting medium is providing nutrients now. If it is not in the potting mix, water-in very dilute liquid fertilizer every two weeks while the plants are blooming.

HELPFUL HINTS

One of the great summer bulb success stories is **lilies**. These summer bloomers are different from most of the other summer bloomers because they are tough enough to withstand real winters in the ground. They have lots of other virtues as well:

- Enormous variety of color
- Fragrance
- Varying heights
- Neat habit
- Formal look (yet they blend with other plants)
- Attract butterflies and hummingbirds
- Make excellent cut flowers

PRUNING

Pick **dahlias** and **glads** for indoor display and to stimulate the plants to produce new blossoms. This also keeps them neat, improving the appearance of the yard and garden as well as the plants. Pinch off shabby leaves and faded flowers and stems of **begonias**.

PROBLEMS

Squirrels may go after bulbs in pots on the ground or patio and tip them over. Group the pots, or raise them from ground level to make them less accessible.

Slugs (snails without shells) are fond of **tuberous begonias**. Raise pots off the ground by setting them on other, overturned pots, bricks or decorative concrete "feet." Sprinkle diatomaceous earth (DE) over the soil around those planted in soil. This sharp material will discourage slugs from slithering over to the plant foliage.

JULY
BULBS, CORMS, RHIZOMES, & TUBERS

 PLANNING

If it has been awhile since you recorded information in your garden journal or notebook, take some time this month—the halfway point of the calendar year—to catch up. Things that are worth noting:

- Major weather events such as late snowfall, late frost, early heat, spring drought
- Which hardy bulbs were a disappointment
- When the first blossoms of **snowdrops**, **iris**, **daffodils**, **crocus**, **tulips**, and **ornamental onions** appeared
- How the tender bulbs withstood winter storage
- If you thinned overgrown clumps of **daffodils** or other flowers
- Things you intended to do, but didn't get to
- When you planted summer-blooming bulbs
- Any significant events in the landscape—large trees removed, construction, flooding

Shopping List: vases for cut flowers, floral preservative

 PLANTING

Allow the bulbs acquired from thinning overgrown clumps of **daffodils** and the early fall-

blooming bulbs (**colchicum**, **sternbergia**, and **fall crocus**) to dry out and rest in a dark place with good air circulation until September.

 CARE

Finish staking tall **dahlia** plants and others that may fall over in storms. Be careful not to poke or damage the tubers when inserting the stake into the soil near them.

Mulch any bare soil around summer bulbs with an inch or two of chopped leaves, dried grass clippings, or similar organic material. It will help prevent the soil from drying out, discourage weeds, and help condition the soil as it decomposes in the summer heat.

 WATERING

Water bulbs in pots if the weather is dry and/or hot. Make sure the pots are draining well so the planting medium does not get soggy. Water summer bulbs in the garden when it becomes necessary to water other plants.

 FERTILIZING

If you have used granular, slow-acting fertilizer when planting

bulbs in containers or garden soil, there is no need to fertilize now, for the bulbs are getting gradual, consistent, uniform nutrition—the best kind. Soil covered by a protective, organic mulch gains fertility over time as the mulch decomposes and nutrients are introduced into the soil.

 PRUNING

Some **dahlia** varieties are dwarf and grow to only 1 or 2 feet tall. The medium and tall varieties, however, reach from 3 to 6 feet tall. Strategic pinching will promote side branching and help keep these taller ones more compact. Begin the process by pinching out the center stem after there are a half-dozen leaves on the plant.

Remove faded **begonia** blooms promptly to reduce disease. Cut off **lily** flowers after all the blooms on a stem have faded. Leave the leaf-covered stem so the foliage can continue to soak up sun for energy that will be stored in the bulb for next season. In a month or six weeks, the stem and foliage will have dried sufficiently so they can be easily separated from the bulb deep in the soil. Cut stems, and discard them on the compost pile.

PROBLEMS

Insects and diseases are more of a problem for tender, summer-blooming bulbs than they are for hardy spring bloomers. This is mainly because the insects and disease spores are not out as abundant in the chilly spring. They share a preference for warmth with the summer bloomers. Handle these problems as you would for any other garden plant.

1. Keep your summer bulb plants as happy and stress-free as possible by giving them proper moisture, nutrition, light, and air circulation.

2. Keep after weeds, which harbor pest insects and disease pathogens and compete with bulbs for nutrients and light.

3. Examine blooming bulbs regularly to discover problems early, before they become severe.

4. Pinch or clip off foliage, blossoms, or stems that are infested with bugs or fungus to reduce the problem and keep it from spreading. Remove them from the garden and put in the trash.

5. Spray affected plants with a strong water spray to dislodge insects. Treat severe infestations with insecticidal soap spray as directed on its label.

HELPFUL HINTS

Like other plants, plants that grow from bulbs, tubers, corms, and rhizomes—collectively referred to as bulbs in this book—have multiple names. Only one is official, and that is the scientific, or botanical, name, which is in formal Latin and is recognized throughout the horticultural world. Other names for bulbs are informal, common names that change from region to region. *Erythronium* is called both **dogtooth violet** and **trout lily**. *Lycoris* is called variously **resurrection lily**, **magic lily**, and **naked lady**, depending on who is talking. When buying bulbs, it is best to use their Latin name as listed in the catalog to be sure you get what you ask for.

Resurrection lily, naked lady, magic lily–it's all the same to *Lycoris*.

AUGUST
BULBS, CORMS, RHIZOMES, & TUBERS

 PLANNING

Enjoy the **resurrection lilies** that pop up in local yards and gardens. Always a bit of a surprise, they seem to appear out of nowhere on tall stems without any foliage. In fact, their foliage bloomed back in spring and died down in early summer. If you decide to plant some in your yard, put them among **hostas** or other companion plants, which can provide some foliage for the charming bare-stemmed flowers.

Fall is a good time to renovate garden beds where the soil has lost its organic content over the years and has become compacted. Plants may be overgrown, the bulbs crowded and tired. Take some time to improve the planting area when the weather cools a bit and before bulb-planting time.

Shopping List: bulb planter, fertilizer, hardy bulbs

 PLANTING

Early this month is a good time to move, or divide and replant, hardy bulbs that have been in the ground so long they have become densely crowded. Smaller blossoms or reduced blooming often signals overcrowding. If clumps of **snowdrop**

bulbs start to rise up from under the soil or if the centers of clumps of **iris** are woody, it is time to dig up the clumps and separate the bulbs. Discard those that look diseased or damaged. Replant the healthy ones, with some space between them.

As soon as pre-ordered hardy bulbs arrive, start planting them. There are several ways to use bulbs in a residential landscape. One way is to naturalize them. This means the planting pattern is random and informal, as might be the case in nature, rather than making official planting beds according to a scheme. This is a great way to improve undeveloped or marginal areas of the yard.

Pop small **crocus** and **glory of the snow** bulbs into an area of the lawn where the soil is damp and easy to penetrate, and next spring they will provide a scattering of color over the green lawn. Plant **daffodils** in a woodland area where they will provide spots of cheery yellow before the leaves come out on the trees. Each year these bulbs will multiply, and the planting will become even more beautiful. Steps for a naturalized planting:

1. Naturalized bulbs do not need to be topsize, which is the most expensive. Use smaller, more economical bulbs that can be purchased in bulk.

2. Scatter the bulbs so they fall randomly over the area to be planted.

3. Dig a hole in the soil where each bulb has dropped, and plant the bulb at the correct depth.

4. Fill the hole with soil, and firm it gently.

5. Water the area if rain is not expected for awhile.

 CARE

Sometimes in summer the mulch layer decomposes and the soil surface dries out and shrinks, revealing piles of tiny bulbs such as **snowdrops** or **glory of the snow** that are shallowly planted. They are dormant and do not mind the dry soil, but they should not be exposed to light and air for long. Poke them back a couple of inches into the soil. They may have surfaced because of crowding, so take this opportunity to thin the clump. Plant the excess bulbs elsewhere.

WATERING

In heat and drought, container bulbs dry out fast! Be sure to check them every day. Water summer-blooming bulbs in the garden when all the plants need it.

FERTILIZING

No fertilizing is necessary this month.

HELPFUL HINTS

Planting time for hardy bulbs is not far away. If you buy bulbs at a store rather than through the mail, you will have an opportunity to examine them closely and select the best quality. How to tell the best? Growers generally grade bulbs by their size, sifting them through holes of various circumferences to sort them. Since the largest bulbs usually perform best—producing larger or more numerous blossoms—they are rated "tops" or topsize. They are usually the most expensive and are ideal for forcing indoors as specimen plants. Bulbs that are somewhat smaller are perfectly satisfactory for gardens and bedding designs. The smallest sizes, which are least expensive, are ideal for naturalizing. If they do not bloom the first year it does not matter, since they are planted randomly with lots of others. Check bulbs for firmness and plumpness. A touch of blue mold on the surface is not a problem; neither is a peeling tunic or dry skin on a bulb.

Cut back iris foliage to prepare for dividing the rhizomes.

PRUNING

Continue to deadhead faded blossoms on **dahlias** and other flowers that are still blooming. The stems of **lilies** will probably be drying and the foliage turning yellow by now. It is okay to cut off the stems at ground level, but do not try to pull them out of the soil, because you may pull up the bulb. If stems are crowded and a lot of them are thin and spindly, make a note to dig up and divide the **lily** bulbs this fall.

PROBLEMS

Deal with annual weeds before they mature and begin to set and spread seed. Pull them promptly. If they have rooted in a mulch layer, they will come up easily.

Mildew problems increase as humidity increases. Look for a telltale gray coating on foliage, especially on **tuberous begonias**. Pinch off any infected leaves, and set pots where plants have good air circulation.

SEPTEMBER
BULBS, CORMS, RHIZOMES, & TUBERS

PLANNING

Plan to plant all your hardy bulbs over the next few weeks as soon as you get them. They store better and more safely in the ground than in the garage, where they may be forgotten. Open the box they arrive in and spread out the packages of bulbs in a dry place so they will have some air circulation.

It really helps to chart where new bulbs are to go in the yard. If you have not done so already, sketch the layout of your existing beds and bulb plantings in your garden journal the best you can remember, and add the locations for the new plantings this year. Consider the height, bloom time, and color of each in the plan. Think about how their ripening foliage might be obscured by perennial plants such as **pachysandra** or **hostas**, which will emerge and grow next spring as bulb foliage dies back.

Spring-flowering bulbs need lots of sunshine, but that does not mean they cannot be planted under trees and in woodland situations. The leaves do not usually emerge on the trees until the bulbs have finished blooming and soaking up sun in their foliage and are ready to go dormant.

If you plan to have **amaryllis** in bloom for Christmas, buy and pot the bulbs now to force their bloom for December (see October for information on forcing bulbs). The packaged planting kits include instructions and make lovely holiday gifts.

Shopping List: shallow pots for forcing bulbs, decorative gravel, **amaryllis** bulb kits

PLANTING

Planting season for hardy bulbs may begin as soon as you buy them at the store or they arrive in the mail. **Tulip** and **daffodil** planting can be delayed until next month if you do not have time to plant all your bulbs now.

Many years ago it was customary to plant bulbs in beds of their own. Carefully spaced in uniform rows for maximum effect, they were separate from other flowering plants, trees, and shrubs. While this "bedding" system of planting is still common for public sites such as parks, malls, corporate campuses, and other formal landscapes, it is less common in smaller contemporary home landscapes. Bedded bulb plantings look best in large, formal landscapes where there are expanses of lawn.

Because spring never comes soon enough outdoors, pot some bulbs to force early bloom indoors in January. Some, such as **tulips**, **grape hyacinths**, or **crocus**, need to have twelve to sixteen weeks of cold temperature to satisfy dormancy before they will bloom. To start the process, imitate these conditions by planting them in pots and storing them in the cold now (see October). **Paper-white narcissus** is the exception, as it will root and bloom without a chill period. Buy lots of bulbs and start some every few weeks as winter closes in.

CARE

When digging or mulching, be especially careful in the areas you have planted **colchicum** bulbs. Unaccompanied by foliage (which emerged last spring and then died back), these fragile-looking lilac crocus-shaped flowers will bloom this month.

Bring last year's potted **amaryllis** indoors so it can have a dormant period of at least six to eight weeks. Withhold water so its foliage dies back, and set it in a cool, dark cellar. Anytime after Thanksgiving, start watering it four to six weeks before desired bloom time.

Soon tender bulbs will face frost outdoors. Decide whether to treat them as annuals and leave them in the ground to succumb to winter, or to dig them up and store them in a cool, dark place where they will be safe from freezing.

WATERING

If it is a dry fall, water tender bulb plants and newly planted bulbs. With only a few exceptions (some kinds of **canna** and **iris** actually prefer to grow in water gardens), bulbs prefer soil that drains well. If you notice that the water pools on the soil over bulbs and takes a couple of minutes or longer to soak into the soil, chances are the soil lacks good drainage. Make a note to correct this situation next summer.

FERTILIZING

Fall is the best time to fertilize bulbs. Add granular, slow-acting all-purpose or bulb fertilizer to the fill soil when planting new bulbs. Sprinkle some over existing bulb beds if you have not fertilized other plants there already.

Be cautious when digging around in the colchicum beds; they don't have foliage yet.

PRUNING

No pruning is necessary this month.

PROBLEMS

Insects often come indoors on plants that were outside all season. When potting up tender bulbs to bring in as houseplants, wash stems and foliage with a strong water spray to remove eggs and larvae. Spray them with insecticidal soap or light horticultural oil to control insect outbreaks.

Slugs like **colchicum** flowers. Sprinkle diatomaceous earth (DE) over the soil around the fragile flower stems if there are signs of slugs. An alternative is to use the new, nontoxic slug baits that contain iron phosphate.

Disease on tender bulbs is best controlled at this point by discarding any bulbs that look suspicious when you dig them up for winter storage. Throw them in the trash, not the compost. Tender bulbs left in the ground will die and decompose.

OCTOBER
BULBS, CORMS, RHIZOMES, & TUBERS

PLANNING

While bulb planting is in full swing, do not forget to save the package labels so you can remember which varieties you have. Store them in your garden journal with the sketch of the bulb locations in the yard.

It is time to set up a storage area for overwintering tender bulbs. The space should maintain about 45 to 55 degrees Fahrenheit and should be dry and rodent-proof. If you are storing other plants—**tropical water lilies**, rooted cuttings—you may need to install shelves or hooks for bags of bulbs. Unheated cellars and garages are often suitable, and so is an old refrigerator in good working order.

Shopping List: shelving, potting soil, bulb fertilizer

PLANTING

Continue to plant spring-blooming bulbs outdoors while the weather is mild and the soil is easy to work. Plant large bulbs in groups or clusters of five, seven, nine or more. Smaller, or "minor" bulbs, such as **crocus, snowdrop, squill,** and **glory of the snow,** look best when planted in large numbers. Their small blossoms make a stronger impact

when they are in patches of several dozen. Mix bulbs into beds of ground cover plants or perennial borders; plant minor ones under trees whose shallow roots will not be disturbed by the shallow planting depth.

To plant bulbs in the ground:

1. Prepare the soil in the planting area by spading and adding organic matter to improve the drainage and friability. Bulbs require excellent drainage.

2. Lay the bulbs on the top of the prepared area checking for design and proper spacing.

3. Using a narrow pointed trowel, insert each bulb to the proper depth (three times the height) while the others remain in place on the soil surface.

4. A light, one inch, layer of mulch will complete the process.

To plant bulbs in pots for forcing:

1. Purchase top size **daffodils**, **crocus**, and **tulips** that are labeled good for forcing (**daffodils** are very dependable).

2. Fill shallow containers with soilless potting mix.

3. Set bulbs in the medium so that tips are even with the edge of the pot. Crowd the pot with bulbs! Then water.

4. Store the pots in a cool (40 to 50 degrees F.) place for several weeks so that roots can grow. Around Thanksgiving, put them where they will experience mild "winter" temperatures (35 to 40 degrees F.) and have their dormant period. A cellar, unheated garage, outdoor cold frame, or old refrigerator will be fine.

5. In about six to twelve weeks you will notice signs of green sprouting. Bring the pans out into a cool room where the foliage will get light and continue devel-

Consider creating raised beds if your bulbs need better drainage.

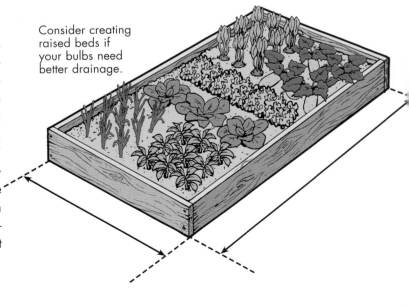

HELPFUL HINTS

If space in the yard is at a premium, you can plant bulbs in an outdoor container such as a windowbox, planter, or half-barrel that has drainage holes. The container must receive normal rainfall during the winter.

1. Fill it with soilless potting medium mixed with granular, slow-acting fertilizer.

2. Plant the bulbs at the correct depth, then fill up the container with the medium.

3. When mixing different varieties of bulbs, first plant the larger, taller ones in a deeper layer, then add some potting medium. Plant the smaller, shorter ones in a shallower layer at their correct depth.

4. Fill the rest of the container with potting medium, and water well.

5. Mulch the medium at the top of the container.

oping. A cool room will lengthen the blooming period.

CARE

Last call to dig up tender **dahlia** tubers, **gladiolus** corms, and other tender bulbs to store them for winter. This must be done after a light frost but before the ground freezes. Examine them after brushing off the soil, and discard any that are injured or diseased. Many bulbs, such as **canna** and **dahlias**, will have multiplied by developing off-shoots, or new bulb segments. Either store the whole clump now and separate them next spring before planting, or cut them into separate bulbs now. After frost, when their tops have blackened and collapsed, you can dig up **tuberous begonia** corms to store indoors over the winter, or you might want to pot them up and use them as houseplants instead.

WATERING

If it is a dry fall, water newly planted hardy bulbs and existing bulb beds. Even though you cannot see them, they are developing roots, and they need moisture.

FERTILIZING

Add a granular, slow-acting fertilizer or a product formulated specifically for bulbs to the soil when planting. Never put the fertilizer in the bottom of the hole—it may burn the bulb root tissues if it touches them. Sprinkle it over the soil of established bulb beds. If you plant bulbs among shrubs and perennials you have already fertilized for the fall, they will benefit from that and no further fertilizing is necessary.

PRUNING

No pruning is necessary this month.

PROBLEMS

Squirrels and other rodents are a real problem with bulbs other than those in the **daffodil** family. They find them, even though they are underground, by smell. Hardware cloth set on the soil over fall-blooming **crocus** will protect the flowers from deer and rodents.

Weeds are fair game if air temperatures are still mild. To prevent them from returning next spring, spray or spot treat stubborn perennial weeds with Roundup™ while the bulbs are safely underground.

November

BULBS, CORMS, RHIZOMES, & TUBERS

PLANNING

Potted bulbs from the florist or forcing kits for **amaryllis** or **paper-white narcissus** make great holiday and hostess gifts during November and December. If purchasing commercially planted bulbs in pots, choose those that are barely sprouting; this way the recipient will have a longer time to enjoy their development and bloom.

Christmas cyclamen (*Cyclamen persicum*) is a perfect holiday gift for all your friends. It likes bright light in a chilly place. This plant that grows from a corm has everything going for it:

- Fragrance
- Silver-mottled green, heart-shaped foliage
- Butterfly-like flowers in a vcariety of flower colors—white, pink, red, lilac, salmon
- Very long bloom time
- Availability in mini-size and full-size 12-inch-wide plants

Check the garage, basement, mud room, or tool shed for any bulbs you may have overlooked and forgotten to plant. As long as the ground is not frozen, you can still plant them. Better late than never is the rule!

Shopping List: hardware cloth to thwart rodents, **paper-white narcissus** bulbs to force for the holidays

PLANTING

Hardy bulbs are better off in the ground than stored, so plant leftovers if you can. If the ground has frozen, you can plant them in an outdoor planter (see October), or pot them up for forcing indoors. Forced bulbs probably will not be finished with their dormant period until about the time their outdoor counterparts are blooming. After they bloom, plant them outdoors for their foliage to ripen and die back. They will be in place for sure for next spring.

CARE

Fall-blooming hardy bulbs such as **sternbergia**, **colchicum**, and most **autumn crocus** have finished blooming by now. The faded blossoms that have collapsed on the ground can remain there, as they will decompose rapidly.

If you have not already mulched areas where you have planted bulbs, do so after the ground freezes, if you can (if your schedule permits you to do it only before the ground freezes, do it then). The mulch is not intended to prevent the ground from freezing; it just buffers soil temperatures during the winter to minimize the extremes of fluctuating temperatures. Alternate freezing and thawing sometimes causes the soil to heave shallow-planted bulbs to the surface. Spread 2 or 3 inches of chopped leaves, pine needles, or shredded bark over the bulb beds.

WATERING

Start watering potted, dormant **amaryllis** bulbs by Thanksgiving to start them growing for late-December holiday bloom. Do not keep their soil soaking wet.

If the soil is not yet frozen hard, use your houseplant water meter probe outdoors to check its moisture where you have planted bulbs if rain has been scarce. Water if necessary.

Use the water meter to check the soil moisture in the pots of bulbs stored for forcing. If they are out in a cold frame, they may have dried out.

If you have dug up and stored tender bulbs for the winter, make it a habit to check them periodically. Some need moist storage; while they must not be wet, they should be protected from drying out completely. Nesting them in damp sawdust, sphagnum moss, or shredded newspaper in venti-lated bags usually does the job. Others, including **gladiolus** and **caladium**, need drier storage. Wrap them in paper or hang them in open netting. Check the instructions that accompany your bulb purchase for guidance.

FERTILIZING

No fertilizing is necessary.

HELPFUL HINTS

Bulb-forcing vases are special glass vases with narrow necks and flaring tops. Available in many colors, they are designed to support a bare bulb so that its base where the roots emerge is just at water level. As they develop, the roots are visible through the glass. Bulb glasses are available in various sizes to accommodate bulbs as small as **crocus** and as large as **amaryllis**. The most common ones are for **Dutch hyacinth**—just a single bulb will fill a room with fragrance.

PRUNING

No pruning is necessary.

PROBLEMS

Once serious frost arrives, most potential problems with bulbs are past. Delaying mulching of bulb beds until the soil is hard forces rodents to nest elsewhere (they may choose evergreen ground cover plantings). When the ground is frozen, though, they will not be able to go after bulbs planted beneath **pachysandra**, **English ivy**, or **spreading juniper**.

Store dahlias in peat moss for the winter.

DECEMBER
BULBS, CORMS, RHIZOMES, & TUBERS

PLANNING

It seems as if **amaryllis**, especially red or red-and-white ones, have become an established winter holiday flower. If you did not plant these large bulbs in pots and start watering them last month, they will not bloom in time for Christmas and New Year's. Fortunately, your local florist or garden-center people did plant and water last month, so **amaryllis** timed to bloom in late December are available in stores for gifts and decorations at home. Purchase pre-potted ones that are just starting to send up their incredible tall stems so the entire process will be on display. Bulbs bought and potted up now can be started for display in February.

Do not be surprised to see that limp, green, grasslike foliage has appeared in the garden. This is the foliage of **grape hyacinths**, which often precedes the flowers by several months. It will survive through snow and ice just fine. **Sternbergia's** foliage emerges with its flowers in October and will remain all winter, even though the flowers die. It will eventually die back in spring.

Catalogs begin to arrive this month. Some mail-order companies specialize in bulbs, and others include bulbs in their line of annual and perennial plants and seeds. Put the catalogs aside in a pile to study and enjoy after the first of the year. Thinking about ordering some tender, summer-blooming bulbs will help the winter days pass faster.

Holiday Gift Shopping List: a book on growing bulbs, a bulb planter, **paper-white narcissus**, garden center gift certificate for tender bulbs this spring

PLANTING

If the ground is not frozen, you can still plant bulbs outdoors.

If you received an **amaryllis** bulb planting kit as a gift, plant it and water it now for bloom in February. Maybe it will be blooming by Valentine's Day.

CARE

Although December is not yet bitterly cold in most parts of the state, assume the worst and check pots of bulbs that you intend to force indoors in February. The planting medium of those stored outdoors in a cold frame or under straw or a tarp for their chill period may be dried out. Make sure their temperature is correct. Do not let the area where forced bulbs are stored drop below 35 or 40 degrees Fahrenheit. If they freeze, they will turn to mush.

WATERING

Moisten the sawdust, shredded paper, or sphagnum moss that tender bulbs are stored in with a spritz of mist if they seem to be drying out. Check the bulbs again soon to be sure that this packaging stays damp without making the bulbs wet.

Bulbs that have been potted up for forcing need some moisture even in cold storage. Check the soil to be sure it hasn't dried out (one clue: the pots are lighter than normal when the soil has dried out). Do not overdo the watering, because too much moisture causes rot. It is important that the bulb pots have drainage holes.

FERTILIZING

No fertilizing is necessary.

PRUNING

No pruning is necessary.

PROBLEMS

Mold is a threat to stored bulbs in overwet potting medium. Remove plastic covers from pots planted for forcing if condensation devlops on their surfaces, allowing better air circulation.

HERBS & VEGETABLES

There are lots of reasons people still grow some of their own food in this day and age of grand supermarkets and farm stands. It certainly isn't to save time and money. Purchasing all the necessary food gardening equipment, seeds, fertilizer, and pest-control products costs a lot more money than you would pay for a season's worth of vegetables at a local farm stand; and creating, planting, tending, and harvesting a garden takes a lot more time than any season's worth of food shopping.

WHY GROW FOOD?

Why, then? Mostly because homegrown food tastes best. The very freshest vegetables and herbs have peak flavor. Fully ripened on the plant and freshly picked, backyard tomatoes have real flavor and more juice. Peppers are crisp with deeper flavor. Fresh basil or parsley picked minutes before it is used provides a whole new taste sensation.

And vegetables grown in the backyard and picked just before they are eaten have much more nutritional value than fresh vegetables from the supermarket. Store-bought produce typically is picked before peak ripeness because it must spend many hours in transit. Then it sits on the store shelf for many more hours; then it sits in a home refrigerator. How can it possibly provide the nutrition of homegrown peas, corn, carrots, lettuce, and other crops?

Then there is convenience—vegetables and herbs growing in the yard means that fresh produce is just a few steps away. Add to that the assurance that there are no unknown pesticide residues in homegrown crops. Better taste, better nutrition, ready access, and control over pesticides make a compelling case for going to the trouble and expense of growing at least some food.

There are also the intangible delights of food gardening. There is always a heightened sense of well-being gained by physical exertion outdoors, of working to understand and harness the natural processes that are part of any kind of gardening. Somehow food gardening intensifies these feelings. Maybe it is because working the soil to produce food puts us in touch with the fundamental experiences of our ancestors in a time when these skills meant survival.

WAYS TO GROW FOOD

Food gardening is not an all-or-nothing thing. It is no longer necessary to garden on the huge scale required to grow enough food to feed the family year-round. Besides, most of us have left behind the rural life and large properties. All the benefits of food gardening can still be enjoyed when done on a more modest scale.

• Grow just for fun. Grow plants in individual containers, or combine several—a tomato plant, some parsley, and a pepper plant—in a large container. When set conveniently on a sunny patio, roof, or balcony, they provide an opportunity to learn about how to grow the particular plants and to enjoy the rewards with little effort.

• Set up a basic bed, a small bed dedicated to a few summer vegetable and/or herb plants. Take the trouble to dig deeply and improve the soil. You may want to box it in with boards for a neater appearance. Planting just a few plants—two tomato plants, two squash, two peppers, or whatever you like—yields substantial food, yet keeps the maintenance and harvesting chores to a minimum.

• Set up a vertical bed. Add a trellis to one side of the basic vegetable bed to take advantage of the airspace above it. Encourage tomato, bean, and cucumber plants to climb. Then there will more space in the same basic bed to try eggplants, carrots, beets, and others.

• Extend the season by adding some cool-weather crops to your repertoire. Start the growing season earlier with lettuce, peas, cabbage, and broccoli. Maybe even plant another round in late summer to grow in the cool fall weather.

With the help of some protective plastic mulch and coverings, you can double productivity from the same basic bed.

• Extend the garden. If you find vegetable gardening satisfying, add another bed or two as space permits, or grow in both beds and containers. There is always a way to grow more herbs and vegetables.

EDIBLES PLUS ORNAMENTALS

The very latest trend is to incorporate food crops into the home landscape as part of the ornamental plantings. Take advantage of the wonderful colors and textures of modern varieties of food plants—purple parsley; red rhubarb; red, yellow, and orange peppers; yellow and orange tomatoes; red cabbages; scarlet-flowered beans; pink eggplants; golden raspberries; and speckled watermelons. Celebrate the shapes—of pear tomatoes, skinny eggplants, softball zucchini, marble-sized tomatoes, and yard-long green beans.

It is possible to grow almost any food plant among shrubs or mixed in with flowers in a flower bed. Plants most commonly planted this way are tomatoes, peppers, lettuce, and parsley. They are annuals, just like petunias and zinnias, and are just as easy to grow. Pick up a few seedlings at the garden

CHAPTER THREE

There are many different kinds of potatoes—even blue ones!—that are not available in the grocery. Yet another reason to grow your own veggies.

center when you shop for other plants and yard-care supplies.

The key to growing food crops among other landscape plants around the property is to provide enough light and space for them to grow to full size without disturbing the appearance of the landscape in general. Like traditional ornamental plants, each vegetable or herb variety has characteristic growing habits and soil needs. Tall, vining tomatoes can form a green foliage backdrop. Beans can climb a trellis to screen a view. Take advantage of dwarf versions of peppers, parsley, and others for small spaces. Use lettuce varieties for edging. Plant a hedge of rosemary or blueberry shrubs. Do

not forget to provide access to those plants for harvesting.

Combining veggies and herbs with traditional ornamental plants makes more efficient use of available space and light and increases the number of different crops you can grow. It maximizes production by extending the space for food crops.

Combining edible and ornamental plants also improves the health of the individual plants and the overall environment. As the diversity of plantings in all parts of the yard increases, so does the diversity of beneficial insects which are the first line of defense against pest insect problems. In smaller yards, your food crops can be rotated more

effectively when you blend lots of plant species in various ways. Take it in stages. Move gradually toward blending edibles and ornamentals:

1. First, add some flowers to the vegetable garden to test the concept.

2. Second, add flowering culinary herbs to flower beds and borders. They are at home anywhere.

3. Third, add a few vegetable plants to a flower bed or border and see how it looks.

4. Fourth, create a new garden using both food and ornamental plants. If that works, do it some more.

JANUARY
HERBS & VEGETABLES

PLANNING

It's time to plan the vegetable garden. Whether it is a sketch on paper or a more formal scheme on a computer program, a plan assures space for all the varieties you want to grow. If you want to extend your garden season by starting cool-weather crops early in the spring and growing another planting of them in fall after the warm-weather crops have finished, you must make several garden plans.

If you already have a food garden, consult last year's plan to make sure you do not plant the same crop in the same place. Rotation of crops, even moving them a few feet, helps reduce pest insect and disease problems.

Whether you will be planting in traditional rows or in modern, boxed, raised beds:

• Draw your garden to scale, orienting your rows or beds east and west to maximize the amount of sun they can receive. Ideally, tall crops or those growing vertically on supports should be on the north side so that they will not shade shorter ones.

• Incorporate vining plants into your garden design. **Cucumbers**, **squash**, **pole beans**, and **garden peas** can all be supported by a fence on the periphery of the garden.

• Plan to fence the garden if there are numerous pest animals in the area. A relatively low fence will thwart rabbits, but groundhogs need a more substantial one (see November Problems). A 7- to 9-foot light-weight fence may be necessary to discourage deer.

• Allow at least 36 inches between rows in a traditional garden where a mechanized cultivator is used. For a modern boxed bed design, allow at least 24 inches for paths between the beds.

• New to food gardening? Start small. Preparing and planting a large area is an enormous amount of work. It takes a lot of knowledge to manage many different vegetable species.

• Think about where to locate herbs. Plant them among the vegetables, or put them in a bed of their own that is convenient to the kitchen.

Shopping List: fertilizer, mulch, fencing. Order seeds, and tools not found locally.

PLANTING

Grow **mushrooms** this month if there is a warm, dark space available in the house. Follow the directions on the label of a commercial planting kit.

It is not too early to begin browsing through mail-order plant and seed catalogs. New gardeners may have to purchase catalogs, but once you are on a mailing list they will arrive frequently, starting in December. Some suggestions:

Design your garden on paper first before you pick up a shovel.

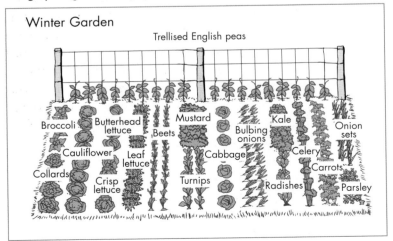

Winter Garden

Trellised English peas

Broccoli · Butterhead lettuce · Beets · Mustard · Bulbing onions · Kale · Onion sets · Cauliflower · Leaf lettuce · Cabbage · Celery · Collards · Carrots · Crisp lettuce · Turnips · Radishes · Parsley

- Don't place an order from the first seed catalog you receive. Other companies may have more popular varieties for Ohio.
- Choose popular varieties for the main crop of each vegetable you grow, and experiment with one other that sounds interesting (see Planting Chart).
- Check records from previous years before ordering plants or seeds.
- Place your orders as early as possible. Some plants or seeds may be in limited supply.

CARE

The sun is moving higher in the sky each day, adding a minute or two of daylight and striking the cold frame more directly. Control heat buildup in the cold frame on sunny days if you are wintering over plants such as **rosemary**. Ventilate gradually as the frost melts on the glass. Leave snow on the glass cover—it is good insulation. If there is no snow cover, cover the glass with a mat or old rug at night to buffer extreme nighttime temperatures.

Rotate herb plants growing indoors on the windowsill so they can receive sun on all sides and grow uniformly. Pinch back leggy stems, and set plants about 2 inches below adjustable fluorescent lights.

HELPFUL HINTS

If you are planting large quantities of any vegetable from seed, such as **peas** or **beans**, don't buy large numbers of small packs of seeds off the rack at the garden center. Bulk buying is often less expensive; order larger bags of seeds from a reputable mail-order seed company.

WATERING

If there has been no rain or snow for the past month or so, unmulched perennial herb and food plants overwintering in the herb garden may need watering. Check their soil.

Water herbs growing in pots indoors when the top inch or so of the soil is dry. Avoid overwatering.

FERTILIZING

Be stingy when fertilizing herbs growing indoors. **Parsley, chives, mint**, and others need nutrition to generate foliage, but too much nutrition causes rapid growth, which dilutes the flavor in the leaves.

Seaweed (kelp), fish emulsion-based organic fertilizer products, and soluble fertilizers are excellent all-purpose fertilizers for indoor plants. They all contain the three major nutrients. Use as directed on the package label.

PRUNING

Pinch off any flowers that are on **basil** and other herbs growing indoors. Flowering alters the flavor of the foliage. Keep pinching off herb foliage for use in the kitchen. Even if you do not intend to use it, pinch anyway to shape the plant and promote compactness and dense foliage.

PROBLEMS

Aphids, mites, whiteflies, and fungus gnats are the usual suspects on indoor plants. Spray insecticidal soap or *Bacillus thuringiensis* on stems and both sides of the leaves. Spray the plant over a box or sink. Follow the directions on the product label, and repeat as needed.

FEBRUARY
HERBS & VEGETABLES

PLANNING

This is inventory month.

- Check your tools to see if any need to be repaired or replaced. Do you need some new tools, perhaps some that are ergonomically designed?

- Check supplies of pest- and disease-control products. Many organic products such as soaps and oils will keep on the shelf for several years. Discard containers of serious chemical products that have been sitting around for years, being sure to follow the instructions for disposal on the product label.

Think about why you grow herbs. Your answers will influence how much space you devote to growing herbs rather than food crops. They will also influence your decisions on which ones to grow. Maybe it is time to get rid of the **mint** that threatens to take over every year! Plant more **basil** if you love pesto!

Shopping List: seeds, soilless potting mix, water-soluble (fast-acting) fertilizer, replacement tools, seed-starting equipment, fluorescent light units

PLANTING

It might still be bleak outdoors in many parts of Ohio. Some diehard gardeners sprinkle **spinach** seeds on the snow so that when it melts they will have a head start.

This is the month to start seeds indoors under lights for cool-weather crops, such as **onions** and **cabbage**, that go out into the garden as early as April. If you are new to gardening or have just a small garden, it is easier to buy young plants than to try to start them in the house.

Plant **chives, cilantro-coriander, dill, fennel, salad burnet, sage, winter savory, French sorrel,** and **thyme** seeds toward the end of the month. For best results, use commercial seed-starting equipment.

1. Fill seed-starter trays or individual peat pots with moist soilless seed-starting medium.

2. Sow seeds in rows in the trays, or individually in each pot or chamber, depending on the type of equipment. Cover them with a bit of the mix, and water lightly.

3. Record the name of the plant on labels (popsicle sticks work well) for each pot or larger container. Use a pen with moisture-resistant ink.

4. Gently cover the tray with plastic wrap or a plastic bag so the moisture is retained until sprouts emerge.

5. Remove the plastic wrapping and set fluorescent lights so they are 2 inches above the sprouts. Make the fixtures adjustable so they can be raised as the seedlings grow, to maintain the 2-inch distance.

6. Water seedlings from below with tepid water when the medium begins to dry out.

Many gardeners prefer to wait and buy commercially raised young plants rather than fuss with raising seedlings. Order them by mail for delivery at the correct time for planting, or wait until they are available at the local garden center.

CARE

Keep an eye on seeds planted indoors so you can prevent them from drying out.

- When sprouts emerge, do not let them push against the plastic over them. Remove the plastic promptly.

- Gently brush your hand daily over the tops of growing seedlings, flexing their stems to help them grow strong.

WATERING

When starting seeds indoors, make certain the medium is moist but not wet. As a general rule it is better to keep plants on the dry side, but do not let the seedlings wilt.

ROWS VS. RAISED BEDS

In the old days when most people lived in rural areas and had plenty of property, vegetable gardens followed the agricultural model—narrow rows of crops with wide paths in between to allow for mechanical tilling and harvesting. These days space is often at a premium in the crowded suburbs, so it makes more sense to have raised beds that are 3 or 4 feet wide with 2- or 3-foot permanent paths between them. While they take more effort to build, especially if you box them, they require less space and less care during the growing season. Once dug, they never need tilling, because they are never stepped on. Carefully nurtured soil within the beds supports intensive planting to produce more food per foot than is possible with traditional rows. Build one and try it.

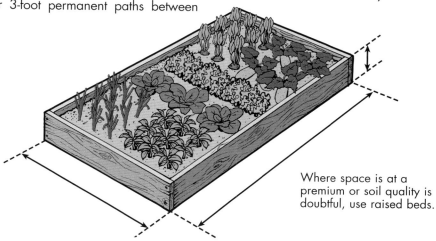

Where space is at a premium or soil quality is doubtful, use raised beds.

The easiest way to water established indoor herb and vegetable plants in pots is to take them to the sink and run tepid water on them. When all the water has drained from the bottom of their pots, return them to their location.

FERTILIZING

Don't fertilize when sprouts first emerge from the growing medium. Wait until stem growth begins and a second set of leaves forms. Use the fertilizer at half the recommended strength for seedlings while the vegetable plants are indoors.

PRUNING

Continue to pinch potted herbs growing indoors to shape them correctly, and to promote dense foliage growth.

PROBLEMS

Damping off is a fungal disease that kills seedlings—their stems weaken and they flop over, dead.

Water seedlings sparingly and from below, and use sterile commercial seed-starting medium. Whiteflies may become a problem, particularly on indoor herb plants. They fly off leaves like dandruff if you disturb them. Use yellow sticky traps, or spray foliage with insecticidal soap or other products listed for whiteflies.

Soluble salts from fertilizer accumulate as deposits of white crust on the pot if plants are constantly watered from the top or if the water is reabsorbed by the growing medium. Repot in fresh medium.

MARCH

HERBS & VEGETABLES

PLANNING

Experienced food gardeners have discovered that there can be as many as three growing seasons in the backyard. Cool-weather crops can be planted in the spring and then again toward fall, adding two more seasons to the main warm-weather one.

After you gain some experience growing warm-weather vegetables during the main season, you may want to experiment with an early-spring cool-weather vegetable garden this year. Buy seedlings for **broccoli**, **cabbage**, and their relatives. Buy seeds for **peas**, **lettuce**, and **spinach** to plant outdoors late this month.

Shopping List: seeds and seedlings for cool-weather vegetables, **onion** sets, herb seedlings

PLANTING

As March progresses, it is tempting to go out and garden, but the soil is usually much too wet to cultivate. Attempts to dig it will leave sticky clods that will later harden into stubborn lumps difficult to work with.

If soil conditions are favorable, however, you may plant dormant **asparagus** roots anytime after March 15, and set out **horseradish**, **onions**, and **rhubarb** plants after the 15th as well. To plant **asparagus** crowns (roots):

1. Soak them in water for several hours before planting.

2. Dig a trench about a foot deep.

3. Set crowns in the trench at the spacing recommended.

4. Cover them with only a few inches of soil, maintaining the depth until stems appear.

5. Gradually fill in the trench with soil as stems grow taller until the soil is level with the surrounding ground.

Tradition dictates that St. Patrick's Day is the time to plant **peas** in the garden. Actually, in most areas of Ohio the soil is still too wet and cold for them to germinate. Wait until the end of the month.

Wait several weeks until the soil is in better condition to plant herbs such as **chives**, **cilantro-coriander**, **dill**, **fennel**, **horse-radish**, **mint**, **oregano**, **salad burnet**, and **thyme**.

CARE

Dig any **parsnips**, **carrots**, and other root crops that may have overwintered in the garden before the soil warms and they rot.

Begin to harden-off seedlings of cool-weather plants scheduled to go into the garden early next month:

• Set them outdoors for a few hours each pleasant day to begin to acclimate them to outside conditions such as wind and sun.

Squeeze a ball of soil; if it sticks together in your hand, it's still too wet to work.

• Increase their exposure gradually over a week or two, bringing them in at night while temperatures are still low.

If you have a cold frame, it is an ideal place to keep seedlings until planting time.

Herbs growing in containers as houseplants will need acclimating to the outdoors, too. If they are not destined to go into the ground, they may need repotting into larger pots with fresh soilless medium. Try planting a large ornamental container with a selection of herbs for the sunny patio later in the season. Be sure the container has drainage holes, and set it on bricks or pieces of wood to facilitate drainage.

WATERING

Make certain any overhead water source for indoor seedlings is a very gentle spray. A hard spray will knock them over, increasing the possibility of fungal disease and harm to the tender stems and leaves.

Water young transplants an hour before they go into the soil, just afterward, and again over the next several days to give the roots a good start. Plants lose a lot of moisture through their foliage because of the temporary stress of transplant shock.

HELPFUL HINTS

Planting **potatoes** this year? Plant part of the crop on top of the ground. No digging required.

Simply lay the cut pieces or seed **potatoes** in a row on top of the soil. Cover them with 8 to 10 inches of organic mulch such as chopped leaves or straw. Make certain it covers the crop at all times through the growing season.

About two weeks after the plants have finished blossoming, lift the mulch on one plant to see how large the **potatoes** are. If they are too small, drop the mulch and look again in two weeks. Do not allow the **potatoes** to be exposed to sunlight because they will form green sections under the skin that are harmful if eaten.

When the potatoes are large enough, pull the plant, harvest the **potatoes**, and enjoy.

FERTILIZING

Either mix a granular slow-acting fertilizer into the garden soil when you are spading or tilling for planting, or add the fertilizer to the soil when you plant each young transplant. If you choose to water in fast-acting (water-soluble) fertilizer every few weeks over the season instead, follow the directions on the product label.

If you have access to fresh animal manure to use in the garden, spread it over and dig it into the soil at least thirty days before planting. The earlier the better (fall is best), so that it will have time to age. Fresh manure will burn tender plants; dried or aged manure can be used immediately.

PRUNING

No pruning is necessary this month.

PROBLEMS

Unexpected late frost may threaten newly planted seedlings. Throw an airy blanket of white, polyspun garden fleece, called floating row cover, over them for protection during the night. Baskets or shade cloth will also work. Remove coverings during the day so the plants can receive sunlight.

Rabbits may eat young plants, causing your plants to disappear overnight or suddenly lose their tops. Protect them with garden fleece, low fencing, or netting.

APRIL

HERBS & VEGETABLES

 PLANNING

Gardening season begins as cool-weather crops begin to thrive outdoors in the garden. To maximize production from your garden space, plan to have young warm-weather transplants ready to go into the empty spots when the cool crops are finished. Buy or raise young **tomato, pepper**, or **eggplant** starts, which need hot weather to thrive.

Shopping List: birdbath, seeds, food dryer, Walls-o-Water™, young transplants

 PLANTING

Finally, outdoor planting time has arrived. The soil should be workable, and the temperatures are moderating. While the possibility of a frost still exists in Ohio, cool-weather crops can handle it.

Among the sure planting bets are **asparagus, horseradish, parsnips, rhubarb**, and **onions**. About mid-April, plant or sow seeds for **beets, cabbage, lettuce, mustard**, and **parsley**. It is not too late to plant **peas**. Plant young homegrown or store-bought cole crop plants such as **broccoli** and **cabbage** outside now, too.

Many herbs and veggies (colorful **lettuces, dwarf parsley**,

Squeeze a ball of soil; if it breaks apart in your hand, it should be workable.

determinant tomatoes, and **thyme**) grow attractively in windowboxes and hanging baskets. Always plant more seeds than needed because there is seldom 100 percent germination.

Lettuce, peppers, radishes, onions, and most herbs need a container at least 6 inches in diameter and 8 inches deep. Groups of plants need larger, 5- to 15-gallon barrels or containers. Later in the season, **tomatoes, squash, pole beans**, and **cucumber** will need containers at least 24 inches deep to handle their larger root mass.

Tomato plants started indoors may be outgrowing their small pots. Transplant them into larger, deep pots filled with soilless medium while they grow until May planting time. Bury their stems a bit so they will develop strong root systems. Plant **sun-**

flower seeds as soon as frost is past in your area. Later, plant **pole beans**, either **snap** or **limas**, so they can climb the sturdy **sunflower** stems. Enjoy the benefits of raising **beans**, as well as pretty flowers and birds in the garden.

 CARE

Thin plants growing in rows to the spacing specified on the seed packet. Snip off or pull excess seedlings so the stronger ones will have room to grow.

To discourage weeds and help retain soil moisture, mulch plants that are more than 6 inches tall. Plant seedlings through a plastic mulch or landscape fabric, which will warm the soil. While black plastic or landscape fabric are commonly used, research shows that the new red plastic (SRM-Red Mulch) may increase **tomato**, **pepper**, and **strawberry** yields by 20 percent. The light wavelength reflected by the red color encourages plant stem and foliage growth, and they bear heavier and earlier crops. Punch holes in plastic mulch to allow moisture to get to the soil.

WATERING

Always moisten transplant root-balls before planting them in the ground. Water them, and the seeds that you plant afterward, too, to settle them in the soil. Follow up with regular watering if rainfall is undependable. Roots of young plants are shallow and dry out quickly until they develop and penetrate more deeply into the soil. Eventually a layer of organic mulch will reduce watering needs.

Watering is critical for seeds and plants in containers. Check moisture levels daily. The soilless medium dries out very quickly, especially if the container is in full sun. Use a watering can or soft sprayer from the hose.

FERTILIZING

Mix a granular, all-purpose (not lawn) slow-acting fertilizer into the soil when you prepare your

---

HELPFUL HINTS

Various **tomato** varieties grow in one of two ways—determinant or indeterminant.
- Determinant types grow to a genetically predetermined height and stop. They typically top out at about 4 or 5 feet and are ideal for use in containers on the patio.
- Indeterminant **tomato** plants grow indefinitely, putting out numerous vining subsidiary stems that grow rampantly. They may extend 10 or 12 feet during a growing season. They need sturdy trellises and frequent pinching of suckers to discipline their spread.

---

beds for planting. This will provide uniform, consistent nutrition for crops planted there for up to twenty four weeks, depending on the product.

Delay using fast-acting (water-soluble) fertilizer products until later in the season when heavy producers such as **tomatoes** need a nutrition boost.

Remember that soilless media in containers has no nutrition because it has no soil. Mix a granular, slow-acting fertilizer into the medium or purchase one that already has it mixed in.

If you prefer to use fast-acting fertilizer, dilute it in water, and water it into the container every few weeks as specified on the product label. Do not overdo, or it will burn plant tissues.

PRUNING

If you did not cut back woody herbs such as **sage**, **rosemary**,

---

and **lavender** last fall when you brought them indoors for the winter, do so now. As soon as they can go outdoors they will begin to generate fresh foliage.

Pinch the tops of young **parsley** plants to encourage them to branch and become more compact. Continue pinching after they are planted outdoors next month.

PROBLEMS

Cutworms are likely to be in your garden soil where they will chew through the stems of young plants at soil level. Protect stems with "collars" made from foam or cardboard coffee cups or similar materials with their bottoms removed. Gently lower the cup over the plant, top down, twisting its rim into the soil around the stems of **tomatoes**, **peppers**, **eggplants**, **cabbage**, **broccoli**, and others.

MAY

HERBS & VEGETABLES

 **PLANNING**

Now that the weather is warmer and the soil has dried out, there is a lot to do out in the garden.

If you have raised beds established, remove any winter mulch remaining on those that do not already hold cool crops planted earlier this spring. Loosen the soil with a rake, add a little granular, slow-acting fertilizer, and you will be ready to plant.

If you have a traditional row garden, it is time to get out the power tiller or spade and cultivate the entire area. Add organic matter and fertilizer, then lay out paths and rows.

Nesting pairs of various bird species have probably already settled in nearby to start their families. This is a plus for your garden, because the parents will seek insects to feed newborns who are unable to digest seeds for awhile.

Shopping List: more seeds, warm-weather vegetable plants, trellis netting, garden twine, bird seed

 **PLANTING**

Direct-seeding into the garden is the best planting approach for many crops. Some germinate fairly promptly and grow so rapidly that there is no real advantage to starting them ahead of time indoors, and others simply do not transplant successfully. To plant seeds:

1. Dig the area to loosen and aerate the soil. Remove stones and debris. Mix in some organic matter such as compost, peat moss, or mushroom soil, and add granular, slow-acting fertilizer. Smooth and level the soil.

2. Create an indentation or shallow trench in the soil, and dribble into it seed from between your thumb and forefinger. Follow seed-packet instructions for depth and spacing.

3. Cover the seed lightly with soil, and water lightly to settle it into the ground.

4. Place a label or seed packet nearby to identify what has been planted.

5. Thin seedlings.

By mid-month it is safe to plant young herb plants such as dill, **sweet marjoram**, and **parsley**. Cut the bottom from a 5-gallon container or use a chimney flue (or any container that won't rot), and sink it into the soil to restrict the roots of **mint** and other invasive herbs. Allow its top rim to protrude from the soil several inches to prevent roots from climbing over the rim of the container. Fill it with soil and plant. An alternative is to plant **mint** and others in above-ground containers.

 **CARE**

Begin to prepare **tomato** plants raised indoors to be moved outdoors. They can go into the garden or containers between the tenth of May and Memorial Day. Set the plants in open shade after the day has warmed, for increasingly longer periods

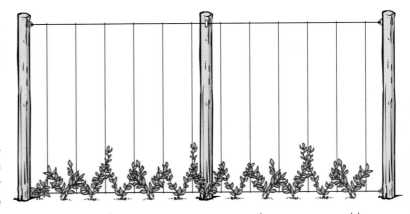

Set up a trellis or fencing to support peas or other vining vegetables.

of time each day, to acclimate them to the outdoor conditions. Bring them indoors at night at first, then allow them to stay outdoors if the weather promises to be mild. Don't set them out in heavy winds or heavy rain.

Many types of **garden peas** need support. Set up temporary fencing or a trellis of some sort to support those that are developing tall stems. Mulch plants over 6 inches tall to keep down weeds.

WATERING

Water newly planted plants regularly if there is no rain, until they show that they are established by generating new stems and foliage. A 2- or 3-inch layer of organic mulch on the bare soil around (but not touching) plant stems will retard water runoff and drying out.

Until plants grow to maturity there is still time (and space) to install drip irrigation in your garden. Porous hose or soaker hose systems made from recycled automobile tires 'leak' moisture along their length. They deliver water directly to plant roots with minimal loss to evaporation. Because foliage stays dry, the chances of mildew diseases are reduced.

FERTILIZING

If there is slow-acting fertilizer in the soil or container mix, there is no need to fertilize plants for many weeks. Later, supplement the slow-acting fertilizer with additions of diluted soluble type fertilizers. Remember, however, that too much nitrogen can promote excessive vegetation growth at the expense of flowering and fruit production.

PRUNING

Pinch herbs to keep them compact and bushy. This will also delay flowering for awhile so you can enjoy harvesting and using the foliage before it gets bitter.

Keep after branch suckers that form on **tomato** plants. Pinch or snip them off to channel energy to developing strong central stems to support the plants all season.

PROBLEMS

Aphids may cluster at the tips of tender new **tomato** stems. Ladybugs will appear later this month to control them. Pinch off infested tips, and put them in a plastic bag for the trash; or wash the aphids off plants with a forceful spray of water from the hose. Use insecticidal soap, as directed, to handle stubborn, well-established infestations.

Slugs, essentially snails without shells, can be a problem on **lettuce**, **beans**, **peppers**, and other crops. They lurk in damp mulch during the day and chew ragged holes in leaves after dark. Pick them off plants or use diatomaceous earth or slug bait containing iron phosphate.

Cabbageworms chew holes in cole crops such as **cabbage** and **broccoli**. These are the larvae of small white butterflies that flit around the garden. When the little worms are feeding on the foliage, spray the foliage thoroughly with a product containing *Bacillus thuringiensis*. The bacteria will sicken and kill them in a few days.

JUNE

HERBS & VEGETABLES

PLANNING

Some gardeners grow food for the joy of it, and to have fresh vegetables for the table during the summer. They give the inevitable excess to neighbors or the local food kitchen to feed the hungry. Others also enjoy "putting food up," storing it various ways for use during the winter. For them, maximum production is a goal, and special gardening techniques increase harvests:

• Plant intensively to use every inch of soil.

• Use clear plastic tunnels to extend the growing season before and after the main season.

• Succession-plant by immediately replacing harvested plants with new seedlings for the next crop.

• Plant vertically to take advantage of airspace above the beds.

• Plant in containers to take advantage of the sun elsewhere on the property.

• Plant food crops among ornamentals to increase the growing area.

Shopping List: sprayer, seeds for fall crops, tomato cages, a book on pest problems

PLANTING

June brings good planting weather for all warm-weather crops. Soil temperatures are high enough for hardened-off **tomatoes**, **peppers**, **beans**, and **eggplants**, and plants that have been displayed outdoors at the garden center are now adjusted to the outdoors. To plant commercially grown or homegrown young vegetable plants:

1. Prepare the soil with organic material and fertilizer (as described in May Planting).

2. Late in the day or on an overcast day, dig holes in the prepared soil, spaced at the distance recommended on their labels. Make the holes the same depth and width as the young transplant's container. (Space plants more closely in raised beds.)

3. Gently tip over the plant, and slide the pot off the rootball. Set the plant in the hole, making sure it is at the same depth in the ground that it was in its pot. Exception: Plant **tomatoes** as deeply as possible without covering their foliage.

4. Press the soil firmly around plant stems, and water gently to settle the plants in the soil.

5. If it is unavoidably sunny at planting time, rig some garden fleece or shade cloth temporarily to reduce transplant stress.

Sow seeds directly into the garden for **corn** and later crops of **beans**, **beets**, **carrots**, **kohlrabi** and **turnips**. If the **lettuce**, **spinach**, **radishes**, and other early crops planted in containers are finished, pull them, and plant a **tomato** or **pepper** plant there.

Purchase seeds of cool-weather plants for a fall garden now. When it is time to plant **broccoli**, **cabbage**, and **Brussels sprouts**, plants may not be available at the garden center. Companies offering seedlings over the Web may have them.

CARE

Mulching plants saves weeding time, conserves water, and protects the soil from compaction by rain and harsh sun. It also prevents dirt from splashing up on plant foliage. Cover all bare soil over plant roots (but not stems) with a 1- or 2-inch layer of organic material. Mulch with your choice of:

• chopped leaves

• dried grass clippings (herbicide-free)

• pine needles

• straw (hay has weed seeds)

• shredded newspaper

• aged sawdust that has been made from untreated wood

Pull up **lettuce** that has bolted, spent **broccoli** stems, and other cool-weather crops that are finished to make way for new warm-weather plants.

Thin the root crops planted earlier in the season. Use the tops of **beets** and **turnips**, and tiny **carrots** in salads.

Start picking **peas** as soon as they appear. They are at their best when they are just barely mature.

Train **tomato** plants onto a fence, stake, trellis, or cage to support them. Fruit held off the ground gets better air circulation and ripens more uniformly, so it is less bothered by pests and diseases.

Train tomatoes to a stake, trellis, or cage to keep tomatoes off the ground.

WATERING

Make certain all crops have sufficient water. **Peppers**, especially, need to be well watered. **Tomatoes** like a steady supply rather than a wet-dry cycle. Avoid hot water from a hose that was lying in the sun.

Water all container plants on a regular basis.

FERTILIZING

If you incorporated granular, slow-acting fertilizer into the soil at planting time, plants should be fine. A periodic watering containing a dilute soluble fertilizer, however, can be beneficial.

PRUNING

Continue to pinch and clip herb plants to delay flowering and encourage denser growth. Removing suckers from **tomato** plants while they are young directs energy and growth to the main stem. Next month, allow a few suckers to develop into real stems with flowers and fruit.

Note: Take care when removing suckers from determinant **tomato** plants. They develop flowers and fruit on thin stems that grow at intersections of main stems which are easily mistaken for suckers.

PROBLEMS

Whiteflies may flit around **tomato** plants. They usually are not a major concern.

Flea beetles are the bane of **eggplants**, as they make tiny holes all over the leaves. Spray foliage with Neem oil or insecticidal soap. Repeat the spray after every overhead watering and when it rains.

Colorado potato beetles are oval yellow-and-black-striped beetles that can be seen on **potato** foliage and lay soft yellow eggs underneath the foliage. Pick them off or spray Neem oil on both sides of the leaves.

Parsleyworms eat **parsley**, **dill**, **fennel**, and **celery** foliage. Because they are the larvae of the lovely swallowtail butterfly, you may want to ignore them or transfer them to a nearby **Queen Anne's lace** plant to eat instead.

JULY

HERBS & VEGETABLES

 PLANNING

Decide whether you want to plant an empty garden spot with a second crop of warm-weather vegetables that will mature before first frost. You might want to leave the soil covered with mulch to prevent weeds, until mid-month when it is about time to plant young cool-weather plants for a fall garden. To time planting properly, check seed packets or plant labels to determine how many days to harvest.

Shopping List: seeds, Neem oil or Neem with soap, deer-repellent, insecticidal soap

 PLANTING

Plant cool-weather **broccoli**, **cauliflower**, and late **cabbage** seedlings by mid-July. Sow seeds for **beans**, **peas**, **beets**, **carrots**, **chard**, **endive**, **kale**, **kohlrabi**, and **radishes** directly into the garden or in containers.

Some new varieties of **lettuce** can handle heat and humidity better than traditional types. Plant a summer salad garden under a shade cloth "awning" to reduce the heat.

 CARE

Stake **eggplants** and **peppers** as they surge in growth.

Mulch all bare garden soil to cool it a bit. The growth of **tomatoes** and some other crops slows down in soil over 85 degrees Fahrenheit. Mulch also preserves soil moisture, discourages weeds, and keeps foliage clean.

Early **corn** matures about three weeks after tassels form. Early **tomatoes** will be ready this month. Dig up **onions** if their tops are dry and bending over.

Keep pinching stems of herbs to delay flowering and loss of foliage flavor. Use them fresh at twice the amounts recommended for dried ones. Freeze or dry extra herbs.

 WATERING

Plants use copious amounts of water when it is hot. Sandy soil or soil that lacks adequate organic matter dries out especially quickly. Water when the soil under the mulch in garden beds is dry an inch or two down.

• Avoid watering in the heat of the day unless you need to cool the soil.

• Water in the early morning to give plants a strong start on the day.

• Use drip irrigation under the mulch for most economical water use.

• Use a timer with irrigation systems for low-maintenance watering.

Water containers set in the sun twice daily, but be sure to check soil moisture first to avoid over-watering.

 FERTILIZING

To give plants that are blooming and setting fruit an energy boost, spray the foliage with dilute liquid fertilizer.

Dig more compost or other organic matter into the soil before planting the next round of crops in the garden.

PRUNING

Continue to pinch suckers from indeterminant **tomato** vines until their main stems are tall enough to attach securely to their support; then pinch suckers according to how much top growth from subsidiary stems you want.

Thin root crops such as **carrots** and **beets** to the correct spacing as indicated on the seed packets.

PROBLEMS

Japanese beetles often emerge during June and July. Immediately start knocking them off plants into a jar of soapy water to control plant damage, and do this several times a day over the next few weeks. Spray heavily infested crops such as **green beans** with Neem oil. Do not use bag traps near the garden—they are so effective they will attract beetles from great distances.

Japanese beetles are beginning to emerge; handpick them to control.

Mexican bean beetles may appear on **green beans** and the foliage of other crops this month. Check the undersides of the leaves for fuzzy little yellow eggs. Mash them between your fingers, or pick them off the leaves before they turn into beetles.

HELPFUL HINTS

• Dry soil sometimes delays seed germination. Soak **corn**, **bean**, **squash**, and other large seeds in water for several hours before planting. Drain them, plant, and then water seed in the row before covering with soil.

• Do not waste food. Use thinned **beets** and **carrots** in salads. Cook **turnip** and **beet** tops from harvested crops for nutritious "greens."

• Pick summer/hybrid **squash** varieties when they are only 4 to 6 inches long. Large **squash** slows down the production of more **squash**. Let them grow a bit larger for stuffing.

• Harvest the main head from each **broccoli** plant before yellow flowers appear. Later, harvest a second, smaller crop from the subsidiary branches of the main stalk.

• Plant **dill** seeds every two or three weeks until early August to ensure fresh **dill** all season.

• Do not mulch with dried grass clippings unless you are sure they are from lawns free of pesticides.

Squash borers attack both **squash** plants and **cucumbers**. A moth lays her eggs at the base of plants, and hatched worms (borers) travel up through the stalk, eating as they go. They also carry a virus disease that infects host plants and causes their stems to rot. To repel the moth, place a piece of aluminum foil around the base of the plant on the ground, or cover young plants temporarily with garden fleece. Many gardeners accept the demise of their **squash** plants at midseason, having had their fill of **zucchini** by then.

Squash bugs, cucumber beetle, slugs, and asparagus beetles are all bad guys. Watch for them, and catch them early before they multiply. Handpick the ones you can reach. Following label directions, spray major infestations with Neem oil or an insecticide product that contains pyrethrum.

Fungal diseases show up as gray coatings or soft, dark spots on foliage or fruit. Pick and discard affected fruit. A mature, healthy plant is rarely affected by mildew on its foliage.

AUGUST
HERBS & VEGETABLES

 PLANNING

The August pause—when just about everything has been planted and is at some stage of development, and the eating is great—offers an opportunity to reflect on the season so far. It is time to catch up on record-keeping in your garden notebook or journal.

- Check those seed packets and plant labels for plant names.
- Recall planting dates, varieties and yields.
- Note any problems and the solutions you tried.
- Remember dates of last frost, heat arrival, and other weather events.

In a short five months it will be time to plan the garden for next year.

Shopping List: bird seed, freezer storage bags and boxes, more slow-acting fertilizer

 PLANTING

There is still time for a second planting of **turnips**, **spinach**, **lettuce**, **beets**, **radishes**, **chard**, and **winter onions** in the garden or in containers. Check the maturity dates against your date for expected first frost. Gardeners in northern Ohio are short on time. Plant seeds more generously,

because germination may be unreliable.

Start seeds for growing herbs indoors under lights this fall for holiday gifts. Plant in 4-inch pots filled with moist, sterile seed-starting medium and some granular slow-acting fertilizer. Then temporarily sink the pots into the garden. Bring the pots inside before first frost.

In most parts of Ohio, **rosemary** will not overwinter safely in the garden. Dig up your plant and put it in a pot to use and enjoy indoors all winter.

 CARE

If it has decomposed in the heat, renew the layer of organic mulch under plants such as **tomatoes**, **cucumbers**, **bush beans**, and **melons**. Mulch helps to prevent fruit from contacting the soil.

When the stalks and foliage of the **potato** plants flop over, it is time to harvest **potatoes**. Dig them up, or lift the mulch from the aboveground pile, taking care not to damage them with the fork or shovel in the process. Allow the **potatoes** to dry, and brush the dirt from them. To avoid rot, do not wash them until you use them.

Dig **garlic** as soon as the leaves start to turn yellow. Dry them carefully and store them hanging in a cool, dry location.

 WATERING

Watering is critical this month. Give each plant at least 1 inch of water weekly. Regular watering will prevent most cracking on **tomatoes** and blossom-end rot on **tomatoes** and **squash**.

Keep newly planted seeds and seedlings moist. While you may have to water both morning and evening in hot, dry weather, you will not have to water for long periods, as the seeds are close to the soil surface.

Containers dry out in no time, especially the clay (terra cotta) ones, because air and moisture can pass through their sides. The hot August sun speeds up this process, and heat from nearby masonry patios, building walls, and paved walkways is much stronger than that generated out in the garden. Water, water, water!

 FERTILIZING

A monthly liquid fertilizer application helps all productive plants. Younger plants will do fine on the granular, slow-acting fertilizer you added to the soil at planting time. Remember each crop utilizes nutrients from the soil, so testing the soil and replacing necessary nutrients becomes important.

If you are growing a second round of **corn**, give young plants some extra fertilizer. **Corn** is a heavy user of nitrogen.

PRUNING

As each crop is completely harvested, take time to pull up plants. Chop or cut them up into manageable pieces with pruners or a spade, and put them in the compost bin.

PROBLEMS

Spider mites curl leaves or make them look sickly or dirty. Pinch off infested leaves. Spray foliage of heavily affected plants with a forceful water spray to wash off mites every couple of days for a week or two.

Viral diseases can attack certain varieties of **tomatoes** and other vegetables. If plant foliage begins to turn brown and die from the bottom up, promptly pull up the plants, and discard them in the trash. Choose disease-resistant varieties next year.

HELPFUL HINTS

To minimize waste from overproduction next year:
- Plant only foods that your family likes to eat.
- Limit the number of different crops to about five until you have learned how to grow and manage them well. Then add two or three new kinds of vegetables and herbs each year.
- Make several successive small plantings of **beans**, **dill**, **lettuce**, and others so that you have some to eat all summer rather than having the whole crop all at once.
- Perfect methods of intensive planting and succession planting for more economical use of space, fertilizer, water, and your time and energy.

Powdery mildew sometimes develops on plant foliage. Ignore it on mature or nearly finished plants. Spray all new and emerging foliage on a newly producing plant with a sulfur-based garden fungicide product according to label instructions. It will protect it from further infection.

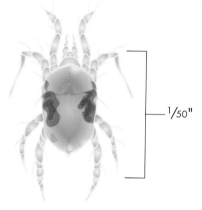

Spider Mite

Bacterial wilt spread by a beetle may infect **cucumbers**, which will dry up and die just as they start to produce fruit. Watch for and control the beetles early in the season. Pull up infected plants, and discard in the trash.

Weeds will soon go to seed. Pull them up before they scatter seeds for next year.

September

HERBS & VEGETABLES

 PLANNING

Labor Day weekend signals the end of summer and, in the minds of many, the end of the vegetable garden season. This month is often seen as a time of harvest and winding up gardening activities for the year—which may be true if you are only interested in a summer garden filled with warm-weather crops.

In large areas of Ohio, however, there are weeks of golden, relatively mild days ahead, even if a light frost visits toward the end of the month. There is ample opportunity for extending the gardening season by growing cool-weather crops. The same plants that did well very early last spring also perform in the fall. With some help from plastic mulches, tunnels, or cold frames, crops can be protected from the frost and nurtured to harvest despite days with increasingly less light.

Shopping List: portable cold frame, clear plastic

 PLANTING

Because there are now fewer hours of daylight, seeds sown directly in the garden will take a bit longer to mature. If you have a cold frame or can rig a clear plastic tunnel, **parsley**, **lettuce**, **chives**, **onions**, and other crops will eventually mature and grow past first frost into November.

To increase your supply of herbs for gifts or for kitchen use, take stem cuttings from outdoor plants before they succumb to frost.

1. Cut off 4- to 6-inch-long pieces of tender stem tips.

2. Remove all but the top three to five leaves.

3. Place the stems in a glass of water on the window sill,

OR

Insert them into a shallow pot or flat filled with moist sand or perlite and cover the container with plastic (with some air holes) to maintain humidity around the cuttings.

4. Check after two or three weeks for signs that roots have developed.

5. Pot rooted cuttings in soilless potting medium with some granular fertilizer mixed in.

Now is the time to plant **garlic** for next year. The secret to growing **garlic** is fall planting and loose soil; add organic matter to make the soil soft and friable.

Get a jump on spring by planting **spinach** now. Sow seeds, and let the new young plants overwinter in a mulched bed. They will resume growing in the spring.

 CARE

Young **broccoli**, **cabbage**, and other cool-weather lovers planted

Plant garlic now to have some next year.

last month may need more mulch. Plan to leave root crops such as **parsnips**, **turnips**, and **carrots** in the ground until after frost; the chill will sweeten their flavor.

Pull up dead and dying plants from containers before real cold sets in later this month or next month. Clean out the planting medium, and mix it into the real garden soil. Scrub the empty containers and store them indoors.

WATERING

Water the soil in the **asparagus** bed either now or next month so it will be moist when cold weather comes.

Unless the fall is extremely dry, there is no need to water the remaining vegetables in the garden, especially if they are mulched. In the absence of rain, moisten materials that you put on the compost pile so that microbial activity will continue deep within it even after frost.

FERTILIZING

When planted beds are cleared at the end of the season, consider spreading a 1 or 2 inch layer of chopped leaves to protect the bare soil from compaction during the winter.

HELPFUL HINTS

Double-digging planting areas—either wide rows or raised beds—is a lot of work, but the improved soil offers great benefits for your plants. The soil has more air and nutrients, and holds moisture better. Do the digging in the fall.

Rather than simply pushing a shovel into the ground, lifting clumps of soil, then turning them over as you deposit them back on the ground, follow these steps:

1. Dig a 2-by-2-foot hole and set the soil aside. Partially fill the hole with organic debris such as chopped leaves, leaf mold, straw, nonmeat kitchen peelings, or prunings.

2. Dig a similar hole adjacent to the first hole, depositing the soil you remove into the first hole to cover the plant waste at its bottom. Partially fill the second hole with organic debris.

3. Dig a third hole next to the second one. Deposit the soil on the debris in the second hole. Continue this process until you've used up your organic material or you have dug all the planting area you want to.

 PRUNING

Cut off tops of **tomato** plants to prevent more fruit production. This will divert energy to those already formed green **tomatoes**, which may still have time to ripen.

Pull stems of other plants such as **corn**, **peppers**, and **eggplants** that have finished producing.

As **asparagus** fronds turn brown and dry out, cut them back, then weed and mulch the bare soil in the bed.

 PROBLEMS

Insect activity virtually halts as temperatures drop. Most have completed their life cycles and have left eggs or larvae to overwinter in the yard. Diseases are not much of a problem as the season winds down. Their spores may winter over in the soil or on nearby organic debris, so clean up the mulch and dead plants where disease problems developed.

Rodents are looking for nesting places. Delay spreading mulch until the ground has frozen. By that time they will have nested elsewhere.

OCTOBER

HERBS & VEGETABLES

PLANNING

Store unused seeds for use next year. Make sure they are not damp from being outdoors during the summer. Tightly seal them in their packets and put them in an airtight tin or other container in the back of the refrigerator to keep them fresh.

If you do not already have one, this is a good time to establish a composting operation on your property. The leaves that fall from trees this month are much too valuable to put in the trash. Collect those that fall in your yard, chop or shred them, and use them to mulch the garden. Use leftovers to start a pile in some out-of-the-way corner where they can sit and decompose over the months to come. Add leaves from the neighbor's yard, kitchen scraps, prunings, dead plants from the garden, straw, dried grass clippings, or any other nonmeat organic material to the pile.

In the spring you can decide whether you want to make compost by one of the following methods:

1. The simple (passive) method means you just allow the pile to perpetually sit and decompose within, while you continually add materials on top during the season. It will begin to yield compost at the bottom of the pile in a year.

2. The managed (active) method means that you build the pile all at once, turn it periodically to make it heat up, and harvest lots of compost halfway through next season.

Shopping List: electric- or gasoline-powered leaf shredder

PLANTING

Other than sowing some **spinach** for next season, there is no more planting to do this season. Place plants such as **lettuce** that are still growing in pots in a cold frame to protect them until you have harvested all the leaves. Tender perennial herbs such as **rosemary** can also winter over in a cold frame if they are in pots. Rooted herb stem cuttings should be ready for potting up any time now.

Last call to bring herbs indoors. Dig up viable **parsley**, **rosemary**, **chives**, **thyme**, **oregano**, and **sage** plants. Shake soil off the roots and plant them in pots of moist, soilless potting mix. Herbs can grow under lights or in a cool, sunny window. (**Chives** that have been frosted already may not grow until next spring.)

CARE

Harvest all remaining vegetables in anticipation of a serious frost, which will blacken **tomatoes**,

If you don't have one yet, start some type of compost pile.

squash, **pumpkins**, **peppers**, and ornamental **gourds**. Root crops may remain in the soil until after first freeze. Cover **carrots** and **parsnips** with a heavy mulch, up to a foot thick. This will protect plants from an early freeze but will not protect them from a constant freeze.

Thoroughly clean up and destroy weeds to control pests and diseases. Remember that pests that annoy vegetable plants are also attracted to many of the weeds growing in and around the garden, and they lay their eggs on them. Compost remaining plant material. Cut or shred the woody plants before dropping them on the compost pile so these tougher materials will break down faster.

Winter squash and **pumpkins** can take a frost but not a freeze. When the **pumpkins** turn solid orange, cut them at their stems with a knife. Cure them in a warm, dry location for a week or two (until they are dried out a bit). Store them cool and dry at 55 degrees Fahrenheit, and they will last all winter. **Winter squash** will be ready to harvest when the **pumpkins** are.

Green **tomatoes** may still be on **tomato** vines, but they require 65 degrees Fahrenheit temperatures to ripen. When the thermometer dips below that, harvest the unblemished remaining ones, and wrap them

HELPFUL HINTS

There are lots of ways to chop leaves for use as mulch or to speed up their decomposition in the compost pile. (Whole leaves tend to mat together and prevent moisture and air from reaching the soil.)

• Mow them with a mulching lawnmower and collect them in a bag attachment.

• Mow them with a mulching mower so that the side discharge blows them toward the center of the lawn as you make your passes. They will become a pile of chopped leaves ready for use.

• Rake them into a pile and run the lawnmower back and forth over them.

• Use a shredder-vac which collects and shreds the leaves into a bag.

individually in newspaper. Place them in paper bags in a cool, dark area such as the basement to ripen. Periodically check to see if any are turning color. Bring pinkish ones into the kitchen to ripen further in the sun and heat.

 WATERING

Make certain all perennial herb plants have been watered in anticipation of winter. Drain all hose and water lines to the garden to prevent damage from freezing.

Moisture is necessary for decomposition of organic material. Water the compost pile only if it is very dry. If the materials were moist when you piled them up, chances are the interior of the pile is still moist.

 FERTILIZING

You might want to sprinkle some slow-acting fertilizer around the **rhubarb** so it will have nutrition for its very early appearance in the spring.

 PRUNING

No pruning is necessary this month.

 PROBLEMS

Squash vine borers winter over in plant debris. Throw suspect debris in the trash.

NOVEMBER

HERBS & VEGETABLES

 PLANNING

Ohio gardeners with extended-season vegetable gardens traditionally have fresh food from their gardens on the Thanksgiving dinner table. What better way to celebrate the harvest!

- Pick **Brussels sprouts**, **lettuce**, **spinach**, **Chinese cabbage**, and **Swiss chard** from under clear plastic tunnels.
- Pull **sweet carrots** and **parsnips** directly from the garden.
- **Pumpkins** and **winter squash** are at their best.

Cover or mulch all the bare soil in the garden. The microbial life in the soil appreciates some winter protection.

Thanksgiving is an appropriate time to take stock of the past gardening year and make final entries in your notebook or journal. Keep it handy to continue to record weather events and information on the birds and other wildlife that visit your feeder during the winter months.

Shopping List: indoor light garden, black oil sunflower seed, suet cakes, birdbath heater, snow fencing

 PLANTING

Plant **Egyptian onions (walking onions)** now. They winter over in bulb form and will begin to grow early next spring. They will be ready to eat two to three weeks earlier than spring-planted **onion** sets.

 CARE

Vent clear plastic tunnels and open cold-frame lids if the weather is mild with strong sun.

If the ground is still workable, this is an excellent time to build a raised bed. Start this first year with just one or two beds; box them with wood planks now so the wood can weather over the winter.

Prepare soil for next spring by incorporating organic material into it now. This will allow time for it to decompose and condition the soil.

If enough manure is available now, this is the best time to dig it into or spread it over the entire garden.

Scrape dirt from the surfaces of hand tools. Wire-brush them, and coat the metal with oil. Follow manufacturers' instructions for winterizing power equipment.

Mulch the herb beds after the first hard frost. By this time rodents will have found homes for the winter and they will not nest in the mulch.

 WATERING

Water any plants growing under clear plastic tunnels, because the rain cannot get at them. Either run drip irrigation, or water by hand with a watering can or hose.

 FERTILIZING

No fertilizing is necessary this month.

 PRUNING

No pruning is necessary this month.

PROBLEMS

Poor crop production may be a result of nutrient deficiencies in the soil. Take a soil sample for laboratory analysis (see December). If the soil is too acid for certain plants, this is a good time to spread lime to "sweeten" the soil. It provides calcium too.

Critters may continue to visit the garden in search of leftovers. An 18- or 24-inch fence with the lower portion snugly against the ground or slightly under its surface will deter rabbits. Groundhogs (woodchucks) are a different matter. Sink their fence in a 12-inch-deep trench and extend it at least 2 feet above the ground. You may want to widen the trench to 12 inches so the fence lies flat under the ground for a foot, then bends upward aboveground for 2 or 3 feet. This is a lot of work, but it is the only effective barrier to these destructive creatures.

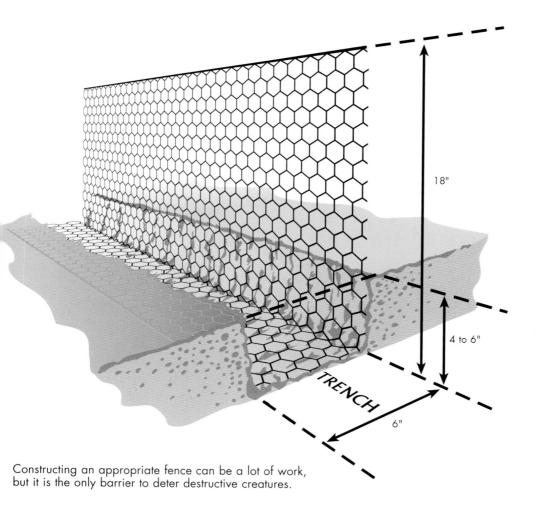

Constructing an appropriate fence can be a lot of work, but it is the only barrier to deter destructive creatures.

December

HERBS & VEGETABLES

PLANNING

Collect new seed catalogs and put them aside for consultation after the hectic holidays are over. There will be lots of enticing new varieties of many of the vegetables and herbs you are already growing. This is where your garden notes will come in handy. They will remind you if you need to try a different variety of a particular plant because the past year's crop was not successful.

Use the off-season to learn more about growing and using herbs. Join a local herb society, and search out herb gardeners who can help you find unusual varieties.

Christmas List: a soil-test kit, a book on vegetable gardening, a rain gauge, a book on herbs, a seed-starting system

PLANTING

Cover cropping is an agricultural technique used by backyard vegetable gardeners to protect and nourish garden soil. A cover crop is a plant that is temporarily grown on idle soil. It will be dug or tilled into the soil in the spring before planting a vegetable crop in that space.

HELPFUL HINTS

If you have a suspicion that the soil in your garden—or some part of it—is not healthy, test it. Production crops are much heavier "feeders" than are most ornamental plants, so their soil is more likely to become depleted of certain nutrients or trace elements even when you fertilize with a balanced, slow-acting product and rotate your crops.

Purchase a soil-sample test kit from your county extension service. Follow the label instructions exactly. A computer print-out will indicate if the soil is overly acid or alkaline; the amounts and proportions of nutrients available to the crops; and any trace elements lacking in your soil. The test will also recommend how to correct deficiencies.

The best cover crops make rapid growth. Grasses are good for producing maximum organic material in a short time. For fall planting, try **winter ryegrass**.

CARE

The ground has frozen hard in many parts of Ohio. If you have not already mulched perennial food and herb crops such as **strawberries**, **rhubarb**, **sage**, **oregano**, **chives**, and **mints**, do so now. Straw, chopped leaves, or pine needles are suitable mulches.

WATERING

No watering is necessary this month.

FERTILIZING

No fertilizing is necessary this month.

PRUNING

Cut back the dead stems of plants in the garden for a final cleanup. To keep the area neat, pick up twigs and branches that drop from trees onto beds.

PROBLEMS

Snow is not a problem. The cover it provides insulates the soil and protects bulbs, seeds, and microbial life beneath the soil surface. It helps hold in moisture and provides more moisture when it melts.

LAWNS

Grass is the number one plant (if you are counting actual numbers of plants!) that we have in our landscapes. And if we are talking about drive-by appearances, we judge the beauty of many homes by the appearance of its lawn. How many times have you said, "My neighbor across the street doesn't do half the yard work I do, and his lawn looks better than mine"? Well, that's because we're not picking up our neighbor's newspaper every morning as we do our own. Every morning we walk out on our lawn and say to ourselves, "Look, I have this weed, this brown 3-inch spot, and oh, what's that?" We can become a lawn fanatic, without becoming a "lawn nut." We view our neighbor's yard from a distance, where his lawn looks better. Want to feel better? Go pick up your neighbor's paper, and you will see the same things—or worse—in his lawn that you see in your own!

WHEN IS THE BEST TIME TO PUT DOWN GRASS SEED?

Fall seeding (mid-August to the end of September) is best. During this period, soil temperatures are high, which promotes quick germination. Annual weeds have already germinated and are less

likely to be a concern. Irrigation may be necessary, however, if natural rains are not available. (See September Planting for instructions on seeding your lawn.)

Dormant seeding (January 1st to March 15th) is second best. Soils are usually freezing and thawing during this time, which works the seed into the soil for great seed-to-soil contact. Remove any fallen leaves or other debris that would prevent the new seed from making seed-to-soil contact. Naturally, seed will not germinate until soil temperatures reach at least 55 degrees Fahrenheit, but having seed in the soil before then can give desirable grasses a head start before spring-germinating weed seeds erupt.

Spring seeding (March 15 to June 15) is third best. Germination can be obtained during these months, but weed competition will be at its highest. Tupersan®, an herbicide that you can use that will not harm the grass seed, should be applied to prevent crabgrass infestation from crowding out desirable grasses. Broadleaf weeds should be ignored until your desirable grasses have matured (or have been mowed two to three times). At that time, weeds should be treated with a selective broadleaf weed con-trol, following the directions on the label.

Summer seeding (June 15th to August 15th) is fourth best. With irrigation, germination will be fast during these summer months, but the high day and night temperatures may result in diseases, such as damping-off, pythium, and brown patch. Crabgrass is also likely to be present. Add to these negatives the fact that tender, young grass seedlings literally cook under the summer sun.

Late-fall seeding (mid-October to January 1st) is the least desirable. It is likely that seed will germinate during this period, but it will not have enough time to develop an adequate root system to protect it from heaving and thawing. In most cases, this seeding will result in seedlings being "popped" out of the ground and just drying out (desiccating).

WHAT'S IN THE SEED YOU'RE BUYING?

All grass seed sold in Ohio is tested by the Ohio Department of Agriculture. All seed that you buy has to have a label. The label information is actually gathered by people working in a lab. They count all the seed and other matter by hand and test that seed for germination. Always check the label, espe-cially if comparing prices. The label should tell you the following (remember these definitions):

• Variety: the correct name(s) of the grass seed you're buying; no common names, such as "super blend," are allowed.

• Seed purity: the percentage of pure grass seed that you're buying; this percentage should always be above 95 percent.

• Other crop seed: the percentage by weight of unlisted grass seed varieties that are in your seed; this percentage should always be 1 percent or less.

• Inert matter: the non-seed count or other non-seed material that you are buying; it, too, should be 1 percent or less.

• Weed seed: the percentage of bad, weed-causing seed that's in your seed. It should be less than $1/2$ percent. Remember, just 1 percent of weed seed can amount to one million chickweed seeds!

• Noxious weeds: should read "none found." You never want to buy any grass seed with noxious weed seed in it.

• Lot number: the number that was assigned to a particular crop of seed that came from the same harvest and the same growing field.

- Germination: the percentage of the seed you're buying that you can expect to grow; it should be 80 to 90 percent.
- Origin: the state where the seed was harvested.
- Test date: the date that the seed from your particular lot was tested.

LAWN FERTILIZER: WHAT THE NUMBERS MEAN

There is a dizzying assortment of lawn fertilizers available at your local garden store. What should you buy? Usually, one pound of actual nitrogen per 1,000 square feet of lawn is applied per application. You will see three numbers on a bag of fertilizer. The numbers (sometimes called the analysis) show the amounts by weight of the nitrogen (N), phosphate (P), and potash (K), always in that order. A 50-pound bag of fertilizer with an analysis of 10-6-4 contains 10 percent nitrogen, 6 percent phosphate, and 4 percent potash and covers 5,000 square feet. You may see an 18-pound bag of lawn fertilizer whose analysis is 20-4-6 and whose directions say it covers 5,000 square feet. Well, let's do some math. If we take 20 percent of 18 pounds (multiply by 0.2), we come up with 3.6 pounds of nitrogen per 5,000 square feet. Not enough. You might find a 50-pound bag of 10-6-4 fertilizer that will cover 5,000 square feet of lawn. Using the same math, 10 percent of 50 pounds is 5 pounds of nitrogen per 5,000 square feet, which is the right amount. Just looking at the numbers on the bag without factoring in the coverage information might have you believe that 20 percent is more than 10 percent, which isn't always the case with fertilizers. Remember, do the math.

A FINAL WORD OF ADVICE

Lots of products are available to simplify your job of maintaining a good-looking lawn. These products will work to your expectations and will be environmentally friendly if you read the label and follow the instructions! And remember, more is not always better.

Lawns can be very challenging, but don't become a "lawn nut." In this chapter, we have listed several varieties of lawn grass. Read carefully and find the one that best fits your growing situation. Don't argue with yourself, hoping to get the grass you thought you wanted and finding it doesn't fit your growing environment. Study and understand the information in this introduction before reading about individual grass varieties. You'll be glad you did.

JANUARY
LAWNS

 PLANNING

It seems that it's finally okay to stop thinking about the lawn. However, January is actually a great time to think about it and your turf management schedule. It is also a good time to maintain and upgrade the equipment you use to care for it. Seeing to this now will reduce the time and effort required to do it during the busy official lawn-care season.

• Check equipment. Have your mower blade sharpened during this slow period. Be sure the gasoline is drained from gas-powered engines, the oil is changed, and the sparkplugs are replaced if necessary.

• Purchase new equipment. If your mower is an older model with lots of engine hours used, upgrade to a modern mulching mower to save future time and effort.

• Evaluate your property. If areas of your lawn are difficult to mow because of steep slopes or hard to reach areas, consider planting ground cover plants to reduce your mowing.

 PLANTING

Fall is the best time to plant grass seed, and January is the second best time. It's called dormant or winter seeding. The only work you have to do is remove any leaves or other debris on the existing areas to be seeded. Mother Nature prepares a natural seed bed and the seed will germinate as the soil warms in the spring. Do not put the seed down on snow covered soil. You want to be able to see what you're doing.

 CARE

Turf grass is vulnerable to damage when the grass plants freeze and we walk on that frozen turf. Really limit the amount of foot traffic when it's cold. Train the newspaper man to have the paper land on the driveway, not the lawn.

Make sure that de-icing salt does not run onto turf areas. While it may be unavoidable along the curb due to municipal plows, use non-salt alternatives on driveways, walkways, and patios. Gritty granular fertilizer will melt snow and ice. The

Review your landscape design to determine if some areas should be planted in ground cover to reduce mowing.

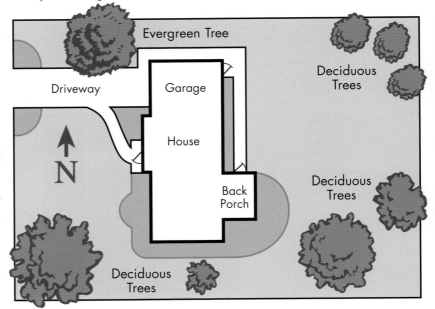

LAWN NOTES TO REMEMBER THROUGHOUT THE YEAR

1. The best fertilization times for all types of lawns are early September (with a high-nitrogen fertilizer), early (zone 5) to late (zone 6) November (high nitrogen), and spring ($1/2$ rate nitrogen).

2. Leave grass clippings. They will continue to release nutrients to the lawn. An exception is the tall clippings due to rainy periods. Collect those that would clump and smother grass plants or wait until the clumps dry and mow again, or spread them out over the lawn using a leaf blower.

3. Choose grass varieties that fit your maintenance schedule. For example, **bluegrass** is high maintenance, **perennial ryegrass** is medium to high maintenance, and **turf-type tall fescue** is low-maintenance.

4. Winter seeding is a great way to go if you can't seed in fall. In late January or early February, go out and remove any fallen leaves and twigs from the areas to be reseeded; this will help ensure that your seeds can make good seed-to-soil contact. Apply your seed to those areas (four to five per inch) and go back inside and watch TV! Freezing and thawing will occur, causing the seed to have a natural seedbed. The seed will germinate in spring when the soil warms to the proper germination temperature.

5. For spring and fall seedings, straw helps to hold moisture around the seed, but you will still have to water daily. If you decide to use straw, a bale should cover 1,500 square feet. This is a very light application. If done this way, no straw removal will be necessary, as the straw will decompose and not inhibit the new grass as it starts to grow.

6. Do I apply fertilizer or seed first? An easy question to ask, an even easier question to answer. When putting down lawn fertilizer and grass seed the same day, always apply the fertilizer first, so you're not walking on the grass seed any more than necessary.

higher the nitrogen (first number), the better the melt.

WATERING

There is usually enough natural moisture in the soil from rain and snow in January. The grass plant is completely dormant and water requirements are minimal.

FERTILIZING

If you fertilized your lawn late last fall with a quick release, high nitrogen fertilizer, you're all set until mid- to late spring. Do not fertilize now as the lawn is dormant and will not benefit. Never use a time- or slow-release type granular fertilizer during late fall or winter as this type of fertilizer needs average temperatures above 55 degrees Fahrenheit to effectively release nutrients.

MOWING

No mowing is necessary this month.

PROBLEMS

Soil compaction underneath the lawn is problematic anytime of the year. This is especially true during the winter due to winter moisture. Discourage everyone, including the mail carrier, from cutting across the lawn.

FEBRUARY

LAWNS

PLANNING

Reminder: take the lawn mower to the dealer for service before the lawn starts to grow. For those with garden tractors and large mowers, many service shops offer pick-up and delivery while others can service the larger equipment at your home.

One of the advantages of cool season grasses such as **turf-type tall fescue** is that they often hold most of their green color during the dormant period in the winter. This is especially true if you applied quick release nitrogen fertilizer last fall. If you notice some of your turf is brown and dried looking, chances are you have some warm season growers like **bermuda**, **zoysia**, and **nimblewill.** These unwanted grasses do not green-up until late May or early June. Check out August in this lawn chapter for

the best way to eliminate these winter browns.

A seven-year study on grass cultivars grown in tree shade in Columbus, Ohio, was recently completed in 2000 by Dr. David Gardner and Jill Taylor. This study tested a total of thirty different varieties of grass seeds, including all species of grass listed in this chapter. At the end of seven years, with the grasses being tested under **sugar maples** and **sycamores**, the scores were as follows (100% being the best):

- **Turf-type Tall Fescue** 84%
- **Fine Fescue** 50%
- **Kentucky Bluegrass** 32%
- **Perennial Ryegrass** 9%

The final results showed that **turf-type tall fescue** did the best; **fine fescue** was a distant second, followed by **Kentucky bluegrass** and **perennial rye**. **Turf-type tall fescue** actually became thicker, while all the others lost as much as 70 percent of their original grass cover.

Are you getting your money's worth when buying grass seed? Not all grass seed is equal. Grass seed is sold by the pound, but the price per pound should not be the determining factor in buying decisions. The number of seeds in an actual pound of grass seed varies with the type of seed you're buying. Example: **Kentucky bluegrass** has approximately one million seeds to a pound, while **perennial rye** and **turf-type tall fescue** have 200,000 seeds to a pound. That means **bluegrass** will cover five times the soil area as the other two. Buy grass seed by the coverage, not by the pound.

PLANTING

If the weather is cooperating and the ground is not frozen, sod could be placed on bare spots or entire sections of the lawn. The soil must be pre-

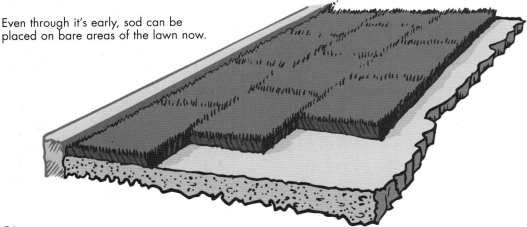

Even through it's early, sod can be placed on bare areas of the lawn now.

pared as you would when preparing for seeding (see September). Keep it moist.

Late winter is the second best time to plant grass seed (see planting times in the introduction to this chapter). Consider spot-seeding bare spots using the following steps:

1. Take a steel rake and loosen the soil.

2. Apply seed with an applicator or by hand at the rate of four to five seeds per inch. Freeze grass seed overnight for faster germination. (This step is not necessary for winter seeding.)

3. Keep soil damp until the seed germinates. Water as much as if you're watering the dust off a ball field. Do this daily. (A light application of straw is optional.)

4. After germination, deep-water the new grass once a week (an equivalent of 1 inch of water minus any rainfall that occurs). Do a complete watering all at one session, or divide it into no more than two watering sessions per week.

5. Mow as soon as the new grass reaches 2½ inches or more. Cut to a height of 2 inches. Raise the mower ½ inch after four cuttings of the new grass.

CARE

Prevent foot traffic when the lawn is frost covered. Grass blades

HELPFUL HINTS

One acre of grass gives off 2,400 gallons of water every hot, summer day. This has the cooling effect of a 140,000-pound air conditioner—a 70-ton machine.

There are some advantages to using sod when installing a brand-new lawn:
- instant green, weed-free lawn
- can be done almost anytime during the growing season
- no erosion problems on slopes
- smothers weed seeds on bare soil
- no need for followup seeding next year

There are some advantages to using seed when installing a brand-new lawn:
- less expensive
- wider choice of grass varieties
- easier to do yourself
- covers a larger area faster

can be easily and permanently damaged during this period.

WATERING

Even though the grass is dormant, it still needs some moisture. If there has been no rain or snow for more than four weeks during the winter and the ground is not frozen, water the grass—particularly the new grass seedlings from last fall.

FERTILIZING

The lawn is in a quiescent state. There is no need for supplemental nutrition.

MOWING

Typically, no lawn mowing is necessary this month.

PROBLEMS

Do not shovel snow into large piles on the lawn that could remain for long periods of time. Given a choice, shovel or blow the snow on areas of the lawn where the sun consistently hits on sunny days. For you procrastinators who didn't "dormant seed" in January, go ahead and do it this month! Just make sure there's no snow cover in place the day you want to seed. Seed when the snow goes away!

MARCH

LAWNS

 PLANNING

If you applied a late fall, high nitrogen fertilizer, you're noticing how much greener your lawn is compared to neighbors who didn't. Please get the lawn mower serviced and be sure to have the blade sharpened! By now, however, the dealer may be overloaded with work, so you can do it yourself:

1. Remove and discard the sparkplug.

2. Uncover the engine, and clean off any accumulated gunk and grass clippings from the fan and engine parts.

3. If the gas tank was not emptied for winter storage, drain it now. Leave it empty while you tip over the mower to access the blade.

4. Remove the blade for sharpening. Reinstall it, or install a new one.

5. Replace the fuel filter, and clean or replace the air filter.

6. Drain the oil from the crankcase (in 4-cycle engines), and refill it with fresh oil.

7. Fill the gas tank with fresh gasoline (and oil if a 2-cycle engine).

8. Install a new sparkplug.

 PLANTING

If temperatures are mild and the soil is not too wet, patch bare spots in the lawn with either patches of sod cut to fit, or seed. Loosen the bare soil with a steel rake or spade. Water these areas daily if spring rains are insufficient to keep them constantly moist.

 CARE

Your lawn will feel "bumpy" to walk on. This is due to the heaving and thawing of the soil all winter. The soil will settle. You might be tempted to roll your lawn, but don't. Let Mother Nature give you a free aeration!

 WATERING

Usually, during the spring there is adequate rainfall to support turfgrasses that are emerging from dormancy. We rarely see a March that doesn't have adequate natural moisture. If you seeded or put down new sod, a light, daily watering should be done on days with no rainfall.

 FERTILIZING

No lawn fertilizer should be applied. Some lawn services will recommend fertilizing, but they're doing it for their cash flow, not the health of your lawn.

Rotate mowing directions and don't cut any more than one-third of the grass blade's length.

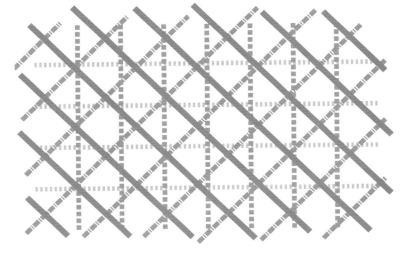

 MOWING

When the grass starts growing, you start mowing! Mow your lawn often enough so that you never remove more than one-third of the grass blades per mowing.

The easiest and cheapest way to have a good-looking lawn is to sharpen the lawnmower blade at least two or three times per season. Have it done professionally (it's cheap) so the blade remains balanced (weighs the same on both sides of the center hole). Grass does not like to be cut. It's a plant genetically programmed to grow to maturity and then produce seed. (Boy, wouldn't our neighbors love that!) We mow to keep our lawns looking neat. Every time we cut the grass, we injure the blade tissue, which is a water and nutrient reservoir. When we cut our grass with a dull blade, moisture and nutrients escape. A sharp mower blade minimizes damage to the cut grass blade.

 PROBLEMS

Early spring fertilization of your lawn is not recommended. You may be tempted to put down preemergence crabgrass con-

HELPFUL HINTS

The best way to discourage weeds in the lawn is to encourage thick, dense turf to crowd and shade them out. Your lawn care practices can reduce weed competition.

1. Core aerate periodically so grass roots can grow deep and support tall, healthy grass plants.

2. To keep lawn grass vigorous, overseed existing turf with new seed every couple of years, if the turf is thin.

3. Mow tall so grass foliage will shade the soil and deny weed seeds the light they need to germinate.

4. Deal with young weeds promptly, before they spread by runners or flower and set seed.

5. After weeds die, fill in bare spots with sod or seed to prevent new weeds from becoming established. Check the herbicide label to see how long you should wait before broadcasting new seed.

trol. Most of these herbicides only work for ninety days. Thus, if they are applied too early, the herbicide will have lost its effectiveness and will not kill crabgrass seeds. Spot treat with a selective broadleaf weed killer any dandelions or other weeds as they start to appear. Make sure air temperature is above 55 degrees Fahrenheit and no rain predicted for 24 hours.

Thatch is a layer of organic material that can buildup between the soil line and the crown of the grass plants. Thatch can be caused by having an incorrect soil pH. Also, certain species of grass (i.e. **bluegrass**) have a greater tendency to produce thatch layers than others.

Minimum amounts (up to 1/2 inch) of thatch are acceptable in lawns. One of the best ways to control thatch is by core-aerating your lawn in late spring and again in the fall. If you have had previous problems with crabgrass and other annual weeds, plan to apply a preemergent crabgrass control that contains Barricade™ or Dimension™. The Barricade™ or Dimension™ will help prevent any unwanted seeds from germinating that are present in your lawn for eight months.

APRIL

LAWNS

PLANNING

The grass is ready to grow. Did you get that blade sharpened? If you were a smart homeowner and fertilized your lawn last November, you now are noticing the benefits of that application. Your lawn is green and no additional fertilizer is needed at this time.

PLANTING

For thin and bare areas of your lawn, seed as early this month as the weather allows. Plant the new seed on the lawn preparing the seed bed with either a slit seeder or steel hand rake. Cover with a little straw on sloped areas and keep the seed moistened daily if no rainfall. April is also a good month to install sod.

CARE

If we are receiving lots of rain this month, limit foot traffic on soggy soil. If the lawn is bumpy to walk on, don't worry about it. That's the result of winter heaving and thawing and the ground will settle soon. Never roll your lawn to make smooth. This practice compacts the soil by reducing air pore spaces.

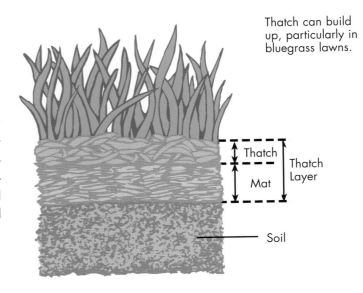

Thatch can build up, particularly in bluegrass lawns.

WATERING

All lawns would like to receive one inch of water per week. This usually occurs from natural rainfall in April. If you seeded or laid sod, water daily to keep the new planting moist.

FERTILIZING

A big mistake that both homeowners and lawn service companies can make is to over fertilize the lawn in April. You only need to apply fertilizer that releases no more than $1/2$ pound of nitrogen per 1,000 square feet. Too much nitrogen at this time can cause grass blades to grow too quickly. This fast growing turf can also be susceptible to disease pathogens.

MOWING

Always try to cut your grass often enough so that you do not remove more than one-third of the blade. The cutting height for your grass should be $2^1/2$ to 3 inches with **turf-type tall fescue** being mowed at 3 to $3^1/2$ inches. Always mow with a sharp mower blade and try to mow when the grass is dry. The clippings do not cause thatch, and they will break down to provide nutrition. Thatch is caused by the natural growing habits of **bluegrass** and certain **creeping fescues**. These plants create thatch as part of their normal growth process. So what to do about clippings? Just leave them. That's right. A full season of grass clippings returned to the soil is the equivalent of one application of fertilizer. If the grass gets extra-long between mowings due to rain, mow the lawn again after the wet clumps dry to distribute the grass clippings uniformly over the lawn. The clippings can also be scattered with a leaf blower.

PROBLEMS

Springtime translates into weed time for a lot of lawns. Unwanted weeds start to appear in lawns in mid- to late-spring. Chickweed, which doesn't become visually apparent until March, is the first unwanted spring guest to appear. It is closely followed by dandelions, then the plantain, wild violets, ground ivy, clover, and so on, and so on. All seed, including weed seed, germinates at different soil temperatures. That explains why chickweed appears in March, and spurge and purslane appear in June and July.

There are many selective—meaning they will not harm grass—broadleaf weed controls on the market. However, there is only one type that will control all the broadleafs, from the easy-to-control ones like dandelions to the tough-to-kill ones like wild violets and ground ivy. That product, Trimec®, is a combination of three different herbicides. Trimec-based products are available as a liquid concentrate, a granular form by itself, or mixed with lawn fertilizer. We always recommend the liquid concentrate as it is more cost-effective and allows you to just treat the weeds and not the entire lawn as you would do when using the granular form.

A word of caution: Remember, weeds die from light contact, not by drowning! Just wet the leaves of the various weeds and move on. Any weed control should be on the plant for 12 hours before rain. Wait 24 hours before mowing. When using the granular, apply it early in the day while dew is still present or if later, lightly water the lawn before applying. Do not reseed treated areas for thirty days.

Insects and diseases can be challenging to lawn management. Generally, **bluegrass** is more vulnerable. **Bluegrass** lawns are prime targets for chinch bugs, grubs, and other insects. Grubs do not cause visually noticeable spring damage to lawns, but new grubs returning to the soil in the fall can be quite damaging. Two new, low-toxicity products have been introduced to reduce grubs and other harmful lawn insects without killing beneficial insects and earthworms. These products, Merit™ and Mach II™, can be applied from May 15th to August 15th. Please read the instructions.

Turf diseases are more difficult to control. Environmental conditions along with natural drought stress and other negative factors can cause many diseases that, for the most part, only do temporary damage. You will find more turf disease problems with **bluegrass** and **perennial rye** than with **turf-type tall fescue**. When in doubt about a turf problem, take a 12-by-12-inch sample that has both healthy grass and diseased grass on it to your garden center or Cooperative Extension office for assistance.

MAY
LAWNS

PLANNING

There is a direct correlation between the height of your grass blades and the depth of your grass roots. This is important to know as we approach what could be the driest part of the growing season, summer. That is why you don't want to over-fertilize your lawn in the spring. Too much nitrogen can cause lots of lush top growth with insufficient roots to support all that growth. When rain days become fewer, the lawn can go into drought stress very quickly. Mow your grass on the high side, 2½ to 3 inches for **bluegrass** and 3 to 3½ inches for **turf-type tall fescue** and **perennial rye**.

PLANTING

It's getting too late for grass seed to grow and mature enough before the heat of summer. It's a suitable time, however, to plant sod. Prepare the soil as you would for seed and firmly place the sod on the soil. Keep the newly installed sod watered daily, for the first few weeks.

A fescue lawn is a good choice for Ohio.

CARE

If your lawn is predominately **bluegrass**, aerating the lawn is a great way to keep the thatch layer under control. This is also a great practice for those lawns growing in heavy clay or compacted soils. This practice over several seasons will continue to improve your soil's texture.

WATERING

Your lawn needs 1 inch of rainfall and/or supplied water per week. If rainfall is insufficient, turn on the hose!

FERTILIZING

If you haven't applied any fertilizer since last fall, a light application ($\frac{1}{2}$ pound of nitrogen per 1,000 square feet) can be applied. If broadleaf weeds are a problem, use a weed-and-feed type product.

MOWING

Keep mowing as often as the grass grows, removing no more than one-third of the grass blades at each mowing.

PROBLEMS

If broadleaf weeds are becoming a problem, the easiest and cheapest way to control the weeds is by using a liquid selective herbicide concentrate that lists the weeds you want eradicated on the label. Follow the mixing instructions and all other information on the label. Make sure no rain is predicted for 12 hours after spraying on a day with little to no wind.

That fast-growing, light yellow-green plant in your lawn that you call a grass is actually a sedge plant, called nut sedge. It gets its name because shortly after germinating from seed, it starts forming little corms on its roots that resemble nuts, thus the name nut sedge. It appears easy to pull, but the more you pull, the more you get because the nuts break off the roots as you pull,

HELPFUL HINTS

One of the best ways to maintain a healthy lawn is to make sure your mower blade is sharp. Sharp blades cut grass foliage cleanly. A dull mower blade will fray the tips of the grass, and the tips will turn brown and unsightly. The ragged tips also promote moisture loss and can offer a way for disease to enter the foliage.

Leaving clippings is one of the best things you can do for your lawn. Modern mulching mowers are designed so that clippings are suspended under the mower deck and then cut several times. Then they are small enough to fall down among the grass blades to avoid clumping. Because clippings are mostly water, they decompose very quickly. The clippings will also provide nitrogen and organic matter to the soil. While they do not create thatch, an existing thatch problem in your lawn will retard the breakdown of the clippings and make them more visible.

creating more plants. Until recently, there was nothing selective over the counter that would control the sedge. There are several products that indicate they do, but they don't. A product is available that provides good nut sedge control. Its trade name is Manage®. Follow the directions completely for excellent control of nut sedge.

Crabgrass can make its presence this month. Crabgrass is an annual grass that returns year after year from seed produced the previous year. Other annual weed grasses, such as goose grass and dallas grass, can be present, too. Annual grasses need warm soil to trigger germination. In Ohio, crabgrass usually starts to germinate near

the end of May in zone 6 and mid-June in zone 5. There are many preemergent crabgrass control products that are available. The vast majority of these products control for ninety days after application. Wet springs can reduce the effectiveness to sixty days, so be careful not to apply too soon in the spring.

Barricade® and Dimension® are both preemergent herbicides that will prevent crabgrass seed and other weed seeds from germinating for several months. Also, there are postemergent herbicides that allow you to spray existing crabgrass during the summer without damaging the desirable grass species.

JUNE
LAWNS

PLANNING

In the warmest areas of Ohio, the great lawn days will soon be over. They will not return until fall. Cool season turfgrasses such as **Kentucky bluegrass, turf-type tall fescue**, and **perennial ryegrass** look their very best when temperatures are cool—daytimes in the 70s and night-times in the 50s and 60s. In the spring and in the fall when these temperatures prevail, these grasses do their serious growing! They send roots deep into moist soil and launch stems outward creating denser turf. Supported by late fall fertilizer or an early spring application, these grasses have been producing lots of foliage which enables them to have energy necessary to support their rapid growth. This translates to frequent mowing!

The spring growth spurt will slow now, as soon as heat and humidity arrive. Grass will need less-frequent mowing and will depend on the vigor it has developed so far to help withstand the tougher summer conditions.

PLANTING

Trying to plant grass seed is a lost cause. If you have bare spots, patch in with sod. Be sure to keep new sod watered during the summer.

CARE

As the temperature climbs and the rains become less frequent, limit the amount of foot traffic on your lawn. Please note that **turf-type tall fescues** hold up a lot better during the summer than any of the other types of cool season grasses.

WATERING

Cool season grasses need lots of moisture to remain green in the summer. Their natural inclination is to deal with heat by going dormant. To help them manage during the summer, encourage them to grow deep roots so they can still get moisture way down in the soil when rainfall is scarce. Make sure that thatch is not preventing moisture from percolating into the soil.

Water established lawns only when it has not rained for over a week or ten days. Then water deeply.

Water new sod daily until it is established. Keep an eye on these areas if rainfall is sparse or temperatures heat up ahead of schedule.

FERTILIZING

If you used a fast-acting, water-soluble fertilizer product on the lawn in the spring, it will probably be time to repeat the application before June is over. It is important that nitrogen continues to be available to the grass. Slow-acting fertilizer applied on the lawn in the spring is still providing nutrition and should last

Encourage grass to develop deep roots so the lawn can withstand dry periods.

anywhere from ten to sixteen weeks, depending on the product. Check the package label.

Never fertilize lawns that are already stressed by drought or heat. Either skip the fast-acting dose, or wait until the weather cools and use it at a reduced strength. Follow the directions on the package label carefully.

MOWING

Unless there is generous rainfall, you will be mowing less often now that warmer weather is slowing grass growth. Make sure your mower blade is set at 2½ or 3 inches so the grass will not brown out in the summer sun.

Alter your mowing pattern to minimize wear on the turf. Mow in horizontal rows one week, in vertical rows the next, and in diagonal rows the third week.

HELPFUL HINTS

There are several good reasons to mow your lawn at a tall setting:

- Tall grass grows more slowly because it does not need to replace so much foliage, which is essential to metabolism.
- Tall grass needs less water because it shades the soil, minimizing evaporation of moisture.
- Tall grass needs less fertilizer and has more leaf surface to capture sunlight to produce its own food.
- Tall grass reduces weed problems because it prevents sunlight from reaching weed seeds in the soil.
- Tall grass has fewer pest and disease problems because it is less stressed.
- Tall grass shelters beneficial insects that feed on pest insect eggs and larvae.
- Tall grass discourages Japanese beetles from laying their eggs in the lawn. This will help control white grubs.

PROBLEMS

Beetles are out and flying about. All of the female beetles will be looking for a nice lawn to lay their eggs for the next generation. When these eggs hatch in June, July, or August (depending on species), the young larvae will start to burrow down in the soil. These larvae will eat grass roots as they bury themselves for winter protection. Their feeding can cause considerable damage to your lawn. There are many brands of environmentally friendly pesticides which contain either Merit™ or Mach II™ to protect your lawn. Apply this month and water in well after application.

July
LAWNS

PLANNING

Plan to have someone mow your lawn if you are going to be away on vacation for more than two weeks. Although grass grows more slowly in hot weather, after ten to fourteen days it will begin to look neglected and reveal that no one is home.

As pest or disease problems appear in the lawn over the summer, give some thought to developing a long-term strategy for preventing these problems. Rather than simply treating them each year, year after year, why not deal with the underlying causes and try to prevent them? The first step is to make some notes about problems that develop—the time of year, the location, the symptoms—to determine if they are chronic. If so, it may be time to change the grass variety to one more resistant to the problem. Consider keeping a lawn notebook or journal to help you track your lawn-care activities.

Reminder: This is a good time to sharpen your mower blade again.

Measure the amount of water you provide to make sure you're not just "sprinkling" the lawn.

PLANTING

Heat is the enemy of all new plantings. Seed of cool season grass varieties does not have a chance to really thrive, even if it germinates and starts to grow. If you need to fill a bare spot to prevent the inevitable opportunistic weeds from taking over, use sod. Water well and often until the roots become well established.

CARE

There is not much to do once summer heat arrives except mow the lawn. Be sure to leave the clippings when you mow (unless you have waited way too long and the clippings are so long that they clump). They will decompose rapidly because they are mostly water. To minimize soil compaction, avoid unnecessary walking on the lawn. Grass is likely to be stressed now, so do not aerate, fertilize, or treat for pest and disease problems while it struggles with heat, humidity, and possible drought.

WATERING

Now that summer is in full swing everywhere in the state, cool season turfgrasses suffer unavoidable stress if they lack regular moisture. (**Zoysia**, however, a southern warm season grass, finally becomes completely green after appearing as a beige carpet since last September!)

Water lawns of cool season grasses every ten days or so, if it does not rain regularly. To encourage grass to develop deeper roots and therefore some drought resistance, water deeply—soak down at least 6 or 8 inches—then do not water again for another ten days to two weeks. Compacted or clay soil may require a pause between watering sessions to allow the water to soak into the soil and avoid wasteful runoff.

Resist the temptation to "sprinkle" the grass daily. This encourages grass roots to stay near the surface, promoting thatch buildup. Having foliage wet all the time may cause fungal disease problems.

FERTILIZING

Even though you may not be actually spreading a fertilizer product, you are providing nutrition to the lawn when you leave the clippings every time you mow. Over the season, their accumulated nitrogen represents one-fourth of the annual nitrogen needs of grass, and the clippings break down into organic matter that will improve the soil.

HELPFUL HINTS

Three ways to tell if your grass needs watering:

1. The grass wilts, acquires a bluish tinge, and the edges of the blades start to curl or fold.

2. The soil is hard and resists insertion of a trowel or screwdriver.

3. Footprints where grass has been crushed from walking on it remain for several hours.

Remember—brown tips do not indicate drought stress. They can be the result of a dull mower blade, which frays the tips. Sharpen your blade!

MOWING

Continue to mow often enough to remove only one-third of the length of the grass blade each time. Keep the mower blade at 3 inches to help grass plants withstand heat and possible drought. If you have **zoysia**, it can be mowed at 2 or 2½ inches tall.

PROBLEMS

Spot treat weeds as they appear. If your lawn has more weeds than grass, consider waiting until August to kill the entire problem area and plant new lawn seed in September, the best month to seed. You still have time to protect your lawn from grubs. Apply Merit™ or Mach II™ following the instructions on the bag.

Weeds can be summer friends! The majority of weeds appear in your lawn in the spring. If you treat large areas of weeds and kill them, you will be left with large bare spots. Remember, you should wait thirty days to reseed. If you kill in late April, that means you should not reseed until late May, a very difficult time to seed and expect good results. Those spring weeds can be summer friends, once they are green when seen from the street and from inside your home. If you have lots of weeds, give serious consideration to lawn renovation in the fall. The best control for any lawn weed is a thick stand of turf that doesn't allow any room for the wind-blown weed seed to land and have space to grow in your lawn.

AUGUST

LAWNS

PLANNING

In the typical lawn, disease problems can begin to show up this month. Many grasses are susceptible to fungal invasions from the extremes of weather. Uncontrolled weeds rapidly move in to fill bare soil.

If your lawn has all these problems, a major lawn renovation might be advisable. If only one or two problems exist, then some remedial measures such as overseeding or aerating may turn things around. In any case, nothing should be done until the second half of this month.

Plan your fall lawn renovation program now, and buy supplies so they will be readily available. The earlier you start, the more time the lawn will have to establish before hard frost arrives. Many regions of Ohio enjoy prolonged, mild autumn weather, which cool season grasses prefer. They can use this time to great advantage to grow deep roots and store energy.

marks the beginning of prime time for overseeding existing lawns or installing new lawns with seed or sod of cool season grasses (**Kentucky bluegrass**, **perennial ryegrass**, and **turf-type tall fescue**). Decide if this is a project you will do yourself, or if you will hire someone to do it for you. The size of your lawn has a lot to do with that decision.

easier for the grass. It is natural for grasses to deal with heat and water shortage by turning brown. Often, sprinklers and hoses water inadequately or intermittently which can cause more stress for grass plants. When normal rainfall resumes, the grass will green up in a matter of days.

Measure the lawn area if you are planning to reseed so you know how much seed to purchase.

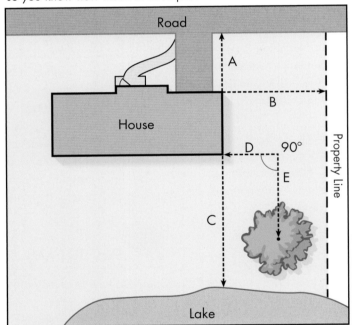

Road

A

B

House

D   90°

E

C

Property Line

Lake

PLANTING

In most of Ohio it is too hot and probably too dry to do any major lawn work. It is best to wait until the end of the month. In the cooler regions, however, mid-August

CARE

If the summer has featured prolonged drought, the best thing for cool season grasses is to allow them to go dormant. Not only will this save valuable water, but it is

WATERING

Water grass deeply if there is no significant rainfall for two weeks or if it indicates by a bluish tinge and curled blades that it is suffer-

HELPFUL HINTS

Theodore Roosevelt once stated, "Grass is what saves and holds the water that keeps life good and going. It keeps the falling rain from flushing away. Blades of grass take water from the air and transfer it into the ground. That works the other way around, too. Because grass blades help put water back into the air so that rain can fall again."

Here are ten ways to conserve water on established lawns during hot, dry weather— and save money on your water bill, as well.

1. Mow as infrequently as possible. Mowing puts the grass plant under additional stress and it will use more water.

2. Mow higher than normal. Larger leaf surfaces shade the root zone. Never remove more than one-third of the leaf blade in one mowing. Longer blades usually mean deeper, more efficient roots.

3. Water and mow in the early evening or morning. Less wind and heat reduces stress on the plant and allows for greater percolation and less runoff or evaporation.

4. Water for deep percolation. Stop watering when puddles or runoff occur, allowing the water to penetrate the soil before restarting.

Light sprinkling may actually bring roots to the surface and do more harm than good.

5. Spot water. Drier areas near buildings and on slopes require more water than flat areas where water doesn't run off.

6. Consider aerifying turf. This process will improve air and water movement in the soil.

7. Use a soil probe. Test the soil moisture with a probe or screwdriver. Water only when the soil is dry or the probe is difficult to push into the ground.

8. Match fertilizer to plant requirements. Extension agents or agronomists can recommend the timing and amounts of fertilizer needed by each grass variety. This will reduce unnecessary fertilization and reduce mowing requirements.

9. Increase disease and insect control with care. Drought stressed turf is more susceptible to pest problems, but too much pesticide will also increase plant stress.

10. Accept a little-less-than-lush lawn. Grass will naturally go dormant during periods of drought, but it will readily regenerate when water becomes available. Reduce traffic on those areas if possible.

ing. The quality of the soil in which grass plants are growing will determine how long they can go between waterings. In good soil, grass will have long roots that can find moisture deep in the soil. In poor soil, grass roots will be near the surface and dry out quickly.

FERTILIZING

Delay any fertilizing until next month when summer tempera-

tures moderate. It is okay to wait until even later in the fall.

MOWING

Continue to mow tall. Taller grass shades the soil to minimize evaporation of moisture, and it is likely to have deeper roots. Leave clippings as usual.

PROBLEMS

This is the longest month for your lawn. Problems, such as disease and drought can affect your lawn aesthetically. This temporary situation will improve as fall weather approaches. Do give thought to renovating your lawn next month by planting **turf-type tall fescue** which doesn't have many of the problems other cool season grasses do.

SEPTEMBER

LAWNS

PLANNING

Traditionally, Labor Day weekend opens the window of opportunity for major lawn-repair work. If sown or sodded at this time, the cool season grasses that are appropriate for Ohio will still have warm weather for germination, then several increasingly cool weeks to develop strong root systems before the ground freezes.

PLANTING

September is the best month to renovate your lawn.

Grass, like any other living plant, will thrive when properly planted in the right location. Many of us think grass seed will grow if we simply throw it on the lawn and walk away. Here are some step-by-step ways to successfully renovate your lawn.

Let's discuss some don'ts before we cover the dos.

1. Don't rototill the soil. This process causes the soil to settle unevenly and allows thousands of weed seeds to compete with the new grass (and it's a lot of unnecessary work).

2. Don't apply topsoil to the overall area unless you spread it to a depth of 4 to 6 inches over the entire area. Use topsoil to fill in any low areas. Settle the new topsoil with irrigation or rain before putting down your seed. Reloosen the topsoil with a steel rake to break up the crust. Then put down your seed.

3. Don't read any further unless you can keep new seed lightly watered twice daily until germination (assuming no rain on a given day). Try the winter seed method if this seems like too much trouble!

Now for the dos—please read carefully.

1. Do kill all existing vegetation in the area to be reseeded. Weeds and other vegetation should be watered well before the application of the herbicide (healthy weeds die faster). In late summer (early August), allow three to four weeks before retreating, as some weeds regrow after initial treatment. The old lawn should be between 2 to 3 inches tall when treating; this is especially true with nut sedge. Great vegetation killers that are safe to use are Roundup® and Finale®.

2. Do rent a slit-seeder or vertislicer. Set the blade to cut a 1/2-inch slit. Run the machine east to west and north to south (a checkerboard pattern). Most machines come with a seed box. If so, set the seeder to drop four to five seeds per inch of soil. For **turf-type tall fescue** and **perennial rye**, make another couple of passes northeast to southwest and southeast to northwest.

3. Do freeze your seed overnight. It can even stay frozen until you're ready to apply it. Do it now before you forget. (This is not necessary with winter seeding.)

4. Do fertilize with a starter-type fertilizer, such as a 9-18-18. Do not mix seed and fertilizer together in the same applicator hopper. Apply the fertilizer first.

5. Do lightly water grass seed daily (assuming rainless days) to keep the seed moist until germination. Then water once weekly with the equivalent of 1 inch of water including any rain. Continue to water during hot, dry weather. In order to tell how much you are watering, place a straight-sided can in the area of the sprinkler and when an inch of water appears in the can, move the sprinkler.

6. Do mow your grass as soon as it reaches 2¼ inches. Mow new grass to 2 inches and mow often. The more mowings, the quicker the new grass will mature. You will get a few new broadleaf weeds. Do not apply a broadleaf weedkiller until you have completed four mowings. Raise the mower ½ inch after four cuttings.

7. Do use high quality grass seed. If you're going to do all the above steps, don't risk failure by purchasing bargain seed. Check the seed label for purity, weed seed content, and inert ingredients.

CARE

If not reseeding or sodding, core aerating your lawn can be very beneficial. If seeding, wait until next season to core aerate.

WATERING

Water newly seeded areas so the seeds stay moist continuously. As sprouts grow into seedlings, water deeply to encourage their roots to grow downward.

Water newly sodded lawns deeply. If it is hot and there is no rain, you may have to water twice a day.

FERTILIZING

For a newly seeded or over-seeded lawn, you should use a seed-starter lawn fertilizer product at sowing time as directed on the package label. Established lawns should be supplied with a high nitrogen fertilizer (at least 1 lb. per 1,000 square feet). Be prepared to repeat this fertilizer in November.

MOWING

As the grass keeps growing, you keep mowing! Mow new grass seedlings as they grow and mow often. The more you mow the new grass, the quicker it matures before its first winter.

PROBLEMS

If mildew has been a problem over several seasons, overseed the affected parts of the lawn with grass varieties that are labeled as mildew resistant. They will thrive and eventually become the dominant species. Treat any broadleaf weeds with a selective herbicide; read the label before applying.

Cut out the bottom of a gallon container to protect any nearby bedding plants when you spot-treat broadleaf weeds.

OCTOBER

LAWNS

PLANNING

This is prime time for all lawns. Existing ones respond to the cool temperatures with renewed growth. New and renovated lawns become greener and healthier daily as the cool season grasses perform well in the increasingly cooler weather. An extended fall season is just the thing for seedlings of **Kentucky bluegrass**, **turf-type tall fescue**, and **perennial ryegrass** planted last month. The goal is to have them well rooted before the soil freezes.

There is no time like the fall to begin to record in a journal or notebook your current lawn-care information, if you have not already done so.

• Record when you fertilize, aerate, topdress, or install a new lawn.

• Each time you purchase and sow a turfgrass seed mixture, keep the label for future reference.

• Note when you purchased and serviced your mower and when you sharpened the blade.

PLANTING

In many parts of the state it is getting past time to plant new grass by mid-month. There is not enough time before serious frost and cold weather for grass seedlings to become established so they can survive the winter. Lawns in areas without snow cover are exposed to harsh wind and sun, too.

CARE

One of the problems with brand new seedlings at this time is that falling leaves from deciduous trees can smother the new, young plants. It is trickier to remove the leaves without damaging the seedlings' tender foliage than it is to remove them from an established lawn.

A shady, peaceful lawn is a great reward for months of hard work. Enjoy it!

Rake or blow fallen leaves from newly sodded or established lawns—do this frequently so that leaves will not mat and smother the grass. To avoid promoting fungal disease, do not allow leaves to accumulate for any length of time, especially if they are wet.

WATERING

If it does not rain regularly, water newly planted lawn areas so that shallow-rooted young seedlings will not dry out and shrivel up.

FERTILIZING

If you were to fertilize your lawn just once a year, this would be an excellent month. Apply a high nitrogen, quick release fertilizer at the rate of one pound of nitrogen per 1,000 square feet.

MOWING

Rake the heavy leaf fall from the turf before mowing each time to assure an even cut. Toward the end of the leaf fall, when the layer of leaves is thin, mow the lawn and leaves with a mulching mower. This will chop the leaves into fine organic matter that will fall between the blades of grass and mulch the grass plants for the winter.

PROBLEMS

White grubs may damage lawns in the early fall. Watch for dead patches of turf. Evidence of skunk visits and/or flocks of starlings on the lawn suggests grubs are present in the soil (both love to eat white grubs)—but if the soil has cooled below 75 degrees Fahrenheit, it is too late to get good control. The grubs migrate deep in the soil below the frost line for the winter.

Broadleaf weeds may still be green and growing. If air temperatures are still mild, it is possible to spot-treat dandelion, plantain, clover, and others with herbicide. This will give you a head start on next season. Check product labels for optimum air temperatures for their use.

Spot treat for weeds as they appear. If your lawn has more weeds than grass, consider waiting until next August to kill the entire problem area and then plant new lawn seed in September, the best month to seed. You still have time to protect your lawn from grubs that will cause damage next season. A quick kill product like Oftanol™ can be effective.

White grub

NOVEMBER

LAWNS

PLANNING

This is a good time to evaluate the size of your lawn. Traditionally, Americans tend to overdo, creating vast swaths of green turf that dominate the landscape. Consider ways to make better use of your yard and reduce lawn care maintenance as well. You might be able to start work on a yard project if the weather is nice.

Identify areas where grass has chronically failed or not performed well. This is often the case under shade trees. Think about giving up on trying to have turf there, and grow ground cover plants instead. Evergreen plants such as **pachysandra**, **vinca**, and **liriope** make great lawn substitutes. They provide interesting green foliage all winter and require less moisture and little fertilizer. Other ways to reduce lawn area:

- Widen shrub borders or garden beds.
- Build a deck or patio.
- Create a dog run.
- Set up an area for a child's swingset or playhouse.
- Put in a pool.
- Widen the driveway or front walk.
- Extend the ring of mulch under a tree as far as the branches reach.
- Establish a water garden.

PLANTING

Delay any planting of seed till January. Dormant or winter seeding is the next easiest time to seed. Continue to install sod until the ground freezes.

CARE

There is little to do for the lawn now. Care for it over the winter by protecting it from damage from shovels, snow blowers, de-icing compounds, and compaction.

Lawn substitutes include vinca, liriope, and pachysandra.

 ## WATERING

Continue to water newly planted lawns if rainfall is scarce. It is important for them to go into the winter in moist soil. If you are lucky enough to be able to count on snow cover during the really cold months, you will not have to think about watering until spring.

 ## FERTILIZING

If you followed our advice and fertilized in September, a follow-up application using the same type of fertilizer that you used then will help to provide a much stronger root system, better winter color, and quicker green-up in the spring.

 ## MOWING

Some years you may find yourself doing the final mowing this month. It is better to cut the lawn again to about 2 inches than to have it go into the winter too long. When covered with snow, overlong grass mats and can develop fungal diseases. Leave the clippings as usual unless they are very long.

HELPFUL HINTS

If you are planning to move to a newly built home, talk to the builder about the lawn. Let him know you want more than the typical "builder's special." This will save you time and energy next season.

• Insist that he replace all the topsoil he removed before construction began. He has probably sold it or used it elsewhere, so request an equal volume of high-quality topsoil instead.

• Ask if there is a seed allowance. If so, ask him if you can add to it so he will buy and sow a premium seed rather than the bargain special which is full of weed seeds. An alternative is to ask for the money, then choose the seed yourself.

• Ask him to have his crew sow the seed thicker than they normally do. Offer to pay for an extra supply of seed so this will happen.

 ## PROBLEMS

Dog urine is a real problem in lawns where owners allow dogs to run in the yard. The nitrogen in their urine can burn the grass foliage and can kill plant crowns, leaving a dead, brown patch in the turf. This happens more often with female dogs because they "puddle" on the lawn, leaving a large concentration of urine in one spot. Male dogs "piddle" at many sites as they mark them, and the nitrogen in any one spot is minimal. To prevent burning of the grass, pour a pail of water on the spot where urine is puddled to dilute it and wash it off the grass and down into the soil.

Weeds that are still obvious will have to remain until spring. Most herbicides do not work when the air or soil temperature is below 55 degrees Fahrenheit.

Erosion of the lawn soil can be a problem in newly built homes where the grass has not yet become established. Often builders rush to complete new construction by the onset of winter and manage to throw some seed on the "sea of mud" around the house at the last minute. It is a good idea to spread some straw over the soil as a mulch to break the force of rain, and reduce runoff and potential erosion.

December

LAWNS

PLANNING

If you have succeeded over the past year in caring for the lawn, it should look pretty good even in December. If there is no snow yet, cool season grasses may even be somewhat green, even though they are essentially dormant. If any **zoysia** grass has invaded, this warm season grass will be clearly visible as dried brown patches. Plan to eradicate it next summer and fall.

PLANTING

If the soil is not frozen, it is still possible to lay sod in limited areas of the lawn that were damaged by construction projects or affected by other events. It is better to lay sod over bare soil than to leave the soil exposed to compaction by winter rain, harsh sun and wind, or foot traffic. Sod will prevent erosion of the soil, too. Be sure to keep new sod well watered. Winter sun and dry, cold air will cause it to dry out quickly, especially along the edges of the pieces and where the sod meets paving. Whether it will actually put down roots and establish before spring depends on the weather over the next couple of months.

CARE

Dormant turfgrass does not need special care. Whether covered with snow or not, the most important thing you can do is avoid walking on it. Alert your family and the mail carrier, and keep walks clear so people are not tempted to take a shortcut.

WATERING

If it has been a dry fall, monitor the soil moisture under your turf. If you are not sure whether the soil is dry, use a soil probe or garden trowel. If the soil is dry, it is time to water. Do not wait more than a couple of days to water young grass that was sown earlier in the fall. It has not had time to develop deep roots and will be in danger of desiccation long before established grass needs irrigation. Water turf near trees, because competition from tree roots for water will have dried the soil under grass even more.

FERTILIZING

If you newly seeded this past fall, consider putting down a "winterizer" type fertilizer. It will be high in potash which acts as additional anti freeze to help the new grass get through its first winter.

MOWING

No mowing is necessary this month.

PROBLEMS

Annual weeds seem to have disappeared, but they have left behind seeds for next year. Perennial weeds are dormant.

HELPFUL HINTS

Salt is a big problem for turfgrasses. Runoff from sodium de-icing products or spray from municipal plows as they scrape salted streets often ends up on the lawn. It dissolves in the melted snow and ice water and is taken up by plant roots, causing plant tissues to die.

- Pour fresh water on turf areas you know have been soaked with salty water. This will help to leach out the sodium and wash it down into the soil beyond plant roots.
- Use non-salt de-icing products—sand, kitty litter, or something similar—on your own driveways and sidewalks.

PERENNIALS & ORNAMENTAL GRASSES

Whether you are a novice gardener or an experienced one, selecting perennials for the garden can be a daunting experience. It may not be difficult to choose an occasional perennial flowering plant to fill a particular space in the garden, but it can be a challenge to buy many plants for a brand-new garden or a renovated bed or border. You should assess the virtues of many different plants and factor color, bloom time, size, and shape into your decisions.

Perennial plants are considerably more expensive than annuals, which means that choosing perennials is a financial as well as an aesthetic decision. Because they can be expected to be around for a long time, making good choices from the beginning makes good sense . . . and cents.

The heart often overrules the head when choosing perennials, so it is important to take time to think about what qualities you want your plants to have before you make the shopping trip. It is tempting to choose the newest or most glamorous plants that are being promoted for the current season. Relatively untested perennials may not be reliable, easy-care choices for your particular garden.

A BETTER PLANT

All gardeners are looking for what horticulturists call a "better plant," one that meets high expectations in the garden. Professional plant hybridizers and growers interpret this to mean a perennial that has attractive foliage, sturdy stems, and handsome, long-lasting flowers. They are constantly trying to find and develop plants that are adaptable to a wide range of soils and various light and moisture conditions. They are always on the lookout for new selections of an existing perennial that display superior qualities. In fact, the running joke is that the perfect perennial blooms all summer like an annual, stands tall without staking, does not need dead-heading, has no pests, never needs dividing, and likes both sun and shade, drought and wet. This "perfect" perennial has not yet been found, but "better" ones are constantly being developed.

A new plant will be evaluated against existing plants to try to determine if it is truly better. Various organizations and plant societies conduct trials in different parts of the country and put promising plants through their paces. Perennials that demonstrate true superiority often win recognition by the Perennial Plant Association or a similar organization. Look for special tags or labels that will indicate if the perennial you are considering has won an award.

Another way to judge whether a certain perennial is reliable and easy to care for is to notice how popular it is with other gardeners. Groups that track sales of various perennials throughout the country year after year report that a consensus exists among gardeners and homeowners about the best garden perennials. While some may shift position over time, the following plants appear on the list time after time:

- Hosta
- Daylily
- Coreopsis
- Geranium
- Veronica
- Ferns
- Salvia
- Ornamental Grasses
- Astilbe
- Purple Coneflower

YOUR BETTER PLANTS

The best way to determine which perennials will be "better plants" in your own garden is to establish your own personal criteria. Growers and evaluators apply good standards to determine a plant's superiority, but they cannot take into account the special circumstances that exist on your particular property. They may assume that easy care, beauty, and reliability are near the top of your personal list of desirable traits in a plant, but they cannot know all the qualities you consider important.

A perennial selected by you must be hardy in the horticultural zone where you garden. Zone numbers traditionally reflect cold hardiness, but plants also have varying heat hardiness. Plant labels are now listing heat-hardiness as well as cold-hardiness information.

Pay attention to the different varieties of a perennial that are available. A certain variety of hosta or phlox may be outstanding in one region, but another variety may do better in your part of Ohio. Every yard has its microclimates—pockets where it is warmer, colder, moister, or drier than conditions that prevail in the yard as a whole. Plant choices must be suited to these sites if they are to perform well. If you garden, you have already been conducting unofficial trials to determine the better plants for your yard.

FAVORITE PLANT CHECKLIST

Take a moment to think about the plants that have done exceptionally well for you, those that come through year after year regardless of the rainfall or heat. Chances are these are your favorites. List the reasons you love them. Chances are this list reflects the qualities you most value in a plant.

Do not be surprised if your favorite perennials are the same ones you see in neighbors' gardens and elsewhere. This is no coincidence. The 'Stella d'Oro' daylily or the 'Sum and Sub-stance' hosta are truly better plants; they perform reliably under a variety of conditions with a minimum of care.

Complete your checklist by checking the qualities you consider virtues in perennials. Then prioritize them to fit the circumstances in your life and in your garden. Take the list with you when you go shopping at the garden center. It will help you narrow your choices in your search for a better plant for your garden.

WHAT MAKES A BETTER PERENNIAL IN MY GARDEN?

- _____ Low water demand
- _____ Tolerates a variety of soils
- _____ Needs little fertilizing
- _____ Likes acid soil
- _____ Deer-resistant
- _____ Dries easily for floral crafts
- _____ Low-growing
- _____ Evergreen foliage
- _____ Variegated/textured foliage
- _____ Native to Ohio
- _____ Good for cutting
- _____ Fragrant (flower or foliage)
- _____ Pest- and disease-resistant
- _____ Does not need staking
- _____ Clumps rather than spreads
- _____ Persistent bloom (more than two weeks)
- _____ Easily propagated
- _____ New or unusual
- _____ Prefers shade
- _____ Attracts beneficial insects
- _____ Attracts butterflies and hummingbirds
- _____ Multi-season interest
- _____ Great flower color
- _____ Other _____
- _____ Other _____

Bleeding heart 'Luxuriant'

JANUARY
PERENNIALS & ORNAMENTAL GRASSES

PLANNING

As the new year begins on the calendar, it is time to think about the garden. Winter weather may just now be truly closing in, with ground-freezing temperatures and some snowfall—nevertheless, the new gardening season has begun! The amount of daylight is gradually increasing, and it's time to follow up on a New Year's resolution and begin a garden notebook or journal. If you already keep one, get it out this month and read the entries from last January.

If you have a sketch or chart of where your perennials are planted in your garden, review it to determine where new ones might be planted this spring. If you do not have a sketch, begin one, and fill it in as emerging plants appear this spring to remind you where they are.

Get out the catalogs that have been accumulating since early last month. Take some time to get acquainted with the featured perennials for this coming season. The wonderful color photographs and information about their cultural requirements will help you identify some that you may want to plant in the garden this spring.

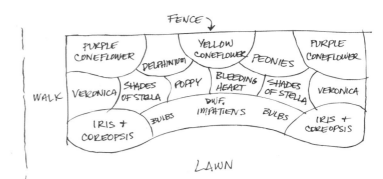

When you sketch your current or proposed perennial beds, take cultural requirements into consideration. That way, you won't place a plant that needs lots of water next to one that does not.

Become familiar with the Perennial Plant Association organization. The organization has grown exponentially during the past two decades. Review the "perennial of the year" list that has accumulated during the past twenty-plus years. Are there ones that you do not have? Are there selections that would be perfect to enhance a location in your garden?

PLANTING

While it is too early to plant any perennials outdoors, it is not too early to select a few varieties from catalogs to start from seed next month.

• Choose perennials that will sprout fairly easily and quickly. Unlike most annuals, many perennials are fussy about their conditions for germination—unless you want a new hobby, let the professionals do the complicated propagation.

• Choose varieties that will come true from seed. Some perennials are hybrids, and their offspring might resemble one of their grandparents rather than their parent.

CARE

At this time of year the soil needs protection from winter weather, because the soil protects the roots of the perennials. If you have not already done so, spread a 2- to 3-inch layer of organic material as a mulch over any bare soil in the garden. Any organic material will work fine.

You can use composted or chopped leaves (whole leaves tend to become matted which then can hold too much moisture), shredded bark, or pine needles.

Some perennials, like **chrysanthemums**, **veronica**, **lobelia**, and others, retain green foliage at soil level during the winter. Make sure this foliage is not under thick mulch. Consider putting some branches of needled evergreens (**pine**, **spruce**, or **fir**) over these perennials if you do not have other organic material readily available.

WATERING

If late fall was extremely dry, check soil moisture around new or divided perennials planted within the past couple of months. Water them if the soil is not frozen and seems dry.

FERTILIZING

No fertilizing is necessary this month.

PRUNING

If you have not already done so, cut back the dead, dried stems from fall-flowering perennials such as **asters**, **mums**, and **goldenrod**.

Leave ornamental grasses uncut to provide some color and movement in the garden for another month or two.

Thirty years ago ornamental grasses were rarely used in the landscape. Today, there are selections for every garden. Using ornamental grasses is one of the best ways to add various levels of movement in our gardens.

HELPFUL HINTS

Some perennials for a winter garden include:
- **Hellebores**—glossy foliage and late-winter flowers
- **Basket of Gold**—gray leaves and stems, trailing
- **Snow in Summer**—mat of gray-white leaves
- **Coral Bells**—variegated, evergreen foliage
- **Lavender**—grayish, thin leaves on straight stems
- **Black-eyed Susans**—black, rounded seedheads
- **Purple Coneflower**—large, rounded, bristly seedheads
- **Sedums**—large, flat, dried flowerheads on dark stalks

PROBLEMS

Deer and rabbits may visit your yard to investigate. Since most perennials are dormant and have died back to the soil, these animals will focus more on the woody shrubs and young trees. **Hellebores** have such leathery foliage, they are usually ignored.

Coral Bells

FEBRUARY
PERENNIALS & ORNAMENTAL GRASSES

PLANNING

Technically, a perennial plant is any plant whose life support system is designed to ensure its survival over many seasons. It's genetically programmed to grow roots and foliage that collect and store energy from the sun in the form of starches that carry it through a dormant season. Woody plants such as trees and shrubs are perennial, of course, but when gardeners talk about perennials, they are usually referring to herbaceous ornamental plants—those whose tops die back with frost but whose roots survive to send up new shoots next year.

Even though they are designed to return each spring, not all perennials are equally capable of surviving cold winter temperatures. Some are genetically more cold hardy than others. To be sure that you select plants this spring that will survive in your garden for years, check the zone number on the plant description in the catalog or the plant label at the garden center. To be successful in most parts of Ohio, perennials should be rated for zone 5. Look at the state Hardiness Zone Map in the Introduction to double-check the zone in which you live. While most garden centers routinely carry only those plants that are suited to the local climate, mail-order companies serve the entire country, so make sure any plants you order are cold hardy for your part of Ohio.

PLANTING

If you would like to try starting some perennials from seed indoors under lights, consult the discussion of seed starting procedures for annuals (see February Annuals). Be sure to read and follow the specific directions on the seed packets as well. Remember that if you are not successful starting from seed, there will be plenty of time to purchase professionally grown young plants in a month or two. Seed starting things to remember:

- Use soilless potting soil or seed-starting mix.
- Cover planted pots or flats to maintain humidity around sown seeds.
- Label the pots or flat with the name of the plant.
- Provide the correct temperature—warmth from beneath is best unless cool temperatures are specified.

As the indoor seedlings grow:
- Maintain fluorescent lights within 4 to 6 inches of the sprouts as they grow.
- Provide sixteen hours of bright light per day.
- Do not let the seedlings dry out.

CARE

Take a tour of the yard to check on current conditions:

1. Where frost has heaved the soil, make sure the crowns and roots of perennials have not been exposed to the drying, cold air. Replant any that have been disturbed. If the ground is too hard to work the soil, carefully place mulch or compost over the plants. Replace mulch that may have blown away in beds exposed to wind.

Young seedlings all look alike; label the seed-starting tray or flats with the name of the plant.

HELPFUL HINTS

Even though you live and garden in a particular cold-hardiness zone, there are several microclimates in every yard—pockets where it is a bit warmer, colder, drier, or more humid than everywhere else. You will become aware of these places and choose plants that can handle the special conditions. Watch the patterns of snow melt this month, which will indicate warmer, more sheltered spots. A few other things to be aware of as you learn the microclimates in your yard:

• Masonry walls absorb heat and reflect light to create a warmer, brighter spot that encourages plants to bloom a bit ahead of schedule.

• Fences and shrub hedges create niches sheltered from harsh winds.

• Low-lying areas tend to trap frost.

2. To prevent early perennials from appearing prematurely during a sunny, relatively warm period, maintain their layer of mulch. It will hold some chill in the soil and delay their growth until there is less risk of damage from late freezes and snow.

WATERING

Mulched beds will not dry out if the soil was moist before the mulch was spread. Often a late January thaw melts any snow cover a bit and the water soaks into the soil. Dormant perennials do not use much moisture, and the moisture in the soil outdoors should be just fine.

FERTILIZING

As soon as seedlings begin to develop the first set of real leaves (not just the initial seed leaves), they will need some nutrition. Because soilless planting medium contains no real soil, it has no nutrients. Every other watering, add some fast-acting (water-soluble) fertilizer to the water. Use it at about half the strength recommended on the package.

If you do not already have a supply of granular slow-acting fertilizer for flowering plants, buy some this month when you buy lawn fertilizer and other supplies for the spring gardening season.

PRUNING

It is tempting to do something out in the garden toward the end of the month. This is a good time to pick up twigs and debris that have fallen onto garden beds, and to check for the first bulbs. To prevent soil compaction if the soil is very wet, avoid walking on the beds.

PROBLEMS

Damping off is a fungal disease that plagues seedlings. To avoid it, plant seeds in sterile potting medium or soilless mix, water sparingly from beneath, and maintain good air circulation around developing seedlings.

MARCH
PERENNIALS & ORNAMENTAL GRASSES

 PLANNING

Early this month there are hints of spring. Out in the woods **skunk cabbage** is beginning to emerge from the soil, and **mayapples** will be along before you know it. In the garden, the flowers on the **lenten rose** are on display, and tiny, delicate stems of **barrenwort** are about to emerge. Most flowering perennials lag behind the early- flowering bulbs. Get organized for the new season!

• Have on hand sufficient supplies of slow-acting fertilizer, soilless potting mix, insecticidal soap, and horticultural oil.

While you wait for the soil to dry out and warm up this month, contemplate new garden projects. Thinking about expanding an existing flower bed or border? How about a new island bed? Pencil it in on the sketch of your garden in your journal. Estimate how many new plants the additional garden space will need.

and dig in the garden the minute the air temperature is milder; the danger is that you will ruin the soil. Do not begin to dig a new bed or extend an existing one until you can grasp a handful of soil, squeeze it, and see it crumble in your hand when you release it.

To establish a new perennial bed:

• Shove the flat blade of a garden spade under turfgrass sod or ground cover plants to break their roots.

Inventory your gardening tools, sharpen blades, and repair handles.

• Locate trowels, shovels, and rakes.

• Sharpen pruners and garden scissors.

• Inventory your supply of stakes, wire cages, and other supports for tall perennials.

• Buy new stakes, garden twine, and plant labels.

 PLANTING

Traditionally, March is "mud" month. Melting snow and early spring rains conspire to turn even great garden soil into sticky slop. The temptation is to get outdoors

• Peel the grass sod or mat of plants off the soil, leaving all valuable topsoil.

• Spade down into the bare soil at least 12 inches. Lift and turn shovelsful of soil back onto the bed to loosen and aerate it.

• Add several inches of organic material such as peat moss, chopped leaves, or compost to the overturned soil.

• Sprinkle granular, slow-acting fertilizer over the newly turned soil.

• Mix the organic material and the fertilizer into the loose soil. Break up the large clods, and remove small stones, roots, and other debris.

• Rake the soil smooth and level to await planting as soon as all danger of frost is past.

Seedlings raised indoors under lights are ready for larger pots if their roots are peeking out through the drainage holes in their current containers:

• Mix some granular, slow-acting fertilizer into moistened soilless potting medium.

• Fill plastic or peat pots half-full of the moistened medium.

• Gently remove each young plant from its container and set it on the medium.

• Fill in around it with more medium. Be sure the plant is at the same depth in the new pot that it was in its former one.

• Water, and return the seedlings to their lights.

CARE

Perennials that are already established in the garden can cope with some chill and the occa-sional setback provided by a late frost. The growth and eventual emergence of their new shoots from the soil is governed by their internal clocks, soil temperature, and the increasing amount of daylight. Plants that you will plant this spring are young and not yet acclimated. Those that arrive mail-order are typically bare-root and dormant. If they arrive this month, delay planting (unless otherwise instructed on the plant label) until next month. Keep them in a cool dark place so they stay dormant until planting time. Make sure their roots stay moist.

WATERING

Perennials that are about to initiate new growth probably have sufficient soil moisture if they have been mulched all winter and there has been normal snow cover or rainfall.

Carefully watch newly transplanted seedlings so that they do not dry out.

FERTILIZING

Granular, slow-acting fertilizer mixed into soilless planting medium for seedlings or into garden soil will provide consistent, uniform nutrition for as many weeks as indicated on the package label.

PRUNING

This is garden cleanup month. Cut back colorful and interesting dried stems of grasses and other plants that you enjoyed over the winter. This will neaten up the yard and make way for the new shoots these plants will be sending up soon.

Do not remove mulch until danger of frost is past. If the sun warms the soil prematurely, shoots of new plants may emerge ahead of schedule and get frosted.

PROBLEMS

Slugs always appear sooner than we expect. Unless there is still snow on the ground, it is not too early to put out some traps. They catch the earliest arrivals so that populations do not become established before their natural enemies are on duty. Slugs typically lurk in damp, shady places where soil is acid; they hide under boards, rocks, and other debris. Set out a shallow pie plate or a commercial slug trap baited with beer or baking yeast dissolved in water. If there are slugs in the area, they will come to investigate, fall in the trap, and drown. Slug deterrents containing iron phosphate will also provide effective control.

APRIL
PERENNIALS & ORNAMENTAL GRASSES

PLANNING

Wonderful shade trees are a hallmark of Ohio landscapes. In residential yards they create shade that cools homes and makes it possible to have woodland gardens. It's here that so many lovely perennial flowers make an early-season appearance, including **bleeding heart**, **Virginia bluebells**, **wild phlox**, **ferns**, and **barrenwort**. If you have trees and do not already have a shade garden, think about adding one.

Other activities for this month:
- Repair nearby walls or walks.
- Evaluate your plants.
- Discard those that have never performed up to expectation.

- Divide overgrown clumps of plants.
  - Introduce new plants.
  - Improve the soil.
  - Change the planting design.

PLANTING

Although the perennial plants in beds and borders dependably return every spring, that does not mean a perennial garden can be taken for granted. After a few years the soil will need attention. Because there is not a lot of planting and replanting activity in long-established beds of perennial plants, their soil is not regularly aerated and conditioned; it becomes compacted and no longer holds moisture or drains as well. Longtime resident perennials will have depleted the soil of certain nutrients, and they begin to show signs of age and lose vigor.

After five or six years, perennial beds and borders need a thorough renovation. Establish a rotation by scheduling renovation of a different bed every year or two. When all danger of frost is past and the soil has dried out enough to be workable, a garden bed can be renovated:

After renovating a perennial bed, rake the surface smooth and replant.

1. Remove existing plants. Dig the rootballs as large as possible to minimize root damage.

2. Set each plant in the shade on a piece of burlap or tarp or in a roomy pot. Cover its rootball to keep it moist and hold the soil in contact with the roots.

3. Spade down into the soil at least 12 inches, if possible. Lift and turn shovelsful of soil back onto the bed.

4. Incorporate organic material and granular, slow-acting fertilizer into the soil.

5. Break up clods; remove stones, roots, and other debris. Rake the soil smooth and level.

6. Replant those plants that you wish to retain; leave space for new ones.

CARE

Mulch the newly replanted perennials in the renovated bed to prevent drying out, and to discourage weeds from seeds that surfaced during the digging and aeration of the soil.

Take care of indoor seedlings:
- Maintain the fluorescent lights at about 4 or 6 inches above their foliage and provide good air circulation around each plant.
- Brush your open hand gently across their foliage daily to promote sturdy stems.

• Inspect regularly for signs of pest or disease problems.

WATERING

April showers should be sufficient for emerging perennials. If it has been a dry spring, check the soil under the mulch to see if it is moist. Water if it is not.

FERTILIZING

If the soil in established beds is not very fertile, sprinkle a little granular, slow-acting fertilizer around newly emerging perennials to get them off to a good start for the growing season.

If you did not mix slow-acting fertilizer into the potting medium when you repotted young perennials growing indoors under lights, add some liquid fertilizer to the water every two weeks. Use it at about half the dilution strength recommended on the package label.

HELPFUL HINTS

Chrysanthemums are familiar favorites in fall perennial gardens or containers. If you planted some last year, they are already developing fresh foliage and new stems. Since they do not bloom until late summer, gardeners handle them several ways.

• Leave them in place and pinch stems often until mid-July.
• Some treat **mums** as annuals. They buy full-grown, budded plants in the fall, plant them in the garden while they bloom, then pull and discard them when they finish blooming.
• Some take cuttings from the young shoots of last year's plants that are still in the garden and discard the plants. They root the cuttings and raise them for planting in the garden late in the summer.

PRUNING

Cut back any remaining dried stems from last season on grasses, vines, and other perennials. When the garden begins to fill in with emerging plants in a few weeks, it will be more difficult to move around in it and reach plants at the back of the border.

If the young perennials raised from seed indoors are developing thin, leggy stems, pinch them back to a place above the second set of true leaves. This will stimulate them to develop multiple stems for a more compact plant.

PROBLEMS

Slugs are the biggest potential problem in shade gardens when the delicate, ephemeral spring flowers appear. Put out slug traps (see March) a short distance from potential target plants.

Deer and rabbits love the tender new shoots of many perennials, but if you have lots of **crocus** and **tulips** on the property, they are likely to focus on them (see Bulbs March).

Squirrels dig in the soil to try to find the nuts they buried last fall or to find bulbs. They do not harm established perennials, but they may expose the roots of newly planted ones. Simply cover any exposed roots.

MAY

PERENNIALS & ORNAMENTAL GRASSES

PLANNING

This is planting month throughout most of Ohio. Local garden centers have lots of fresh new perennials available in different sizes. Small young plants in 4- or 6-inch pots are least expensive. Larger plants in individual quart, 1-gallon, 2-gallon, and larger pots cost more, but these plants have more of an immediate presence in the garden. Unlike annuals, perennials are slow to establish, and don't reach full potential until their second year. It is vitally important to choose healthy perennials at the garden center. Their stems and foliage will indicate if problems exist:

- Wilted foliage—improperly watered
- Yellow, limp foliage—insufficient light or fertilizer
- Holes in foliage—insects
- Dark blotches or gray coating on foliage—possible fungal disease
- Blotches on the stems—injury or disease
- Tiny pale spots or dark specks on leaf undersides—insects
- Thin, lanky stem—insufficient light

PLANTING

A new perennial will not thrive unless you have met its cultural requirements. Check plant labels and other resources for the correct cold hardiness zone and specific requirements.

Keep newly purchased perennials moist until planting time. Then dig a hole as deep as the plant's container and slightly wider. Make sure the plant is at the same depth it was in its pot. Fill in loose soil around the rootball, and firm it around the stem. Water well.

You can plant perennials in large decorative outdoor containers as you would plant annuals, perhaps combining them so the annuals can provide colorful flowers during the time the perennials display foliage only. Use soilless planting medium and incorporate a granular, slow-acting fertilizer.

CARE

Established perennials send out stem or root runners to form new plants nearby, or they develop larger clumps as their crowns enlarge and send up more stems. Either way, they will reach a point when they are too large for their space in your garden bed. They are crowding neigh-

boring plants, and may begin to die out in the center of the clump. To renew the plants, divide them. The best time to divide perennials is in either spring or fall after they bloom.

1. For easier handling, try to time the division so emerging shoots are only 2 or 3 inches tall.

2. Dig under the roots and their soil, and lift the plant from the soil.

3. Use a sharp knife or garden spade to cut through the clump of roots to make "rooted chunks" of plant.

4. Discard woody, thin, or dead centers of old plants.

Divide established perennials by digging up a large root clump and separating it into several sections.

5. Replant one of the viable rooted chunks in the former planting spot, and plant the others elsewhere or in pots for gifts.

Mulch all newly planted perennials with a 2- to 3-inch layer of organic material such as shredded leaves, pine needles, or compost.

Some perennials will need support as they mature. Individual, unobtrusive green bamboo stakes are suitable for single-stemmed plants such as **delphiniums** and **foxgloves**. Use several with a matrix of twine to support large clumps of stems of plants such as **beebalm**, **asters**, and **black-eyed Susans**. The stakes should be just slightly shorter than the plant's maximum height when they are inserted into the soil 10 to 12 inches.

By month's end it should be safe to acclimate the young perennials that were raised indoors to the outdoors. Set them in a shaded place for a few hours daily, gradually increasing the light and outdoor time. After a few overnight stays, they will be ready to be planted in the garden or in a container.

WATERING

Water newly planted perennials well at planting time. If rainfall is unreliable, check them every four or five days—more often if you have not mulched.

FERTILIZING

Perennials planted in beds where granular, slow-acting fertilizer has been added to the soil do not need fertilizing this spring. Check the product label for the number of weeks the fertilizer will last.

PRUNING

Some spring-blooming perennials will have finished blooming by now. Removing their faded flowers neatens their appearance and sometimes stimulates a few more blooms later in the summer. Use hedge shears to clip off the small flowers from low-growing mats of **candytuft**, **pinks**, and **phlox** quickly and evenly. Use hand pruners for larger, faded blossoms.

The flower spikes of **lamb's ears** and some kinds of **coral bells** and the flowers on **coleus**

and **artemisia** are regarded by many as dispensable. Cut them off as they develop over the season.

PROBLEMS

Skunks leave small conical holes in the lawn or garden soil and paths where they dig for grubs. The occasional plant they might disturb is a small price to pay for the service of grub control!

Ants may crawl all over the swollen buds on **peonies**. They are not harming them—they are seeking the sweet juices that healthy buds secrete.

Aphids will probably show up clustered at the tender growing tips of certain perennials. Until their natural predators arrive in your yard, you can control them by pinching off the infested stem tips. Insecticidal soap or a product containing Neem oil will also work well.

Plants may disappear after blooming. This is normal for **bleeding heart**, **Virginia bluebells**, **oriental poppies**, and certain other early-season perennials. They go dormant for the summer and they will return next year.

JUNE
PERENNIALS & ORNAMENTAL GRASSES

PLANNING

It's important to record in a garden notebook, calendar, or journal when your perennials begin to bloom and how long they bloom. Because most perennials bloom for a relatively short time, each typically shows mostly foliage for much of the season. Without planning and careful choice of plants, the garden is likely to be mainly green foliage for the bulk of the season. If your records indicate that you have mostly spring-blooming perennials, plan to acquire some later-season bloomers now while there is still a good selection at the garden center. To assure some color in the garden all summer:

- Select perennials that bloom in midsummer, late summer, and early fall.
- Choose a few plants with variegated foliage.
- Plant annuals among the perennials.
- Choose perennials that have long bloom periods.
- Cut off faded flowers and stems to promote repeat bloom later in the season.
- Record those companion plants that look good together.

PLANTING

Plant perennial plants as soon as possible after you purchase them. If they sit around in pots, they are likely to dry out or become potbound, stressing them unnecessarily. Any perennials that you grew indoors from seed should be planted early this month.

Plant any divisions of plants that you have made or have been given as soon as possible. They dry out very easily, and they need as much growing season as possible to get well established in the soil.

CARE

Make sure the mulch layer around perennials is no thicker than 2 to 3 inches. That is sufficient to discourage weeds and maintain soil moisture, while still providing oxygen to the root system.

Do not delay setting up supporting stakes for plants that will develop tall stems or clumps. Once the stems fall to the ground or begin to develop crookedly, it is difficult to train them to grow straight.

WATERING

Established perennials need about 1 inch of water per week. Those in sandy soil need more because the soil drains so quickly. Mix in some organic matter at planting time to help the soil hold more moisture. Perennials that are mulched need less-frequent watering because soil moisture is not lost to evaporation and runoff.

Check soil moisture around newly planted perennials every week or so if it does not rain; their soil dries out a bit faster than that of established plants.

Unpack mail-order plants as soon as possible and hydrate them to prepare for planting.

FERTILIZING

The granular, slow-acting fertilizer you added to the soil when preparing the garden bed or at planting time will continue to offer nutrition to perennials for several weeks, as indicated on the package label. If there is no granular fertilizer mixed into the potting medium of perennials in containers, remember to water-in some diluted fertilizer every two weeks all season long, or as recommended on the package label.

PRUNING

Pinch back the lengthening stems of **chrysanthemums** by half to encourage denser branching and more flowers in the fall. Because this practice also delays the development of buds, do so every few weeks until the middle of next month if you want the **mums** to bloom in October.

To guide and control the growth of other summer- and fall-blooming perennials that tend to become tall and lanky— **beebalm**, **artemisias**, **asters**, **goldenrod**, and others—cut back newly developing stems by about half after they grow to about 10 or 12 inches long. This will delay flowering somewhat,

ARRANGE PERENNIALS

There are all kinds of perennial gardens. The classic one is the perennial border. Typically a potentially stunning, high-maintenance effort, it features many perennials planted in a long, relatively narrow bed along a fence, hedge, walkway, or building. More common is the mixed border, which features many herbaceous perennials, foliage plants, and small shrubs. There are other types of gardens where perennials are very effective:
- an island bed that is viewed from all sides
- a naturalistic woodland/shade garden
- a rock garden
- a meadow
- a cutting garden for producing flowers, foliage, and dried pods for bouquets

but it will result in shorter, fuller plants that may not need staking.

Cut off stems of **daylilies** whose flowers have faded. In reblooming varieties, this will encourage the continuous development of new stems and buds. It improves the appearance of any **daylily**.

PROBLEMS

Leafminer activity is usually obvious on plant foliage (especially **columbine**) after flowering. Their tunneling in leaf tissues makes visible white serpentine trails. Cut back the infested foliage to the ground, and put it in the trash.

Slugs may be making inroads on shade-loving perennials. Look for chewed leaves and shiny mucous trails. Turn over boards and other debris to find them hiding during the day, and put them in a plastic bag for the trash. Set out traps (see March) to catch others.

Weeds steal nutrients and moisture in the soil intended for your cultivated plants. Pull them or spot treat with Roundup™. Use mulch to cover bare soil and prevent other weed seeds from germinating.

Runaway plants spread so rampantly that they crowd out their neighbors and monopolize soil moisture and nutrients. Known offenders are **running bamboo**, **mint**, **Japanese loosestrife**, **glory bower**, and **creeping lilyturf**. Plant them where their growth is restricted, perhaps in containers or between paved areas and walls.

JULY
PERENNIALS & ORNAMENTAL GRASSES

 PLANNING

Typically, during July, the spring blooming perennials are slowing in blossom production and the summer bloomers are just getting started. If this creates a noticeable pause in the flower display, you might want to choose some plants to fill in the gap. Adding some annuals will do this nicely.

Some plants are attractive all season long. These are the perennials that provide interesting and colorful foliage rather than only fancy, striking flowers. They provide nonstop color to bridge the peak flowering times of other perennials. Plants with silver-and-white or bright-yellow foliage add to the color mix even if their flowers are absent or insignificant.

Many familiar perennials are also available with variegated foliage in green-and-white or green-and-yellow (or cream) stripes, speckles, or blotches, doubling their color contribution to a garden. Certain **Jacob's ladder**, **hosta**, **phlox**, and **ornamental grass** varieties are good examples.

 PLANTING

Once summer heat arrives, it is not advisable to transplant perennials if it can possibly be avoided. Either they are about to bloom, or have just bloomed and their vigor is already being drained. Adding the stress of being uprooted and then planted in a new environment while trying to cope with heat and humidity may compromise their appearance for the rest of the season. Although many perennial plants might survive summer transplanting, this is not the best time.

To avoid as much transplant stress as possible:

- Plant on a cloudy day or in the evening.
- Shade new transplants for a day or two if they are in a sunny site.
- Consider delaying planting until the heat breaks and temperatures are cooler.
- Cut back foliage by one-fourth to minimize moisture loss through transpiration.
- Water and mulch new transplants to assure sufficient soil moisture.

 CARE

With the onset of summer heat, the organic material in the mulch around perennials and other plants begins to decompose, and the layer will grow thinner. Spread fresh material to main-tain 2 to 3 inches in depth. Pull or spray any weeds that may have become established when the mulch was thin.

Stake plants before they grow so wide or tall that their stems fall. It takes only a few minutes for a summer rainstorm to flatten stately stalks of **phlox**, **beebalm**, **meadow rue**, and similar plants. Plants that are growing upright have cleaner, healthier flowers and foliage, and a better appearance.

 WATERING

If the summer is going to be dry, it is usually apparent by mid-July. Well-mulched, established perennials growing in decent soil can manage a week or ten days between rainfalls or waterings. Check the soil moisture of recently planted perennials more frequently. Dig an inch or two down in the soil under the mulch layer with a garden trowel to determine if the soil is dry. Pay particular attention to shallow-rooted plants and moisture lovers such as **astilbe**. They may need watering more often.

 FERTILIZING

As organic mulch gradually decomposes in the hot weather, it adds valuable humus to the soil around perennials. The humus also stimulates the activity of the soil's resident microbial life, which maintains the fertility of the soil.

If more than ten weeks have passed since a slow-acting product was added to the soil, late-summer bloomers will benefit from a light application of granular fertilizer worked into the soil now.

 ## PRUNING

Clip off dead flowers to prevent disease and stimulate new bloom. With plants like **coreopsis**, where the flowers are at the ends of bare stems, cut the stems off as well, back to where some leaves appear. This will keep them looking nice by removing the unsightly stem ends. With rebloomers like **daisy** and **purple coneflower**, cut back to a leaf node, where another flower may be formed already.

If plants that have already bloomed are looking unkempt, cut them back to the ground and they will develop fresh, new foliage for the remainder of the season. Sometimes they even manage to bloom again before frost.

Continue to pinch back stems of **chrysanthemums** to delay their blooming until mid-fall.

Coreopsis 'Early Summer'

 ## PROBLEMS

Japanese beetles usually are active this month in many areas of Ohio. Make a note of when you first spot them in the garden, as they return every year at almost the same time. Look for chewed leaves and flowerbuds, and you will find the metallic-colored beetles nearby. Start control with the first arrivals; knock them from plant foliage into a jar of soapy water. Check the plants they seem to favor several times a day, if possible. The more you destroy, the fewer will have an opportunity to lay eggs to become next year's pests.

Mites may infest plants such as **chrysanthemums** that are stressed by heat and drought. Look for light stippling on the leaves and fine webbing around stems. Control mites with insecticidal soap or a miticide. Check after a week or two to be sure they have not returned.

Powdery mildew may develop on the foliage of certain perennials like **phlox**, **beebalm**, and **veronica**. The fungus forms a gray coating on the foliage in humid weather. It is unsightly, but rarely life-threatening. If the plants have bloomed, cut back stems to the ground to promote uninfected new growth. Try plant varieties that are labeled disease-resistant.

133

AUGUST
PERENNIALS & ORNAMENTAL GRASSES

PLANNING

One of the many things to consider when planning and managing gardens that feature perennials is that many plants self-sow their seeds. Plants such as **black-eyed Susan**, **columbine**, **coreopsis**, **fringed bleeding heart**, **purple coneflower**, **hardy begonia**, **goldenrod**, **hellebore**, **Shasta daisy**, and others do this to varying degrees. Some gardeners welcome this—new young plants that appear in the garden next season are easily pulled up and discarded, dug up and moved to a desirable location, or potted for friends. To encourage perennials to seed themselves, leave faded flowers on the plants so seeds will dry and scatter.

Another good reason to leave seedheads on late-season perennials is to provide seed for visiting wildlife. Finches of all kinds love the seeds of **purple coneflower** and **black-eyed Susan**.

PLANTING

While the weather is typically too hot and oppressive for planting in the garden this month, you might want to propagate some favorite perennials from soft-stem cuttings.

This can be done almost anytime during the growing season.

1. Cut each stem about 6 inches back from its tip just above a node, the point where leaves emerge from it. Choose stems tipped with foliage only, or pinch off any flowers or buds.

2. Remove the lowest leaves so that $1/4$ to $1/2$ inch of stem is bare. Dip the cut end into rooting hormone powder (available at most garden centers).

3. Insert a pencil into a pot filled with moist sand, perlite, or soilless potting mix to make a hole for the stem cutting. Then stick the powdered end of the cutting into the moist rooting medium.

4. Water well, and cover the pot with clear plastic wrap or a plastic bag to maintain a moist environment around the cutting.

5. Set pots of cuttings in light, but not direct sun. Make sure they do not dry out. When small leaves begin to emerge, that is a signal that roots have established.

6. Remove the plastic, and increase the sunlight. Water-in a very dilute fertilizer when you

This is a good time to root stem cuttings.

134

water, as the rooting medium has no nutrients in it.

CARE

Toward the end of the growing season the number of daylight hours decreases daily, and new young plants made from rooted stem cuttings will not have the luxury of a full growing season in the garden to build their vigor. Rather than plant them directly into a garden bed, provide a temporary winter location where they are more protected. Designate a sheltered area as a nursery bed, and either set their pots in the soil or remove them from the pots and plant them in the soil.

WATERING

Perennials in decorative containers will dry out in a day or two if it is hot. At this point in the season their root systems are crowding the pot and the planting medium dries out even more quickly than it would in June or July.

Ways to conserve water:

• Group plants by water preference. Locate low-water-demand plants farther from the house and water source.

• Mulch garden beds well to reduce evaporation of moisture from the soil and prevent runoff from rain or watering.

• Use drip irrigation systems, which leak water slowly directly into the soil.

• Plant perennials that do not require lots of moisture— **yarrow**, **artemisia**, **coreopsis**, **baby's breath**, and **daylilies**.

FERTILIZING

Do not fertilize perennials after mid-month. Except for those that bloom in the fall, most perennials are now preparing to enter dormancy. Unless plants have six weeks or more before frost arrives in your area, the new growth stimulated by the fertilizer will likely be damaged by frost.

PRUNING

As the summer wanes, the perennial garden may begin to look a bit shabby. Some pruning and maintenance will soon restore a pleasing look.

• To neaten their appearance, cut back stems of plants such as **black-eyed Susan**, **daisy**, **bee-balm**, and **baby's breath** after they bloom.

• To improve the appearance of plants such as **lady's mantle**, remove aged, discolored foliage, allowing younger, fresher foliage to show.

• Clip off the spent flowerheads on **phlox** to stimulate a second flowering.

• Cut off flower stems from **hostas** and **daylilies** as soon as the flowers fade.

PROBLEMS

Mites love the dry, hot conditions that stress plants. Check perennials for pale, stippled leaves and fine webbing on stems. Wash mites off infected plants with a forceful spray of water or spray with a product labeled for mites.

Fungal diseases, usually in the form of mildews, thrive in heat and humidity. They appear on plant foliage as a gray or white coating and cause leaves to droop, shrivel, and eventually dry out and drop off stems. At this point in the season it is easiest to cut off plant stems to the ground. Pick up fallen leaves and debris, and discard in the trash.

Viral and bacterial diseases sometimes attack perennials. When they do, symptoms such as wilting foliage seem to appear suddenly. These diseases typically infect the roots or crown of the plant, causing it to rot. Since cures are difficult for these diseases, prevention is the key. Immediately dig up the plant, including as many roots as possible and the soil surrounding them. Put it in a plastic bag and discard in the trash.

September
PERENNIALS & ORNAMENTAL GRASSES

 PLANNING

Traditionally, Labor Day weekend marks the end of summer. That may be true for schoolchildren, but it's not true for gardeners. Often this is one of the best times in the perennial garden, as the cooler temperatures intensify colors and crisp up foliage. The golden light created by the changing angle of the sun casts a warm glow on your yard. Many earlier-blooming perennials may produce pods or seedheads that accent beds displaying **boltonia**, **asters**, **perennial sunflower**, **turtlehead**, **tall sedums**, **mums**, and other late-season bloomers. Since many annuals will still be going strong, a mixed border can be as exciting now as at any other time during the season.

Try to find time to visit nearby public gardens and arboreta to see how gardens are designed for the fall season. Write down the names of the plants you like, and note the conditions where they are growing. You can find out more about them from resource books and catalogs.

 PLANTING

Fall is a great time to plant perennials. Those in pots at the garden center may not look great this time of year, because they are starting to die back for the winter. Some may have spent the season in their pots and are rootbound. However, they may also be on sale!

Planting or transplanting perennials now affords them several weeks to become established before the ground freezes. This time of year they do not have to produce foliage and flowers, so they can concentrate on expanding their root systems.

Take special care if plants have roots that are matted and wrapped around themselves from long confinement in their pots. Tease apart the roots, or pry them loose so that they hang free before you set the plant in its hole.

Perennials with single, long taproots like **balloon flower**, **globe thistle**, **columbine**, and **butterfly weed** are particularly tricky to transplant and moving them now should be avoided.

This is also a good time to divide clumps of perennials that have grown too large over the summer. Wait to divide spring bloomers until after they bloom next spring (see division steps in May).

 CARE

Stake tall plants that are blooming or are about to bloom. If they have already started to fall over, prop them up the best you can so their flowers are visible.

If plants in certain areas of the yard have not performed well this season despite your attention, there may be a problem with the soil. The problem is often signaled by off-color foliage and lack of vigor. Take a soil test to determine if it is deficient in one or more essential nutrients. Call your county agriculture extension office for a list of companies who perform soil analysis in a laboratory.

 WATERING

Water potted **chrysanthemums** and other perennials. They will dry out very quickly if the weather is mild and they are in the sun.

Water newly planted divisions and transplants well if there is not enough rain to provide about an inch of water a week.

If it has been a dry late summer, garden areas that are usually damp, or even boggy, may dry up. Remember to check moisture levels so that **turtlehead**, **lobelia**, **astilbe**, **Joe-pye weed**, **swamp**

milkweed, and **red (swamp) hibiscus** do not suffer.

FERTILIZING

No fertilizing is necessary this month.

PRUNING

If the birds have pretty much eaten all the seeds from **purple coneflowers** and **black-eyed Susans**, cut back the stems to the ground. To maintain the appearance of the garden, continue to deadhead faded flowers from plants that are still blooming.

PROBLEMS

Weeds become very obvious now that garden perennials and

Plants in containers still need watering as long as they are thriving.

TOP TEN PERENNIALS

The Perennial Plant Association (PPA), located in Hilliard, Ohio, is an organization of producers, growers, and sellers of perennial plants. They promote the use of perennial plants in civic spaces and public and private gardens. In an effort to educate gardeners about perennials, each year the membership selects a Plant of the Year, a perennial which is exceptionally hardy, beautiful, and easy to grow.

1995 *Perovskia atriplicifolia*
1996 *Penstemon* 'Husker Red'
1997 *Salvia nemerosa*
1998 *Echinacea* 'Magnus'
1999 *Rudbeckia* 'Goldsturm'
2000 *Scabiosa* 'Butterfly Blue'
2001 *Calamagrostis* x *acutiflora* 'Karl Foerster'
2002 *Phlox* 'David'
2003 *Leucanthemum* 'Becky'
2004 *Athyrium niponicum* 'Pictum'
2005 *Helleborus* x *hybridus*

---

other plants are dying back. Many of the perennial weeds such as nutsedge, wild grape, plantain, and smartweed are still green. As long as the weather is mild and they are growing, they will be susceptible to herbicide. Spray them now with Roundup™ or a similar product that kills their roots.

Pest insects normally represent only about 10 percent of all the insects in your yard. The others are either beneficial or benign. Chronic pest insect infestations on perennials suggest that populations of beneficial insects in your yard might be low. This may be caused by a number of garden problems:

1. Plants have been unusually stressed and are more vulnerable. Think about the possible causes of the stress—poor site or soil—and correct it for next season.

2. Frequently used general insecticides have killed off many resident beneficial insects. Use methods that target specific pests.

3. There is not enough diversity of plants in the yard to support a healthy population of beneficial insects.

OCTOBER
PERENNIALS & ORNAMENTAL GRASSES

PLANNING

The one thing gardeners can count on this month is a fresh supply of leaves. What a gift! The trees that grow so well here have been providing humus from their decomposed foliage in the forest for ages. Utilize this resource to build and renew your soil so it will resemble the soft, rich soil in the woods. Ways to use fallen leaves in the landscape:

• Chop or shred them to spread as a mulch on all bare soil on the property.

• Chop or shred them, and mix them into soil to create or renovate planting beds.

• Pile them to partially decompose into leaf mold for mulch or soil conditioning.

• Pile them with other organic materials such as weeds, prunings, kitchen peelings, or straw to completely decompose into compost.

• Mow them with a mulching mower as they lie on the lawn, and bag them with grass clippings for use as mulch or compost.

Cool weather inspires outdoor projects now that plant maintenance is reduced for the year. This is a great time to build or repair a walk, fence, or patio. Dig new beds or renovate exist-ing ones so that you will be ready to plant in the spring.

PLANTING

Theoretically, you can plant perennials that are in containers practically anytime the ground is not frozen. It is better to plant them than leave them in their cramped containers all winter.

If one of your fall landscape projects is building a stone wall or laying a stone terrace or patio, try planting some plants among the stones:

• Choose sturdy, low-growing perennials such as **moneywort** or **moss pinks** that love the excellent drainage of coarse or sandy soil.

• Tuck plants like low-growing **sedums** in the crevices created when you lay a course of rock in a dry wall, or plant them as you build the wall in spaces you purposely leave between the stones.

CARE

Herbaceous perennials disappear with the arrival of frost, although their roots still grow underground. Clean up dried leaves and stems, then mulch the soil over their roots for the winter. Do this after the ground freezes hard. If you live in the southern part of the state, sometimes that does not happen until January—in that case, spread winter mulch around Thanksgiving to have the job done.

Some plants in your garden will continue to show green foliage close to the ground over the winter. These are not true perennials. These basal rosettes are formed at the end of the growing season and will continue to manufacture sugars from the weak winter sunshine. **Asters**, **goldenrods**, and **lobelia** overwinter this way. Don't cover these rosettes with heavy mulch, which will prevent them from receiving sunlight, and may cause them to rot.

WATERING

Water any plants you have moved or added to the garden if there is not sufficient rainfall.

When the perennials have died back to the ground, install drip irrigation. Consider installing lengths of porous hose through beds among the plants, and attach them to a feeder line that links them to an outdoor faucet. Then spread fresh winter mulch, which will cover the irrigation lines. Water leaking slowly from the entire length of the hose and soaking slowly into the soil near plant roots can reduce fungal disease due to wet foliage.

FERTILIZING

No fertilizing is necessary now.

PRUNING

Frosty mornings blacken annuals dramatically, but perennials preparing for dormancy may have already begun to turn brown and die back. First frost is a signal to gardeners that it is time for major cleanup.

• Cut back remaining soggy or dried stems, and clean up fallen leaves that may harbor fungal spores. Pull or dig up weeds.

• Leave ornamental grasses in full-blown glory. Their bleached stems and fluffy seedheads will provide something interesting to see in the garden over the winter.

• Pick up boards, twigs, old pots, and other debris.

• Pull out stakes and other supports, and store them.

• Bring in any decorative pots, statuary, and birdbaths that may crack in cold weather.

HELPFUL HINTS

Hellebores and their hybrids provide interesting evergreen foliage and flowers when most garden perennials are dormant.

• **Christmas rose** (*Helleborus niger*) forms clumps of dark-green leaves with toothed leaflets that spring directly from the soil. In late December, purple stems arise among them, bearing saucerlike white or pink-tinged flowers with greenish centers.

• **Lenten rose** (*Helleborus* x *hybridus*) forms open mounds of glossy, leathery, deeply divided leaves year-round. Slightly nodding flowers in wonderful variations of cream, pink, and maroon—with and without speckles—appear mid-winter.

• **Bearsfoot hellebore** (*Helleborus foetidus*) features a burst of narrow, rich-green, toothed leaves at the top of sturdy stems. About midwinter it produces stalks of yellow-green, bell-shaped flowers that sometimes have purple edges.

PROBLEMS

Rodents like to nest in deep, soft mulch. If you have vole, mice, or chipmunk problems, delay spreading winter mulch until the ground freezes. By then the rodents will have found alternative nesting sites.

Fallen leaves lying on garden beds may mat together and prevent moisture from soaking into the soil. Rake or vacuum up leaves and shred them. Then cover the beds with them.

Bearsfoot hellebore

NOVEMBER
PERENNIALS & ORNAMENTAL GRASSES

 PLANNING

It is possible to have a winter perennial garden. It does not feature flowers, but it offers a welcome alternative to the typical winter garden. With judicious selection of plants and careful planning, you can create a garden that is interesting during the winter months when there is sparse snowfall. Choose a site that is visible from the windows of the house so you can enjoy it when you're shut in by the weather. A winter garden might include:

- Colorful evergreen foliage of **hellebores**, **ivy**, **European ginger**, **pachysandra**, and **hardy ferns**
- The semi-evergreen foliage on **barrenwort** and some other perennials—it turns purplish or yellow and persists for many weeks
- Bright berries from plants such as **Jack-in-the-pulpit** and **arum**
- Interesting dried stems of **ornamental grasses**, **Russian sage**, and **dwarf astilbe**
- Silver foliage that persists on some **artemisias**
- Architectural lines provided by dried stems topped with seedpods and seedheads of **yarrow**, **tall sedums**, and others.

 PLANTING

Outdoor planting time is past in parts of the state where hard frost has shut down the season. Because the roots of any perennials still in pots are vulnerable to freezing if they are aboveground, do not leave them outdoors over the winter without protection. Temporarily bury the pots in an existing bed, compost, or mulch pile. Mulch over the container to provide further winter protection.

If you feel the urge to plant, try planting some seeds. Certain perennial seeds require a period of moist cold in order to germinate. After frost arrives, conditions are good for planting seeds in pots or flats filled with moist potting medium. Cover the pots with hardware cloth to avoid rodent damage. Place in a cold frame or similar location for four to eight weeks. Seedlings will begin to emerge during late winter or early spring.

1. Cover the pots with plastic to help maintain moisture.

2. When sprouts emerge, move them into bright, indirect light, and begin to water them. Make sure they continue to experience roughly the same air temperatures of perennials outdoors.

3. As seedlings develop in late winter or spring, provide dilute doses of fertilizer every few waterings, as well as larger pots. Plan to plant them in late spring—or early fall if they have not grown large enough to go into the garden safely.

A cold frame is helpful for hardening off plants in spring and for starting seeds that require a cold spell to germinate.

CARE

Spread winter mulch up to 3 inches deep on the soil over the root zones of perennials. Use pine needles, shredded leaves, decayed wood chips, or shredded bark. Spreading the mulch after the soil is cold or frozen will:

• insulate soil by buffering temperature extremes of freeze-thaw cycles that heave soil and disturb plant roots.

• help soil absorb and retain moisture.

• keep soil cold in early spring to avoid premature emergence of perennials.

• discourage early growth of weeds.

To reduce the recurrence of disease problems next season, pick up all fallen leaves from the areas where infected perennials grew.

WATERING

If there is a lack of rainfall, continue to check soil moisture and water perennials as needed. Though they are going dormant, they are still in danger of drying out, especially newly planted additions. Every so often Ohio autumns are mild and dry, and a prolonged Indian summer occurs. When this happens, water perennial gardens and

THE BENEFITS OF COMPOST

Compost is a wonderful garden resource for improving the soil. It is easily made at home from yard and some kitchen vegetable waste and is free, making it even more valuable. Whether your soil tends toward clay or sand, the humus that compost provides creates a better environment for most plants. When mixed into soil, it improves the soil's ability to hold air and water, and simultaneously helps it drain better. The microbial life that lives in soil transforms its nutrients into a form that plant roots can easily take up, and these microbes thrive when soil provides oxygen and some (not too much) moisture. When the microbes are on the job, soil is fertile and plants thrive.

other planted areas well before the ground freezes hard.

Pay particular attention to newly planted and transplanted perennials.

FERTILIZING

No fertilizing is necessary this month.

PRUNING

Garden cleanup should finally be finished by Thanksgiving. Except for those plants that will provide some winter interest, cut back the dried stems of all perennials. There is no need to cut them off at ground level—in fact, it is a good idea to leave short lengths of stem on plants to mark where they are located. This is especially helpful for late spring

arrivals such as **balloon flower**. Otherwise, there is a danger of forgetting that they are there and digging or planting on top of them in spring.

PROBLEMS

Diseases can be carried over winter on plant parts and infect them next year. Remove fallen leaves and dead stems from perennials before applying mulch.

If mice appear to be a problem, set out bait stations when applying mulch. Be careful that the bait stations are not accessible to other wildlife. Boxes with holes large enough for mice, but too small for others, are acceptable.

December

PERENNIALS & ORNAMENTAL GRASSES

 PLANNING

A review of your notes from the season just past will remind you of some of the changes you want to make next year. The health of certain perennials which are not quite in the ideal spot can be improved by moving them during the next growing season. They may need more sun, better soil, or more room than you anticipated. Perhaps you will want to add more plants to improve bloom sequences or color coordination. Sometimes a garden bed needs more variety in plant height or foliage color or texture to look its best. Make a list now of changes you are considering before end-of-year holidays divert your attention.

Some ideas for a holiday gift list:

- certificate for a purchase at a favorite garden center
- membership at the local botanic garden or arboretum
- comprehensive reference book on perennials
- book on designing a garden
- new garden journal for the coming year

One way to learn more about gardening is to enroll in the Master Gardener program. Call your local county agriculture extension office to inquire about classes.

 PLANTING

As you planted and transplanted perennials last season, no doubt you became aware that soil type varies somewhat at different locations on your property. There are probably places where the soil is less than ideal, possibly areas near the house that feature builder's fill, silty subsoil laced with pieces of mortar, bricks or stone, and the occasional nail or piece of glass. Other areas may be sandy, soggy, or rock-hard clay.

Take this into account when choosing and locating perennials next year. Some plants actually prefer soggy, boggy soil. Others love sandy, fast-draining soil. On the theory that it is easier to adapt the plant to the soil, rather than vice versa, try to plant the right plant in the right place.

 CARE

- Have you groomed and mulched all perennial beds?
- Have you planted outdoors or protected all container-grown perennials?
- Have you collected and stored all stakes and other plant supports?
- Have you brought indoors all ornaments and pots that are vulnerable to winter weather?
- Have you set up and filled bird feeders and birdbaths?

 WATERING

Until and unless there is a major freeze in the forecast, keep the outdoor water turned on in case you need to use the hose or drip irrigation. If the soil in perennial beds was moist before it was mulched, plants should be fine if there is a week or two of dry weather. Check unmulched areas, especially if temperatures are mild for an extended period.

 FERTILIZING

No fertilizing is necessary this month.

 PRUNING

If the pods, seedheads, and berries that remained on perennials have already been depleted by the birds and other wildlife, cut back the stems to neaten the yard.

PROBLEMS

No problems this month.

ROSES

Until relatively recently, the only rose for home gardeners was the hybrid tea rose and bush roses such as grandifloras and floribundas. Devoted rosarians knew about other kinds of roses.

So did horticulturists and world-class gardeners. Now you can, too.

The rose is our national flower, and it deserves to be—but in the past, the rose family has been a very challenging group of plants to grow successfully in Ohio. Fortunately, it's getting a lot easier. Many, many new varieties have been produced over the last twenty to thirty years. Add to this original list the Meidiland® landscape roses, shrub roses of all colors, and mini-flora (a cross between a floribunda and a miniature). We will discuss each in this chapter.

A LITTLE BIT OF TLC

Yes, roses do best in a full day of sun. If you don't have this type of exposure, morning is the better half to have. Morning sun dries the dew off the plants, and that's important for reducing the risk of diseases, such as blackspot and mildew.

Roses like to be planted in an open area where they can get good air circulation among the individual plants.

Plant your roses 3 to 5 feet apart to give each plant good growing space and air space.

Many of the newer rose varieties are more disease and insect resistant. But certain groups—especially hybrid teas and grandifloras—still need a little assistance. There are spray products that can be used to protect these roses from disease and insect attack. Roses in general prefer good, loamy soil. They will, however, tolerate clay soil as long as the soil drains well.

HOW TO SELECT A ROSE

Roses are available three different ways: (1) bare-root plants whose roots are packed in moist packing material and wrapped in a plastic or foil-type bag; (2) "boxed" potted roses that are available in early spring; and (3) roses that are already growing in their own soil medium in 2 or 5 gallon pots. The latter is the absolute best way to buy rose plants. These roses are usually potted during the winter and are well established by the time they're available for you to buy. They'll cost more, but their value is much greater.

Be wary of the "boxed" roses. These are basically bare-root plants that have had their canes and roots pruned (which is good), but the roots are placed in the cardboard box with moist sphagnum peat. The canes have been coated with wax to keep moisture from escaping the rose while it is being stored and offered for sale. Here's the problem: you can't water the roots because that would ruin the box. These plants have a very short shelf life; they just don't stay viable for long. And too often, these roses remain for sale for several months, daily increasing the desiccation of these roses.

Remember, as is true of any living plant that you want to purchase, it won't get any better looking during the ride home! Always buy healthy, vigorous plants, including roses.

PLANTING BARE-ROOT AND POTTED ROSES

Bare-root roses come from the nursery with their roots in a plastic-coated paper bag or a cardboard box. Take the wrapping off the roots. Prune the roots back to 8 inches in length. If they are already at 8 inches, put a fresh 1/4-inch cut in the root ends. Prune off any broken roots just above the break. Soak the roots in a bucket of water for 6 hours; then you're ready to plant. Dig a hole 16 inches wide and as deep as the roots are long. Break up all the soil particles so that none are bigger than a golf ball. Now, in the center of the hole build a pyramid of soil that ends at the top of the hole. Spread the roots over the pyramid and backfill the balance of the soil. This process ensures complete soil coverage around the roots. Water-in very well to settle the backfilled soil. If no new buds or shoots are growing on the canes, cover the canes with additional soil to help push out new growth. Remove this excess soil as new growth starts to appear.

Potted roses are those roses already growing in their own soil. To plant, dig a hole as deep as the distance from the bud union (that swollen area joining the rose graft) to the bottom of the soil clump. Dig your hole twice the width of the pot. Slide the pot off and backfill with the soil that you've broken up so no clumps are bigger than a golf ball. Water-in well to settle the backfilled soil.

THE KINDEST CUT

There is plenty of misinformation out there about how far to cut your roses back to encourage more repeat bloom. We'll try to make it simple.

For long-stem cutting roses (hybrid teas and grandifloras), when the flowers have finished blooming on a particular stem, cut back the stem 20 to 40 percent of the way, making the cut just above a five leaflet leaf which is growing away from the center of the plant.

For cluster-blooming roses (all the rest), wait until each cluster has finished blooming then cut

the stem halfway back, cutting just above a set of leaflets growing away from the center of the plant. Stop pruning back all rose stems in September and allow the seedheads (rose hips) to form, which signals the roots that it's time to get ready for winter. Let the roses continue to put on new blooms on their own. Just don't remove the spent flowers. Don't be surprised to see Knock Out™ roses blooming in November, maybe even December. Do not fertilize roses after September 1st.

Do your heavy pruning of rose canes in early spring as the new buds start to swell. On all roses but climbers, prune all canes back to 8 inches or lower, depending on whether or not any winter dieback has blackened your canes closer to the ground than 8 inches. In this case, prune back to good green cane color. Cut them back so no cane is longer than 8 inches.

Climbers will have the majority of their bloom during the current year on canes that grew the prior year. Do not prune except for removing winter-damaged canes, or you will cut off the canes that are carrying this year's flowers.

HOW WILL MY ROSE STAY WARM FOR THE WINTER?

Many roses need to be protected from cold Ohio winters. The base of each plant, known as the bud union, is the most vulnerable part. Leave the rose canes long, at least 3 feet tall. Do not prune climbers at all. Buy or make rose collars that are 8 inches high to encircle the base of each plant; you can use any material that will hold together for the winter. Fill the collar with any well-draining material, such as pine bark, chips, or compost.

HOW MANY ROSE VARIETIES ARE THERE?

There are literally thousands of rose varieties . . . more than we could count. Most garden centers and nursery stores try to sell roses that come from some of the best growers, such as Conard-Pyle's Star® Roses, Weeks, and Jackson and Perkins®. Buying roses grown in these great nurseries gives you greater assurance that you are buying high-quality plants, representing high-quality varieties.

Go ahead and try a rose—and enjoy!

'The Fairy' is a magnificent shrub rose.

JANUARY
ROSES

PLANNING

It takes some imagination to visualize lovely roses out in the yard where now there are only some humps of mulch and soil around stubby canes. Exercise your imagination by browsing the new garden catalogs that have started to arrive in the mail. If you do not yet have any roses in your yard, why not try some? This New Year's resolution will be easy to keep.

Roses are actually many different kinds of shrubs of different colors, sizes, and habits. They do not have to be planted in a bed of their own—or even in a garden. The key to selection is identifying the reasons you want to grow roses. Some reasons might be:

- cutting for indoor display
- drying for floral crafts
- fragrance in the garden
- season-long color in the yard
- solving a landscape problem
- an enjoyable hobby

Look for improved varieties that are low-maintenance, hardy, and disease-resistant. Think about where there is lots of sun in your yard or garden and whether there is sufficient room there for a full-sized shrub. Otherwise, you may want to consider growing a rosebush in a container on a deck or patio.

Miniature 'Rise 'n Shine'

Miniature roses are ideal for balconies and windowboxes. Think vertically, and consider **climbers** or **ramblers** on trellises or arbors where space is limited.

It is time to start a new garden journal or notebook for the new year. If you have lots of roses on your property, you may want to devote your journal exclusively to your experiences over the coming year with roses. Otherwise, keep records for all your plants to help you remember names, weather events, planting times, and pruning and blooming times.

PLANTING

No planting is necessary at this time.

CARE

If you are growing **miniature roses** indoors as houseplants, keep a close eye on them. Their environment is very stressful because of cold drafts from opening doors, low humidity from central heating, and low light. Stress makes them vulnerable to pest and disease problems.

If possible, set potted **miniature roses** under fluorescent lights to increase the amount and duration of their daily light. Group them (but don't crowd them) to promote ambient humidity, and check their soil moisture often.

Outdoors, check to be sure rose shrubs are still nestled deeply in mulch, soil, or other protective materials. Replace protection that has blown away and exposed the rose crowns to harsh wind and sun. In most parts of Ohio, January will be the coldest month.

WATERING

Monitor indoor **miniature roses** closely for sufficient soil moisture. In heated homes where humidity is low, the soil medium can dry out quickly, and the plants may need watering twice a week or more. Beware of overwatering, which will induce root rot and kill the plant.

The pencil test will determine whether the soil is dry and watering is needed. Insert a sharpened pencil point about 2 inches into the soil, then remove it. If wet soil sticks fast to the pencil, check again in a few days. If there's some soil on the pencil, check again in a day. If the point comes up without any soil, it's time to water.

Ways to increase humidity:
- use a room humidifier
- cluster plants
- keep plants in the kitchen or bathroom
- set plants on shallow trays of damp gravel

FERTILIZING

If **miniature roses** are actively blooming indoors, they will need nutrition. If you mixed some granular, slow-acting fertilizer into their potting medium when you potted them last fall, it will suffice. Otherwise, water-in some liquid fertilizer as directed on the product label. It is a good idea to dilute it more than suggested if plants are only producing new foliage.

PRUNING

During the period that **miniature roses** bloom indoors, pinch off the faded blooms. This will improve their appearance and encourage more buds to form.

Pick off any yellowed leaves, and remove fallen leaves from the soil surface promptly to prevent disease problems.

Sometimes high winds outdoors will cause breakage on dormant roses, especially on long canes of **climbing roses** that come loose from their supports. Prune off any broken or injured canes on outdoor rose shrubs as soon as you notice them.

PROBLEMS

Spider mites are problems for all indoor plants, especially **miniature roses**. Too tiny to detect without a hand lens, these spider-like pests cause pale stippling on foliage. Sometimes their fine webbing is visible among the stems. The simplest solution for these small plants is to wash them thoroughly in tepid water from the kitchen faucet every couple of days for two weeks. Persistent infestations may need a spray of insecticidal soap or a miticide.

Aphids may also attack **miniature roses** growing indoors. They cluster on tender new growth at tips of stems and on buds. Pinch off stem tips. Wash insects off the plant with tepid water from the faucet. Spray stubborn infestations with insecticidal soap as directed.

Powdery mildew appears on foliage of **miniature roses** as a gray or whitish coating. There is no cure for already infected leaves, but you can spray uninfected foliage and new foliage with a garden fungicide listed for this use. Follow the label directions. Promote better air circulation around your roses with a small fan.

FEBRUARY

ROSES

PLANNING

This month roses are in the minds of many who hope to be in the hearts of others on Valentine's Day! While bouquets of long-stemmed beauties are a classic gift of love, the gift of a rose shrub is a more enduring expression of affection. A gift certificate for a garden center or mail-order rose supplier tucked in the Valentine card may be just the thing to touch his or her heart all year.

It is time to plan where to locate new roses in your garden. If you want them for flower production for cutting, crafts, competition, or a hobby, you may want to establish a separate rose garden on your property. This requires significant space and sunshine.

Roses are also easy to integrate into the yard like any flowering shrub. As they beautify a home landscape, the many kinds and sizes of rose shrubs also solve problems. Roses can:
- make a hedge to enclose an area.
- screen a view.
- mask an eyesore.
- anchor a mixed flower border or cover and soften an arbor or pergola.
- replace your lawn as a ground cover.

Heavily mulching is one way to protect the graft union.

- cool a wall.
- accent a doorway.
- soften architectural lines.
- serve as barrier plants along the property line.

PLANTING

Although it is too early to plant rose shrubs outdoors, it is time to order roses by mail. Suppliers will send the plants to you about the time it is safe to plant in your area. They will arrive packaged bare-root. A bare-root plant is dormant. It is just three or four bare, stubby brown stems joined at the plant crown. Its exposed roots are temporarily covered with moist sawdust, sphagnum moss, or shredded paper, all covered by a plastic bag with a few air holes.

Store bare-root roses in a cool (above freezing), dark place so they will remain dormant. Make sure the material around their roots stays moist. Soak their roots in water for about twenty-four hours prior to planting (plant as soon as possible after they arrive in March or April).

CARE

If the winter weather is severe, check to make sure there is still plenty of insulating mulch piled

generously around the crowns and stems of rose shrubs out in the yard and garden. **Hybrid tea roses** are at special risk for winter damage because they are typically grafted. The bud union, or graft, where they meld is a small "knob" low on the stem near the soil. If it is not well protected against winterkill, the top part of the rose shrub might die and the new growth will come from the root stock. **Shrub roses** that are typically on their own roots may suffer some winter damage, but as long as their roots and crown survive, they will regrow true to variety.

This is also a good time to spray horticultural oil on the bare, stubby stems of rose shrubs that have a history of insect pest problems. It will smother any overwintering eggs. Follow the directions on the product label. Spray heavy, or dormant, oil only before leaves appear. Spray light, or superior, oil at any time during the year.

 WATERING

Continue to watch soil moisture in potted **miniature roses** indoors. Do not let them dry out.

Dormant plants do not require much moisture. Unless there has been an unusual drought period, there is no need to water rose shrubs outdoors.

 FERTILIZING

Miniatures that have been coping with less-than-ideal indoor conditions would appreciate a boost from a soluble fertilizer. Mix with water as directed. There is no need to fertilize plants to increase blooming until the return of bright sun and warmer temperatures signal a new bloom period.

If you are suffering from cabin fever and feel you must get outdoors and do something for the roses, spread a thin layer of some organic matter such as rotted manure or compost on the soil over the root zone of the rose shrubs.

 PRUNING

Indoors, carefully check **miniatures** for insects and diseases. Remove and discard any dropped, discolored leaves that could harbor black spot fungal spores or insect eggs. Prune away bare stems and excess twigginess from plant centers to encourage good air circulation.

 PROBLEMS

Rabbits and deer may nibble the bases or tops of rose canes. To protect shrubs, either surround them with wire cages tall enough so that deer cannot reach down inside, and/or spray stem surfaces with a repellent.

Mice and voles may be nesting in the mulch piled up around dormant rose shrubs. They will chew on the bark and damage canes. To prevent this in the future, delay mulching until after the ground freezes hard so the rodents will seek another place to nest. For now, use a repellant product as directed.

HELPFUL HINTS

All-America Rose Selections (AARS) is a nonprofit organization dedicated to introducing and promoting exceptional roses to homeowners. Its members represent more than 90 percent of the total garden rose production in the United States. AARS has more than 130 official test gardens throughout the country where they test new rose varieties in a wide range of soil and climate conditions for two years. The AARS website, **www.rose.org**, contains a list of winning roses, test gardens, monthly rose-gardening tips, and more.

MARCH

ROSES

PLANNING

This is a good time to examine your pruning tools. They will be in use before you know it. Sharpen or buy replacement blades for handpruners. Shop for loppers, handpruners, and pruning saw. You might also pick up some supplies such as:

- granular, slow-acting fertilizer formulated for roses
- shredded bark mulch
- tough gloves for handling thorny rose canes

Soak the roots of bare-root roses before planting. You can add a little liquid fertilizer to the soaking water.

- bags of compost or peat moss if you do not have another source of organic material for improving the soil

PLANTING

Planting roses begins this month wherever the soil has thawed and is not too wet to be worked. It is important to plant rose shrubs ordered by mail while they are still dormant. To plant a bare-root rose shrub:

1. Set the plant in a pail of water so its roots are immersed for up to eight hours prior to planting.

2. Dig a saucer-shaped hole about as deep as the roots are long, and 2 feet wide.

3. Mix some slow-acting, granular fertilizer for shrubs or roses into the soil you remove from the hole. Add organic material such as peat moss or compost to improve the tilth and drainage. Reserve this to fill the hole later.

4. From the regular soil at the bottom of the hole, form a mound to support the crown of the rosebush so the bare roots descend down along its sides. The bud union (graft) on the main stem should be at ground

level when the plant is correctly planted.

5. Fill the hole with soil, firming it gently around and over the roots. Water well.

6. Hill more soil or some mulch up over the crown and base of the stubby canes until temperatures moderate and leaf buds start to swell.

CARE

When leaf buds start to swell, begin gently removing the piled protective soil or mulch from around the canes of both established and newly planted rose shrubs. Use gloved hands or a soft water flow from a hose. Wait until temperatures are consistently above freezing at night and at least 45 degrees Fahrenheit during the day.

Check the canes, especially at crown level, for rodent damage. Spread the mulch in a 2-inch layer over the shrub root zone out as far as its potential branching area.

WATERING

If less than an inch of rain falls weekly, water newly planted roses deeply. Water the soil, not the leaves, to minimize the potential for fungal disease. Properly mulched shrubs will manage longer between rains than unmulched ones.

FERTILIZING

If you haven't yet done so, consider spreading organic matter such as rotted manure and compost around the bushes. Spring rains will soak nutrients in. If you do not have these materials, simply mulch the soil.

Established rose shrubs will need an application of granular, slow-acting fertilizer. Following package directions, sprinkle the granules over the entire root area, and mix them into the mulch. The rain or your watering will soak them in.

PRUNING

When all winter protection has been removed, prune rose shrubs. Cut out all dead and damaged canes on all types of roses. If some canes show winterkill at their ends, cut them back to live wood; cut as low as you must.

Use sharp pruners, loppers, and pruning saw blades for a clean cut. Further pruning can be done now or early next month for the health and beauty of the roses. How much and what you do depends on

---

HELPFUL HINTS

When working with roses (and sphagnum moss), a gardener should be aware of the potential for contracting the fungal disease sporotrichosis. Rose thorns can carry this fungus, which enters the skin through small cuts and punctures. The first symptom of infection is usually a small painless bump (red, pink, or purple) resembling an insect bite on the finger, hand, or arm. Sporotrichosis can be serious, so contact your doctor. For more information, see the Center for Disease Control and Prevention's website at **http://www.cdc.gov/ncidod/dbmd/ diseaseinfo/sporotrichosis**.

---

the type of rose shrub. Always pick up and discard fallen debris. New roses arrive from the nursery pruned properly.

- **Hybrid teas**, **floribundas**, and **grandifloras** require hard pruning. To keep the center of the shrub open to light and air, select three to six healthy young canes spaced openly to form a vase shape. Cut them back to 8 to 12 inches tall. Cut off all other canes at the base. Make the cuts about 1/4 inch above an outward-facing leaf bud.
- **Landscape roses** need renovating. Prune away about 1/3 of their older canes and weak branches. Reduce the length of remaining canes by 1/3 their length.
- **Polyanthas** and **miniatures** need grooming. Prune back stems to 3 to 5 inches. Prune off twiggy growth, especially from the center.

- **Ground cover** and **hedge roses** need shearing. Cut all canes to about 6 inches.

PROBLEMS

The early season is a time for prevention measures. Proper pruning assures removal of dead and diseased tissues and possible overwintering insect eggs. It also establishes good air access to prevent fungal disease on foliage.

Fungal diseases plague certain types of roses. Spray new foliage with the antidesiccant spray used on evergreens to limit moisture loss. The coating will discourage fungal spores from attaching to leaf surfaces. Choose disease-resistant rose varieties.

APRIL
ROSES

 PLANNING

As the season unfolds, consult your garden notebook or journal to refresh your memory about your roses. Were there trouble spots in the bed of **hybrid teas**, or with the rose shrubs elsewhere in the yard? Did you identify any new opportunities for using roses in the landscape?

Hybrid teas, **miniatures**, and others adapt well to planters on the sunny deck or patio. When pruned as standards, each on a single stem like a small tree, **hybrid teas** provide a formal touch. **Miniatures** can go in windowboxes and hanging baskets. Their colors blend well with tropical plants such as **canna** and **hibiscus**, possible neighbors on the deck. Plant fragrant roses where you sit to relax and entertain so the fragrance can be fully appreciated.

 PLANTING

Plant **container roses** anytime when the ground is not frozen.

1. Keep the soil in the container moist until planting time. Temporarily tie overlong canes up out of your way with twine to prevent damage to you and the shrub.

2. Dig a saucer-shaped planting hole as deep as the rootball is high and about twice as wide. The sloping sides will encourage roots to spread into the natural soil around them.

3. Slide the rootball out of its container, taking care not to break up the soil or damage the roots. Prune or untangle any roots that are matted or circling due to confinement in the pot.

4. Set the rootball in the hole. Check that the top of the rootball is level with the surrounding ground.

5. Fill the hole with the soil you dug out of it. Mix in some granular, slow-acting fertilizer formulated for woody plants, or for roses specifically. If your soil is heavy clay, add some organic matter such as chopped leaves or compost to improve its drainage.

6. Water the entire area thoroughly. To help reduce transplant shock and safely stimulate root and leaf growth, add some water soluble fertilizer to the water.

7. Spread a 2- or 3-inch layer of some organic material over the root zone. If more cold weather is a possibility, add some mulch over the crown and lower stems temporarily.

 CARE

By month's end it is probably safe to remove winter protection from rose shrubs. If an overnight frost threatens, throw some garden fleece or a light blanket over vulnerable shrubs for a few hours.

As the leaves begin to show on rose shrubs, softening their profile in the wake of severe early-season pruning, spruce up their beds by spreading fresh mulch under them. Add only enough to make the total mulch 2 or 3 inches in depth. The mulch will discourage weeds and help control leaf diseases by reducing splashing of fungal spores from the soil onto the leaves. It also reduces water loss from runoff and evaporation, and insulates roots from extreme summer heat and winter cold.

Begin to train **climbing roses** as their canes grow. They produce the most blossoms on canes that grow horizontally, within a 45-degree angle of the ground.

 WATERING

Remember to water newly planted roses deeply every week or so if less than an inch of rain falls. Check unmulched soil to determine its dryness after about five days without rain. When watering, avoid wetting the rose foliage.

 FERTILIZING

If you have not already sprinkled a granular, slow-acting rose or nursery fertilizer into the fill soil of newly planted roses or onto the soil of established shrubs, do so now. The package label will indicate how long it is effective. Later, when warm weather arrives and plants have been flowering for a time, a nutritional boost from fast-acting (water-soluble) fertilizer is desirable.

 PRUNING

One pruning rule of thumb is: Prune when the **daffodils** bloom. If you have not done the job yet, do it this month. It is best done just as the leaf buds are beginning to enlarge, but it is better to do it later than not at all.

Prune **climbing** and **rambling** roses this month. Because **climbers** take two years to establish themselves and bloom, wait three seasons after planting to do the maintenance pruning described below. It's okay to prune dead and damaged canes anytime.

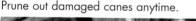
Prune out damaged canes anytime.

- **Ramblers** flower on one-year canes, so prune all canes that are two years old or older—prune them away at the crown.
- Flowers on **climbers** develop on short, 6- to 12-inch laterals on two- to three-year-old canes. Keep all tall canes except the oldest (dark brown). Prune off dead ends to just above a healthy, outward-facing bud. If the long canes have come loose from their support structure (trellis, fence, etc.), reattach them.
- Just before spring budbreak, prune the short laterals to 3 to 6 inches or three to four buds.

 PROBLEMS

Aphids may cluster on tender new growth at the foliage tips or flowerbuds of rose shrubs. Masses of these pear-shaped, soft-bodied insects are visible to the eye. Pinch off infested shoots, and discard tips. Spray more serious aphid infestations with insecticidal soap or Neem. Spray the aphids directly.

Blackspot is a major fungal disease that attacks the foliage of many rose varieties, especially **hybrid teas**. Watch for sunken black rings and then yellowing in lower leaves. Limit its spread by spraying healthy foliage with a rose fungicide product.

MAY

ROSES

 PLANNING

May is a feast for rose gardeners. By mid-month, garden centers are stocked with the latest varieties such as 'Knock Out™', 'Chuckles', and other favorites. Take the trouble to seek out disease-resistant varieties. The AARS label attached to the stem of a rose shrub indicates that it is a good choice.

'Heritage' is one of the David Austin roses.

While you are at the garden center, take a look at rose accessories. You might need a sturdy trellis or handsome arbor for your **climbing rose**. Any of the new lightweight planters that resemble terra cotta or concrete would make a wonderful Mother's Day gift for a special lady. So would a good book devoted to the history, selection, and cultivation of roses.

 PLANTING

Cool nights and comfortably warm days make this an excellent planting time for roses as well as gardeners! Follow the March and April planting directions for container-grown rose shrubs. You may see some at the garden center that are packaged in card-board containers intended for planting directly into the planting hole. Follow the instructions on the package label.

Roses thrive in rich soil and open space with good air circulation. Place bushes 3 to 5 feet away from surrounding plants in a garden bed with other flowering plants in it. If they are in a bed of their own, be sure to allow enough space to move among them to prune and harvest flowers without getting pricked by the thorns. Those planted as hedges

should be far enough apart so their fully-grown branches just barely touch. **Climbers** should be at least 1 foot from a wall or trellis to allow room for air circulation and pruning.

As spring becomes warmer, consider taking stem cuttings from your favorite **miniature rose**. They root easily and make delightful gifts throughout the summer.

 CARE

Spread fresh mulch or augment existing mulch on the soil around all roses in the yard. Do not make it deeper than 2 inches. Shredded leaves, leaf mold (partially decomposed leaves), or dried grass clippings are perfectly fine. For specimen plants or entire beds devoted to roses, you may prefer something a bit more elegant such as:

- shredded bark
- pine straw
- cocoa bean hulls
- wood chips
- bark nuggets

The coarser the material, the longer it takes to break down during the hot summer.

The long canes of **climbing roses** will need fastening to their supporting trellis or arbor as they grow. They are not able to cling or twine on their own. Use brown or green jute twine ties or commercial plant ties. Loop them around the cane, then around the trellis, and fasten. Do not tie them tightly; leave a bit of flex in the ties.

Warm weather brings indoor **miniature roses** outdoors. Acclimate them gradually by setting them outside for just a few hours daily, extending the time every couple of days until they are comfortable staying out all night, too. Do not put them in the sun immediately; it will burn their foliage.

WATERING

Be sure to water new transplants generously until new green sprouts show they're getting established. Because they are in the sun a large portion of the day, rose shrubs need to be watched for water when the weather warms. Well-mulched established roses will manage fine with the usual spring rains, but they, too, will need supplemental watering in the summer sun and heat.

If there's no rain, water all young plants and continuously blooming roses thoroughly once a week. Using a water wand rather than a hose sprayer will help direct water to the soil and root area, not the leaves. Wet leaves can lead to fungal diseases. If you must use an overhead sprinkler, try to water early in the day so that any damp leaves will dry before nightfall.

FERTILIZING

If you haven't yet sprinkled a granular, slow-acting rose or nursery fertilizer on the mulch and soil around rose shrubs, do so now. They will need the consistent, uniform nutrition because warm weather promotes vigorous growth. Follow label instructions. Because **hybrid tea roses** demand heavy nutrition, they also benefit from some supplemental foliar sprays of a fast-acting fertilizer every few weeks over the summer.

PRUNING

Once rose foliage fully emerges, basic maintenance pruning should be finished. If stems are beginning to grow from below the graft, clip them off promptly.

Their foliage will look different from that of the main plant. Remove all fallen leaves and plant debris, and discard them in the trash, as they might harbor insect eggs and fungi. Trim the edges of rose beds to create an attractive border and to halt encroaching weeds and grasses.

PROBLEMS

Leggy stem growth along with few or no flowerbuds usually signals that a rose shrub is not getting enough sunlight. Trim overhanging tree branches that may be shading its site. Move the shrub to a sunnier place.

Canker causes canes to turn brown in the spring or fall as if winterburned. It is caused by a fungal infection which is encouraged by poor air circulation. Remove canes showing signs of canker by cutting them off well below the infection. Improve air circulation.

Pull weeds or carefully spot treat them with Roundup™ as soon as you notice them. Be certain to never allow Roundup to contact any part of the desirable rose.

JUNE
ROSES

PLANNING

Many rose varieties—the older one-time bloomers, the **hybrid teas**, the continual bloomers, the rebloomers—begin to flower in early to mid-June in most of Ohio. This is the peak time for roses. The first flushes of blooms are the freshest and most abundant. It is a perfect time to plan leisurely visits to public (and private) gardens where roses abound. Keep notes on the roses that appeal to you. Are you attracted to their color, fragrance, or flower form?

Later this month there are usually a few steamy days, advance warning of the summer heat and humidity to come. While the bush roses that are integrated into your landscape as ground covers, hedges, or screens will manage pretty well on their own, expect to devote considerable time to **hybrid tea** specimens. Careful tending will yield the best, healthiest flowers over the weeks ahead. When several rosebushes are planted in relatively close proximity, the incidence of pest and disease problems is greater. Having resistant varieties helps a great deal.

PLANTING

It is best to have planting and transplanting of roses completed well before their major bloom time this month. This is especially important for bare-root shrubs. If they are planted when dormant early in the spring, new acquisitions can concentrate on growing roots and foliage all spring. Then they will be ready to produce buds and flowers on schedule now in June.

Many **rose shrubs** are available in containers at the nursery or garden center this month. By this time they have already produced foliage and flower buds. They will transplant fairly well over the next few months as long as it is not too hot. If you want to plant, do so on an overcast day to reduce transplant stress.

CARE

Since this is display time for your roses, take some time to enhance their surroundings. Make sure the mulch is fresh and the edges of beds of **rose shrubs** are trimmed. Treat for weeds, and mow adjacent lawn areas.

Check **climbers** and **ramblers** to make sure they are securely fastened to their supports. Rapid early-season growth sometimes loosens the ties. Newly planted **climbers** may need some guidance as their canes grow long enough to reach the bottom of the trellis or arbor they are intended to climb.

WATERING

If less than an inch of rain per week falls, water newly planted roses deeply every week. Properly mulched, established roses can go longer between waterings—as long as two or three weeks.

FERTILIZING

Sprinkle a granular, slow-acting rose or nursery fertilizer product on the soil around any roses newly planted. Scratch it into the soil surface. The rain or your watering will soak it in.

All roses that will continue blooming over the summer might need a follow up fertilizer application. Most slow-acting products last 2 to 4 months.

PRUNING

Cut and enjoy your **hybrid tea roses** indoors in bouquets. Clip off all spent blossoms that remain on the rosebush. Cut stems back to just above a point where a second five-leaflet leaf faces outward on the stem. This practice stimulates repeat bloom and controls the shape of the shrub.

Continuous bloomers such as 'Meidiland', 'Carefree', and 'Knock Out' varieties do not require deadheading of spent blossoms to maintain flowerbud production—however, it does improve their appearance and helps keep the shrubs compact.

PROBLEMS

Mites infest roses stressed by heat and drought. Disrupt light infestations with a vigorous water spray from the hose on leaf undersides every day or two for a week. Established, stubborn mite infestations, as evidenced by fine webbing on twigs and leaf stems, may require further treatment with insecticidal soap, Neem, or a miticide.

Thrips may become a problem when heat and drought arrive. These tiny insects target rose flowerbuds—especially light-colored ones. They burrow into the unfurled petals, which become deformed and fail to open properly. Hang a yellow sticky trap near plants where they are suspected. If thrips appear on the trap, spray buds with a pyrethrum-based insecticide as directed on the label or a systemic pesticide labeled to control thrips.

HELPFUL HINTS

To prolong the life of cut roses, cut them in early morning or at dusk when the air is cool. Cut flowers that are in the late bud stage, open just enough so you can see their colored petals. Carry a bucket of tepid water into the garden with you. Use sharp pruners for a clean cut, and cut each selected stem at a 45-degree angle back to where a five-leaflet outward-facing leaf joins it. Immediately immerse the cut stems in the container of water. Set the cut roses aside in a cool, shaded place for a few hours to allow them to take up water. Then re-cut the stem ends and arrange them in a vase of tepid water containing floral preservative.

Caterpillars such as the rose budworm or fall webworm or rose slugs sometimes chew leaves and buds of roses. Tent-like webs among the foliage may be the first clue that they are present. Destroy the web nests, pick off visible caterpillars, and clip off ruined buds and leaves. Spray the foliage of heavily infested rosebushes with a product containing Neem oil. Neem works on all caterpillars, including the rose slug.

A well-placed rose can enhance any garden setting.

JULY
ROSES

PLANNING

Now that your continuous-flowering roses are in full show and early bloomers are on the wane, take time to enjoy and evaluate. While the garden's display is fresh in your mind, make a few notes on the highlights and disappointments.

If certain rose shrubs have died or their health has been seriously compromised by winter conditions or chronic disease and pest problems, dig them up and throw them away. This will make space for one of the newer interesting varieties. At least you'll have room for a 'Knock Out™' or two!

PLANTING

You can still plant **container roses** in the ground (see steps for planting **container roses** in April Planting). Now that summer has arrived, sufficient soil moisture is even more important. Put extra effort into follow up watering. If rainfall is scarce, keep up the extra watering until you see the plants are growing new foliage;

> Tree roses are not hardy in Ohio but they make wonderful container plants. You can bury the entire rose—pot and all—to protect it from winter weather.

water-in some dilute soluble fertilizer to help them withstand transplant stress.

Miniature roses are as at home in a pot (indoors or outdoors) as they are in the ground. **Rose standards**, the tree forms with single stems, usually are grown in pots here in Ohio. Just winter over in an unheated garage.

CARE

A layer of organic mulch on the soil beneath rosebushes will cool the soil and also keep weeds to a minimum. When weeds do appear, they will pull out easily from the mulch.

Landscape or **shrub roses** are typically much tougher than the classic traditional bush types such as **hybrid teas**. Freer in habit, more rambunctious, they can handle a wider range of soil types and conditions. As long as they get sufficient water, they can pretty much manage on their own.

WATERING

Check moisture of **container roses** with a garden trowel. If soil is dry, water. Be sure containers have good drainage holes.

If less than an inch of rain falls, continue to water newly planted roses deeply every week or so. Give established roses a good soaking every two or three weeks during summer drought.

FERTILIZING

Don't fertilize roses in extremely hot weather. Their slow-acting fertilizer from earlier in the season will sustain them nicely through these hot weeks.

PRUNING

Routinely check rosebushes for damaged canes, dead twigs, and faded flowers. Remove them promptly to improve their appearance. Remove dead leaves and other debris on the ground to prevent splashing soilborne fungal spores onto the lower leaves of rose shrubs.

Prune varieties such as spring-flowering, **perpetual hybrid**, **early-blooming climbers**, and some **rambling roses** shortly after the flowers drop. This will give the bushes time to set buds on new wood for next year.

PROBLEMS

Japanese beetles love roses. In July they emerge from the soil, where they have lurked in their larval (white grub) stage since last year, to feed on rose leaves, flowers, and buds. Be on the lookout for the early arrivals, and start picking them off plants and dropping them into a jar of soapy water. Patrol your rose garden several times a day, if possible. If their numbers overwhelm, spray them with an insecticide product containing pyrethrin, making sure it contacts them directly. Do not hang bag traps near roses or anywhere else on your property, because their lures will attract even more beetles to your property.

Rose midge larvae cause deformed buds and dead stem tips. They can quickly infest and devastate an entire rose garden. Prune off and destroy infested buds and stem tips. Spray with Neem every five days, as directed on the package.

Leafcutter bees cut precise ovals and circles from leaf surfaces, sometimes causing stems to die back. Just prune off the dead and dying stems, and remove dead debris. As pollinators, leafcutter bees are beneficial to the garden environment, so don't treat them with a pesticide.

AUGUST

ROSES

PLANNING

It takes a sturdy plant to flower with gusto during this month of serious heat and, perhaps,

Rosa rugosa develops colorful hips as well as decorative flowers.

drought. Some roses take this in stride. In fact, they are just getting their second wind about this time. Take note of those roses blooming in yards this month as you travel in the neighborhood and on your way to work.

Typically, it is the informal landscape types rather than the formal display type of rose shrubs that are most visible. Plan to integrate some of these roses into your landscape if you like what you see this month.

When you go on vacation, watering your roses will be a concern if rainfall has been scarce all summer. While established **landscape roses** can manage for several weeks, others may not be able to. Try to arrange for a neighbor to water, especially those roses planted in containers. Think about installing a drip irrigation system on the property this fall to handle the roses and other plants as well.

If you vacation at the seashore, you may be familiar with **rugosa roses**. These sturdy plants are adapted to coastal conditions and can handle drought well. By late this month they will be showing gorgeous bright-orange hips that are as decorative as their flowers.

PLANTING

By late August and through September as summer heat subsides, you can plant **landscape shrub roses**. If they have been sitting in a garden center in a container all summer, it is best to get them into the ground as soon

as possible. They are tough enough to manage in any residual heat and drought.

- Follow the instructions on planting container rose shrubs in April Planting.
- Untangle and clip off matted or circling roots caused by confinement in the pot for an extended period.
- Prune off flower buds that are close to opening. The shrub can then concentrate its energy on growing new roots to withstand the winter.
- Do not add fertilizer at planting time.

CARE

Maintain a 2- or 3-inch layer of mulch over the soil in beds where roses are planted. Chopped leaves tend to decompose quickly in the heat, so you may have to spread a fresh layer to keep down weeds and help the soil retain moisture. The decomposed material is excellent for conditioning the soil over shrub roots.

Many varieties of roses will develop rose hips where flowers fade on the stems—this is their way of setting seed. By late this month, stop deadheading faded flowers, and allow the hips to form. This, combined with the increasingly fewer hours of daylight daily, will signal the shrub to slow its growth and prepare for winter. Later in the season, the hips will provide a nutritious meal for birds and other wildlife.

Check **climbers** to be sure their new growth is securely fastened to their trellis or arbor. The high winds that accompany late-summer storms will loosen the long canes and thrash them about, causing major damage.

WATERING

Continue to water if rainfall is sparse.

FERTILIZING

A rule of thumb is to stop any fertilization of rosebushes six weeks before first frost is expected where you live. There is no point in stimulating tender new foliage growth which will not have time to mature before cold weather.

PRUNING

Routinely remove dead, diseased, and dying branches from rosebushes that are in full view in the garden.

Prune off any suckers that may have originated from below the bulging bud union on the bush stem. Suckers have a different look from the flowering plant—coarser or different-colored foliage.

PROBLEMS

For answers to specific disease or insect problems or other questions, check with your local rose society, county agricultural agent, or horticultural society. You can learn about local trends and conditions and receive the latest information on solutions and research.

Mites, aphids, and Japanese beetles may still turn up on rose foliage. They will focus on those shrubs that are stressed or weak for some reason. Consider their appearance an alert, and try to discover why the plant is struggling. It may just be in the wrong place. If so, you can move it in the fall. Neem is effective for all these problems.

Viral diseases such as rose mosaic virus occasionally appear in rosebushes. Infections are systemic, established throughout the plants. The plants' growth will be stunted and they will develop increasingly more splotchy colored, puckered leaves and malformed buds. Infected plants decline over time. There is no cure for plant viruses. Dig up the shrub immediately and discard.

SEPTEMBER

ROSES

PLANNING

While we think of fall starting after Labor Day, summer actually continues for several weeks on the calendar, and good weather continues in Ohio. Expect to enjoy your roses during this time. They will respond to a break in the heat with a fresh flush of blooms.

A season's experience with roses yields a lot of helpful information on how to grow these wonderful shrubs even more successfully next year. The key to their health is proper siting. Plan now, so when the weather cools and plants begin to go dormant, you can move those that did not perform well because they were in the wrong place. The various **landscape** or **shrub** types generally tolerate a range of soils and moisture conditions and less sunlight. However, high-performance **hybrid tea roses** have stricter requirements. Do yours have:

- at least six hours of sun (more in the morning so some shade cools them in summer afternoons)?
- excellent soil drainage?
- a soil pH of about 6.5?
- good air circulation?
- at least 2 feet of distance from walls and solid fences?

Garden centers hold fall sales to clear their merchandise, and bargains are to be found. Here are opportunities to acquire garden accessories inexpensively.

PLANTING

Plant **container roses** from the garden center now through the fall until the ground is frozen. Sooner is better, because their roots will have more time to adjust to the new soil and site and begin to grow. Follow the planting steps in April Planting. Do not fertilize until next spring.

Some of the roses growing in planters and decorative pots may be outgrowing them. Either repot them into larger planters, or put them in the ground in an appropriate place in the yard. In the case of **miniatures**, either plant outdoors, repot for outdoors, or repot and bring them indoors for the winter.

CARE

Topdressing the soil around roses with compost or composted manure is not essential, but it is a good thing to do if you have a source of these organic materials and the time! Combine this task with season-end cleanup. Remove the thinning, old mulch that may be contaminated with fungal spores and pest

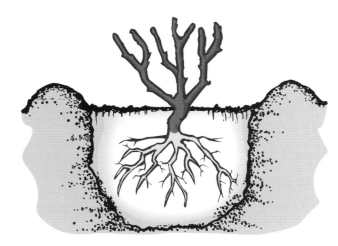

Plant grafted roses so that the graft union is at ground level.

insect eggs. Spread the organic material, then spread a thin layer of fresh mulch over it.

Shortly you will be placing more mulch up over the crowns and lower stems of the roses for

HELPFUL HINTS

One way to enjoy your roses long after the season is past is to dry some of their petals for use in potpourris. Pick opened blossoms of fragrant varieties after morning dew has evaporated, but early enough in the day so their essential oils are still strong.

• For a moist potpourri, pull the petals from the blossoms. Then spread them on a drying rack away from the light for a few days until they are limp. The petals will retain their color well.

• For a dried potpourri, pull the petals as above. Set them on a cookie sheet in a warm oven. Keep the oven door ajar to allow the moisture to escape. Stir the petals occasionally so they dry evenly and completely. They will lose some color intensity with this technique. Drying the petals in the microwave oven is faster, and the color holds better. Experiment with timing, because each appliance is somewhat different.

winter protection. Delay doing so until plants are dormant and freezing is imminent.

Prepare any **miniature roses** destined to overwinter indoors:

1. Wash their leaves and stems with water, then spray their foliage with horticultural oil to eliminate any residual insect life, including mite eggs. A repeat spray a week or so later will reduce the next generation.

2. Reverse acclimate them to help them with their adjustment to indoor conditions—particularly the reduced light. Bring them in gradually, before the heat goes on in the house. Have them spend just a few hours at a time indoors—more every few days—for a week or more. Eventually they will stay overnight and settle in at your sunniest (usually south-facing) window.

WATERING

When rainfall is limited, continue to water container and garden roses while the weather is mild and they are still blooming. It is important that they go into the winter in as healthy condition as possible.

FERTILIZING

Do not fertilize outdoor roses. Newly planted ones will do fine, and all rose shrubs on your property will get their fertilizer next March.

PRUNING

Continue to pick up and discard any dropped foliage or other debris. Prune only damaged twigs or canes now; delay other pruning a few weeks until the rose shrubs have dropped their leaves and are dormant.

PROBLEMS

Weeds may be a problem now. If the mulch over beds of rose shrubs has decomposed and thinned, perennial weeds can enjoy more light, and annual weed seeds may germinate in the rich residue. Hand pull them if there are only a few. Carefully use a post-emergent herbicide if weed growth is significant.

Powdery mildew is a potential problem as long as there are leaves on the rosebushes. At this point in the season it is not practical to treat it. Soon the leaves will drop. Clean them up promptly.

OCTOBER

ROSES

PLANNING

It has been customary in this country and abroad to plant **hybrid tea roses** in beds of their own. In their own bed they are easy to prune, spray, and, of course, pick. Their typical stiff, upright posture makes them difficult to blend in with other shrubs or flowering plants, so a separate bed makes sense.

This is a good time of year to make a rose garden or to renovate an existing bed to be dedicated to **hybrid tea** and other **specimen roses**. Establishing it from scratch provides a great opportunity to create optimum conditions—strong light, good air circulation, and great soil.

1. Choose a site that receives at least six hours of direct sunlight daily in the summer.

2. Designate a measured area. Remove the turf or other existing plants to expose the soil.

3. Dig down at least 2 feet, and turn over the shovelsful of soil in place. If the soil is hard and clayey, improve its drainage. Dig a deep trench and lay drainage pipes or tiles and gravel beneath the bed. An easier method is to build up the bed a foot or two above ground level to facilitate drainage.

4. Add an inch or two of some organic material such as compost, peat moss, or mushroom soil over the soil, and dig it in to improve the soil's ability to drain well yet retain moisture. Rake the soil smooth and level.

5. Move rosebushes from elsewhere in the yard, or plant new ones now, or wait until spring to plant.

6. Cover the beds with a 3- or 4-inch layer of winter mulch in the form of pine needles, chopped leaves, wood chips, or shredded bark.

PLANTING

It is still okay to transplant rosebushes. This is also a good time to remove poor quality plants. This will make room for new plants next spring. Transplant roses when the soil is moist:

Imagine a bed devoted to hybrid teas, such as 'Marijke Koopman'.

1. Prune out dead wood, and cut back long canes to 2 or 3 feet.

2. Tie the canes together with twine for better access to the plant crown and root zone.

3. Estimate a distance of 8 to 10 inches out from the shrub crown on all sides. Shove a sharp spade or shovel into the soil around this perimeter so that it cuts through roots. This will create a soilball with the roots embedded.

4. Lift the rootball out of the ground with a shovel or spading fork. Try to keep the soil around the roots, and set it on a tarp or piece of burlap. (If the soil falls off the roots, proceed to plant as you would a bare-root rose, described in March Planting.)

5. Dig a saucer-shaped hole the depth of the rootball. Use the tarp or burlap to lower the rootball into the hole, and position it as you wish. Then lift the plant slightly to remove the fabric.

6. Check to be sure the rosebush is at the same depth in its new hole that it was in its former one.

7. Fill in the hole with soil, water, and mulch, as you do when planting any shrub. Remove the twine. Do not fertilize until next spring.

CARE

Rose trees, also known as **rose standards**, aren't hardy in most of Ohio. They involve two grafts, so they have two bud unions, and are therefore doubly vulnerable to weather extremes. For winter protection, place the entire plant, pot and all, horizontally in a trough, and cover it with mulch. An alternative is to put it in a cold frame or cool shelter, such as an unheated garage, where the temperature never drops much below freezing.

Light frost is usually not a problem with roses. White polyspun garden fleece is an excellent material to protect the last remaining flower buds.

WATERING

If keeping up with summer watering of roses has been a problem, consider installing an irrigation system where roses are planted in beds. This is a good time of year to do the job, because it is cool and the plants are dormant.

Snake porous hoses over the bed between the rosebushes, where they will sweat moisture along their entire length. Because it delivers water slowly and directly into the soil, a porous hose system conserves water. It also avoids wetting rose foliage. Once the length of hose is installed, cover it with mulch. Next season, attach a timer to the faucet.

FERTILIZING

Do not fertilize any outdoor roses. Delay fertilizing newly planted ones until next spring.

If you have brought **miniature roses** indoors and they are producing new foliage, water-in a very dilute fast-acting fertilizer every couple of weeks.

PRUNING

Mulch leaves that are falling from trees promptly. If allowed to lie on the ground and mat together, they may slow rain from access to the soil around rose shrubs in the landscape. When leaf fall is finished, mulch any bare soil around roses.

PROBLEMS

Deer may nibble on rose canes and any foliage that remains on shrubs prior to hard freeze. Given alternatives, they typically avoid plants with thorns, but if there is not much else available, they will go for the roses. Spray roses with repellent, or cage them.

November

ROSES

PLANNING

Before the extended end-of-year holiday period begins with Thanksgiving, take some time to review your experiences with your roses this past year. Have you:

- updated your notebook or garden journal?
- built or renovated a bed for **hybrid teas** and other **specimen rosebushes?**
- removed any dead or dying rosebushes?
- transplanted roses to better sites?

Soil may be heaped over cut-back canes to protect the rose.

- installed drip irrigation in rosebeds?
- winterized the roses?

PLANTING

If you have decided to pot up a **rose shrub** that has been growing in the ground, it is best to do it this month after a hard frost. Otherwise, wait until spring. Dig only when the shrub is fully dormant.

1. Water the soil around the shrub the night before to soften it and hydrate the roots.

2. Tie the canes of the rose shrub to prevent damage while you dig and move it.

3. Dig a rootball as described for transplanting roses (see October Planting). Pots should have a drainage hole and be roughly 6x8 inches for **miniature roses**, 14x18 inches for standard-size roses.

4. Set the rosebush in the pot so the top of the rootball is an inch or two below the edge. Fill in the edges with soil if necessary.

5. Water well. Remove the twine.

CARE

Rose shrubs in containers are more vulnerable to winter cold than those in the ground, as their roots are aboveground and subject to drying and cold. There are several ways to overwinter them safely:

- Set them in a cold frame.
- Sink the container into the ground out in the garden.
- Leave it in place, and pile up mulch around the container and over the soil around the shrub crown.
- Bring it indoors. Treat **miniature roses** as houseplants.

The conclusion of leaf fall from shade trees and the arrival of hard frost signals time to winterize roses. They are now fully dormant.

- **Landscape type roses** on the property are pretty tough and need minimal care. Water them well if rain has been sparse, and mulch them appropriately.

- **Hybrid teas** and other grafted roses need more care. Cut back any long canes that might whip around in the winter wind. No canes should be shorter than 24 inches or so.

Pile up soil or other organic material such as pine needles, wood chips, shredded bark, or chopped leaves over the crown and lower parts of the canes. Be sure to cover the knobby graft with mulch.

• **Climbing roses** need protection if winter temperatures dip below zero with any regularity. Unfasten the canes from their support, and gather them in a horizontal bundle on the ground. Cover them and the plant crown with soil, straw, leaf mold, or other organic material. If it is too difficult to remove the canes, tie them very securely to their support, and mound soil or mulch as high as possible on the plant.

Check any nametags wired on new and existing rose shrubs. Make sure their wires are not girdling the canes as they mature and grow thicker.

Miniature roses kept indoors as winter houseplants need lots of light to avoid the loss of vigor that invites pest and disease problems. As the sun drops lower in the sky and the number of daylight hours shrinks, they cannot get the requisite minimum of four hours of direct sunshine on the windowsill. Set them under fluorescent lights to compensate. Rig the lights so they are about 2 or 3 inches above the tips of the branches. Use a timer to assure that the lights are on sixteen hours a day.

HELPFUL HINTS

Flowers are not the only ornamental assets of roses. Many kinds of roses develop large, colorful hips after their flowers fade. Their rich orange color enhances the autumn landscape well into early winter if the local wildlife does not eat them first.

Rose hips are a source of seeds if you want to try to propagate roses yourself. Remember that seedlings of hybrid varieties of roses will not resemble their hybrid parent.

Rose hips are also a rich source of vitamin C. In fact, the vitamin C in commercially produced natural vitamin supplements is made from them.

 WATERING

If it has been a dry fall, water all shrubs in the yard and garden before the ground freezes hard.

Check soil moisture for **miniature roses** growing indoors. They tend to dry out quickly when the indoor heating runs regularly. Do not let them dry out.

 FERTILIZING

If budded or blooming indoor **miniature roses** do not have slow-acting fertilizer in their potting mix, fertilize with a water-soluble fertilizer when you water.

 PRUNING

From now until spring, limit any pruning to removing injured canes from dormant rose shrubs. Resist the urge to neaten them up ahead of schedule. There will be some winterkill at the tips of canes, so they should remain at 18 to 24 inches. That will assure there is live, healthy wood lower on them when official pruning time arrives in the spring.

 PROBLEMS

Spider mites are always a potential problem on indoor **miniature roses**. They love hot, dry conditions, and these are often the norm inside homes when cold weather arrives. To catch infestations early, regularly check for pale, fine stippling on leaves.

DECEMBER

ROSES

PLANNING

An appropriate year-end activity is to revise the sketch of your yard and garden. Before the possibility of a cover of snow, tour the property and identify changes that have occurred during the past season. Alter the drawing of your landscape to reflect:

- new planting beds
- roses and other shrubs that have been moved
- any trees that were removed (affects available sunshine)
- changes in walkways, and grades (might affect rainfall drainage)
- drip irrigation installed
- any arbors or pergolas established
- new pools, decks, or patios

If you have been taking photographs of your roses over the past season, label them and put them in your journal for future reference.

PLANTING

If the ground is not yet frozen, it is still possible to plant or transplant rosebushes outdoors. It is not recommended, however.

HELPFUL HINTS

Gloves that best protect against thorns are usually made from heavy canvas or leather and/or are coated with a rubber type compound. The best have generous cuffs that reach up the arm toward the elbow to protect against scratches. Maybe new gloves for rose care should be on your holiday gift list!

CARE

For winter protections, hill up mulch—chopped leaves, shredded bark, pine needles, wood chips—over the crown graft and bottoms of the canes of **hybrid tea** and other grafted rosebushes. A 3- or 4-inch layer over the ground around and between bushes in a bed will insulate the soil so it does not alternately freeze and thaw and disturb the roots over the winter.

WATERING

Water **miniature roses** wintering indoors. Check their soil every few days for adequate moisture.

FERTILIZING

If there is no granular, slow-acting fertilizer in the soil of indoor **miniature roses**, incorporate some in the upper inch of soil.

PRUNING

No pruning is necessary this month.

PROBLEMS

Wind is the enemy of roses in the winter. Check to be sure **climbers** are securely tied to their arbors and trellises. If the canes of other rose shrubs are becoming too battered, tie some twine around them all to steady them.

Lack of sufficient light will stress **miniature roses** growing indoors. Make sure there are only 2 or 3 inches between stem tips and the fluorescent lightbulb. Set a timer to run the lights for sixteen hours daily.

Insufficient humidity is a problem for all indoor plants. Put them in a cool room, or set them in a tray of moist gravel. If they are located in the bathroom or kitchen, they will get more humidity.

CHAPTER SEVEN

SHRUBS

It is something of a mystery to us why caring for residential lawns is virtually a national pastime in this country, yet caring for shrubs seems to have such a low priority on the homeowner's to-do list. These incredibly important landscape plants are typically taken for granted. The fact that many shrubs survive years of neglect is a tribute to their genetic makeup. When someone does pay attention to them, it is often to prune them incorrectly. With utilitarian rather than artistic effort, the pruning often distorts the natural habit.

Yet shrubs are so essential to our sense of a residential landscape that builders always put a few around newly built homes that need buyers, even before they seed-in lawns. These perfunctory shrub plantings are serviceable evergreens familiar to one and all. They do the job and grow reliably over the years, until one day they completely obscure the house from the view of the street. Unless and until there are new owners or the house desperately needs painting or repair, the faithful shrubs continue to grow wildly, unnoticed and neglected.

CHAPTER SEVEN

What's wrong with this scenario? It reflects an unfortunate failure to appreciate shrubs both as handsome plants of enormous variety and as important ornamental assets to every property. When carefully selected and strategically planted around the yard to showcase their beautiful foliage, flowers, bark, fruit, and shapes, shrubs contribute significant monetary value to a property. Shrubs also feed and shelter wildlife, they screen wind, and they soften architectural lines of buildings.

Shrubs are woody plants. This means they have stems that do not die back every fall, but instead develop thick tissues that survive year after year, growing harder as they age. Shrubs are usually distinguished from trees, which are also woody plants, by their smaller size and multiple stems. Like trees, shrubs may bear deciduous foliage that drops every fall, or either needled or broadleaf evergreen foliage that remains throughout the winter. Many shrubs are valued for their blooms in spring, summer, or fall. Others offer unusual growth habits or foliage shapes and textures. Still others withstand shearing and make great formal hedges.

Shrubs provide an infrastructure for the landscape. They unify its disparate elements— low ground covers, lawn, plants, buildings, and tall trees. They do lots of things, sometimes all at the same time. They:

- soften hardscape features.
- define spaces.
- punctuate doorways.
- screen utilities.
- delineate property lines.
- buffer noise.
- anchor flower beds and borders.
- provide winter interest.
- produce flowers and fruit.

ASSESSING YOUR SHRUBS

The first step in appreciating how shrubs can enhance your landscape is to identify the ones you have. Enlist the aid of a knowledgeable friend, landscape design professional, or horticulturist to help you answer the following questions about a shrub you are considering to purchase:

1. What is the common name of this shrub?
2. What is the formal scientific (botanical) name of this shrub?
3. What are its ornamental qualities?
4. Is this a high- or low-maintenance shrub?

5. What is the mature height and spread of this shrub?

The next step is to evaluate the condition of each existing shrub on your property:

1. How old is this shrub?
2. Is the foliage healthy?
3. Are there any signs of girdling roots?
4. Do the stems have dead bark, insect holes, or fungal disease?
5. Has either over pruning or neglect compromised this shrub's aesthetics?
6. Is this shrub worth keeping, or should it be replaced?

Evaluate the shrub's location on your property:

1. Is this shrub in the best site for the light it needs?
2. Is it too close to another shrub? to a building or wall?
3. What function does this shrub perform here?
4. Would the ornamental features of this shrub show better elsewhere in the yard?
5. Will this location still be suitable when the shrub grows to mature height?
6. Is this shrub able to tolerate the soil conditions at this site?

UPGRADING YOUR SHRUBS

The answers to all the foregoing questions will help you make some decisions about the shrubs on your property.

CHAPTER SEVEN

Removal. It may be clear that certain shrubs should be removed and discarded. They are either old, diseased, or so overgrown that efforts to reestablish their shape will unavoidably ruin their health. In some cases there are modern cultivars or new varieties of a shrub that are so superior, there is no point in keeping the older one.

Rejuvenation. Shrubs that are healthy, not too old, and appropriately sited are worth the trouble it takes to restore. Since most often the problem is tangled, woody overgrowth, the solution is to revitalize the shrub by pruning. This is not pruning to control its size, this is pruning to remove its old, overgrown stems and stimulate new stem growth. The pruning can be pretty radical, involving either cutting all the stems back to the ground all at once, or cutting back one-third of the oldest, thickest stems each year for three years.

Transplanting. Some shrubs may be perfectly fine but they are not in the best location. Many can be transplanted fairly easily to another site in the yard. The best site for an existing shrub may not be available on your property, so it may make sense to give it to a friend.

Once the existing shrubs on a property have been inventoried and noted in your journal, there remains the wonderful task of purchasing new ones. If this seems like a daunting task, seek the advice of a professional landscape designer or horticulturist who may be especially helpful if your plan is to add many shrubs over a newly developed area. It is certainly not difficult to choose a few shrubs on your own. Just be sure that when you go to the nursery you have in mind the specifications for the site—the mature size, the ornamental features, and the purpose the shrub must serve.

JANUARY

SHRUBS

PLANNING

If you didn't have a chance to do so last month, this is a good time to study your yard and appreciate the role shrubs played. What do you see from the various windows in the house? Are shrubs in view, or are they all up near the house to be viewed and appreciated only by passersby on the street? Here are some other questions to answer:

• Do your shrubs have ornamental features—fruit, cones, interesting bark, dark or golden evergreen foliage—that relieve the winter bleakness?

• Do your shrubs have a variety of sizes and shapes?

• Are there some evergreens? They are particularly nice this time of year, softening the scene and providing color, plus shelter and food for wildlife.

• Are there places on the property where shrubs would help define its border, screen an unattractive view, or block the wind?

Make a New Year's resolution to plant at least one new shrub this year.

Shopping List: an illustrated book on shrubs; admission to the local arboretum or park

Firethorn produces ornamental berries that persist through the winter.

PLANTING

This is not a good time to plant, even if the soil is not frozen. The possible exception might be a living Christmas tree. It is better to get it into the ground to keep the roots moist and safe from frost than to let it sit around until spring. Timely planting is important enough that if you live in areas where the soil is usually frozen by late December, it is advisable to dig the hole in the fall or cover the fill soil so it will not freeze. Then you can plant the tree as soon as possible after the holidays (see Trees January).

CARE

Renew the antidesiccant spray on any evergreen shrubs in sites exposed to harsh winter sun and wind. Choose a mild day, and follow the directions on the product

label. This coating on their leaves will reduce moisture loss from evaporation and transpiration.

Check the winter mulch under shrubs for signs of rodent nests. If some of the lower branches are buried in deep snow or bent over with ice, leave them as is to prevent injury to brittle stems. The snow will protect them, and gradual melting will release them gently.

Shrubs that are located just at the edge of a roof overhang are vulnerable to damage by sliding snow. Snow that accumulates on the roof will gradually slide off as temperatures moderate. It can fall as a clump, splitting and breaking branches. Try to avoid planting vulnerable shrubs in these locations.

WATERING

If it has been a mild, dry winter and the soil has not frozen, check under the mulch around shrubs to see if the soil is still moist. If it is not, water the shrubs. Foundation shrubs near the house, garage, or other buildings often dry out because they are partially under a roof overhang, which may block rain or snowfall. Check them often.

SUNBURNED AND WINDBLOWN

Winter damage to shrubs and other landscape plants does not come from bitter cold, frozen ground, or lots of snow. If they are correctly selected for the cold-hardiness zone, shrubs can handle all these winter conditions. Damage is more likely to come from bright, glaring sun that reflects off snow or glossy evergreen leaf surfaces and dries foliage and tender bark. Strong winds whip branches around so that they break, or cause broadleaf evergreen foliage to puncture itself and lose excess moisture. Frozen soil prevents shrub roots from absorbing moisture from the soil. Fluctuating temperatures can cause soil to alternately freeze and thaw around shrub roots— as it expands and contracts, it shifts, damaging roots or even heaves recently planted shrub rootballs out of the soil altogether. Snow cover or winter mulch insulates soil against these freeze-thaw cycles.

FERTILIZING

No fertilizing is necessary this month.

PRUNING

Limit pruning to cutting off injured and broken branches. Make clean cuts back where the branch joins a larger branch or a main stem. Take care not to cut into tissue on the main branch or trunk. Leave the wound as is so that closure will take place.

PROBLEMS

Deer and rabbit damage peaks these next few weeks as natural food supplies are depleted or covered with snow. Deer will be bolder about venturing into your yard, even if they have not previously been much of a problem. Make sure protective wire cages around shrubs are high enough to deter deer standing on deep snow. If you are depending on spray repellents to protect evergreen foliage, renew the sprays. Alternate taste and odor repellents every couple of weeks to maintain their effect. Power up the electric fence!

FEBRUARY

SHRUBS

PLANNING

As the late-winter planting time approaches, it is a good idea to look closely at the shrubs already on your property. If there are some that are obviously in the wrong place (bumping into the sides of the house, so tall that they have covered up windows), think about moving them. If they are otherwise healthy and lovely, give them a new site where they have room to grow. Move them yourself, or hire a landscape contractor to do it for you. If you decide you do not want them at all, consider giving them to a friend. Other questions to think about before the season commences:

- Is this the year to deal with the growing deer problem?
- Will a border of shrubs make the property line more pleasing or private?
- What shrubs will encourage more birds to visit the yard?
- Would shrubs with colorful foliage improve the yard?
- Are all the shrubs spring bloomers, or do you have some that bloom in summer?

- Would a hedge help to define a garden area?

Shopping List: a good pair of work gloves, floral preservative, more birdseed and suet, a platform feeder for birds

PLANTING

Even though the soil may be thawing, there is no need to rush to plant new shrubs or transplant existing ones. Wait until the local nursery or garden center has its new stock—that will be a signal that the time is about right to plant. It may not be until next month.

1. First, dig up and discard very old, dead, or diseased shrubs.

2. Then, transplant existing shrubs that are too big for their site to new locations in the yard to make way for new plantings in their former locations.

3. Finally, plant newly acquired shrubs in their designated spots.

Bare-root shrubs that come in the mail can be planted any time now, but it is easier when the weather is a bit milder (see March for planting steps). Store the bare-root shrubs in a cool place, and keep their roots moist until planting time.

Many summer-blooming shrubs are not available for planting until later spring. In the warmer regions of Ohio, **crape myrtles,** **hydrangeas,** and **rose of Sharon** arrive in garden centers in May.

CARE

Remove snow from heavily laden conifer boughs with a broom, to avoid compounding the weight problem. Using upward strokes from beneath, start knocking the snow from the lower branches first. If you do this, snow knocked from above will not overburden, and possibly break, the lower branches. Work toward the upper branches, bumping them upward from underneath to dislodge and scatter the snow. If shrub stems or branches are iced over, do not disturb them—they may be so brittle they will break. When the ice melts, they will resume their former position.

WATERING

Water shrubs whose soil is not frozen, if there has been no appreciable rain or snow for a month or more. Well-mulched, established shrubs usually can go that long in winter. If shrubs are not mulched, are newly planted, or are under a roof

HELPFUL HINTS

To force branches of spring-flowering shrubs for indoor bloom:

1. On a relatively mild day, cut branches that have flowerbuds on them. The more swollen the buds, the sooner they will open in the warmth of the house.

2. To maintain its pleasing natural shape, choose branches that will not affect the shrub's form. The longer the selected branches, the more flowers there will be. Long stems are also more versatile for indoor arrangements.

3. Once indoors, cut off the ends of the branches for a fresh cut, and immediately immerse them in a container of tepid water containing commercial floral preservative.

4. Set the branches in their temporary container in a cool room away from direct sunlight. When the flower buds swell so much that you can see their color, put them in fresh water with more preservative in a nice vase. Move them into a warmer room, and enjoy the unfolding display.

overhang or other structure that may deflect rainfall from their soil, check under their mulch to see if the soil is still moist.

FERTILIZING

No fertilizing is necessary this month.

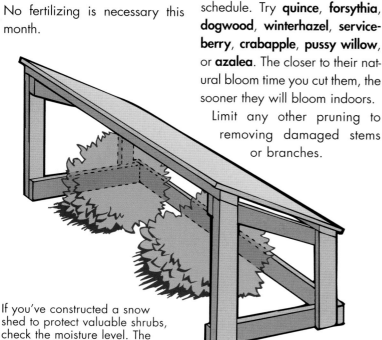

If you've constructed a snow shed to protect valuable shrubs, check the moisture level. The overhang will deflect rain or snow.

PRUNING

To get that spring feeling, clip off some budded branches from spring-flowering shrubs to bring indoors to force bloom ahead of schedule. Try **quince**, **forsythia**, **dogwood**, **winterhazel**, **service-berry**, **crabapple**, **pussy willow**, or **azalea**. The closer to their natural bloom time you cut them, the sooner they will bloom indoors.

Limit any other pruning to removing damaged stems or branches.

PROBLEMS

Deer continue to be a potential problem, especially if there is snow on the ground. They will nibble on tender branch tips and twigs of young shrubs. Those under extreme pressure from starvation will eat almost anything, even **holly** and other plants with prickly foliage. The only truly dependable deterrent is a fence. Electric fences or ten-foot-tall black polynetting around the perimeter of the property are effective. Some electric fences can be easily reconfigured around limited areas of the yard to protect groves of certain vulnerable shrubs such as **yews** or **rhododendrons**. If relying on repellent sprays, change the type every two weeks. Many products require repeat sprays after it rains.

175

MARCH

SHRUBS

 PLANNING

It's time to get serious about choosing new shrubs for the yard. Start with a particular site in mind, and choose a shrub whose mature size will not overwhelm the space available. If the site receives lots of sun, mostly shade, or some of each, choose shrubs accordingly. If the soil is usually soggy, very acid, or very sandy, choose a shrub that can handle those special conditions.

Shopping List: a new shrub, bark mulch, granular, slow-acting fertilizer, bird-bath, sharp replacement blades for handpruners

 PLANTING

Like trees, shrubs are sold retail either in containers or with their roots in a ball of soil wrapped in burlap and sometimes a wire cage. If ordered by mail, they will likely arrive bare-root—stubby, leafless stems with roots wrapped in damp paper, moss, or sawdust. Keep the plant cool and the wrapping moist until you can get it outside and into the ground when it thaws. To plant a bare-root shrub:

1. Dig a hole with sloping sides, slightly more than wide enough to accommodate the root system. Make it about as deep as the roots measure from their tips to the crown of the shrub (the knob where its roots join its stems).

2. Take some loose soil, and build a cone of packed soil in the center of the bottom of the otherwise empty hole.

3. Set the shrub in the hole so its crown rests on top of the mounded soil and the roots fall down along its sides. Check that the shrub crown is level with, or slightly above, the surface of the surrounding ground.

4. Fill the hole with plain soil, intermittently firming it lightly around the roots. Then water well to eliminate air pockets in the fill soil. Check the shrub depth again to make sure it has not settled below ground level.

5. Spread a 2- or 3-inch layer of organic mulch over the planting area. Do not pile it against the stems of the shrub.

CARE

It's time to deal with neglected shrubs that are tired, overgrown, tangled, and showing lots of dead wood or twigginess. Basically healthy shrubs will respond to rejuvenation. One way to

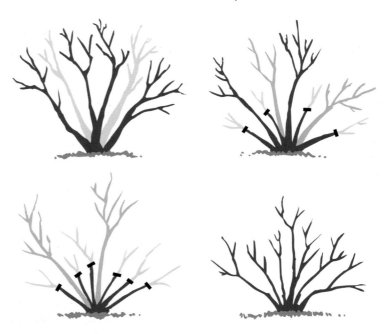

Over a period of three years, gradually prune back the oldest stems to rejuvenate the shrub.

renew them is to gradually prune out dead wood over several seasons (see Pruning, this month). In cases where the entire shrub is a mess, the best way to renew it is to cut all the stems back severely. This radical measure stimulates vigorous growth of new shoots, rejuvenating the shrub.

1. Rejuvenate before spring growth begins, either before leaf or flower buds break or new soft needles form on evergreens.

2. Using sharp pruners or pruning saw, systematically cut back every stem.

3. When young replacement shoots begin to appear, signaling renewed growth, you might need to prune off some of the weaker ones to encourage the development of fewer, but stronger, remaining ones. These will constitute the basic architecture of the shrub.

4. If the shrub is a naturally well-balanced and full plant, every time stems grow 5 to 8 inches, pinch out the terminal bud to promote branching. New branches will emerge just below the cuts.

WATERING

Water newly planted shrubs well. Follow up every week or so if rainfall is limited. To avoid overwatering, always check soil moisture under the mulch layer first.

FERTILIZING

When signs of new growth appear, fertilize shrubs, if you did not do so last fall. Sprinkle a granular, slow-acting fertilizer formulated for nursery stock on the soil over the shrub root zone. Use the amount suggested on the package label, or less—never more. Evergreens and some other shrubs such as **holly**, **rhododendron**, and **azalea** like acid soil, so you might use a product formulated for acid-loving trees and shrubs.

PRUNING

This is a good time to do cosmetic pruning of spring-blooming shrubs. Remove those twigs that you determine are diseased, damaged, or dead. Do not assume evergreen foliage that has pale or dark blotchy foliage is dead and remove a branch without testing it to see if it is brittle and dry—it might just be wind or sun damage. Wait until after shrubs bloom to prune for size or shape, if it seems necessary.

With certain rejuvenation techniques, you renew neglected shrubs a step at a time. This gradual process allows you to enjoy the shrub while it is undergoing renewal. **Spireas**, **viburnums**, and **lilacs** (which produce many stems at soil level) tolerate this technique well.

• This spring, identify and cut back the oldest, thickest, woodiest stems to 4 to 6 inches above the soil level (do only about one-third of the total number of stems).

• Cut back another third next year.

• Cut back the final third the year after that.

PROBLEMS

Rots may develop in roots planted in overly wet soil during the cool early spring. Plant shrubs a bit above ground level if soil is heavy clay.

Brown needles dropping from **pines** and other evergreens are not necessarily cause for alarm. This is older foliage that has been around for two or three years, giving way to new replacement leaves.

APRIL

SHRUBS

 PLANNING

Over the next few months, take some photographs of the shrubs in your yard and other gardens. If taken every couple of weeks, photographs make a terrific record of the succession of bloom and foliage over the growing season. Sometimes a picture helps us be more objective about the problems in the landscape.

Watch the flowers on the conifers develop—**pines** and **spruces** first. On a windy day you can see the pollen float toward the female flowers. Later in the season the flowers will become cones.

Shopping List: rain gauge, garden sulfur, insecticidal soap

 PLANTING

To plant or transplant balled-and-burlapped shrubs:

1. Loosely tie the shrub stems together so the rootball is visible and easier to lift and move. Keep the rootball moist prior to planting so the soil stays in contact with the roots.

2. Dig a saucer-shaped hole with sloping sides about twice as wide as the rootball and only as deep as the rootball is high.

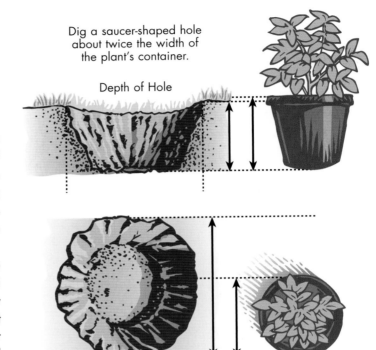

Dig a saucer-shaped hole about twice the width of the plant's container.

Depth of Hole

Width of Hole

3. Set the shrub in the empty hole, oriented as you wish. Make very sure that it does not sit lower than the surrounding ground level. (Set it slightly above level if the soil is clay.) Cut away as much of the burlap wrapping as you can reach. If there is a wire cage, remove as many rows of wire as you can. Brush off the soil at the top of the rootball until the root flare at the base of the stems is exposed and level with the ground.

4. Fill the hole with plain soil, and firm it around the rootball.

5. Spread a 2- or 3-inch layer of organic material such as chopped leaves, pine needles, compost, or commercial bark product over and slightly beyond the planting area.

6. Water the planting area well so that the soil is moist down at least 10 inches. If soil is clay, water for a while; then stop for a half-hour; then resume for a while longer.

 CARE

Mulching shrubs is one of the best ways to care for them. Spread a 2- or 3-inch layer of organic material over the bare soil under and around shrubs. If there are no chopped leaves left from last fall, use pine needles or wood chips, or buy a commercial bark mulch. The mulch layer discourages weeds, holds in soil moisture, and enriches the soil with nutrients and microbial organisms as it gradually decomposes in warm weather.

WATERING

Most shrubs are fairly shallow-rooted, so they tend to get dry quickly. They need, on average, about 1 inch of water a week from you or the rain—more in the hot summer months, less when it is cool. Mulched shrubs may go two or three weeks before their soil begins to dry out. April showers should take care of watering the newly planted shrubs, too.

FERTILIZING

If you did not fertilize established shrubs last fall, do so now. Recently planted shrubs need at least a season to begin to grow roots outward into the soil before they need much fertilizer. Use a granular, slow-acting "nursery" product labeled for the shrubs you have, in the amount suggested on the label.

Because they also produce a berry crop, **blueberry** bushes need fertilizer every year in spring or fall. Use a product for acid-loving plants to assure rich foliage color and good fruiting.

PRUNING

Prune shrubs soon after they flower if you feel you need to either shape them or gradually renew them. Now that they have leaves, lightly prune hedges that were cut back severely for rejuvenation last month. This will encourage uniform growth and narrower tops. Subsequent prunings should never cut off all this season's new growth.

If you did not do so last fall, prune the stems of **butterfly bushes** back to within 4 to 6 inches of soil level.

PROBLEMS

Aphids and other pest insects that have wintered over as eggs will begin to appear at this time. They will cluster on the tender new growth at the tips of shrub branches and suck their juices. You may see ants running along stems because they like the sweet honeydew aphids create. Unfortunately, the beneficial insects that prey on aphids are not usually appearing just yet. Until they appear, you can: 1) wash aphids off stems with a strong water spray from the hose; 2) clip or pinch off infested stem tips, and toss them in the trash; 3) spray the aphids with insecticidal soap or a product containing Neem oil as directed on the label.

Spot-spray stubborn, perennial weeds such as poison ivy, thistle, and dandelion, with Roundup™, which will kill their roots.

STRESS-FREE GROWING

The key to healthy shrubs is keeping them free of stress. If they are in the right location—one that provides excellent soil, enough moisture, correct light, and room to grow—then they will be at the peak of their form. They can defend themselves against most insect and disease attacks. When injury or environmental conditions such as drought, pollution, compacted soil, or excessive heat stresses them, they become vulnerable to pest insects and diseases. When there is a problem, treat the pest or disease, then address the cause of the underlying stress. Otherwise, the problem may return.

MAY

SHRUBS

PLANNING

May is when spring really happens in most of Ohio. The air softens, and the warm days gradually begin to outnumber the cool ones. Shrubs respond to this weather by growing vigorously. Spring bloomers follow up their gorgeous show by pushing foliage and extending their stems. Later bloomers are developing and displaying larger buds. The paler, soft needles at the tips of needled evergreen limbs signal that they are growing, too.

Because there are lots of species and cultivars of shrubs such as **viburnum** and **hydrangea** that bloom at slightly different times, these wonderful spring bloomers decorate landscapes over many weeks. Watch as some of the early species of **hydrangeas** bloom, followed by the **peegee hydrangea** and **climbing hydrangea**. When you think about purchasing a new shrub, consider the bloom period of the species and related cultivars.

Shopping List: a new hose, a hat for sun protection

PLANTING

Many shrubs are grown and sold in containers these days. They are easier to handle and can be planted almost any time of the year except during severe heat and drought or when the ground is frozen. Planting them is slightly different from planting bare-root (see March) or balled-and-burlapped shrubs (see April). To plant container-grown shrubs:

1. Dig a hole with sloping sides somewhat wider and just as deep as the container that the shrub came in from the nursery.

2. Remove the shrub from its container, and gently knock or brush off excess potting medium from around the roots and the top of the rootball onto a tarp.

3. Set the rootball in the hole, positioned as you prefer, and level with or slightly above the surrounding soil. Make sure the root flare at the base of the stems is visible at the top of the rootball.

4. Mix the excess potting medium from the container with some of the dirt dug from the hole, and fill in around the rootball. This soil mixture provides a transition zone for the roots before they extend into the existing soil. Shrub roots need encouragement to venture beyond the medium in which they have been growing.

5. Firm the soil around the rootball. Spread a 2-inch layer of mulch over the planting area up to the root flare, and water well.

Oakleaf hydrangea

CARE

Is it dead? Browned or dried-looking foliage on some or all branches of a shrub does not necessarily mean that the shrub is dead. Bend the stem or branch. If it is flexible rather than dried and brittle, it may still be alive. Scrape a bit of bark off the stem with a fingernail. If there is green or pale moist tissue beneath, it's still alive. Cut back the stem about halfway, and see if it generates new growth.

Add some fresh wood chips, chopped leaves, pine needles, or shredded bark, if the mulch layer under shrubs has thinned to less than 2 inches.

Many shrubs grow well outdoors in decorative containers or planters. To prevent loss of water from the potting medium, mulch the top of the planting medium with chopped leaves, sphagnum moss, decorative pecan shells, or cocoa hulls.

If a shrub has a poor appearance and suddenly dies, several consecutive summers of drought may be the reason.

WATERING

Water shrubs when rainfall is unreliable. If they are well mulched, they should be able to go two to three weeks without water.

Newly planted shrubs and those in containers will need more-frequent watering, especially if it is hot.

FERTILIZING

Any fertilizing of shrubs in the ground should have been done by now.

If you did not mix a complete granular, slow-acting product into the potting medium of shrubs that are in decorative containers and planters, sprinkle it on top of the medium now. Rain and watering will activate it over time. Otherwise, add a dilute water-soluble (fast-acting) fertilizer intended for shrubs to the watering can every couple of weeks when you water these shrubs. Measure it according to package directions. Do not overdo.

PRUNING

Prune **quince, azalea, daphne, forsythia,** and any other spring bloomers after they have finished blooming.

Deadhead faded blossoms from **rhododendrons** as they finish blooming. This is an opportunity to make them denser by clipping off individual branches to encourage branching. Do not shear these plants. In a few weeks many of these shrubs will set buds for next year, so don't delay—later pruning will cut off the buds and reduce flowering next year.

PROBLEMS

Deicing-salt problems may show up now as scorched lower leaves or twig dieback on shrubs that are near the street or sidewalk. The sodium chloride gets into the soil and absorbs the moisture, dehydrating shrub roots. If you suspect this problem, drench the soil with lots of water to leach out remaining salts.

Pine sawfly larvae are brownish-black caterpillars that resemble the bark on branches of **mugo pine** and some other needled evergreens. They chew on the needles, denuding branches. Look closely to detect their movement, and knock them off into a plastic bag, or squish them between thumb and forefinger. Spray a product containing Bt (*Bacillus thuringiensis*) on the infested foliage you cannot reach while the sawfly larvae are eating it. They will sicken, stop eating, then die in a matter of days.

JUNE

SHRUBS

PLANNING

This month is a transition time. Late spring gives way to true summer and things are, literally, heating up. This is when shrubs demonstrate their versatility and dependability, providing dense, colorful foliage to cool the yard. They have many other jobs in the landscape as well. They define borders, enclose spaces, screen views and noise, and form a pleasing backdrop to showcase the herbaceous annual and perennial flowers that are going strong now. During this pause before summer-flowering shrubs begin to bloom, take note of how your shrubs look.

It is not too late to add some summer-flowering shrubs to the yard if you have none. If all you have are spring bloomers, many that bloom later in the summer and into fall are available in containers at garden centers:

- **Annabelle Hydrangea** (*Hydrangea arborescens* 'Annabelle')
- **Butterfly Bush** (*Buddleia* spp.)
- **Crape Myrtle** (*Lagerstroemia indica*)
- **Fringe Tree** (*Chionanthus* spp.)
- **Peegee Hydrangea** (*Hydrangea paniculata* 'Grandiflora')

- **Rose of Sharon** (*Hibiscus syriacus*)
- **St. Johnswort** (*Hypericum* spp.)

The flowers on the following summer bloomers are small, but their fall fruit is wonderful:

- **Beautyberry** (*Callicarpa* spp.)
- **Chokeberry** (*Aronia* spp.)
- **Winterberry** *Ilex verticillata*)

Shopping List: hose storage reel, new watering can, house-plant water meter

PLANTING

It's the last call for safely planting or moving shrubs. Theoretically, you can plant container-grown plants all summer, but it's a lot more stressful for both the shrub and you after heat arrives!

If the shrubs in a border or hedge are too close together now that they have matured a bit, thin them by digging up and transplanting every other one. Take care to minimally disturb the roots of those that remain in place. They will welcome the improved air circulation and room to grow.

Shrubs that have drooping branches, such as **forsythia** and **deutzia**, sometimes root where their tips touch the soil. If you notice this, clip off the main branch above the rooted tip to separate it from the main plant, then dig up the small rooted

Gradually move tender shrubs in containers, including citrus, back outside.

piece and pot it for a gift, or replant it elsewhere.

CARE

Gradually move tender indoor potted plants—**gardenia**, **Norfolk Island pine**, **fig**, **citrus**, and others—to the porch. Allow them a few days to acclimate to outdoor conditions by returning them indoors at night if it is cool. Do not set them immediately in sunlight, or their foliage will burn. When they are acclimated to the outdoors, place them in spots around the property that have their desired light conditions. Tender tropicals are really useful for filling in spaces in planted beds vacated by spring-blooming bulbs and other plants that disappear when heat arrives. Mulch the soil in each container to help it retain moisture.

WATERING

If it has been a moist spring, soil moisture will probably be fine. Check the soil under the mulch of recently planted ones, and water if it is dry. Do not forget those in large planters and containers that are out in the garden.

Do not automatically water if a shrub's foliage is wilted. Wilt can also be a reaction to excessive heat, direct sun load, or a root rot problem. Later in the day, check to see if foliage is still wilted. If not, it was the heat.

FERTILIZING

The main growth period for most shrubs has passed, so there usually is not a need to fertilize now. It will stimulate excessive stem and foliage growth.

PRUNING

Continue to prune any late-spring bloomers, such as certain **rhododendrons**, after their flowers fade. Other evergreens to prune are **pines**, **yews**, **juniper**, **boxwood**, **pieris** and evergreen **viburnum**. Otherwise, limit pruning to cutting off broken or diseased stems and branches from now until fall.

Remember, once you give your hedge its major cutback in the spring, subsequent pruning should be light. Do not keep cutting or shearing back to the major cut and eliminating all new growth.

PROBLEMS

Chlorosis causes foliage of **rhododendrons**, **mountain laurel**, and other acid-loving shrubs to become pale or yellowish between dark-green veins. This is usually due to iron deficiency. Although there may be iron in the soil, the soil environment may not be acid enough to convert it into a form these shrubs can use, so they become iron-deprived. Acidify the soil by sprinkling powdered garden sulfur on the area over their root zones and watering it in. If the leaves do not grow darker green in a few weeks, add iron to the soil with a product from the garden center. A soil test will confirm if soil problems are serious.

Pest insect activity in the yard is to be expected now. As soon as you notice aphids, whiteflies, or mites, either wash off or use an appropriate insecticide. Do not assume that all insects are pests! Most insects are either benign or beneficial. If your yard has diverse plantings and some bird feeders, beneficial insects and birds will keep most problems under control.

Scale may turn up on evergreen **euonymus** and other shrubs. Either powdery white spots or waxy hard bumps will dot leaf and stem surfaces. Spray affected shrub foliage thoroughly—top and bottom—with light (superior) horticultural oil as directed on the product label.

JULY
SHRUBS

PLANNING

One of the ways shrubs can be used to enhance a landscape is by forming hedges. Hedges along property boundaries are gentle fences. They provide privacy, enclosure, barrier to foot traffic, and are less isolating or intimidating to people on the other side. Hedges along planted beds add color and definition to gardens. They enhance them as a frame does a picture.

While low hedges that edge formal beds typically require frequent close pruning, hedges in general are not necessarily high-maintenance. If the shrubs are properly chosen and sited, their natural growth habit will create a soft continuous row of dense branches and foliage of the desired height when they are mature. Periodic intense pruning is necessary only in situations where large shrubs must be forced to stay short or where a strictly classical, formal sheared hedge is the goal.

Think about planting shrubs this fall to form a hedge on your property. Observe hedges this summer to get some ideas. Many kinds of shrubs make good hedges—they don't have to be **privet** or **boxwood**. Consider plants such as:

- **Deutzia**
- **Forsythia**
- **Virginia Sweetspire**
- **Viburnum**
- **Cotoneaster**
- **Yew**

Shrubs that have thorns also can be used for edges and they serve as barrier plantings:

- various **Barberries**
- various **Hollies**
- **Pyracantha**
- **Quince**
- **Shrub roses**

Shopping List: polynetting to deter birds and squirrels from edible fruit crops, drip irrigation system, mechanical timer

PLANTING

It is probably too hot to plant shrubs now. If you must, arrange for temporary shade at the site to reduce transplant stress.

CARE

Blueberry shrubs serve double duty. They are wonderful landscape assets when they bloom in the spring and then, again, when their leaves turn a rich red color in the fall. In between, they yield wonderful berries. As **blueberries** ripen, pick them promptly. Discourage birds from stealing the harvest by draping netting over the shrubs.

Check the organic mulch layer under shrubs. As heat accelerates its decomposition, the layer of leaves, wood chips, or pine needles gets thinner and gradually disappears. To discourage weeds and cool the soil, mulch should be 2 or 3 inches. If it is thicker, it may reduce oxygen in the soil.

Be careful with the weed-trimmer. Avoid damaging the bark and cambium of young shrubs.

A soaker hose, mulch, and a rain guage will be your helpers in the fight against drought.

WATERING

If there is to be a drought, it is probably already apparent by mid-month. Because drought conditions often become the norm in summers, it makes sense to invest in a simple irrigation system for shrubs. In the long run it will save money, water, and time.

Choose the porous-hose type of drip irrigation made from recycled automobile tires; it sweats water along its length for hedges and shrub borders. Another type that has individual emitters every 12 to 18 inches or more is good for shrubs that are planted farther apart. Nestled under the mulch, these systems use water efficiently because they deliver it directly to shrub roots, and there is minimal loss from runoff or evaporation.

FERTILIZING

No fertilizing is necessary this month.

PRUNING

Limit any pruning to removing dead or injured branches.

IDENTITY CRISIS?

Some woody plants are both trees and shrubs. How can that be? Well, it is mostly an arbitrary matter. If they have several stems instead of a single leader, or trunk, and if they are smaller than about 20 feet, then most horticultural authorities call them shrubs. There are also some plants, such as **juniper**, that exist as both trees and as shrubs. Even more confusion results because certain shrubs are grown as single-stem plants. Some have a few stems, but they are limbed up so their branching canopy resembles a tree. Some examples of shrubs that are often made into trees are:

- **Crape Myrtle**
- **Fringe Tree**
- **Witchhazel**
- **Serviceberry**
- **Smokebush**
- **Juniper**

PROBLEMS

Japanese beetles can be a problem this month. Watch for them, and start knocking them off shrub foliage into a jar of soapy water immediately. Avoid pheromone traps that lure beetles from other yards into yours. Not all the beetles will fall into the bag that is a part of a pheromone trap. Spray major infestations with a product containing pyrethrum, according to label directions.

Lacebugs may appear on the foliage of **rhododendron**, **azalea**, **pieris**, and other shrubs that are stressed by exposure to too much sun. Leaf surfaces are dull, pale, and speckled, and the undersides are littered with dark specks of insect excrement.

Install some temporary shade for now, and plan to move the plant to a shadier site in the fall. Spray infested foliage periodically with insecticidal soap or horticultural oil to catch the inevitable next generation of lacebugs.

Bagworms and other worm/caterpillar pests may feed on foliage of shrubs. Spray heavily infested foliage with Bt (*Bacillus thuringiensis*) as directed—the caterpillars in the remaining, out-of-reach bags will eat it as they feed on the foliage. They will sicken and die within days.

Aphids should not be much of a problem now, as their beneficial insect enemies are out in full force. Check tender new growth tips that have developed on recently pruned shrubs to make sure.

AUGUST
SHRUBS

 PLANNING

Of all the plants in your yard, shrubs are among the most self-reliant. If you are planning to be away on vacation for several weeks during this hot and possibly dry month, your established shrubs will do fine. As long as they have been watered well and properly mulched, they can go for quite a while without rain.

This is a good time to think about buying a shredder-chipper or chipper to turn the leaves and branches pruned from shrubs into valuable mulch. Shredders also help with composting. If you have lots of trees and shrubs on the property, it makes environmental and economic sense to have this equip- ment. Think about owning this equipment cooperatively and splitting the cost with one or two neighbors.

Shopping List: a shredder-chipper, composting fork, safety glasses, ear protection

 PLANTING

This is not the best time to plant shrubs, since high soil temperatures can reduce root growth in many plants. Container grown plants will be available for sale at the local nursery or garden center. If you find one you like,

bring it home and water it, but consider waiting to plant.

After Labor Day, nurseries will be getting new shrubs. Even then, there will still be several weeks for newly planted ones to develop extended roots and become established before the ground freezes hard. Deciduous shrubs will not use energy to make leaves until next spring—by then, they should be established.

 CARE

Shrubs planted last fall should be strong enough to cope with heat and drought if necessary. Those planted this past spring or early summer may be struggling a bit. If they are in very sunny sites, you might erect some temporary shade for them during the really hot weeks.

 WATERING

Watch newly planted shrubs to be sure they have enough water. Proper mulching will retard evaporation of soil moisture and help cool the soil.

Understory shrubs such as **bottlebrush buckeye** that nestle partly under large shade trees often lose their share of the soil moisture to nearby tree roots. Light rains may not fall through the leaf canopy to saturate the

soil under a large tree. When it's hot, check the soil moisture around these shrubs often.

Shrubs in planters around the pool or patio are very stressed by August sun. Check frequently to make sure their planting medium is still moist. Shrubs in clay (terra cotta) pots tend to dry out more quickly than those in plastic or wooden planters. Mulch the planting medium, or add some low cascading plants to the container to cover the soil. Experiment with fancy mulches such as cocoa or pecan hulls, sphagnum moss, or special decorative wood chips. Do not use stones or gravel; they absorb and hold heat.

 FERTILIZING

Delay fertilizing for another few weeks until shrubs go dormant. Fertilizing now will only stimulate tender new growth that will get caught by the first frost. Never fertilize a shrub that is stressed by heat or pest problems. Wait until the stress is reduced.

 PRUNING

Continue to limit any pruning to removing dead or injured branches from shrubs.

PROBLEMS

Mildew month has arrived. If this grayish-white coating on the foliage of **common lilacs**, **Exbury azaleas**, and other victims has not yet appeared, it will now. While it mars the appearance of mature shrubs, it does not harm them. In a few weeks the leaves will drop anyway. If it threatens to overwhelm young, new shrubs, thoroughly spray all uninfected foliage with an antidesiccant product or wettable garden sulfur to reduce the spread of the fungus. Make sure shrubs are not too close together. Good air circulation helps control fungal diseases such as mildew.

Mites on **junipers** and other conifers are more likely if you routinely spray your property with the chemical pesticides that also kill the resident beneficial insects that prey on mites. Mites thrive on plants stressed by heat and dryness. Look for sickly or dried foliage and thin webbing among twigs or foliage. Use a strong water spray from the hose to wash them off. Horticultural oil sprays and miticides are effective, too. Use as directed on the product label.

You can mix your own solution to combat powdery mildew if it's threatening the health of new shrubs.

HELPFUL HINTS

Shrubs may be used as ground covers! The typical image of a ground cover plant is something low-growing, green, and crawly. However, lots of different kinds of plants—grasses, annual flowers, wildflowers, perennial flowers or foliage plants, flowering bulbs—do a good job of covering bare soil and protecting it from compaction and erosion, and lots of shrubs make great ground cover plantings, too. The carpet types of **junipers** that grow horizontally in colorful, textured mats over the soil are standouts. Here are some others:

- **Cotoneaster** (*Cotoneaster salicifolius* 'Repens')
- **Red Twig Dogwood** (*Cornus sericea*)
- **Shore Juniper** (*Juniperus conferta*)
- **Slender Deutzia** (*Deutzia gracilis* 'Nikko')
- **St. Johnswort** (*Hypericum calycinum*)
- **Wintercreeper** (*Euonymus fortunei*)

Weeds do not seem to mind heat and drought. Keep after them to reduce developing seeds. The tough ones (dandelion, thistle) will probably need an herbicide such as Roundup™ to kill the deep taproot that is almost impossible to dig out completely.

SEPTEMBER

SHRUBS

PLANNING

In some areas of Ohio it still feels a lot like summer, but the number of minutes of daylight each day is shrinking rapidly with every passing week. As shrubs and other plants respond to this and prepare for their upcoming period of dormancy, it is time to do the jobs that have been delayed until cooler weather prevails. This is a good time to start a compost pile, if you have not already done so:

1. Designate an area away from obvious sight—behind the garage or tool shed will do—for depositing yard waste.

2. Collect prunings, weeds, dead plants, and fallen leaves, and throw them into a heap.

3. Cut or shred the organic debris into small pieces to speed the action of the microbes, whose eating and reproducing activities will promote decomposition.

4. To improve the appearance of the compost pile, enclose it with chicken wire, wooden pallets, or a commercial bin.

5. Next spring, harvest the material at the bottom of the pile that has been transformed into compost.

Shopping List: potting mix, a book on composting, a compost fork, granular slow-acting fall fertilizer for shrubs

PLANTING

Coming up soon—last opportunity to move or add shrubs to the landscape for this year. Nurseries and garden centers are well stocked with supplies and plants with signs to remind that "Fall is for Planting."

Since there are no flowers to guide your choice, read the plant labels carefully to ascertain the flower color and variety name of flowering shrubs. **Viburnums**, for instance, are available in many species. Note the shrub's light and soil requirements. While conifers and flowering deciduous shrubs usually love sunshine, many broadleaf evergreens prefer woodland settings and need some shade. Be sure to note each shrub's mature height and width.

Review the steps for planting container and balled-and-burlapped shrubs (see April and May). Bare-root shrubs will not be available now, as they are usually planted in the spring.

If you haven't started a compost pile yet, it's a good time to start one.

CARE

Tender plants—**gardenia**, **citrus**, **fig**, and others that have summered outdoors—must come indoors before frost. Check to see if they need repotting after a season's growth. Increase the size of the pot an inch or two, and make sure it has a drainage hole. Fill it with fresh soilless potting medium mixed with a complete granular slow-acting fertilizer. Set the shrub at the same level in the new pot that it was in its previous one, add extra medium to fill in the space, and water well.

Before bringing tender plants indoors, check each one carefully for signs of insects or disease. Wash their foliage well with water. Assume there are likely to be pest insect eggs somewhere, and thoroughly spray the stems and foliage with light horticultural oil.

Gradually acclimate them to reduced-light indoor conditions by setting them in the shade for a few days, then moving them indoors to a location with bright light.

If you have acquired a bonsai specimen, keep in mind that it must stay outdoors for the winter if it is a hardy shrub. It needs the same conditions to thrive that its normal-sized counterparts need.

However, if a plant is in a container you must protect the roots from freezing temperatures. Put the container in a cold frame or sink it down in the ground.

WATERING

When rainfall is scarce, water shrubs if the soil under the mulch is dry. Do not forget that shrubs in containers in the sun will dry out more quickly than those in the ground.

FERTILIZING

Fertilizing is okay only if frost arrives in your yard this month and shrubs begin their dormant period. It's better to wait a few weeks more to be sure. Delay fertilizing newly planted shrubs until next year.

PRUNING

Cut off cleanly any branches that are snapped off in a storm. Make the cut back at a joint where the branch joins a larger stem. This avoids unsightly stub ends of branches. Delay other pruning until late winter or early spring.

PROBLEMS

Keep after the weeds. Pull easy ones as you notice them. Perennial weeds will be alive until frost. Roundup™ or a similar herbicide product works best when weeds are actively growing, so spray them as soon as possible—hopefully before they release seed for next year. Be especially careful around poison ivy, which will be developing berries and lovely purplish-red or yellow foliage. All parts of it are poisonous to those who are sensitive.

Deer will reappear if they are in the neighborhood. Set up the electric fence or make other preparations. Put wire cages around newly planted young shrubs. Young stems and twigs are the tastiest.

Rodents will be nesting soon. To force them to nest elsewhere, delay renewing the mulch under shrubs until after the ground freezes. Pull ground cover plantings away from shrub stems. If rodents are a chronic problem, set up wire cages around shrubs to protect the bases of the stems from their gnawing.

Pest insect populations will diminish as the month progresses. Do not worry about those on deciduous shrubs, which are about to lose their leaves anyway. Pluck off any bagworm cases dangling on needled evergreens.

OCTOBER

SHRUBS

PLANNING

While you are outdoors doing yard chores, be sure to take time to notice the shrubs in your yard and the neighborhood. Note which ones are developing wonderful fall foliage and fruits. A trip to a nearby arboretum or an illustrated book on shrubs will help you identify them. If you would like to add them to your landscape, look for them at the garden center now, or plan to check for them next spring. Shrubs such as **viburnums** are especially wonderful because they have both outstanding fall color and fruits.

Shopping List: antidesiccant spray, burlap or other wind-screen material, hardware cloth, animal-repellent spray, birdseed

PLANTING

This month is a great time for planting or transplanting shrubs in Ohio.

Transplanting requires the extra planting step of first digging up the shrub. Use a good long-handled shovel, and wait until the ground has softened a bit from a recent rain.

1. Moisten the soil the day before. Loosely tie the stems of the shrub together to enable you to see the ground to dig.

2. Dig around the roots as far out as you can and still have a manageable rootball. The larger the better, so that fewer roots are cut or disturbed, making an easier transition for the shrub. However, you need to be able to lift the shrub without ruining your back!

3. When the shovel can go completely under the shrub, the roots are free. Shove a piece of burlap under the rootball from one side, then tip it to the other side to allow you to pull the burlap completely under it.

4. Use the burlap to lift the shrub out of its hole, then wrap it around the rootball to hold the soil on the roots while you dig a saucer-shaped hole at the new site.

5. Follow the steps for planting balled-and-burlapped shrubs (see April).

CARE

Plant some tiny hardy bulbs under your newly transplanted shrubs before spreading winter mulch. **Crocus, snowdrops, squill**, and others go only an inch or two into the soil, so this will not disturb the shrub roots. You'll be glad you took the time when spring comes.

To prevent pest eggs or spores from overwintering and causing problems again next year, clean up fallen leaves and fruits from under shrubs that have suffered from disease or pest problems. Put them in the trash, not the compost. Then spread fresh mulch.

Collect the leaves that fall from deciduous trees this month for free mulch.

• Mow over them with the mulching mower when you cut the lawn the final few times, and collect them in a bagging attachment;

• OR use the mower side discharge to blow them toward the center of the lawn as you make passes, then collect the pile after you cut the final swath of lawn;

• OR rake the leaves and chop them with an electric leaf-shredder, or string-trimmer or mower.

WATERING

Water all recently planted shrubs and established evergreens, which continue to lose moisture through their foliage all winter. They need as much moisture as they can absorb before the ground freezes.

At right: Beautyberry

FERTILIZING

Spring-planted shrubs and those that went in last fall but have not yet been fertilized will benefit from some granular slow-acting fall-season fertilizer formulated for nursery stock. After deciduous shrubs drop leaves and enter dormancy, their roots will grow actively until the ground freezes hard later in the fall. Follow package directions.

PRUNING

As a precaution, cut back extremely long branches of shrubs if they are likely to whip in winter wind. Reduce their length to that of the rest of the branches.

A HOME SWEET HOME

The backbone of any backyard bird habitat is its shrubs. They provide all-important shelter and, in many cases, nuts and berries for food. Attract a variety of bird species to your yard to help you with pest insect problems.

1. Learn about birds. The more you know about their lifestyles and food preferences, the easier it will be to please them.

2. Plant for diversity. Choose a variety of shrubs of different types (evergreens and deciduous), sizes, and site preferences (woods, sun, wet).

3. Provide a source of fresh water year-round for birds to drink and bathe in. Use a heater, dripper, or other device to keep it thawed in winter.

4. Let part of the property become a bit wild. Birds need brush and the food sources that hide there. Let flowers develop seeds at the end of the season.

5. Set up bird feeders. Birdseed supplements natural food sources as they become depleted.

Cut and bring indoors some berry-laden branches for harvest season arrangements. **Winterberry holly**, **beautyberry**, and **viburnums** are real standouts in vases when added to the silvery plumes of ornamental grass.

PROBLEMS

The condition of no or few berries on a **holly** may have several causes. The plant may be male. It may be too young. It may be too far from a pollen producing male. It may have been so rainy and chilly last spring that the bee pollinators were unable to visit the flowers. Wait until next year.

Beautyberry

NOVEMBER

SHRUBS

PLANNING

November is a transition month in much of Ohio. It bridges a possible Indian summer and the first real snow in some parts of the state. Plan to have shrubs set for the winter by Thanksgiving so they will be prepared for any eventuality.

Get out the binoculars and a notebook so you can watch the birds that visit the bird feeder and the berry-laden shrubs in the yard. Mockingbirds will be very interested in holly berries. Keeping fresh water available for birds in freezing weather is a challenge. Site a birdbath in the sun so the water will melt for parts of some days. Float a table tennis ball in it to keep some movement to retard freezing. There are birdbath heaters if all else fails.

Shopping List: suet for birds, birdbath heater, bark mulch

PLANTING

It's last call for planting and transplanting shrubs in areas where the ground has not frozen. Store balled-and-burlapped shrubs safely while they wait for planting day. Keep the rootball moist. Even though their branches or evergreen foliage can withstand the considerable cold, their roots cannot. They are accustomed to being safely in the ground by now. Plant as soon as possible.

If the ground is already frozen hard, it is too late to plant. Store the shrub in a cool space that does not freeze in the winter, such as an unheated garage. Keep the rootball moist. An alternative is to dig a hole in the compost pile or a mulch pile and temporarily bury it there, its pot or burlapped rootball well covered with organic material as insulation.

CARE

Once the ground has frozen hard, spread mulch over shrub root zones to insulate the soil during the winter season. The layer of organic material should be 2 or 3 inches. Mulch will buffer temperature fluctuations in the soil that may disturb roots.

Winter protection measures may be necessary for some broadleaf evergreens that must endure direct winter sun and wind where they are located. Spray foliage surfaces and undersides with antidesiccant spray (Wilt-Pruf™ or similar product) to minimize moisture loss. Use this spray on your living or live-cut Christmas tree as well, to prevent it from drying out while it waits to come indoors.

WATERING

If there is not much rain, continue to monitor soil moisture under evergreens as long as the ground is not frozen. Water where the soil is dry. Check shrubs that are not mulched for some reason, because their soil will dry out faster if there is minimal rainfall. Keep the hose handy until serious cold arrives.

FERTILIZING

By now shrubs are dormant. If you haven't done so yet, sprinkle some granular, slow-acting fall/winter fertilizer for nursery stock over their root zones so that the snow or rain can activate. Use the amount indicated on the product label. If you fertilize this fall, you will not have to do it in the spring. Fall is an outstanding time to fertilize both shrubs and trees.

PRUNING

Corrective pruning or the removal of dead, diseased, or damaged branches is the only pruning necessary this month. However, it is a good time to identify branches that might be used next month for decoration inside or outside in window boxes.

Consider pruning a few shrub branches for an arrangement that will be placed on the Thanksgiving table.

This is also a good time to clean and sharpen the pruners.

PROBLEMS

Even though this is deer hunting season, deer still dare to visit yards in Ohio as fall becomes winter. Prepare according to the seriousness of the problem. Experiment with repellent sprays, bars of soap, and other measures if deer are a minor nuisance. Up the ante with wire cages around individual shrubs and maybe even electric fencing if they threaten nice ornamentals. If deer are constant intruders, consider installing black-mesh polynetting fencing around the perimeter of your yard (and across the driveway) to deter them. The ultimate defense is to wrap your property in 10-foot-high wire or polynetting with electrified wires running through it about 4 feet off the ground.

MULTISEASON SPLENDOR

The ultimate shrub in the eyes of many homeowners and gardeners is the one that is attractive almost year-round. Sound impossible? There are some shrubs that actually fit this description. Here are some shrubs with multiseason interest—flowers, berries, colorful foliage, great bark, and interesting shapes.

- **Cornelian Cherry Dogwood**
- **Crape Myrtle**
- **Oakleaf Hydrangea**
- **Oregon Grape Holly**
- **Red Twig Dogwood**
- **Southern Magnolia**
- **Viburnum**
- **Virginia Sweetspire**
- Most needled evergreens

Rodents such as mice and voles like to chew on the tender bark of shrub stems. When they chew enough to girdle its stems, a shrub will die. If you detect rodent damage on plants, protect them by surrounding the shrub or individual stems with cages of hardware cloth (wire mesh) or with commercial tree-guard products. Make sure they are high enough so that a few feet of snow under a mouse or chipmunk will not boost it high enough to reach its target.

Deer deterrents can include sprays, screens, cages, bars of soap, polynetting fencing, and even electric fencing! You will have to experiment.

December

SHRUBS

PLANNING

The catalogs that arrive in the mail this month will remind you of the new gardening year coming up. Spend time at your front side, and back windows and notice whether there are shrubs in view. Notice areas where new shrubs might be attractive.

This is a good time to bring your gardening journal or notebook up to date. Record the names and planting times of new shrubs, weather highlights, fertilizing times, and major pruning efforts. It is helpful to note which shrubs have performed particularly well and which had problems. Since pest insects arrive at nearly the same time each season, a record of when they arrived last year will give you early warning next summer.

This is the traditional time to make New Year's resolutions. A good one is to resolve to be sure that the soil under shrubs is mulched with a layer of organic matter year-round. Another is to resolve to sharpen your pruners and loppers at least once each season. See how many resolutions you can come up with.

Holiday List: a good forged-steel, long-handled shovel, an indoor-outdoor thermometer, a good pair of pruners, a gift certificate for a new shrub

PLANTING

If you plan to have a living Christmas tree, select its site and dig the hole where you intend to plant it, so you can do so immediately after the holidays even if the ground has frozen by then. Cover and store the loose soil in pails where it will not freeze.

CARE

If you haven't already set up protection for shrubs against sun, wind, snow, rodents, and desiccation, do so now. Evergreen shrubs with flexible branches that might flop or break off in a heavy snowfall may benefit from tying. Loosely gather the branches against the stems, and loop some twine around the entire bundle. Tie them so that air and light can penetrate the interior of the shrub.

Low-wattage outdoor holiday lights will not harm shrubs. Wrap or drape the strings of lights loosely. Be sure they are UL approved for outdoors.

WATERING

There is always a possibility that a fall drought will endanger evergreens. Check soil moisture under the mulch layer if there has been no rain or snow.

FERTILIZING

No fertilizing is necessary this month.

PRUNING

Cut a few branches from shrubs for use as holiday decorations. Try some new ones in addition to the traditional **holly** and needled evergreens. Various shrub **dogwoods** offer bright red and yellow bare twigs. Leafless **winterberry** branches are literally crusted with red berries. The corky stems of **burning bush** and the kinky ones of **curly willow** will add interest. Various **junipers** have blue, silver, or yellow foliage. Don't forget that **yew**, **rhododendron**, **cherrylaurel**, **arborvitae**, and **pine** are great additions to wreaths and bouquets.

PROBLEMS

Toward the end of the month, check for signs of rabbits, voles, chipmunks, and mice. Look for deer hoofprints in the snow or mud and gnawed bark on shrub stems and low-hanging branches. Reinforce barriers or other protections you installed last month.

TREES

Trees have practical as well as aesthetic functions in the landscape. Judiciously sited trees can moderate the climate indoors. The leafy canopy of a tree on the south side of a house will block the hot sun in the summer, and a row of sturdy needled evergreens planted to the north or west will alter prevailing winds in the winter.

From the beginning, trees have been an integral part of life in Ohio. Their silhouettes form a backdrop to the lives of the generations that have lived among them for centuries. Today, trees are so much a part of our sense of place that they are still everywhere, despite urbanization and suburban sprawl. Remnants of the great forest that reside in our cultural memory preside over municipal parks, corporate campuses, schools, and churchyards.

Trees line the streets of our cities. And, of course, it is the rare home landscape that does not feature at least one tree. In the past, the local builder who was most respected was the one who took the trouble to save the trees on the lots where he put houses. Other builders scrambled to plant a tree or two on each of their lots in an attempt to make their houses as desirable.

TREES IN THE HOME LANDSCAPE

As much as we love our trees, we do tend to take them for granted. That's partly because they have always been a part of the landscape and partly because they have been, until recent times, quite self-reliant. They aren't benefiting from living in a community of trees. They must compete with turf-grasses for water and nutrition in the soil. They must cope with air pollution, damage from yard-care equipment, compacted soil, and utility company pruning. The list of insults goes on. The net result is that these trees live shorter, more stressful lives.

It takes only one experience of having to cut down a large shade tree in your yard to realize the significant role trees play in a landscape. After the sound of huge lengths of trunk and limbs falling with concussive thumps onto the ground, then the noise and commotion of the chain-saws and chipper, then possibly the whine of a stump grinder . . . there is a profound silence. There is also a huge hole to the sky, and the familiar is forever changed.

Large shade trees form a vertical framework for your outdoor living space. They establish and define its scale and create a balance for its overall design. Trees link the sky with the ground, roofing it with their canopies. Smaller trees soften the edges of the yard and buildings. They provide ornamental features such as colorful flowers, berries, fruit, and bark. Their wonderful variation in foliage color, texture, and shape is appealing throughout all the seasons.

And that's just the beginning. Trees have practical as well as aesthetic functions in the landscape. Judiciously sited trees can moderate the climate indoors. The leafy canopy of a tree on the south side of a house will block the hot sun in the summer, and a row of sturdy needled evergreens planted to the north or west will alter prevailing winds in the winter. Trees also protect other plants. Large ones shelter smaller shade-loving understory trees, flowers, and shrubs from exposure to harsh winds and heavy rain. Their leaf canopies create microclimates by transposing light, filtering it, or blocking it to create textured shade. An assortment of both large and smaller trees provides diverse niches in a landscape that attracts a diverse population of beneficial insects and other wildlife. This fosters a healthy balance of predator and prey, thus a healthy environment for everyone.

Trees increase the monetary value of your property. Ask anyone who has put a house on the market recently, or who has suffered fire or hurricane damage to his or her property. While the value of shade trees varies with their location, age, species, and condition, realtors estimate that each healthy specimen on a property can add significant monetary value. It is worth the time to inventory and photograph your trees every few years. Store the information in a safe place so it will be available to insurance adjustors if necessary.

A TREE CARE PLAN

Trees are not demanding, but they need attention from time to time. Considering their value, it's worth the money to hire a professional consulting arborist to inventory and evaluate your trees. A tree-care service will also do this for you; bear in mind that they will have an understandable expectation that they will be doing any work they recommend.

Knowing the answers to the following questions will help you plan a care program for your trees:

- What is the name of this tree (common and scientific)?
- How old is this tree?
- What is its life expectancy?
- Is it a desirable tree species?
- Is this tree in a good location for light, air circulation, and soil?
- Does this tree need pruning? Why?
- Are the roots girdled or on the soil surface?
- Are there signs of injury, pest infestation, or disease?

The recent summers of drought remind us that trees in a residential landscape benefit from human assistance. A basic-care step from the minute they are planted and throughout their lives is to make sure trees have sufficient water. They lose an enormous amount through their foliage daily, especially on a hot day.

Another step is to make sure they have adequate nutrition. This is largely a function of the health of the soil they are growing in. If the soil is full of organic matter from decomposing organic mulch, then supplemental fertilizing might be necessary only when trees are very young. If trees receive adequate light and have room to grow, then they avoid common causes of stress and will be able to resist most common pest and disease problems.

Finally, do no harm. Do not pile soil on tree roots, do not compact the soil over their roots, and do not injure the tender bark with weed-trimmers and mowers.

Trees anchor a landscape, much as this white oak does.

JANUARY
TREES

PLANNING

Trees stand out in bold relief in the bleak days of winter. The evergreens soften the landscape and offer shelter to birds and other wildlife. The varied bark patterns and branching architecture of leafless deciduous trees have a beauty that is obscured other times of year. Observe the trees on your property closely this month. Look for:

• broken branches that have not yet fallen through the canopy to the ground (a potential hazard to pedestrians below).

• stubs where branches have broken off and need a smooth cut to close the wound.

• dry, cracking bark that is located low on the trunk and exposes the wood beneath.

• trees or limbs where the leaves are brown but have not fallen as usual.

• holes bored in limbs or trunk, and sawdust visible nearby.

• "shelf type" fungi growing from the trunk or base of the tree.

Have a certified arborist examine trees that have these problems, older trees, or those that suffered serious pest, drought, or disease problems last season. Make a date for follow-up care.

Shopping List: bird seed, anti-desiccant (also called antitranspirant) spray, gasoline for the chain-saw

PLANTING

Plant your living Christmas tree in the ground as soon as possible.

1. Remove the tree from the heated house as soon as possible, and store it in a cool, protected area such as a closed-in porch or unheated garage.

2. Allow the tree several days of transition time to acclimate to cold weather at the sheltered, unheated location. Keep its soilball moist and protected from freezing.

3. Dig the hole if the soil is still unfrozen, or pull off the tarp and mulch from the hole you dug last month. On a relatively mild day, plant the tree. Check to be sure that the top of the rootball is slightly higher than the surrounding ground. Fill in the hole with plain loose soil, and firm it around the rootball.

4. Water the planting area thoroughly. Then spread 2 or 3 inches of organic mulch such as chopped leaves, pine needles, straw, or wood chips over the soil out beyond the branches. This will insulate the soil from extreme temperature fluctuations

There are many types of organic mulch, including straw, pine needles, chopped leaves, and even grass clippings.

that may harm the tree roots. Do not fertilize at this time.

CARE

Take the opportunity during a "January thaw" period when temperatures moderate somewhat to spray antidesiccant on the foliage of evergreens that are exposed to harsh winter sun and wind. A product such as Wilt-Pruf™ coats the leaves to reduce moisture loss but does not harm the tree.

WATERING

If the ground is not frozen and there has been little rain or snow, check to see if the soil around newly planted trees is still moist. Using a garden trowel, make certain that the rootball and surrounding soil are moist.

FERTILIZING

No fertilizing is necessary now.

PRUNING

Cut injured or dead limbs from trees with a smooth cut just past the ridge of branch collar tissue where they attach to the trunk (see February for detailed instructions).

HOW TO SPOT A DEER

Increasingly, deer are at the top of homeowners' lists of yard and garden problems. You may notice their damage before you actually see deer on your property. These are the most obvious signs of deer.

• Tender new growth at tips of small, young trees and shrubs are nibbled off.

• The lower stems of shrubs and trees are stripped of foliage.

• The bark of small trees is torn by bucks rubbing the velvety covering off their antlers in the fall.

• Lower limbs of small shrubs and saplings are broken or trampled by young bucks who are rehearsing fierce combat as rutting season approaches.

• Tall weeds are crushed where the deer have bedded down.

When you see these signs, it is time to think about barriers or other controls.

If a pruning job requires a ladder or a chain-saw, consider hiring a professional arborist to do the job quickly and safely.

Cut down old and injured trees, and cut them up for firewood. Cut up fallen limbs that are lying around. Let the wood dry out for a year.

• Stack logs away from the house to prevent bug and rodent problems. Lay them bark side up so that air can circulate around them.

• Cover just the top of the pile with a tarp to keep rain and snow off it.

PROBLEMS

Heavy snow and ice are potentially damaging to trees. Knock snow from evergreen boughs, starting with the lower branches. Use a broom to gently push up the branches to dislodge the snow. Repeat the action, moving upward until the upper branches are snow-free. Then redo the bottom branches where snow has accumulated again during this process. Do not try to remove ice from tree branches or to free trees that are bent over to the ground (such as **birches**) with ice and snow. Allow it to melt on its own.

Deer and rodents may nibble on bark and tender shoots of young trees. Wrap tree trunks in hardware cloth (wire mesh) or other protective material. Make sure it is high enough to protect the trees even if there is a layer of snow.

FEBRUARY

TREES

PLANNING

One of the toughest things to decide is whether to take down a large tree. Evaluate your trees and resolve to remove and replace any that are not doing well. Candidates are those that are old, diseased, too big for their location, disturbing sidewalks, or unsightly from repeated severe pruning by utility companies or injury from passing cars or lawn-care equipment. The sooner you make the decision to remove the tree, the sooner a new young replacement can start to grow in that spot. Consult books and visit your local arboretum for ideas. Check mature size to be sure possible choices are appropriate to the space.

Do not plant or replace a street tree in the area between the curb and the sidewalk, called a "tree lawn," without consulting appropriate municipal officials. In the early days of suburbs, new developments had tree-lined streets. Sixty or eighty years later, those trees are aging prematurely because of compacted soil, surface roots that bulge in the confined space, and injury from passing trucks. Now, many communities have requirements about planting trees in tree lawns.

This is the time of year to order a fruit tree from a mail-order catalog if you have always wanted an **apple** or **pear** tree in the yard. Some **apple** trees are small enough for hedges, screens, and container growing.

Check pruning equipment, and sharpen loppers and saws for the new season.

Shopping List: tree fertilizer, tree-staking kits

PLANTING

No planting is necessary now.

CARE

Spray horticultural oil on fruit trees to smother overwintering eggs and larvae of insect pests. Heavy dormant (Volck) oil is traditionally used early this month while trees are dormant. If you do not have a chance to spray before leaf buds start to swell, use light (superior) horticultural oil. This coats the bark and foliage as well, and is safe for use on foliage and flower buds.

Check any trees that were staked when planted last year. Sometimes alternately freezing and thawing soil heaves and shifts soil, disturbing the supporting stakes. Make sure the ties are not rubbing the tender young tree bark.

WATERING

Check the soil under the mulch of newly planted trees and evergreens if snow cover or rainfall has been limited. Broadleaf and needled evergreens continue to lose moisture through their foliage during the winter, and those in containers are in particular danger of drying out. Water them if necessary.

FERTILIZING

If you did not get around to fertilizing trees in the fall, do so this month or next. Wait for a year before fertilizing recently planted or transplanted trees. Fertilize relatively young trees every couple of years until they are fully established and about ten years old. After that, soil testing should help to determine the amount and schedule of fertilization needed.

Use a slow-acting, granular product formulated for trees and other woody plants. It may say "nursery stock" on the label. There are also products labeled for acid-loving evergreens—**hollies, camellias, pines, oaks**, and others. Broadcast it on the mulched soil beyond the branch dripline. Eventually snow or rain will soak it in. Follow the label for the correct amount.

HOW TO PRUNE

Proper pruning contributes greatly to a tree's health and welfare. That is never more true than when cutting off a good-sized limb. It takes three separate cuts to do it properly.

1. First, cut partially into the underside of the branch to be removed about a foot or so out from where it attaches to the limb or trunk. This will assure that when the limb is cut through from the top, it will not strip off bark as it falls.

2. Next, cut entirely through the limb from the top a few inches beyond the undercut. By removing the bulk of the limb, you will reduce the weight at the place where you will make the final smooth cut near the trunk.

3. Finally, locate the ridge or collar of bark tissue where the limb joins the main trunk or larger limb from which is being removed. Make a smooth cut just on the outside of this branch collar, so that it remains around the cut. The specialized callus tissue there will grow around and over the exposed wound to compartmentalize and close it.

PRUNING

Begin major tree pruning this month while deciduous trees are still dormant. Cut away branches that rub against one another. If a young shade tree has a double leader, cut away the less dominant one. This will establish a single strong trunk and avoid the possibility of splitting in the future.

PROBLEMS

Root problems compromise the health and vigor of trees. One problem is confined roots due to poor planting technique. Failure to remove some of the burlap wrapping or the wire cage from the rootball can cause problems several years in the future. Roots can become so large that they are constricted by the wire. (See April Planting for instructions on planting balled-and-burlapped trees.)

Rodents are a real nuisance.

Watch for signs of voles, mice, chipmunks, or rabbits near young trees. Stamp down the snow around the tree to collapse voles' burrows near the tender bark on tree stems. (See September for rodent controls.)

MARCH

TREES

PLANNING

As important as their beauty is, trees are not just beautiful. They are also useful to indoor and outdoor environments. Think about how a new tree might provide shade for a patio area, or screen the noise and eyes of the street to create family privacy. A large deciduous tree located on the south-facing side of a house cools it with its leaf canopy in the summer. Then in the winter, its bare branches allow the sun to shine on the house to warm it. A row or grove of tall evergreens on the north side alters the cold wind in the winter.

Choose a new tree carefully, since it will be part of the landscape for a long time. Look for specific cultivars and varieties of trees that are known to do well in Ohio and are known to be more disease-resistant or problem-free than others.

- For a more disease-resistant **dogwood**, choose a **Chinese dogwood** or **Cornelian cherry dogwood**.
- For a shade tree, visit a park or arboretum to determine reliable species.
- Choose fruit trees and **crabapples** that are noted as disease-resistant.

Shopping List: new tree, tree-staking kit, shovel, organic mulch, all-purpose spray for fruit trees

PLANTING

It is okay to plant trees now where the soil is no longer frozen. They come from the nursery either in containers, or with their roots in a ball of soil wrapped in burlap and sometimes a wire cage. If ordered by mail, they will likely arrive as small whips that are bare-root and nestled in damp sawdust, wood chips, or newspaper. Keep young trees cool and their soil moist until you can get them into the ground. To plant bare-root trees:

1. Dig a hole with sloping sides, wide enough to accommodate the root system on the young tree. Make it about as deep as the roots measure from their tips to the crown of the tree where they join its main stem.

2. Take some loose soil, and build a cone of packed soil in the middle of the bottom of the hole.

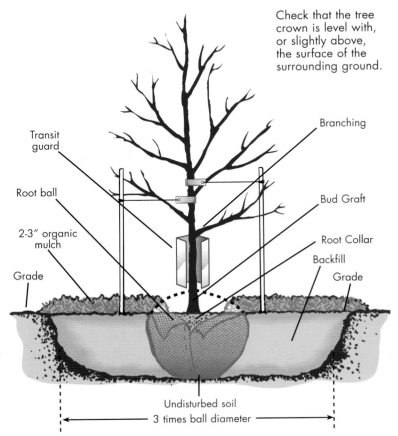

Check that the tree crown is level with, or slightly above, the surface of the surrounding ground.

Transit guard

Branching

Root ball

Bud Graft

2-3" organic mulch

Root Collar

Backfill

Grade

Grade

Undisturbed soil

3 times ball diameter

3. Set the tree in the hole so that its crown rests on top of the mounded soil and the roots fall down along its sides.

4. Fill the hole with soil, periodically firming it around the roots with your hand. Water well to eliminate air pockets.

5. Check that the tree crown is level with, or slightly above, the surface of the surrounding ground. If it is not, tug it upward, and firm the soil around and under where the roots are so it is at the correct level. Spread a 2- or 3-inch layer of organic mulch over the planting area. Do not pile the mulch against the tree stem.

CARE

Sometimes, but not always, newly planted trees require staking for their first season. Insert two sturdy posts equidistant from the tree, just beyond the planting hole. Loop a wire or rope through an old piece of garden hose and around the stem, about one-third the way up. Allow some flex in the ties to allow the tree stem to move a bit so it gains strength. Make sure the ties do not damage the tender bark. Plan to remove the stakes and ties within six to nine months.

Spray fruit trees with light horticultural oil if you missed the dormant oil spraying last month.

WATERING

Water newly planted trees well if rainfall is sparse. Don't forget those that were planted last fall. Established trees that are well mulched can manage for several months without rain, especially in cool weather.

FERTILIZING

While this can be a good time to fertilize established trees, do not fertilize newly planted ones until they have been in place for at least a year. It is not always necessary to fertilize every tree. A soil test is a valuable tool to help you decide. The organic material in mulch improves soil texture and fertility as it decomposes over time, and trees continue to benefit from that.

PRUNING

Continue winter pruning jobs. This is a good time to remove lower limbs of the larger shade trees that may be obstructing pedestrians or the view of traffic. The younger and smaller they are when cut, the faster the wounds will close over. Raising the canopy a bit this way allows more light to reach ground cover plants below.

PROBLEMS

Birds are great allies in the campaign against pest insects in trees. Woodpeckers, flickers, and others remove borers and bugs from tree bark. Robins feed on tent caterpillars; wrens eat tons of tiny bugs. Even seed-eating birds hunt for bugs to feed their babies in the spring. Invite birds to set up housekeeping in your yard by putting up birdhouses (nesting boxes) for those that prefer houses. Those that prefer open-air living will build nests in the branches of your trees, and will be on the job when the pest insects begin to appear.

APRIL

TREES

PLANNING

Ohio celebrates Arbor Day this month. Observe this occasion by planting a tree or visiting your local arboretum for festivities. Spend some time looking at a book about trees to become acquainted with some of the wonderful ones that are ideal for home landscapes.

When choosing a tree to plant in the yard, consider its size. While it may take many years to fill the space where a mature tree once stood, a younger tree with a smaller trunk diameter will often grow faster than a larger one. A larger tree usually takes longer to recover from transplanting.

Shopping List: a good pruning saw, mulch, more light horticultural oi

PLANTING

Most nurseries and garden centers will plant trees that you purchase from them and guarantee them for a period of time. Choose from freshly dug trees whose soil balls are wrapped in burlap, twine, and maybe a wire cage, or select from those growing in containers (see planting steps in May). Certain trees, such as **oaks** and **birches**, prefer spring planting.

Appropriate tree-planting techniques encourage the roots to grow laterally into the soil surrounding the planting hole as soon as possible. If the surrounding soil is not the greatest, this will come as a bit of a shock to the tree. To plant balled-and-burlapped trees:

1. Dig a saucer-shaped hole about twice as wide as the rootball and as deep as it is high. Keep the rootball moist prior to planting.

2. Set the tree in the empty hole on firm soil and orient as you wish. Take care not to damage the tender bark on the trunk while moving it. Cut away as much of the burlap wrapping as you can reach. If there is a wire cage, remove as many rows of wire as you can. Brush off the soil at the top of the rootball until the root flare at the base of the trunk is exposed.

3. Adjust the rootball so that its surface is level or slightly above ground level. Fill the hole with plain soil, and firm it snugly around the rootball.

4. Spread a 2- or 3-inch layer of organic mulch such as pine needles, chopped leaves, wood chips, or commercial bark prod-

Birches prefer spring planting.

uct over and slightly beyond the planting area.

5. Water the planting area well so that the soil is moist down at least 10 inches.

CARE

Wrap the trunk of the new tree with tree wrap to protect its tender bark from sun exposure. The bark will "toughen up" as it ages, and the wrapping will not be necessary after a year.

Stake a newly planted or transplanted tree only if it is vulnerable to windstorms or other harsh weather (see March).

Remove any staking from trees planted last spring. Check others to see if the ties are too tight for the growing tree.

Take care not to damage tree trunks with lawnmowers and weed-trimmers. A ring of mulch or ground cover plants over the tree roots will help to protect them.

WATERING

April showers will probably take care of watering your trees this month. Keep an eye on newly planted ones, and check their soil if there is no rain for two weeks.

PROTECT FROM LIGHTNING

Lightning is attracted to tall, isolated targets such as telephone poles, tall buildings, and, of course, trees. Big old, valued specimen trees are frequent victims, especially those whose branches overhang buildings. Trees protrude into the air and are better conductors than air, so they are "sitting ducks." Since wood resists conducting the charge, tree tissues can suffer severely as their sap boils and becomes steam, bursting apart the bark and stems. As it dissipates, the electric charge will rupture cell tissues, scorching them. Lightning protection cables are intended to conduct lightning to the ground where a metal rod is buried. Professional arborists will install and check these systems.

FERTILIZING

Finish any fertilizing you intended to do last month but did not get to. Spring is the peak growth time for plants of all kinds, so nutrients need to be available.

PRUNING

Prune out vertical suckers and water sprouts from along the branches of fruit trees, **magnolias**, **crabapples**, and others that tend to produce them.

Most needled evergreen trees have symmetrical natural habits, so pruning for shape is not needed. Occasionally the brittle branches of **pines** break in a storm and must be removed as soon as possible. A smooth cut near the branch collar will promote closure.

PROBLEMS

Aphids may cluster at the tips of tree branches where tender new leaves emerge. Spraying them with a forceful stream of water or insecticidal soap should provide good control. To avoid harming pollinating bees, delay spraying aphids on fruit trees until after blooming has ended.

Tent caterpillar nests are visible in tree branches by the end of the month. Either cut off the branches they are attached to and put them in a plastic bag in the trash, or poke the tents open with a long stick so the young worms are exposed for birds to eat. *Bacillus thuringiensis* or a product containing Neem oil will give excellent results.

Weeds begin to grow now. Use mulch to discourage them around trees.

MAY

TREES

PLANNING

In addition to their ornamental value, trees have significant economic value. At selling time, trees certainly add to the property's curb appeal. Keep records of when you buy and plant new trees, and record the names and approximate ages of the ones that are already on your property as you learn their identities. Photograph them over the years, and note any special care that they have required, such as major pruning, cabling, or spraying. This documentation is also useful for insurance purposes if trees are damaged by storms.

A young tree makes a nice gift for a special family event. Give a tree (and a gift certificate to have it planted) to commemorate the arrival of a new baby, a marriage, a death, an anniversary, or holiday. Make planting it the centerpiece of a family reunion.

Shopping List: ground cover plants, tree wrap to protect trunks

PLANTING

Many trees are raised and sold in containers. Container trees are easier to handle and can be planted almost any time of the year except during severe heat and drought or when the ground is frozen. Planting them is slightly different from planting bare-root (see March) or balled-and-burlapped (see April) trees. To plant a containerized tree:

1. Dig a hole with sloping sides, making it twice as wide and just as deep as the tree's container.

2. Remove the tree from its container, and gently knock or brush off excess potting medium from around the roots and on top of the rootball.

3. Set the rootball in the hole, positioned as you prefer, and level with or slightly above the surrounding soil. Make sure the root flare at the base of the trunk is visible at the top of the rootball now and after the tree is planted.

4. Mix the excess potting medium from the container with some of the soil removed from the hole, then put it in the hole to fill in around the rootball. This soil mixture provides a transition for the roots from the "ideal" potting mix to the real soil in your yard as they grow outward.

5. Firm the soil over the rootball. Spread a 2-inch layer of mulch over the planting area up to—but not on top of—the root flare, and water well. Repeat watering weekly until it rains generously.

Many trees grow well outdoors in decorative planters year-round, especially on narrow city streets and in malls. Plant a tree that seems too small for the yard in a container for a few years before putting it in the ground. If you are not sure where to plant a new tree, or if you plan to move to a new property in a year or so, plant it in a decorative container for the interim.

By month's end it should be safe to move outdoors the tender trees that lived as houseplants all winter, so they can enjoy the summer. Give them a few hours outdoors in the shade over a week or two, gradually increasing their exposure until they can stay out all night. **Ficus** and **citrus** like sun, but do not put them in direct sun immediately or their foliage will scorch.

CARE

Renew the mulch layer to 2 or 3 inches under trees where it has begun to decompose and has become too thin to deter weeds and hold moisture.

Successful pollination of fruit trees may burden their branches with excessive numbers of fruits. Over the next six weeks thin crowded **apples**, **peaches**, and **pears** so that fruits are 4 to 6 inches apart for larger, healthier fruits.

Thin crowded branches of immature fruit so fewer—but larger— fruits develop.

WATERING

In the absence of rain, water young mulched trees when their soil is dry down several inches. Water slowly and deeply with a dripping hose, soaker hose irrigation, or sprinkler.

FERTILIZING

Do not fertilize newly planted trees.

PRUNING

When spring-flowering trees bloom this month, notice any flowering branches that do not resemble the majority of those on the tree. On grafted trees, the rootstock sometimes sends up branches that flower among those of the desirable tree variety grafted on top of it. Look for branches growing from below the graft union.

While it is still okay to do major pruning this late in the spring, some trees "bleed" sap so profusely that it is better to do it earlier or later. **Maples, yellowwood, styrax, birch,** and **elm** have this tendency. Bleeding does not harm them—after all, certain **maples** are purposely tapped to make maple syrup—but it is messy and easy to avoid.

PROBLEMS

Woolly adelgid is a serious pest of the **Canadian hemlock**. It attacks those in the wild as well as those planted in yards and gardens. The insects appear as soft, white dots at the base of the narrow-needled foliage on the undersides of branches. Infested branches start to look brownish and thin, and eventually, the entire tree will die. The best control for this problem is to limit the use of **hemlocks**. Horticultural oil will provide control on existing **hemlocks**.

JUNE
TREES

PLANNING

Part of the fun of moving to a new home is getting acquainted with the plants in the yard. When you agree to purchase a property, ask the current owners to provide a list of the names of the trees, as best they can. Enjoy observing and learning about them. Keep track of the history of the largest or most valuable trees during the time you live in the house. Record information about:

- name and approximate age
- when a tree leafs out
- ornamental features
- major pruning events
- major pest problems and outcome of treatments
- wildlife living on tree
- service the tree has rendered (held a swing, treehouse)

Shopping List: wettable sulfur for fungal disease protection, insecticidal soap

PLANTING

It is okay to plant containerized trees this month as long as it is not too hot and dry (see May).

Have some fun rooting a tree yourself. Insert a freshly cut stem from a willow tree into moist soil, first removing its leaves. It will root in a few weeks. Not many trees are this easy to root!

CARE

- Remove support stakes from trees planted a year ago. Their roots have had time to grow and can support them now.
- Protect trees from lawnmower and trimmer injury.
- Forbid parking of any vehicles or heavy construction equipment within several feet of the outer edge of the branch canopy of any tree. They will compact the soil, depriving tree roots of oxygen and stressing the roots.
- Try to avoid fastening anything to a tree—birdhouse, child's swing, fencing, clothesline, or treehouse that would cause a major wound. When in doubt, consult a tree expert.

WATERING

This may be the year to address the water needs of your trees. They need about 1 inch of water a week in the heat of summer.

- Install soaker hose drip irrigation under small, medium, or young trees.
- Mulch the soil under the trees to retard evaporation of moisture from the soil and prevent runoff of excess water from hard rains.
- Aerate the soil over the root zone of trees so that it can absorb and hold water well.

- Water slowly and deeply by dripping hose, drip irrigation, or low sprinkler.

Newly planted trees will need lots of moisture to compensate for the normal loss through their foliage to help them cope with the stress of transplanting. If rainfall is scarce, check soil moisture for mulched trees every ten days or so. Do not overdo irrigation. Puddling water will compact the soil and deprive tree roots of oxygen.

FERTILIZING

Limit routine maintenance fertilizing to spring or fall. Never fertilize trees and other plants when they are stressed by heat, drought, or pest and disease problems. Granular slow-acting products release nutrients consistently and gradually over the season as the trees need them, so the fertilizing you did in spring will sustain the younger ones just fine. Older trees are able to manage on their own under normal conditions.

PRUNING

Some tree branches are still bare. Do not assume they are dead and prune them off. To determine whether a bare branch or young tree is still alive, bend some twigs or branches to see if they are flexible. Scrape the bark with a fingernail to see if there is moist, green tissue beneath. Brittle, browned twigs are dead—prune them back to where wood shows signs of life.

PROBLEMS

Trees that drop bark, fruit, and leaves this early in the season may or may not be in trouble. Some trees are just messy and constantly drop twigs, fuzzy balls, seeds, flower bracts, last year's leaves, or excess fruit set. Many routinely slough off strips or patches of bark. Evergreens are constantly shedding older leaves and needles to make way for fresh ones to maintain their green foliage year 'round.

Anthracnose and wilt diseases cause dropping leaves. **Sycamores** and their **planetree** cousins may be infected with anthracnose, a fungal disease. Younger, healthier trees are able to withstand anthracnose by producing a second flush of foliage. Trees infected with wilt diseases may lose leaves from a branch or side of the tree permanently. When trees shed leaves from the tips of branches only, that is a sign they are stressed by something. Make every effort to keep your trees stress free. Plant them in the right place, water them during drought, mulch their soil, and protect them from injury by lawn-care equipment and competition from turfgrass over their roots.

IS IT HASSLE FREE?

Not all trees are equally desirable in a home landscape. Certain ones are real problems because they are breakage-prone, messy, smelly, or weedy. The **box elder maple** is an example of a weedy tree. Landscape bullies, they quickly develop wide-ranging root systems that invade areas where moisture is available. Because they are able to handle poor soil, crowding, and drought, they compete successfully against other woody plants, even natives that are well adapted to local conditions. Their seedlings turn up in the middle of otherwise civilized hedges, ground cover patches, and shrub borders. Do not be charmed by their quick growth. They thrive at the expense of other trees and shrubs.

Norway maple (*Acer platanoides*) is also not a good choice for many areas of Ohio.

JULY
TREES

PLANNING

Nice shade trees make the yard a pleasant family retreat in the summer. Even family pets are grateful for their cool shade. As you watch the birds and butterflies and hear the bees busy at their honey-gathering (**black locust, sourwood, black gum**, and **linden** flowers make great honey), think about how adding more and different kinds of trees

might create an even more inviting habitat for a variety of species.

Environments that are healthy for all—humans, plants, and pets—always have lots of different kinds of plants. A diversity of trees, shrubs, flowers, vegetables, and herbs feeds and shelters a diversity of organisms. This assures that populations of pests and predators stay pretty much in balance. A healthy yard is easier to take care of. Take an informal inventory:

• Does your yard have some conifers such as **pine** and **spruce** that will provide shelter and food to birds and squirrels?

• Does it have some small flowering trees to attract pollinators and add fragrance over the season?

• Does it have some fruit- or nut-bearing trees such as **crabapple**, **kousa dogwood**, and **buckeye** that support birds and squirrels?

Shopping List: netting for fruit trees, drip irrigation hoses and fasteners

PLANTING

Delay planting trees, if possible, until fall. Container-grown trees can manage, but it is very stressful for them to endure transplant shock during the hot months, even though their roots suffer minimal disturbance. With its foliage canopy that emits moisture in the heat, a tree newly planted this month must also begin generating root cells in unfamiliar soil. This takes an enormous amount of energy, which would otherwise be devoted to maintaining its vigor and growth. To minimize summer transplant shock:

• Plant when several days of overcast, relatively cool weather are predicted.

• Water generously, but not excessively! Mulch the soil to keep it cool.

CARE

Certain backyard fruit trees may be about to produce fruit. Check frequently, and pick the fruit as it ripens. Do not allow overripe fruit to fall on the ground and rot. It will attract bees and pest animals.

Sourwood not only produces flowers to support bees, it has fantastic fall foliage.

WATERING

If rainfall is scarce, check soil moisture under mulch around young and newly planted trees weekly. Mulch will effectively cool the soil and deter runoff of valuable moisture when it does rain.

Eliminate the grass over tree root zones. Turfgrass roots grow in the same top 6 to 12 inches of the soil that tree roots do. Guess which grabs most of the moisture? Chances are the grass is struggling anyway because the tree shades it too much.

• Replace the turfgrass with a ring of organic mulch, about 2 or 3 inches thick, which will protect the roots and trunk from damage from yard-care equipment. It will also improve the soil as it decomposes over the summer.

• OR plant a nice ground cover such as **pachysandra**, **liriope**, or **vinca** over tree roots (this will protect the tree and the soil while providing more plant diversity in the landscape).

FERTILIZING

If you did not mix a complete granular, slow-acting fertilizer into the potting mix in the containers for potted trees, be sure to water-in dilute, fast-acting fertilizer containing minor nutrients periodically. Potting mixes are usually soilless, so they have no nutrients in them.

PRUNING

Clip off water sprouts and suckers along branch surfaces of **crabapples**, **magnolias**, and others. Except for removing broken or diseased branches, delay other pruning until trees are dormant to avoid stimulating more growth.

Remove dead branches in the canopies of older trees. Often summer storms break them off. They may get caught in the tree for a while and then suddenly drop. Prune off these dangerous limbs as soon as you notice them.

If new growth on nearby trees shades a flower or vegetable garden, prune off lower limbs or thin some branches from the canopy to permit more light to reach the garden. This is best done in the spring or fall rather than the summer, but sometimes the problem is not obvious until the middle of the growing season. Follow the steps for cutting off a tree limb carefully (see February).

PROBLEMS

Japanese beetles may be a problem during July. Although they prefer roses and other flowering plants, they may be attracted to the foliage of young, new trees. They particularly like **linden** trees. Look for them, and knock any you can reach into a jar of soapy water. Do not put out pheromone bag traps. They will attract beetles into your yard from elsewhere, and there is no guarantee that the beetles will all end up in the bag. For long-term control of Japanese beetles, control their white grub larvae in your lawn.

Noxious weeds really take off this month. Wild grape, poison ivy, bittersweet, and wild honeysuckle will climb up trees right before your eyes. They eventually spread over leafy canopies, blocking foliage access to the sun. Cut main stems to deprive them of support from their roots, and they will die up in the tree. Paint the stems and lower foliage with an herbicide such as Roundup™.

Birds and squirrels can be pests when **cherries** and **pears** ripen. Throw netting over fruit trees to foil the pests.

AUGUST

TREES

PLANNING

As back-to-school time draws closer, thoughts eventually turn to cooler weather and fall yardwork. Those trees that did not survive transplanting, injury, or the cumulative effects of stress such as drought, poor pruning, or compacted soil will need to be replaced, and there are probably other places on the property where new trees might be attractive, too.

Studies show that patterns of family outdoor life change every seven years or so as children grow up, dogs are acquired, and adults develop new interests. Perhaps it is about time to rethink your backyard's suitability as an outdoor room. Think about how the addition of some trees would contribute to the diversity and functionality of your yard. How would they affect both the outdoor and indoor climate by shading the sun and modifying the wind?

If you are tempted to cut down a large, attractive tree to make room for new construction or reduce shade or for some other practical reason, think twice. Good, mature trees are in demand for large properties, and you may be able to sell it. Call local arborists and nurseries, and tell them about it.

Professionals have equipment called a tree spade which enables them to transplant a large tree.

Plan to plant and transplant trees starting in September.

Shopping List: commercial bark mulch

PLANTING

Delay purchase of balled-and-burlapped trees for several more weeks. As the weather cools, growers dig and wrap new ones to sell at the nursery this fall. They are likely to withstand transplanting better than those that have stood around above ground all summer with their rootballs wrapped in burlap, at risk for drying out.

Meanwhile, research the tree species you are interested in to determine their requirements for light, soil, and moisture. Learn about their growth habits, and their mature sizes and shapes. This way you can make sure there is an appropriate site on your property for a tree's mature height and spread.

CARE

Trees cultivated in a landscape typically experience more stress during their lives than those growing in the wild. Therefore, they usually have a shorter life. This is especially true of street trees and trees in urban environments. In the wild, they grow in communities; their soil is not compacted, and is constantly renewed by decomposing organic debris on the forest floor; and they do not have to compete with grass for water and nutrients. To lengthen the life of your trees, try as much as possible to reproduce similar conditions for trees on your property.

WATERING

If it is a dry summer, there may be water-use restrictions. If there are, implement a triage system for watering plants in your yard:

1. Water trees first since they are the most expensive, most permanent, most difficult to plant and to replace, and contribute more to the value of your property.

2. Water newly planted trees, then older trees.

3. Water recently planted shrubs and any unmulched shrubs.

4. Water perennial flowers, then annuals which are less expensive and easier to replace.

5. Finally, water lawns.

Of course if you have food crops, they will go to the top of the list, especially since it is likely to be harvest time.

FERTILIZING

Hold off fertilizing any trees until late September or October when the deciduous ones have lost their leaves. While evergreens do not go as dormant, they too will slow down. The nutrition will support the vigorous root growth that trees develop in the fall and spring.

PRUNING

Leave most pruning until fall or winter—the exceptions are certain fruit trees. Seasonal pruning of fruit trees requires special knowledge, so it is important to read a good book on their care.

Pruning landscape trees in summer helps maintain their shape, especially of dwarf trees. Prune out water sprouts from along branches and any suckers that grow from below the knobby place where a tree may have been grafted to special rootstock.

PROBLEMS

Fall webworm tents are often quite visible at the branch tips of trees near the edges of highways. If they appear on your trees, either clip off the branches to which they are attached, or poke open the tents with a stick. The birds will eat the young

HELPFUL HINTS

Some trees that tolerate wet soil:
- **Alder** (*Alnus* sp.)
- **Baldcypress** (*Taxodium distichum*)
- **Swamp Red Maple** (*Acer rubrum*)
- **Sweetbay Magnolia** (*Magnolia virginiana*)
- **Black Gum** (*Nyssa sylvatica*)
- **Willow** (*Salix* sp.)

Swamp red maple

caterpillars once they are exposed to view.

Bagworm infestations on needled evergreens such as **spruce**, **juniper**, and **arborvitae** show up as dangling, twiggy bags that hang like Christmas tree ornaments. The bags shelter the bagworms, which venture out of the bags to feed on tree foliage, then withdraw into them for protection. Pull off or cut off the bags you can reach. Spray the foliage where they are feeding with a product containing Bt (*Bacillus thuringiensis*). When the caterpillars ingest the bacteria they will sicken, stop eating, and die in a few days.

Watch out for poison ivy climbing up tree trunks. All parts of it are toxic—leaves, berries, stems. Use an herbicide such as Roundup™ on it.

September

TREES

PLANNING

Prepare for this year's leaf fall. Leaves are a wonderful source of free organic mulch for use under trees and shrubs. Leaves can be mulched in place where they fall or added to a compost pile.

If you do choose to create a compost pile, designate an out-of-the-way spot on the property as a collection area for organic debris from planted beds, pruning, and leaf fall (leave the grass clippings on the lawn). Even if you do nothing more than pile it all in a heap and let it sit and decompose, you will get wonderful compost next season. There are a few ways to speed up decomposition of organic yard waste:

- Shred or chop materials into small pieces.
- Turn the pile every month or two.
- Add special composting worms called "red wigglers."

In the colder areas of the state, homeowners might get a frost at the end of this month. It is time to clean up, repair, and refill the bird feeders.

Shopping List: new rake, compost fork, chipper/shredder or shredder-vac, fertilizer, hardware cloth, birdseed

In spring, you'll be glad you planted spring-flowering bulbs under a deciduous tree.

PLANTING

In the colder parts of Ohio, tree-planting time begins just after Labor Day. Elsewhere, wait until deciduous trees lose their leaves and go dormant.

If you plan to plant a new tree this fall, consider hiring the local nursery staff or a landscape contractor to plant it for you. It is worth the money to have it done quickly and properly. It is certainly easier on your back! Professionally planted trees are often covered by warranty for a year or two. Read the tree-planting instructions (April) to be sure it is done correctly.

CARE

Plant some spring-flowering bulbs under deciduous trees, either in the soil under the mulch or among green ground cover plantings. Because minor bulbs such as **crocus**, **squill**, **glory of the snow**, and **snowdrops** are planted shallowly, they do not disturb tree roots, and look lovely against the dark tree trunks in early spring. They get enough sun when they need it before the trees leaf out. When the leafy canopy has fully emerged, they are ready for dormancy.

Make certain that ties on staked spring planted trees are firmly fastened but at the same time are allowing some tree movement. Remove supports from trees planted last fall.

WATERING

Continue to monitor soil moisture under the mulch of spring planted trees. Water them if the soil is dry.

FERTILIZING

Fertilize young trees that have been in the ground for a season. Granular, slow-acting fertilizer needs a few weeks to move into the soil and be available to the roots. Sprinkle a granular slow-acting product formulated for shade or flowering trees and shrubs on the soil out at least as far as the dripline. Use just the amount suggested on the package label.

Trees that are over eight or ten years old and are growing well might not need fertilizing every year. Their root systems have spread sufficiently wide to access nutrients. Decomposing organic mulch improves the soil over their roots and provides some nutrition throughout the year.

PRUNING

Delay most pruning until late fall or winter when deciduous trees are leafless. An exception is when some strange-looking foli-

TECHNICOLOR TREES

Ohio residents are treated to a gorgeous show every fall as the forest that covers part of our state is ablaze with color. Many of the trees that we see in native tree stands will also grow in our home landscapes, so it is possible to enjoy a show in our own backyards. Some trees that offer richly colored fall foliage are:

- **Aspen**
- **Birch**
- **Flowering Dogwood**
- **Linden**
- **Maples—Sugar, Red**
- **Sweet Gum**
- **Sourwood**
- **Black Gum**
- **Oaks**

A couple of needled evergreens are deciduous, and their foliage turns color before it drops:

- **Baldcypress**
- **Larch**

age alerts you to the presence of a reversion or a witches' broom.

1. Reversions are situations when a branch of a plant develops foliage of a different color or texture than the rest of the plant. Something triggers it to produce branches that resemble one of its parents. Although a reversion does not harm the tree, if left alone it may eventually take over the entire plant. Prune it out to maintain the uniform appearance of the tree.

2. A witches' broom develops when a branch produces a tangle of immature-looking suckers covered with stunted, congested foliage. This is an alteration of normal growth caused by genetics, disease, insect attack, or unknown factor that changes normal branch development in this one place. Arborists and horticulturists often try to start new

varieties from this altered tissue, but homeowners usually prune them from the tree because they are unsightly.

PROBLEMS

Fall webworm nests may still be around. Open them up, prune them out of trees, or use an appropriate insecticide such as *Bacillus thuringiensis*.

Rodents such as mice and voles are also getting ready for colder weather. Delay renewing thin mulch around trees until after the ground freezes to force rodents to make their cozy nests elsewhere. Remove ground cover plantings within a foot or so of the trunk. Protect trunks of young trees by encasing them in hardware cloth or commercial tree-wrap products.

215

OCTOBER

TREES

PLANNING

Frost arrives in Ohio this month, signaling the beginning of dormancy. First, however, deciduous trees will excite us with fall color! As the foliage of various deciduous trees turns color over the next few weeks, visit your local arboretum or take a drive in the countryside, and enjoy the glorious color. Make a note of which trees might look good in your yard.

Season's end is a good time to update your tree records. Note major pruning, problems, and observations for each tree. Jot down flowering or fruiting dates as well. This information and a brief summary of the weather over the season may be helpful in the future.

If you do not have room in your own yard for trees, you can still plant one. Arboretums, botanic gardens, cemeteries, and many communities have memorial tree programs through which you can donate a tree in the name of a loved one. You pay for the tree and (usually) a sign or plaque with the name of the tree, the person, and other information. The staff plants and cares for it.

Shopping List: animal repellent, deer fencing

PLANNING

This is a good time to plant many tree species, as this is their best root-growing time. The ground is still friable, and there is no heat to stress them. Since the deciduous trees are dormant and have no leaves, they can devote their energy to producing a good root system to get a head start on next season. Many kinds of trees are dug this time of year and are available in nurseries.

The planting techniques previously outlined (see April) are designed to encourage trees to send their roots out into the soil beyond the planting hole as soon as possible.

• Cut off most of the burlap and twine after placing the tree, since they may be synthetic and resist decomposition.

• Cut off as much of the wire basket as possible, because most tree roots grow laterally rather than downward.

• Give the hole sloping sides to encourage outward root growth. Otherwise, the roots might prefer to stay in the hole, which will act like a container.

Fall is a glorious time in Ohio.

• To be sure the rootball does not sink below level, do not put loose soil at the bottom of the hole under the rootball. The roots must grow outward at the right depth.

• To force the tree to accept the new soil environment, use only plain soil when filling the hole (unless the soil is extremely heavy clay).

• Remove any excess soil at the top of the rootball to expose the root flare or crown so you can accurately determine the planting depth.

CARE

Wrap or otherwise protect the tender bark of young trees from possible damage by rodents and deer.

Mulch newly planted trees of all kinds through the winter. Spread a 2- to 3-inch layer of organic mulch such as chopped leaves, pine needles, wood chips, or commercial bark products on the soil over the root zone. Mulch is not intended to prevent the ground from freezing. It insulates it once it is frozen, so that fluctuating winter temperatures do not alternately thaw and then refreeze the ground and disturb tree roots. As it slowly breaks down, organic mulch also improves the fertility, texture, and aeration of the soil.

Trees that have evergreen ground cover plants growing over their root zones already enjoy a "living mulch."

WATERING

Evergreens of all kinds need good, moist soil going into winter. If rainfall is scarce, water the trees before the ground freezes when they will have more difficulty absorbing moisture from the soil. They will continue to transpire and lose moisture through their foliage all winter.

FERTILIZING

Fertilize any young trees that you did not fertilize last month. Skip those newly planted last spring and fall. This is an excellent time to fertilize established trees. A 3-2-1 ratio of nitrogen, phosphorous, and potassium is excellent. A common and readily available formula of 10-6-4 will be close to the suggested ratio. This fertilizer is quick in release and will leach into the root zone during the next three to four months. Using a broadcast method will be the most cost effective way to distribute the fertilizer. Other methods of tree fertilization include soil injection, vascular injection, and vertical mulching techniques. A certified arborist can assist with these application procedures.

PRUNING

Remove any limb that is rubbing against another, and prune lower branches that might be obstructing pedestrians or blocking a view. Prune injured or diseased branches on all trees as soon as possible.

PROBLEMS

Heavy thunderstorms and the occasional tornado that affect Ohio pose enormous threats to trees. Large, well-established specimens can lose limbs or literally fall over, their rootballs torn from oversaturated soil. Consider thinning the canopy of densely branched trees to reduce 'sail' resistance. Professional arborists will evaluate special trees for you. They may recommend cabling to support heavy, extended limbs, or install ground wires to protect against lightning.

Weeds like fall weather. Take advantage of any mild weather to deal with stubborn perennial weeds and invasive vines around trees. Spray them with an herbicide such as Roundup™, as directed on the label.

NOVEMBER

TREES

PLANNING

Roosting boxes shelter small birds when winter really closes in. Designed to be mounted on poles or trees, they are open at the bottom, their inside walls lined with pegs for perches. Many birds will seek refuge in them in severe winter weather; their collective body heat keeps a box warm and snug.

Plan to purchase a live-cut or living Christmas tree as soon as it is available for sale. The sooner you get it off the sales lot and home, the better. Since it may have been cut weeks ago, it is already drying out.

• Immediately cut off an inch or two from the base of the trunk of a live-cut tree, and set the tree in a pail of water outdoors in a sheltered spot. Check it often, and refill the pail when the water gets low. It is surprising how much water a tree will quickly take up.

• Set the soilball of a living tree in a large container such as a galvanized metal tub, and pour water over it. Lay damp burlap or some other covering over the top and sides of the rootball in its container to keep the rootball moist. Do not let it sit in water; just keep the soil moist.

Shopping List: bird food, new feeder, Christmas tree stand that has a large water reservoir,

Some trees, including pines, prefer acid soil; adjust your fertilizing regime accordingly.

hardware cloth or commercial tree trunk protectors

PLANTING

You can still plant a tree if the soil is not frozen. If you acquire one, it is better to plant it than to try to store it over the winter.

Overwinter small trees in pots, one of three ways:

1. in a cold frame or unheated garage or porch if the ground is frozen

2. buried in the ground, pot and all, and mulched

3. semi-buried in a sheltered place in the yard with wood chips,

bark mulch, or other organic material piled over the pot

Water if it is a dry winter.

CARE

Spray antidesiccant on the tops and undersides of the foliage of evergreens that are exposed to harsh winter sun and wind. A product such as Wilt-Pruf™ coats the needles on conifers and broader leaves on **hollies** and **rhododendrons** to reduce the amount of moisture they lose from transpiration. This coating does not harm the tree. It will eventually wear off, so a second spray will be necessary during the January thaw. Follow the directions on the product label.

WATERING

Water needled and broadleaf evergreens if there is no rain after two or three weeks.

FERTILIZING

Fertilize young trees over a year or two old now, if not done in October. Use a slow-acting, granular product formulated for trees and other woody plants. There are also products labeled specifically for acid-loving evergreens. Follow package instructions to determine the amounts.

PRUNING

The only pruning to do now until year's end is to remove broken or diseased branches. Anytime the protective bark covering of a tree is cracked or broken open, there is a potential for disease spores or insects to penetrate its interior. By promptly removing injured or diseased branches with a smooth cut through healthy tissue just beyond the branch collar, you will help the closure and compartmentalization process of the tree.

A LIVING CHRISTMAS TREE

The time to decide on which kind of Christmas tree you will have is this month, when trees go on sale. The idea of a living tree is very appealing. Rather than watching the gradual desiccation, decline, and death of this lovely plant during the holidays, why not consider one that can be planted outdoors in the yard to grow and prosper in the years ahead?

The reality of a living Christmas tree is something quite different.

The fact that you must keep the tree healthy during the holidays adds excitement to the experience.

• Because it is alive and transpiring, a living tree needs constant moisture—more so the minute it is brought indoors.

• A living tree has a heavy rootball. The more soil it has, the better for the tree, but the harder it is to move and maneuver in the house.

• Provide a large container for the rootball.

• To minimize stress on the tree, keep it in a heated room no more than three or four days.

• Acclimate it gradually by bringing it inside in steps over several days: first to an unheated porch, then to a cool indoor room, finally to the main display area.

• Keep the soil in the rootball and the wrappings moist at all times.

• Light the lights as little as possible.

• Reverse the acclimating process when it's time to take it back outdoors.

PROBLEMS

The following is a troubleshooting pre-winter checklist:

____Any bagworms on needled evergreens?

____Any perennial weed growth in garden beds?

____Any dangerous or hanging branches visible now that leaves have fallen from trees?

____All trunks of young trees protected against rodents and deer?

____Any weedy vines climbing trees?

____Any ragged stubs where branches have broken off?

____Any trees that do not have a protective winter mulch or ground cover planting?

____Gutters free of late-falling deciduous tree leaves and evergreen needles?

DECEMBER

TREES

PLANNING

If you decide to have a living Christmas tree this year, make arrangements ahead of time for planting it. Choose a sunny site that is roomy enough for the tree at maturity. Plan carefully to assure it will survive the indoor experience in good health.

Have your camera ready to record fresh snowfalls on evergreen boughs out in the yard. Take pictures of the lovely branching patterns of deciduous trees now that the leaves have fallen. Photographs are a great way to enjoy the season in your yard and consider how you might improve it.

Shopping List: tub to hold rootball of living Christmas tree, antidesiccant spray, animal-repellent spray

PLANTING

Dig a hole for transplanting a living Christmas tree before the holidays if the soil is likely to be frozen at planting time. Make a saucer-shaped hole, twice as wide as the rootball on the tree and exactly as deep as the rootball is high. Cover the hole and the fill soil nearby with straw or insulating mulch to keep the soil from freezing. Throw a tarp over the hole and soil to keep them relatively dry. If the ground is not frozen, any balled-and-burlapped trees can be planted this month.

CARE

To ensure that a living Christmas tree does not dry out, set it up for display in a heated house for a maximum of only three or four days. (See November Helpful Hints.)

WATERING

Mulch or snow cover should keep the soil over tree root zones moist even if rain is scarce. Deciduous trees do not use as much moisture when they are dormant. Check evergreens. Soaker hoses covered with mulch are not affected by winter weather.

FERTILIZING

No fertilizing is necessary this month.

PRUNING

Although this is not official pruning time, it is a great time to lightly trim **hollies**, **pines**, and other evergreens to acquire boughs and cones for holiday decorations. Put the cut ends in tepid water immediately so that they take up moisture. Keep them in water until it is time to use them.

Spray wreaths and other live greens with an antidesiccant to reduce drying out during the festivities. Do not use live greens around fireplaces, lighted candles, and other potential fire hazards.

PROBLEMS

Mice may be attracted to the thin tender bark and stems of young trees when their normal food sources are under snow or out of season. Tall wire cages may be necessary to protect young trees if deer are a major concern. Stamping down the snow around tree stems may reduce access by burrowing voles. Try sprays that repel by taste or odor too. Respray as recommended on the product label. Alternate products to maintain effectiveness.

Strong winter winds threaten young and newly planted trees in exposed sites. Either stake them or erect wind barriers of burlap or other material to block the worst of its force. Do not use plastic.

VINES & GROUND COVERS

Beyond their individual beauty, beyond even their collective beauty in a garden design, plants contribute many things to residential landscapes. This is why even non-gardening homeowners value and enjoy plants in their yards. Plants play a practical as well as an aesthetic role, as they improve a yard's comfort, health, and value. They can also make a yard easier to care for—and no plants do this better than those that function as ground covers, especially those that climb or crawl. Vines, grasses, and other plants that grow well planted in large masses are enormously useful for solving common landscape problems that make yard care difficult or even unsafe.

SOLVING YARD PROBLEMS

Too much lawn to care for? A patch of evergreen ground cover is ideal for reducing lawn size, yet retaining the green look. Plant liriope, pachysandra, vinca, or something similar in generous islands out in the existing lawn to reduce the overall turf area. Create groves of ferns or ornamental grasses in turf areas, or fill in remote or undeveloped areas of a large property with naturalized plantings of wildflowers.

Tough terrain? Steep slopes or uneven grades on properties make mowing lawns difficult and dangerous, and the unevenness promotes soil erosion wherever turf breaks down. Replace the

turfgrass with a self-reliant perennial ground cover plant with a deep root system that holds the soil. Use smaller, finer-textured plants such as liriope or lily-of-the-valley in small areas. Use larger plants such as daylilies or ornamental grasses in broader areas. Often low-growing shrubs such as carpet-type junipers, azaleas, or dwarf deutzia are effective on hill-sides. Choose sun-lovers for a sunny bank, shade-tolerant plants for slopes that face north or for those under trees.

Tree surface roots? Beeches and certain other trees typically have surface roots. Others develop them because the soil is so compacted their roots must gravitate to its surface to obtain oxygen. Piling soil on them endangers the tree. Instead, plant ivy, minor bulbs, or tiarella among the roots to obscure them, yet allow them the air they need. Shallow-rooted plants minimize disturbance to the tree roots.

Too much shade? Trying to grow turfgrass in shade is an exercise in futility. Plant instead a ground cover plant that toler-ates shade.

Use annuals such as impa-tiens, begonias, or coleus for a colorful and different summer look in that spot every year, then mulch the area with chopped leaves in the winter. Or go with a more permanent perennial

plant such as evergreen helle-bores. Try moss if the soil is both compacted and acidic.

Tree and shrubs dry out quickly? Only recently has it been understood how shallow the root systems of many trees and shrubs really are—typically only 8 to 12 inches deep. Those in poor soil are at constant risk of drying out whenever rainfall is scarce. A living mulch of ground cover plants is excellent at helping the soil absorb and retain moisture.

Use evergreen, perennial plants such as liriope, lamium, vinca, or pachysandra, which do not need much moisture for themselves.

Difficult soil? The typical resi-dential property has soil that is less than ideal. Some areas may be too sandy, others too clayey. Some may have that special mix called builder's fill, which features construction debris! Low parts of the yard may be chronically damp and boggy. Again, ground cover plants can come to the rescue. Carpet these areas with plants that appreciate the unique soil conditions, making a virtue of necessity. Use ornamental grasses, potentilla, and yucca in sandy soil. Use red twig dog-wood, astilbe, iris, Virginia sweetspire, or forget-me-nots in the low-lying wet areas.

Unsightly ripening bulb foliage in spring? The gradually

ripening foliage of tulips, daf-fodils, hyacinths, and others always presents a problem. Many plants used as ground covers are effective at obscur-ing the unsightly foliage until it is time to clean it up. Evergreen ivy or pachysandra foliage will complement the bulbs during their bloom period and then cover their dying foliage. Herbaceous plants such as hosta, ferns, or sweet woodruff emerge just in time to cover the bulb foliage as it dies back.

Stem or trunk damage on woody plants? Landscapes are easier to maintain with power tools, but more and more trees and shrubs are sustaining injury from string-trimmers and mow-ers. A simple nick in tender bark can reduce the plant's life expectancy. Replace the turf around the stems of trees and shrubs with a ground cover planting to create a barrier so that passing equipment cannot get close enough to harm them.

Compacted soil? Unless soil is aerated periodically, it gradu-ally becomes compacted from the weight of pounding rain, foot traffic, or construction equipment. Areas between step-ping stones, paths where the kids or the mail carrier take shortcuts, and edges of walks and driveways where traffic strays from the pavement are chronically compacted. Carpet these areas with low-growing

Hostas (here shown with maidenhair fern and Solomon's seal) make a great ground cover.

plants or ornamental grasses that cope with compacted soil better than turfgrasses do.

Unsightly areas? Every property has its eyesores—both temporary and permanent. Once again, ground cover plants and grasses can save the day. Let vining plants trail over crumbling walls or fences, decaying stumps, and rock piles. Send them up drainpipes and over utility boxes. Use foliage plants to obscure drains, septic zones, and air-conditioner compressors.

Limited growing space? Many newer homes are located on smaller properties, and many older ones have lost their sunny expanses as trees have matured. The best way to take maximum advantage of limited growing space is to grow plants vertically. Use flowering vines to provide color for the landscape, as well as vertical interest.

Yard lacks interest? The absence of traditional garden beds does not mean a yard must have boring green grass and a few unexciting shrubs.

Planting ground covers is another way to add color, texture, and variety to a property. They are, in most cases, relatively care-free. Many are essentially the same plants found in a mixed flower border, or even a vegetable garden. Climbing up or covering the ground to solve landscape problems, they still attract birds, butterflies, and beneficial insects and enhance the entire property.

JANUARY
VINES & GROUND COVERS

PLANNING

After the activities of the December holidays, it's time to relax and enjoy some reading. The pile of catalogs that has been accumulating for weeks beckons, so why not indulge? Among the excellent choices are lots of perennial and annual plants of all kinds that can be used as ground covers or vines. Think about how interesting it might be to use plants that you routinely use in a mixed flower border, massed instead as a ground cover. The plants will look striking while they protect the soil.

Study your winter landscape from windows in various rooms in your house.

• Is there some vertical interest in the form of tall grasses or woody vine stems wrapped around arbors or posts?

• Is there some foliage color and texture on the ground, relieving a unexciting expanse of lawn?

• Is there the sound and movement of the wind stirring brittle grass stems?

Vines are popular these days, exceedingly adaptable, and lovely for smaller properties where horizontal growing space is limited. They can offer architectural interest, foliage color, flowers, berries, pods, food and shelter for birds, and screening for privacy. Why not make a New Year's resolution to grow at least one new vine this year?

PLANTING

No planting is necessary this month.

CARE

One of the great things about **ornamental grasses** and other perennial plants that are suitable for use as ground covers is that they are self-reliant. If they are hardy in Ohio (check the zone number on the plant label or in a book on garden and landscape plants), they will not need additional care in the cold and frost.

It is a good idea to mulch the soil in beds where ground cover plants (or bulbs) were planted last season and have not yet knitted together. A 2- or 3-inch (maximum) layer of organic mulch such as chopped leaves, pine needles, or wood chips will buffer extreme temperature fluctuations, which sometimes cause the soil to heave plants to the surface. Make sure vines are securely attached to their supports. If you planted **pansies** in the fall to make a headstart ground cover, mulch or snow cover will protect the **pansies**, too.

Spray antidesiccant spray on evergreen ground covers such as **carpet junipers**, **skimmia,** and **English ivy** that are exposed to harsh, bright winter sun and wind. This will help them retain moisture and prevent their foliage from drying and turning brown. In areas where there is dependable snow cover, this is not necessary.

WATERING

If the late fall and early winter have been dry, water recently planted evergreen vining plants, as well as evergreen perennials and shrubs that serve as ground covers, will need watering. This is especially true if they are not mulched. They are still transpiring through their leaves, which cause them to lose moisture and dry out. Take advantage of a winter thaw, and run the hose on the soil for a while.

FERTILIZING

No fertilizing is necessary this month.

PRUNING

Pruning time does not officially begin until next month, but be sure to remove broken branches any time you discover them.

Clean cuts prevent further tears on the bark and will close faster. Cut back any branches of vines that are whipping around in winter wind because they are too long or will not stay attached to their support.

Ornamental grasses still look attractive in the winter landscape. Delay cutting them back for a few more weeks.

PROBLEMS

Rodents are always a potential problem during the winter. They nest in ground cover plantings or in the mulch at the base of woody vines. Their chewing on the tender bark of woody vines and ground covers can girdle stems and kill the plants. To reduce the problem, delay mulching until the ground freezes hard, forcing them to nest elsewhere. Install wire wraps around vulnerable stems, or spray them with repellent.

Deer are the other big problem. If they are in the area, they are on the lookout for tender leaves, berries, and shoots to sustain them. Spray vulnerable patches of ground cover with

Deer often avoid plants that have fuzzy leaves or aromatic stems; try planting artemisia as a ground-cover if you have a deer problem.

HELPFUL HINTS

Because they are naturally vertically oriented, vining plants need little encouragement to climb. The trick to growing them successfully is to match each vine to a support that displays it attractively yet is sturdy enough to hold it securely until season's end, when many vines are heavily burdened with multitudes of branching stems weighted with blooms and/or seeds. As a rule, annual vines such as **morning glory** develop less weight than perennials such as **wisteria**. Make sure the support is sited where light conditions are correct for the particular vines you plant. Here are some suggestions for supports:

- arbor
- downspout
- fence
- light post

- mailbox post
- pergola
- shrub
- tree

- utility pole
- tree stump
- trellis
- wall

repellent spray. Alternating products that repel by smell or by taste every two weeks is more effective than using the same one repeatedly. Follow the directions on the product labels. Lay chicken wire over beds of ground cover, or use to fashion temporary fencing around vines and low shrubs.

FEBRUARY

VINES & GROUND COVERS

 PLANNING

Winter is a good time to study gardening topics that you are too busy to research during the season. Make notes in your journal for later reference. You may need to learn more about deer; maybe a fence will be necessary. If a review of your garden notebook indicates deer problems in several previous seasons, it is time to address the situation before you lose too many more plants.

Barriers are the only truly effective way to control deer. Some work by simply screening the view so deer are not aware of the menu in your yard. Others are so tall that deer cannot jump them. In the face of heavy pressure by starving deer, the most effective fences are polynetting around the perimeter of your entire property, or electrified fences. A combination is the best.

If there's not much snow, late winter is a good time to put up deer fencing. The leaves are off the trees and plants have died back, so access is easier, and it's easier to see where to erect the poles or fasten netting to existing trees. Remember to gate the driveway, too!

Visit a local arboretum or botanic garden, and get to know winter-blooming vines and ground cover plants such as **winterhazel** (*Corylopsis pauciflora*), **winter jasmine** (*Jasminum nudiflorum*), **windflower anemone** (*Anemone blanda*), and **Christmas rose** and **lenten rose** (*Helleborus* sp.).

 PLANTING

The only planting that might go on this month will occur indoors toward month's end. Get a jump on the season by starting annual vines from seed under lights, rather than waiting to direct-sow them outdoors in April or May. A head start is not necessary for many annuals, because they germinate quickly once the soil is warm outdoors. Others, such as **moonflower**, are slower to germinate outdoors, so it helps to get them going early. To raise sturdy, healthy seedlings you will need some special equipment:

- seeds
- peat pots or other containers
- soilless potting medium
- adjustable fluorescent lights
- heat mat (optional)
- some counter space or a seed-starting table (see Annuals January)

Here are the steps:

1. Fill each peat pot with moistened soilless potting mix.

2. Drop one or two seeds in each pot, and cover with more mix.

Thin extra seedlings so there is just one per pot.

3. Water each pot, then set all of them on a tray for easy transport.

4. Cover the peat pots with plastic wrap to prevent the mix from drying out.

5. Give the pots warmth from a heat mat, radiator top, or incandescent light until they sprout.

6. Remove the plastic, and set the tray of peat pots under fluorescent lights that can be adjusted so they are consistently about 2 inches above the seedlings as they grow.

7. Snip off the second, less vigorous seedling so there is just one per pot.

8. Water when the potting mix seems dry.

Also by month's end, **pansies** will start to appear at garden centers. Pick some up if you didn't plant them last fall. Plant them as soon as you can work the soil. They can go into pots sooner.

CARE

Look closely to see if bulbs are beginning to emerge in patches of **ivy**, **vinca**, or **pachysandra** as the month progresses. They add welcome color to the yard, and later the ground cover plants will hide their ripening foliage. Remove any large fallen leaves from last fall that may threaten to smother their progress.

Check **pansies** planted last fall to be sure they are not smothered by mulch. They will be raring to go.

WATERING

No watering is necessary this month.

FERTILIZING

Late winter is a good time to fertilize woody vines and ground cover plantings, if you did not do so last fall. Use a granular, slow-acting product labeled "nursery" or "for trees and shrubs." Sprinkle it on the soil over each plant's roots as directed on the label for the rain or snow to soak in. Well-established vines and shrubby ground covers such as **junipers** do not need regular annual fertilizing. By all means, do not encourage **wisteria**! It overgrows automatically and does not need more nutrition.

PRUNING

If you did not cut back your **ornamental grasses** last fall or during the winter, do so in the next few weeks. If left alone, the tall stems will flop over and provide a self-mulch as new shoots push their way up from the clump to form this season's plant. Cutting them back will make for a neater plant in a garden setting. If you wait too long, you risk inadvertently cutting the tops of the new shoots as well.

PROBLEMS

Deer will continue to visit. If your defenses are not in place, refer to January. If they do damage, take notes. Record which plants seem to be their favorites and which ones they ignore. Note their location in the yard. Spray repellent on remaining targets.

Rabbits do their share of damage to a winter landscape, too. They might nibble the tender bark of a young shrub or vine all the way around the stem. They strip fleshier-stemmed plants apart, sometimes nibbling off the tender tips. Wrap exposed stems in chicken wire, or spray them with repellent, as directed on the product label.

MARCH
VINES & GROUND COVERS

If you have a spot that you don't want to mow, then an appropriate groundcover such as pachysandra can be a landscape solution.

 PLANNING

Now is the time to choose plants to cover those areas in the yard where grass won't grow or locations you do not want to mow. Traditional choices are the low-growing, tough, permanent evergreen standbys such as **English ivy**, **liriope**, or **pachysandra**. They are great for under trees where there is shade and frequent replanting of annuals may disturb roots. There are also lots of other kinds of plants that, planted en masse, can make great ground covers:

• Annuals are a great choice for sunny sites where flowering plants thrive. They bloom with gusto all season, providing color and sometimes fragrance. They attract butterflies and other wildlife, as well. **'Purple Wave' petunias** and **trailing nasturtiums** are examples of trailing annuals, particularly effective for covering the ground.

• **Moss** is great for shade areas with chronically acidic, compacted soil. Rather than fight **moss** where it has appeared on your property, encourage it!

• Many herbs are great at spreading and blocking weeds. They smell good where you step on them. **Creeping thyme**, **oregano**, and **globe basil** are good choices.

• Sometimes food plants are good ground cover choices. Ornamental and edible plants such as **alpine strawberries**, **low-bush blueberries**, and **lettuce** need sun.

• Shrubs do a great job covering the ground with foliage, fruit, and flowers. They hold the soil and prevent erosion on slopes. Consider **carpet junipers**, **cotoneaster**, **dwarf deutzia**, and a host of others.

 PLANTING

Sweet peas prefer chilly weather, just as their edible cousins do. Plant these vines at the same time you plant **peas** in the food garden—near the end of the month.

Shrubs that come by mail are likely to be bare-root. Keep them moist until the soil is workable, then plant them over the area they are intended to cover. Follow the steps for planting shrubs (see Shrubs March).

 CARE

Mulch newly planted ground cover plantings to discourage weeds until the plants have a chance to knit together and cover the soil. Spread a 2- or 3-inch layer of chopped leaves, pine needles, or wood chips over the soil between the plants.

Dig up and divide overgrown clumps of **ornamental grasses** as their new shoots begin to appear.

First cut back last year's stems if you haven't done so already. Then:

1. Dig down in the soil around the grass clump until you dislodge it from the soil.

2. Lift the entire rootball out of the ground.

3. Cut it into manageable rooted sections by slicing down through it with a sharp spade.

4. Replant one, then give away the extra sections.

Perennial vines resume growth following dormancy soon. Check trellises and other supports to be sure they are ready to meet the challenge of vigorous vines. Be forewarned: the first year perennial vines sleep, the second year they creep, and the third year they leap!

WATERING

It is more than likely that the soil on your property will be too wet rather than too dry this month. If it is dry, water newly planted **pansies** and **sweet peas**, as well as any biennials and plants planted last fall. Mulched plants will survive a bit of dry weather just fine.

FERTILIZING

Well-established beds of evergreen ground covers do not require annual fertilizing. Com-

HELPFUL HINTS

To get rapid ground coverage:

1. Plant annuals. Perennials take at least one season to get established before they start to spread.

2. Plant large plants—either shrubs or more-mature plants in larger pots from the garden center.

3. Plant lots of plants—small plants close together cover the ground well.

4. Plant aggressive spreaders. This is a calculated risk, because most do not know when to put on the brakes!

pared to turfgrasses, they need less nutrition, and the leaves that fall down among the foliage of the planting provide some nutrients when they decompose.

PRUNING

Mow beds of **liriope** to cut off the evergreen foliage. Set the mower at its highest setting to avoid inadvertently cutting new **liriope** shoots or the emerging foliage of bulbs that may also be planted in the bed. Mulching-type mowers cut the **liriope** foliage into small pieces that fall back down on the bed to serve as a mulch and a source of nitrogen for new growth. Mowing also renews **vinca**, **ivy**, and **pachysandra** every few years.

PROBLEMS

Rot diseases are common in certain low-growing ground covers

that grow in soil that does not drain well. **Ajuga** is an example. Every so often, patches of it will "melt" away. Usually enough remains to spread and fill in again with time. Organic matter or fine gravel added to clay soil at planting time helps soil drain better to reduce rot.

Slugs become active before we expect them. The trick to controlling them is to put out traps early. They overwinter in moist, acidic organic debris in shady areas in the yard. Set out a shallow pie plate or a commercial slug "bar" trap filled with beer (they are attracted by the yeast) in the area where vulnerable ground cover plants such as **hostas** will be emerging. Check it daily for slug bodies to pinpoint when they start feeding. Set out more traps (a slight distance from vulnerable plants) to lure more slugs once you know they are active.

APRIL
VINES & GROUND COVERS

PLANNING

Lawn-mowing season begins this month. Think about reducing the size of your lawn and the amount of time, energy, and money it costs. Replace some of the turfgrasses with other ground cover plants. Patches of different plants provide texture and color variety to the landscape. By adding to the plant diversity in your yard, you will create shelter and support for more beneficial insects for a healthier, lower-maintenance environment.

One area where a permanent ground cover planting rather than turfgrass makes sense is on a steep slope. It is dangerous and difficult to mow such sites. Another area is under trees and shrubs. When planted in a ring over their root zones, ground covers fend off injurious mowers and weed trimmers. Ground cover plants do not compete with trees at the same level as turfgrass.

PLANTING

Before the month is too far along, plant **ornamental grasses** in beds, borders, or areas where they are to serve as ground covers. They are easiest to manage when their new shoots are just starting to emerge:

1. Remove weeds, then aerate the soil by digging and turning over shovelsful to break it up.

2. Add some organic matter to the soil if it is clayey to help it drain well. There's no need to add fertilizer, as **ornamental grasses** (unlike turfgrasses) do not need high nutrition.

3. Rake the soil smooth, and mark where each grass plant will go. In ground cover plantings, make sure they are equidistant from each other and spaced to allow for their mature spread.

4. Dig a hole for each plant as deep as its pot is tall. If the area is sloped, dig the hole straight up and down so the plant will sit vertically.

5. Slide the plant from its nursery pot after a tap on its bottom. Set the plant in the hole, and fill in with plain soil dug from the hole.

6. Water well for good root-to-soil contact. Mulch between plantings to discourage weeds until the grass foliage grows and shades the soil between the plants.

CARE

Established evergreen ground cover plantings of **ivy**, **pachysandra**, **liriope**, and **vinca** need very little routine care, but periodically they will need renovation.

Mow them every six or eight years—more often if the plants lack their customary vigor and color.

1. Set the mulching mower at its highest setting, and mow to cut off the bulk of the ground cover foliage.

2. Topdress the exposed tangle of soil, bare stems, and chopped foliage with some organic matter. Compost, chopped leaves, topsoil, or mushroom soil will do fine.

3. While it is not essential, you might also sprinkle a small amount of granular, slow-acting fertilizer over the area.

4. Water if it does not rain.

In a few weeks the ground cover plants will generate fresh new foliage and look terrific.

WATERING

This is the month that is famous for its showers, so it is tempting to assume there will be no need to drag around the hose yet. But if it has been an unusually dry winter, your plants are not mulched, or you have newly planted areas—and two weeks pass without significant rainfall—water ground covers and vines in dry soil.

FERTILIZING

As planting season gets under-way, incorporate some granular, slow-acting fertilizer into the soil each time you plant new vines and ground cover plants. This will provide consistent, uniform nutrition over many weeks.

PRUNING

Before you are quite ready, leaves will start to emerge along the woody stems of your **hybrid clematis**. Use them as an indication of how healthy the old wood is. Cut back the stems as low to the ground as you can and still have some leaves sprouting. This will stimulate vigorous growth and flowering in another month or two.

Thin out dead and injured stems and branches from perennial vines that have endured winter. **Kiwi**, **autumn clematis**, and others respond with vigor to late-winter pruning.

This month begins the **wisteria** pruning season. For this first pruning, just remove excess growth along the main stems—cut back to the already formed flower buds on the spurs on last year's wood.

HELPFUL HINTS

As a group, ornamental plants are more adaptable than turf-grasses as ground covers. Ornamental plants:
- are more disease-resistant.
- need less fertilizer and water.
- are available for every situation—sun, shade, wet, dry.
- provide a variety of textures, colors, and habits.
- shelter more kinds of beneficial insects.
- prevent soil compaction.
- discourage weeds.
- protect trees and shrubs from being injured by mowers and trimmers.

PROBLEMS

Shade presents a problem some-times because it seems as if most plants prefer sun, or at least significant light. Increase available light under trees by limbing them up or thinning their branch canopy. This will allow more light to reach the soil.

Weeds emerge as enthusiastically this month as do desirable plants. Pull them when they are young after a rain moistens the soil. It is impossible to get the entire root of taprooted dandelions and thistle. Spot-treat them with herbicide such as Round-up™, which systematically kills the entire plant.

Spot treat dandelions and thistle with an herbicide that kills them to their roots.

MAY
VINES & GROUND COVERS

PLANNING

Vines add a new dimension to the yard. They also represent an opportunity to try new plants without taking up a lot of space. Many perennial and annual flowering plants are willing climbers. Annual vines grow fast and bloom steadily all season, but they have to be replaced each year. Perennial vines survive winters and grow thicker and stronger every year. Typically, they bloom for a short time, then produce fruit later in the season. Think about how you can use their attributes to your advantage:

- screening a view or noise
- creating shade for a shade garden
- disguising a drainpipe or other eyesore
- attracting hummingbirds and butterflies
- adding drama and four-season interest to the yard

Plan ahead. Any plant raised or kept indoors will need a period of gradual adjustment to the outdoors before planting. The acclimating process takes a week or ten days because the weather is still likely to be erratic. Take flats or trays of plants outdoors for increasing lengths of time during mild days, returning them to the house at night.

PLANTING

The appearance of young transplants at the garden center signals that planting time is near. By mid-month, seedlings you started indoors are also ready to be planted outdoors.

Once the danger of frost has passed and the soil has dried out and warmed a bit, start preparing the soil for planting. Plant annuals intended for ground covers as you would any annual (see Annuals May).

Perennial vines and shrubs will probably be in sizable containers in which their roots have become accustomed to soilless mix and lots of fertilizer. Planting them in the existing soil may slow the roots from growing outward. To prevent this and ease their transition, loosen the roots when you remove each plant from its container. Mix any potting medium that falls away with the regular soil. After setting the plants in their holes, fill them in with this soil combination, and firm it around each plant before watering (see Perennials May).

Most annual vines are best grown by seed, directly sown where they are to grow. Follow the instructions on the seed packet. It does not take long or take many seeds to start some **morning glories** or **hyacinth (lablab) beans**. Certain favorites such as **moonflower** take additional time to germinate.

CARE

Mulch newly planted plants over 6 inches tall with a 2- to

Daylilies like this 'Stella d'Oro' can be used as ground cover.

3-inch layer of organic material such as chopped leaves or shredded bark.

Make sure trellises are fastened out from walls several inches to allow air circulation behind the vine. This will protect wall surfaces from mildew and marks from the vine. Trellises should be detachable to allow for painting or repairing the supporting wall surface.

Large clumps of **hostas** and **daylilies** used as ground covers usually do not need dividing.

WATERING

Water all newly planted plants if it does not rain regularly. If the plants are mulched, the soil will not dry out so fast. Use a moisture meter probe or garden trowel to check the soil at a depth of 2 to 3 inches for annuals and perennial transplants.

FERTILIZING

If you did not add some granular, slow-acting, all-purpose fertilizer to the soil when you prepared it before transplanting new plants, sprinkle a little on the mulch around them now for the rain to soak in. Established ground cover plantings and **ornamental grasses** do not need supplemental nutrition.

HOW VINES CLIMB

- "Clingers" attach with anchorage roots generated from stems. They can damage mortar if it is soft or old.
- "Grabbers" latch on to the nearest support with special tendrils they produce from their leaf stems. They like relatively thin supports such as wire or netting.
- "Sprawlers" lean against or lie across whatever is handy. Stems must be fastened with twine or woven between rungs of a support.
- "Twiners" wrap themselves around supports. They need very substantial, sturdy structures.

 ## PRUNING

Perennial vines will already be off and running! Prune off dead stems and twig tips injured in winter dieback. Clip off unruly stems to train the development of the vine and encourage fullness.

Trailing ground cover plants such as **vinca** and **English ivy** enjoy a growth spurt now. Cut back any stems that venture out into the lawn or up a nearby tree, to keep them in bounds. If **ivy** is growing on the house, trim it so that it does not encroach on chimneys, windows, or gutters at the roofline.

 ## PROBLEMS

Aphids show up pretty early in the season. They fancy the tender flowerbuds and the succulent new growth at the tips of plant stems and vine tendrils. Until beneficial insects arrive to deal with them, pinch off aphid-infested plant tips, or wash off the pests with a strong water spray from the hose. Insecticidal soap or a product containing Neem oil is also a very effective control.

Tent caterpillar nests in trees shelter tiny caterpillars. These larvae will soon leave the tough, weblike nests to feed on vine and ground cover plant foliage. Clip the supporting branches of the nests to remove them, and put them in the trash. Products containing Bt (*Bacillus thuringiensis*) or carbaryl will also provide effective control.

JUNE
VINES & GROUND COVERS

 PLANNING

As newly planted vines begin to grow, some pre-planning will prevent frustration.

• Ensure that a supporting structure is in place and is appropriate for the type of vine you have.

• Examine the bolts, eye hooks, or other type of fasteners that you use to hold a wire matrix or wooden trellis out from the wall. Make sure they are secure.

• Check the footings on arbors and pergolas that must bear the weight of a heavy **wisteria** or **climbing hydrangea**.

• Have soft twine or cloth ties handy for tying the stems of any vine that leans to its support as soon as it reaches it. Proper training now saves time and trouble later.

 PLANTING

By now it is safe to bring tender annual or tropical vines outdoors to spend the summer. Acclimate them gradually to the fresh air and sunshine. Plant **mandevilla**, **plumbago**, or **bougainvillea** in the ground next to a mailbox post or other structure it can climb or cover. If you intend to keep a plant in a pot, remove it to check the roots.

If the roots are winding around the base of the soil ball, it's time for repotting.

• Choose a somewhat larger pot—but no more than 2 inches wider—with a drainage hole.

• Fill it with fresh soilless mix, and add some complete granular, slow-acting fertilizer.

• Set the plant in the pot at the same depth it was in its previous pot.

• Fill in with mix, and then water well.

If you do not intend to position the pot near a post or fixture for it to climb, insert a stake into the pot to make a free-standing vine.

Here's a different idea. Try setting a potted vine on top of a sunny wall or deck edge and letting it fall downward instead of climb upward. **Sweet potato vine, jasmine**, and others look lovely when displayed this way.

 CARE

Expect young vine stems to take a while to grow up to the bottom of their supporting structure and grab hold. Temporarily stake them to train them in the right direction until they are able to grab on or you can tie them on.

Some ground cover plants are valued more for their foliage than for their flowers. To maintain foliage production and a fresh look, routinely pinch off the new young flowers of **coleus, lamb's ears,** and **artemisias**.

Pull up any **pansies** that did ground cover duty early in the season! As the heat arrives, they become lank and leggy. Replace them with heat-loving annuals such as **creeping zinnias, nasturtiums, portulaca, salvias,** or **lantana** 'New Gold'.

 WATERING

If rain is scarce, newly planted ground covers and vines may need extra water—especially if they are not mulched. Established plants and **ornamental grasses** should be fine for at least two weeks between rains or watering. Vines in pots and planters will need checking frequently because soilless potting medium dries out quickly in the hot sun.

 FERTILIZING

The dose of granular, slow-acting fertilizer mixed into their soil or added to their containers during repotting provides sufficient nutrition to vines and ground cover plants for the season. It releases nutrients gradually over the number of weeks indicated on the package label. Resist the temptation to fertilize more, which will stimulate rampant foliage growth at the expense of flowers. More pruning and maintenance will be necessary, and the risk of attack by pest insects will be greater.

PRUNING

After the **wisteria** finishes blooming, it will generate a lot of leafy stems. In no time it will engulf its support and anything in its vicinity! Prune this excess greenery back before the buds for next year start to form in July. Try to shape and control the size and direction of the vine until the next pruning in late summer.

Regularly deadhead faded **daylily** blossoms to improve their appearance and promote rebloom over the season. Pull or cut drying stems.

PROBLEMS

Slugs are out in force by now in the moist, shady parts of your yard. Use traps (see March) to catch as many as you can. Sprinkle diatomaceous earth (DE) powder over the soil in a circle around vulnerable plants. Slugs will be injured if they try to slither over these sharp microscopic particles. Slug products containing iron phosphate will also be effective.

Wisteria is a very heavy vine; make sure you have adequate support for it.

HELPFUL HINTS

Ground cover plants need not be trailing and low growing. Almost any plant will cover the soil when planted en masse. Whether it is annual or perennial, evergreen or deciduous, shrub, herb, wildflower, or bulb, a good ground cover plant has certain attributes:

1. It grows and spreads fairly rapidly, but in a disciplined manner and is easily removed if it outgrows its intended space.

2. It does not require constant pruning, watering, and fertilizing.

3. It holds up over many years (or, if an annual, over the entire season) with minimum care.

4. It is ornamental in one or more ways—foliage, flowers, or fruits.

Aphids are everywhere, but in a healthy landscape, beneficial insect populations are sufficient to control them. Pick off infested leaves and flowers to reduce their numbers.

JULY
VINES & GROUND COVERS

PLANNING

This month the areas converted to attractive, relatively low-maintenance ground cover plantings are becoming effective. You will appreciate having less lawn to mow.

Where annual vines have stretched to several feet tall, they define and enclose spaces for quiet and privacy. Those covering light-colored walls are reducing the reflected light and heat to help keep things cool around a pool or patio. Watch for hummingbirds around the **mandevilla**, **morning glory**, **honeysuckle**, and **trumpet creepers** that flaunt tubular, brightly colored blossoms.

Remember to take some photographs of the early-summer landscape, and record what's blooming in your journal.

PLANTING

Soon it will be too hot to plant perennial vines and ground cover shrubs or ornamental grasses without risk. Although they are available in containers at the garden center or nursery all summer, they will have difficulty establishing new roots and top growth in the heat and possible drought. If you do not have

them in the ground shortly after the Fourth of July weekend, consider waiting until fall.

Annuals planted for ground cover duty this month will have to play catch-up. Shade them from the sun for a few days after planting, and mulch them well. Those planted in late May are already knitting together.

CARE

Certain ground cover plants have difficulty with heat. After flowering and by mid-month, cool shade-lovers such as **lily-of-the-valley**, **deadnettle**, and **sweet woodruff** begin to look shabby and may collapse and give up. **Tiarella**, or **foamflower**, may melt away in patches. Clean up dead leaves, and cut back limp stems to help them regenerate fresh foliage or wait out the weather in dormancy. Fortunately, annual plants such as **Madagascar periwinkle**, **impatiens**, and **trailing petunias** love this weather.

Keep an eye on the vines. Tie or wrap rapidly extending stems to their supports before they reach out and embrace some neighboring plants. **Moonflower** vines and tropicals such as **mandevilla** need major heat before they are interested in growing and blooming.

WATERING

New, mulched ground cover patches and those that are well established in decent soil can go a week to ten days without rain before they need watering. **Ornamental grasses** can go longer. If it is terribly hot, check soil moisture every few days. Even plants in shaded areas, such as **ferns**, may dry out because nearby trees take most of the soil moisture and their leaf canopies block light rains.

FERTILIZING

No fertilizing is necessary this month.

PRUNING

After large-flowered **clematis** blooms in June, cut back the stems at least halfway to stimulate possible repeat bloom later in the summer. Alternatively, just a light pruning of rampant stems will neaten its appearance and leave some of the interesting seedpods to enjoy.

Climbing hydrangea takes several years to start producing flowers. Once it does, prune it each year just after it blooms. Cut back branching stems that extend outward more than 15 inches from the main stem. Otherwise, they will become so heavy that their collective weight may pull the vine from its support altogether.

Pinch back **impatiens** stems that may be growing leggy. This will keep the plants bushy and compact so they do a better job of covering the ground.

PROBLEMS

Japanese beetles are apparent this month. Since they are so punctual, if you record the date, you will know when to expect them in your yard every year. In no time it will be clear what their favorite plants are, so patrol that area frequently with a jar of soapy water. Knock them from the foliage into the jar. They do not bother **ornamental grasses**.

Scale is likely to appear on certain **hollies** and **euonymus** species. Watch for the waxy or whitish bumps under the leaves and along the stems. Spray all surfaces of affected plants thoroughly with light horticultural oil to smother the insects.

HELPFUL HINTS

People assume that **English ivy** strangles and kills the trees when it climbs up their trunks. So many dead trees are covered with ropes of **ivy** stems, it seems like a logical conclusion—but **ivy** is not the culprit. Typically, the trees are already dead before the **ivy** adopts them as a convenient place to climb.

English ivy is not a twiner. It does not climb by wrapping itself around the trunks; it crawls up tree bark by means of its anchorage roots. The only time **ivy** might threaten harm to a tree is if it climbs into its foliage canopy and spreads over it thickly. By denying it essential sunlight, the **ivy** could conceivably harm the tree. Since **ivy** prefers partial shade, it is not likely to do this on large trees.

Spider mites thrive in hot, dry weather. Often they are associated with stressed plants such as **ivy**, **azaleas**, and **junipers**. They cause pale stippling on leaves, and sometimes their fine webbing is visible among the twigs and branchlets. Spray infested foliage with a strong water spray every other day to disrupt the mites' life cycle. Insecticidal soap and miticides will also provide excellent control.

Weeds mar the appearance of a patch of ground cover. They also steal soil moisture and nutrients from the desirable plants. Spot treat with Roundup™ for excellent control.

English ivy

AUGUST
VINES & GROUND COVERS

 PLANNING

August is grass, vine, and ground cover appreciation month! A landscape that has ground covers, vines, and ornamental grasses is more self-sustaining than others. This is a particular advantage when it is too hot to take much pleasure in working outdoors, and when it is time to go away on vacation.

Like turfgrasses, **ornamental grasses** may be cool-season or warm-season types.

- Because they do not mind spring chill, cool-season grasses mature faster and bloom earlier. Look for their flowerheads now.
- Warm-season grasses usually start later because they wait for warmer weather. Consequently, they take a bit longer to reach their mature height and to flower. Look for their flowers late this month and next month.

Grasses produce stems tipped with feathery flowers that resemble nodding bottlebrushes, plumes, or sheaves. Flowers eventually mature into bristly seedheads and feathery tassels that capture the late summer sunlight. Bring some indoors to add to flower arrangements.

 PLANTING

It is too hot to plant this month. Wait a few weeks until after Labor Day. Hold plants in containers in the shade, and water them well while they wait.

 CARE

Check vines to be sure they are securely fastened to their supports. The pounding rain and gusty winds from our classic late day summer thunderstorms might break long stems or even whip a vine off its trellis or wall.

You may discover some ripening fruits on the **kiwi** vine. Wait until they are very soft before picking and eating them. **Lablab** vines develop shiny, reddish-purple pods that dangle attractively near clusters of small purplish flowers. Allow the pods to remain on the vine until they dry out. Then pick them, pop them, and save the interesting seeds you find inside for next year.

Weed ground cover beds to reduce plant stress. Desirable plants should not have to compete with others for water and nutrients in the soil.

 WATERING

Do not worry if the **moss** you have started as a ground cover seems to dry up. It will revive as soon as it gets moisture from your sprinkler or the next rain.

Be aware that many **ferns** prefer cool, moist conditions, so they will have a particularly difficult time during heat and drought. Their ideal soil has lots of organic material in it to keep moisture available to **fern** roots even if there is no rain. If possible, water them every four or five days if rainfall is scarce. Make sure the moisture soaks in several inches each time.

 FERTILIZING

No fertilizing is necessary this month.

 PRUNING

Impatiens will bloom well into October if there is no frost. Give them a new lease on life by pinching them back, watering them, and providing a very dilute liquid fertilizer.

Keep after aggressive vines to direct their growth and control their spread. If known invasives are growing on your property and you do not want to abolish them, prevent their escape into the wild by cutting off their flowers before they make seeds. **Porcelainberry**, **oriental bittersweet**, and **akebia** are notorious for spreading rampantly and driving out native species in our parks and open spaces.

Japanese honeysuckle is a major invader also.

PROBLEMS

Wilted foliage may be apparent during the hottest part of the day. To confirm this normal reaction, check wilted plants after the sun and heat of the day have passed. If the foliage has recovered, the problem is heat. If it has not gained turgidity, chances are that dryness is the problem. If it does not perk up within a half-hour after a good watering, then look for signs of disease.

Phomopsis twig blight sometimes affects carpet-type **junipers** and other needled evergreens. The fungus attacks branch tips in the spring, eventually killing them. Prune out the dead, gray-brown branches to get rid of fungal spores that remain, before they spread to healthy branches. Consider spraying a commercial fungicide if shrubs are severely affected.

Fungal diseases can be prevalent this month because plants are often under stress from heat and humidity. Visible signs include spots, blotches, or cankers on plant foliage, killing the tissues and threatening the stems with dieback. Prune any affected leaves or stems. Clean up old mulch under infected plants to remove a source of repeat infection. To protect surrounding healthy perennial plants in ground covers where air circulation may be limited, spray their foliage with a sulfur-based, general garden fungicide as directed on the product label. Repeat the spray as new foliage emerges. If annuals are infected, it is probably easiest to remove them and discard them in the trash. They are temporary anyway. Clean up the mulch, and replant the area with fall annuals.

HELPFUL HINTS

When is an **ivy** not an true **ivy**? When it is poison ivy. This plant masquerades as a shrub, a ground cover, or a vine, so it is often hard to identify. Its resemblance to **Boston ivy** confuses the issue even further. Both have three-lobed leaves, fall berries, and lovely fall color. Look closely at **Boston ivy**. You will see that its leaves are actually a single leaf with three pointed lobes rather than a group of the telltale three separate leaflets of poison ivy.

Remember: "Leaves of three, let it be."

Boston ivy

SEPTEMBER
VINES & GROUND COVERS

PLANNING

"Fall is for Planting" signs are up at the garden center. Fall begins right after Labor Day for gardeners. Think ground covers:

• This perfect time for renovating lawns is also a perfect time to consider whether more lawn area might be devoted to ground covers instead of high-maintenance turfgrasses.

• Areas under trees where grass struggles mightily are good candidates for alternatives such as **moss, pachysandra, liriope**, or other shade-loving plants.

• Planting new trees and shrubs? This is the perfect time to start a ground cover planting in the soil over their root zone.

• In cases where shrubs have spread wider, allow the ground cover planting under them to expand outward.

Flowering continues. Enjoy **mums, asters, black-eyed Susans, celosia**, and other fall bloomers planted as ground covers. **Autumn clematis** will spill over everything. **Autumn crocus, colchicum**, and **sternbergia** bulbs will appear.

PLANTING

Most woody plants—including perennial vines and shrubs

Cotoneaster can take many forms including a creeping one. Some also produce colorful berries.

suitable for ground covers—respond well to fall planting. Plant low-growing shrubs that will cover and hold the soil on slopes. Some, such as **cotoneaster** and **beautyberry**, produce berries and foliage color in the fall. While you are planting, pop dozens of small **crocus** or **snowdrop** bulbs in the ground for a great spring ground cover show.

Moss is a ground cover alternative. The many different plants that belong to this plant phylum like the type of environment that is common in Ohio. Some kinds will exist in sunny locations if there is adequate humidity. If you already have some growing on your property, you can assume that the conditions are good. Properly prepared ground invites

transient **moss** spores to invade:

1. Clear the area of weeds, and rake debris off the soil. Rake the soil smooth.

2. Sprinkle powdered sulfur to increase the acidity of the soil to the ideal pH of 5.5. The rain or your sprinkler will soak it in.

3. Keep the soil weed-free because **mosses** like barren soil.

Another way to introduce **mosses** is to invite them to expand from where they are already growing in a lawn or elsewhere in your yard by preparing adjacent soil as above.

Yet another way is to plant small patches of **moss** as **moss** "sod," in prepared soil. Transplant these from other parts of the yard. If you can find several different types, they will make an interesting tapestry. Plant them with space between, and let them knit together.

CARE

Bring in the potted tropical vines that you intend to overwinter indoors as houseplants. They need warmth, and there is the possibility of a light frost in northern Ohio before the month is over.

1. Clip the longest climbing stems back to about 2 feet.

2. Dig the plant out of the soil, disturbing the roots as little as possible, and put it in a pot filled with soilless potting mix. Wash off the plant with a forceful water spray when you water it in the pot.

3. Leave the plant outdoors while it adjusts to its pot. Spray it with insecticidal soap to eliminate pests.

4. Bring it indoors gradually—for increasingly longer times over a week or two—so it can adjust to stressful indoor conditions. Set it where it will receive bright sunshine until the shorter days of fall will trigger its quiescent stage.

5. Reduce watering, and do not fertilize. Locate the plant where night temperatures are 60 to 65 degrees Fahrenheit, until late winter when growth will begin again.

HELPFUL HINTS

Many vines and ground cover plants end the growing season aglow with brilliantly colored foliage and berries. Two outstanding vines are **Boston ivy** (*Parthenocissus tricuspidata*) and **Virginia creeper** (*Parthenocissus quinquefolia*).

Many shrubs suitable for ground cover also feature colorful berries:

- **Bayberry**
- **Beautyberry**
- **Chokeberry**
- **Cotoneaster**
- **Dwarf Barberry**
- **Nandina**
- **Skimmia**

WATERING

If rainfall is limited, water all newly planted ground cover shrubs and vines. Well-mulched, established plantings can manage several weeks between rainfalls.

FERTILIZING

When planting woody shrubs and vines, delay fertilizing until at least next spring.

PRUNING

To prevent their self-sowing all over the yard, cut seedheads from **northern oat grass** before they release seeds. Cut off maturing berries on **porcelainberry, akebia**, and other vines that are known invasives before birds spread them into the wild.

Prune the **wisteria** one more time. Cut back wildly rampant stems, taking care not to clip off buds that formed in July.

Ornamental grasses will begin to lose their color and turn beige or pale yellow, their seedheads bursting into fluffy plumes as they release their seeds. Wait to cut them back until late winter.

PROBLEMS

Insect problems should be about over, since insects are preparing for winter. Many leave behind eggs or larvae safely secreted in organic debris around the yard. The good news is that beneficial insects are doing the same thing.

Weeds persist. Take advantage of warm days to spray the tough perennial ones with herbicide to prevent their return in the spring. Continue to pull annual ones before they release their seeds.

OCTOBER
VINES & GROUND COVERS

 PLANNING

First frost signals a slowdown out in the garden. Annual ground cover plants are likely to succumb to the brief chill and die, leaving a bare expanse of ground that will need a protective winter mulch of straw or chopped leaves. Perennial grasses, vines, and ground covers put on their final show of the year with an explosion of foliage color, late flowering, and fruit production.

Get out the camera again to capture the changing scenes as golden light backdrops the show. Record any sightings of new birds that may stop off during migration to sample the berries growing in your yard.

Cooler weather makes this month an ideal time for accomplishing major landscape projects that require a fair amount of physical labor.

• Repair walls and re-attach trellis supports.

• Reinforce trellises and fences that support heavy vines.

• Build or repair arbors.

• Build a pergola.

• Set stepping stones for a walkway with spaces between for ground cover plants.

• Expand ground cover beds.

• Terrace slopes with landscape timbers.

 PLANTING

This is a good time to plant bulbs intended for ground cover. Either naturalize them by casting them freely over the intended site and then planting them where they fall, or insert them among established ground cover plants such as **ivy**, **vinca**, **hosta**, or **liriope**. Various kinds of **daffodils** or minor bulbs such as **crocus**, **snowdrops**, or **wood hyacinths** are best suited for this use. Over the years they will spread to form large patches of color in the spring.

Plant shrubs like **juniper** for ground cover. Choose containerized plants, making sure they are all the same variety and color and roughly the same size. Clear the area of weeds, rocks, and debris, and spade into the soil some organic material such as chopped leaves, compost, or mushroom soil to improve drainage and moisture retention. Set the potted shrubs over the area to determine desirable spacing, then dig saucer-shaped holes at the exact spots.

 CARE

Remove frost-blackened annual vines from trellises and other supports.

Lay netting or garden fleece over **moss** and other ground covers to catch leaves that might mat and block moisture and smother the plants over the winter. After leaf fall is over, roll up the leaf laden netting, carry it

Variegated liriope

to the compost area, and dump its contents on the pile. Store the netting until it is time to protect berry patches from birds next summer.

Spray needled evergreen shrubs that are exposed to drying from harsh winter wind and sunshine. Use an antidesiccant spray according to label directions.

WATERING

Install a drip irrigation system in certain areas that are difficult to water or where plants depend on regular moisture. There is better access to the open soil now that plants have died back. Snake "leaky pipe"-type soaker hoses through ground cover plantings. Emitter-type hoses are better for shrub and vine plantings that are less closely planted. Mechanical or digital timers are useful but not necessary. Cover the hoses with winter mulch. **Ornamental grasses** do not need much water, so they do not need an irrigation system.

Drip irrigation is ideal for shallow-rooted plants that dry out quickly during hot, dry summers. It delivers water directly to the soil so that none is lost to evaporation. The water enters the soil slowly for maximum absorption so none will be wasted in runoff.

HELPFUL HINTS

If certain varieties of annuals such as **geraniums, wax begonias,** or **impatiens** became ground cover favorites over the summer, bring them in to overwinter indoors. Either dig up existing plants and pot them in soilless planting mix to serve as houseplants, or take stem cuttings from them to root and make new plants (see Annuals October).

FERTILIZING

After established deciduous trees and shrubs lose their leaves, it is okay to spread over vine and ground cover soil some winter-type fertilizer formulated for woody or nursery plants. It will help with root growth during the time when the ground has not yet frozen, and will be there to start off next season. Wait until next year to fertilize recently planted plants.

PRUNING

Unless vines and ground cover plants are a danger to themselves or others, delay pruning until late winter or early spring. You do not want to risk stimulating new growth during a possible period of Indian summer, as the growth would be killed back immediately with a hard frost.

PROBLEMS

Although your summer mulch is probably pretty thin by now, wait until the ground freezes before spreading a fresh winter layer.

Poison ivy gives itself away at this time of year. If you have not noticed it in the yard all summer, you will now. Deal with it before birds carry its berries away to start even more plants. All parts of the plant are poisonous. Pull up small plants with a long plastic bag covering your hand and lower arm. Once the plant is out of the ground, pull the plastic bag off your arm over the plant as you hold it, effectively turning the bag inside out with the plant ending up inside. Cut larger vines and spray the basal portion with Roundup™. After the vines have died and dried, carefully cut up the remaining plant.

NOVEMBER
VINES & GROUND COVERS

 PLANNING

Enjoy harvest season indoors with berry laden branches taken from vines and ground cover plants. Dried pods and bleached stems of **ornamental grasses** topped with airy, spent seed-heads also make wonderful floral displays for Thanksgiving.

Outdoors there is much to enjoy. After **Boston ivy** and **Virginia creeper** drop their leaves, the delicate tracings of their dried stems stand out on walls and tree trunks. Grasses become carefree, their stems flexing in the increasingly chilly wind, adding movement and sound to the autumn landscape.

Take a few moments to record in your notebook or journal the dates of first frost and hard frost, what continues to bloom in November, and things you would like to do with vines, grasses, and ground covers next year.

 PLANTING

Dig into unfrozen ground to plant minor bulbs that will create displays under trees and shrubs, between stepping stones, and elsewhere.

If you have not yet planted **pansies**, put some in where the ground is still workable, and they will have a head start for spring. In and around areas where **forget-me-nots** bloomed last year, tufts of narrow dark-green leaves will persist through the winter and bloom next spring. If you want to relocate them to a better place, transplant them now if the ground is still friable.

 CARE

Leave small leaves that fall between **pachysandra, ivy,** and beds of similar evergreen plants as a natural mulch. They will decompose and add nutrients to the soil so you do not need to routinely fertilize these ground covers. Remove larger leaves (**sycamore** leaves are the size of dinner plates!) to prevent their matting and blocking moisture from penetrating the soil beneath the ground cover. Either capture them in netting spread over the top of the ground cover planting, or dislodge and remove them with a rake or powered blower/vac. Most vacuums simultaneously shred the leaves into a bag so that you have instant mulch to return to the plantings or to spread elsewhere.

This is a good time for final fall cleanup in the yard.

• Cut back dead plant stems, and discard them on the compost pile.

• Pull up stakes, remove temporary fencing, and bring in any ornaments that may crack in cold weather.

• Set up a winterproof container to hold water for birds. Locate it in the sun so its water will be melted at least part of the day when temperatures really drop and winter closes in.

Fasten the thick, woody stems of long-established perennial vines such as **kiwi, wisteria,** and **climbing hydrangea** securely to their supports. Check ties to be sure that they are not too tight around stems after a season's growth.

 WATERING

Only if it has been a dry fall is it necessary to water plants this month. Lack of rainfall will most affect recently planted shrubs and vines, or those that are not mulched. Do not let evergreen shrubs—either broadleaf or needled—go into the winter in dry soil. Before the ground freezes, soak it well so that these plants can take up the moisture they need for the winter. Because they are never entirely dormant, they continue to transpire and lose moisture through their leaves.

FERTILIZING

While it is okay to sprinkle a granular, slow-acting product labeled for woody or nursery plants around established shrubs and vines now, delay this job until late winter or early spring for recently planted ones.

PRUNING

Cut back the tall stems of **ornamental grasses** now if you want to—but if left in full-blown majesty, the larger ones can be a real asset to an otherwise bleak winter landscape. Snow sets off their subtle beige, golden, or parchment foliage and fluffy seedheads.

Limit any pruning to removal of injured or dead branches on vines or shrubby ground cover plants. In a few months you can prune for shape and to renovate plants.

PROBLEMS

Deer will continue to be a problem through the winter. If they are desperate for food, they may go to great lengths and risk to reach the plants in your yard. Occasional casual visitors can usually be thwarted by wire used as cages around individual plants or laid over patches of ground cover. Various repellents sprayed on their foliage may work. Desperate or regular visitors can only be deterred by an effective high fence. Use 10-foot-high black polymesh mounted on trees or posts around the perimeter of your property. Electric fences can also be effective.

HELPFUL HINTS

Throughout this book fertilizer recommendations are for slow-acting rather than fast-acting products. The difference is primarily in the form of nitrogen they contain. In slow-acting products, the nitrogen is water-insoluble. Whether its source is natural or chemical (synthesized in a laboratory then coated), nitrogen dissolves gradually over time. In fast-acting products—either liquid, granular, or powdered to be dissolved in water—the nitrogen is water-soluble and is immediately available to plant roots.

While there are many situations when immediate nutrient availability is desirable, in most landscape situations plants benefit from slow release products that provide nitrogen over a longer period of time. Perennial plants, both woody and herbaceous, benefit from consistent uniform nutrition available all season. Slow acting fertilizers provide this steady, long term nutrition.

Fertilizers come in different forms.

DECEMBER
VINES & GROUND COVERS

 PLANNING

As winter closes in and holiday activities monopolize time and energy, take a moment to reflect on the year's gardening successes and failures. Jot down some ideas for acquiring and planting more grasses, vines, and ground covers next year.

Drop daily catalog arrivals in a designated box until you have time to look through them. Their many color photographs and great descriptions are really helpful for learning to identify plants. Good ones have lots of information about suitable planting locations and how to grow and care for the plants.

Think about what to put on your holiday gift list. Perhaps a good book on vines and ground covers? How about an arbor for the garden? Gift certificates to garden centers and nurseries are great to give and receive.

 PLANTING

If the ground is still soft, get any leftover unplanted bulbs into the ground. They will cover the ground with color in just a few months.

 CARE

Cover bare soil in the yard with 2 to 3 inches of organic mulch such as chopped leaves, wood chips, pine needles, or shredded bark to maintain an even soil temperature. Plant roots perform better if the soil stays at about the same temperature rather than repeatedly freezing and thawing.

 WATERING

It seems as if there is not as much snow during Ohio winters as there used to be. It has always been a source of moisture during winter thaws and in the spring. If it neither snows nor rains for an extended period of time, water evergreen vines and ground cover plantings.

 FERTILIZING

No fertilizing is necessary this month.

 PRUNING

If wet snow or ice snaps off branches from vines and ground cover shrubs, saw or cut off the branch cleanly back where it joins another one.

 PROBLEMS

Rodents of various kinds may try to nibble on the tender bark of young shrubs and vines during the winter. If you anticipate problems, wrap hardware cloth or a commercial tree-wrap product around vulnerable stems. Remember, rabbits, deer, mice, and voles can reach pretty high when standing on a foot or two of snow.

Road salt pushed by snow-plows onto ground cover plantings near the street causes them to desiccate and turn brown. The salt absorbs the moisture in the soil and plant roots dry out. Pour pails of water on areas where salt has been deposited to leach it into the soil past plant roots.

HELPFUL HINTS

Nothing improves a nighttime winter landscape more than holiday lights. Low-wattage lights that are rated for outdoor use do not harm shrubs and vines, but the way they are attached may cause problems if they are left up for several months. Never wrap the light wires snugly around shrub and vine stems and branches. Drape, rather than wrap, the strands of lights over and among the branches. It is okay to wrap them around a trellis or arbor that a vine is climbing.

WATER &
BOG PLANTS

It is no surprise that the popularity of water gardening—growing aquatic and bog plants in ponds or containers—grows and grows each year. Of course long-time gardeners are going to enthusiastically embrace the opportunity to learn about and acquire a whole category of new plants. For them, water gardening is a natural extension of terrestrial gardening, and they welcome the opportunity to extend the skills they have into a new arena. It's a wonderful way for plant enthusiasts to indulge even more in their favorite pastime.

The surprise is the popularity of water gardening among those who are not experienced with plants and who have not learned the basic skills of growing and nurturing them. Often it's the very people who announce they have brown thumbs when the conversation turns to gardening who are not at all shy about putting a pond in the yard. Many take confidence from recollections of childhood adventures with aquariums: Others draw on memories of summer vacations at the lake. They may start with fish in the pond, then they add a few plants, then they add some more plants. Perhaps water seems more forgiving than soil—maybe growing plants in water seems less permanent, so it is less daunting.

WATER GARDENING

We think the best explanation for the appeal of water gardening to everyone, gardener or not, is that the activity has to do with water as much as it has to do with plants. Those who garden in water often talk about the serenity they feel when they work near their ponds and containers, caring for their water plants and the wildlife this environment attracts. Literally and figuratively, a water garden is an oasis.

This oasis can be an ecological paradise! It is a place where all creatures come, depend on— prey and predator alike. A water garden oasis is also a zone of serenity in our residential landscapes. The surface of the water offers a visual tranquilizer, the ripples from the foliage of water plants and the darting of fish providing constantly changing patterns in the light. The sound of a trickle from a fountain or waterfall or a gurgle from a bubbler is restful. Here is an opportunity to play. Permission is granted to get wet and muddy. Add to that the sense of well-being gained from creative expression in designing the water garden and the sense of physical well-being gained from the exercise while planting and lifting pots and tending plants. Certainly gardening in water is a powerful antidote to the daily stress that is part of contemporary life.

WATER GARDENS

Not too long ago, only wealthy people grew water lilies, lotus, and other exotic water plants. They could afford to buy large properties with natural ponds or to build swimming pool-like water gardens. Aquatic plants were not commonly available for sale, and there were not many kinds to choose from.

Today, water gardening is within the reach of everyone. Modern technology has provided inexpensive materials and equipment for building ponds. There are now several types of sturdy, flexible poly liner materials, as well as stiff, preformed fiberglass liners that will last for years and years. One can buy PVC tubing, efficient sealed pumps, easy-to-handle filters, netting, lighting, and a host of other products that homeowners can afford and install themselves.

With plants, the choices seem infinite. Driven by the upsurge in consumer interest, growers have produced many colors and forms of water lilies and lotus. Plant enthusiasts have searched out interesting new aquatic plants from all over the world. Closer to home, many plants that grow in local lakes, creeks, and wetlands have been given a second look and a new appreciation. Now they are part of a rich selection of native water plants available to homeowners. Most recently, the trend has been to discover terrestrial plants that double as aquatic plants. Both professional growers and home gardeners are identifying certain hibiscus, canna, hostas, ornamental grasses, ferns, lysimachia, lobelias, and others that do not just tolerate wet soil but will actually grow in water. The possibilities seem endless.

There is no denying that water gardening is strenuous at times. This is especially true if you garden in an inground pond. Fortunately, more and more landscape service companies are offering to do pond design, construction, repair, and maintenance for homeowners. If your enthusiasm for water gardening gets out of control (not uncommon!), there is help at hand to build a second pond, or to clean the ponds. Companies that specialize in these services sometimes offer to take care of your tender plants in their greenhouses for the winter, or to take extra or large fish off your hands. They also troubleshoot when problems develop.

There is no excuse for putting off trying this wonderful kind of gardening. Start small with just one or two plants and a large decorative jar or half-barrel of water. Experiment, play, learn, find peace!

JANUARY
WATER & BOG PLANTS

 PLANNING

Even in winter, a water garden has a special appeal. The surface shimmers in the cold light of winter, threatening at times to ice over completely when temperatures drop very low. Beneath the surface rest dormant perennial aquatic plants, safely below the frost line waiting for the lengthening hours of sunlight that will signal the return of spring. Like their counterparts in the soil, they are poised to send up tender new shoots in just a few weeks. Fish are dormant too, their cold-blooded systems responding to the low water temperature, their metabolisms virtually stalled.

If you have not gardened in water, this month is a good time to think about starting. If digging a pond seems too big an undertaking, plan to experiment with growing some aquatic plants in ornamental containers aboveground on a porch or patio this coming season. Following this opportunity, you may decide to create an entire garden in water.

Seasoned water gardeners can review last year's experiences in their journals this month. Consider how nice the pond might look on winter nights with landscape lighting.

Shopping List: a de-icer or heater for water garden ponds, a journal for recording this year's events in the water garden

 PLANTING

This is a good time to divide or take cuttings from tender aquatic plants that are overwintering indoors under lights as houseplants.

• Cut sections of stem from plants such as **parrot's feather**, **water mint**, or **snowflake** that are in pots in water or in an aquarium. Put them in water to root, then pot them in soil, and immerse the pots in water.

OR

• Slip **taro** (or other plants that have developed rooted runners) from its pot, and separate the tiny rooted offshoots from the main plant. Take care to preserve as much root as possible. Plant the offshoots in small pots, and immerse in water again.

 CARE

Check those tender water garden plants that are stored indoors in a cool, dark space. Make sure the potted ones are still wet and that the wrappings of tubers and rhizomes of **water lilies** are still damp. If they have dried out, moisten them and put them in a plastic bag. Leave it open at one end, or puncture some holes in it to allow air circulation.

 PRUNING

To provide winter interest, the attractive leaves or stems of **grasses**, **cattails**, and other hardy perennials planted near the edge of the water garden can be left unpruned. If snow or ice makes them fall into the water, however, cut them back.

 PROBLEMS

Frozen pond surfaces can cut off gas exchange between the air and water, threatening fish and plants at the bottom of the pond. Install a de-icer device, or melt a portion of the ice by gradually pouring boiling water over it. Keep a bubbler or waterfall running. Electricity for pond lighting or a pump may fail because of damage to the wiring. Check for signs of rodent gnawing or loose connections.

FEBRUARY

WATER & BOG PLANTS

PLANNING

Aquatic nursery catalogs are wonderful sources of information about aquatic plants and how to grow them. The best catalogs offer detailed instructions for creating a water garden—digging a pond or setting up ornamental containers such as half-barrels. Experienced water gardeners will want to spend time looking at current catalogs because so many new plants are available. Dwarf versions of traditional favorites make water gardening in containers even easier and more fun.

It is not too soon to plan an inground water garden or to think about purchasing a new container for aboveground water gardening.

Shopping List: pots and heavy soil for potting plant divisions, fertilizer tabs, plants from mail-order aquatic plant nurseries

PLANTING

Check stored, tender aquatic plants to be sure their soil or wrappings are still moist and that the temperature in their storage space is between 40 and 50 degrees Fahrenheit. They must not freeze.

By the end of the month, tender plants that have over-wintered in a greenhouse or as houseplants—their pots in water and under lights—may start to send up new shoots. If they begin to crowd their pots, transplant them into larger containers. If a plant is already large, divide the plant and repot the divisions. While large immersed plants are nice, remember that they are heavier to raise and lower into the water; and **papyrus**, **taro**, **lotus**, and others that are allowed to grow too large may be out of scale in a typical backyard pond. Either divide them, or put them in an ornamental jar or tub of their own for display aboveground.

CARE

Birds and other wildlife need a source of fresh water, and water gardens are a perfect source. Prevent the pond surface from freezing over entirely by:

• installing a de-icer or heater designed for use in water garden ponds.

• running the pump to power a bubbler or waterfall to maintain water movement.

• gradually melting one area by pouring boiling water over it each day.

If any debris from trees or shrubs has fallen onto the pond surface, remove it to prevent decomposition. Leaving the net-ting from last fall across the pond will prevent wind-blown debris from falling in the water.

Water plants that are growing indoors under lights for the winter will need just a bit of fertilizer to keep their foliage healthy. If you included some granular, slow-acting product or fertilizer tabs in the soil when you potted them, that should be sufficient. If you did not, sprinkle just a trace of water-soluble fertilizer into their water.

PRUNING

As snow and frost begin to recede toward the end of the month, tidy up the planted areas around the edge of the water garden pond or containers. If you have not already clipped off dead stems from marginal plants and cut back nearby **ornamental grasses**, do that soon. Minor bulbs such as **crocus** and **snowdrop** will be appearing soon.

PROBLEMS

Pest insects may attack tender water plants overwintering indoors under lights. Like other houseplants, they are vulnerable to problems with scale or aphids because they are stressed by the less-than-ideal conditions indoors. Watch for these pests and treat with horticultural oil or Neem oil.

HELPFUL HINTS

A healthy, attractive water garden is a diverse ecological niche where various kinds of water plants function in concert with wildlife. Increasing the diversity of plants in the water garden, balances the interaction between beneficial and pest insects. A greater diversity of plants can also improve water quality for plants, fish, snails, frogs, snakes, and other wildlife that require an aquatic environment. Each plant contributes toward a balanced, self-sustaining system.

Some plants reduce algae in the water, some attract beneficial insects, and others provide shelter for fish. All this, and they look attractive, too! When planning a water garden, select many types of plants. Just as when you garden in soil, you will need tall ones at the back or edge of the pond, others to be specimens or accents, and others to act as fillers and ground (water) covers. You will need the following kinds of plants:

Taro

Submerged plants are barely visible under the water. They do the behind-the-scenes work of generating and maintaining oxygen in the water. (Example: **anacharis, cabomba**)

Floating plants bob untethered on the water surface. As carefree as they look, they are also at work, shading and filtering the water to discourage bright-green algae. (Example: **water hyacinth, azolla, duckweed, snowflake, water clover**)

Immersed plants have their roots, crowns, and part of their stems in water. Their main job is to look (and smell) gorgeous to attract insects. (Example: **lotus, water lilies**)

Marginal plants prefer their roots and crowns just at the water surface. They hold the soil in natural ponds, shelter wildlife, and provide a transition from water to soil. (Example: **canna, papyrus, pickerel weed**)

Bog plants need soggy mud around their roots to thrive. They are not actually in the water—in fact, they may be in a separate boggy place of their own. They attract insects and wildlife, and hold the soil. (Example: **iris, taro, lobelia, grasses, marsh marigold, Japanese primrose, sedges, pitcher plant, ferns**)

MARCH
WATER & BOG PLANTS

 **PLANNING**

Anytime after the ground thaws is a good time to dig a pond for an inground water garden. Growing aquatic plants aboveground in large ornamental containers is a way to garden in water in a small yard, balcony, or patio near the house. Aboveground water gardens are easier to work with, especially for gardeners with bad backs!

Shopping List: ornamental containers for aboveground water gardening, water-conditioning crystals or "tonic" for the water and the fish; for a new inground pond, flexible or preformed liner, pump, edging material

 **PLANTING**

Soon it will be time to pot up plants that have recently arrived mail-order or that have been stored since last fall and need dividing. In cultivated water gardens, aquatic plants are planted in soil in plastic pans, baskets, or nursery pots. Even if the water garden pond has a natural soil bottom, gardening with potted plants is easier.

- They are not able to spread beyond their designated spot.
- They are easier to move and remove from the garden for maintenance.
- Their height can be adjusted to assure correct water depth over their roots.

- They facilitate cleaning the water garden pond.

 **CARE**

Examine and repair the edges of the water garden pond, if the winter freeze thaw cycles have disturbed the soil.

To dig a new water garden pond:

1. Clear the area of plants, rocks, and debris. Check to be sure there are no utility wires or pipes underground. The ground must be level. For a flexible liner: outline the pond's dimensions with a hose or rope to guide the digging. For a preformed liner: position the liner in the desired spot, then trace its outline on the soil to guide the digging.

2. Dig from the edges toward the center. Excavated soil goes into a cart to be deposited at a predetermined spot. Dig the sides fairly straight (unless the soil is silty or sandy) to a depth of at least 2 feet if you plan to have fish. Preformed liners need holes that are 2 inches deeper and 3 or 4 inches wider around the sides than the form measures. Preformed ponds are usually not deep enough to allow overwintering fish in Ohio.

3. Create a shelf for marginal plants along one side (usually the back, because plants may be

---

HELPFUL HINTS

To learn more about water gardening and the culture of aquatic plants, join a society.

Miami Valley Water Garden Society
P.O. Box 13293
Dayton, OH 45413
www.mvwgs.org

Aquatic Plant Management Society
P.O. Box 821265
Vicksburg, MS 39182
www.apms.org

International Water Lily and Water Gardening Society
6828 26th Street West
Bradenton, FL 34207
www.iwgs.org

tall). Make it about 12 inches deep and 15 or 20 inches wide, then dig down to the main depth. Preformed liners will have a built-in shelf.

4. Line the bottom of the hole with 2 inches of sand to protect flexible or preformed liners from punctures by sharp stones. Make sure the preformed liner is level in the soil, its rim just above soil level.

5. Fill the preformed pond with water once it is settled in the soil. If using a flexible liner for the garden pond, spread it on the ground to allow the heat of the sun to soften it. Then, EITHER

(a) Center it over the excavated hole and temporarily anchor its corners with rocks. Run the water into its center, and allow the gradual weight of the water to carry the liner down into the hole, while you monitor and release the corners. As the pond fills, the weight of the water forces the liner to conform to its shape.

OR

(b) Center the liner over the hole so that it can easily sag into the space. Step into the hole, and fit the liner to its shelf and sides, pleating excess material where it curves.

DETERMINING POND LINER SIZE

1. Measure the width and length of your pond, and draw a sketch to scale of its general outline with those two dimensions. Then draw a rectangle that encloses the pond outline.

2. Determine the length and width measurements of that rectangle.

3. Determine the depth of the pond at its deepest point

4. Calculate liner length as: Pond Length + twice its depth + 2 feet for edging.

5. Calculate liner width as: Pond width + twice its depth + 2 feet for edging.

OR

Take the pond measurements to the garden center, and ask someone on staff to calculate the appropriate size.

6. Trim the edges of the liner, but leave a generous 4 feet to allow for laying it under the first row of edging material. Fold the liner over the first course of edging, then, lay the second course. It must bear your weight when you haul heavy pots out of the water.

 PRUNING

Cut back **ornamental grasses** at the water garden's edge to make way for their new sprouts. Dig up and divide overlarge clumps. Prune other perennials and shrubs which may have winter injury to twigs.

 PROBLEMS

When a pond is new, the water will look dirty and clouded for several weeks while it achieves biological balance. Resist the temptation to drain and refill the pond. Time will solve the problem.

Various species of algae are always present in water gardens. Early in the season, the stringy bright-green type may appear. Murky "blooms" will clear up as a biological balance is achieved over time. Meanwhile, do not feed fish until the water is warmer. Remove accessible strands of stringy algae with a stick or net.

APRIL
WATER & BOG PLANTS

PLANNING

When properly in balance, the pond life does most of the work to maintain water quality. Fish eat mosquito larvae, and oxygenating plants offer food, shelter, and oxygen for fish as well as aid gas exchange for plant roots. Snails and other scavengers eat algae and debris from the bottom of the pond.

Of course, a water garden is not a totally natural environment. A certain amount of maintenance is necessary to keep everything balanced. The pond will need cleaning periodically because organic debris can accumulate at the bottom and deplete the oxygen in the water. Cleaning is usually done in the fall (see October), but it can be done in spring if necessary.

Water gardens are a potential danger. While they are a marvelous nature lesson, children have a great affinity for water and are attracted by fountains or waterfalls and colorful fish. Consider some sort of decorative fencing around the water garden to alert visitors they are near the edge. Local municipal ordinances may require more substantial fencing.

Shopping List: pots for divided plants, water thermometer, new plants, decorative fencing, snails

PLANTING

Divide and repot hardy water garden plants that have over-wintered at the bottom of the pond. Pot up plants ordered by mail. Wait another month before dividing and potting up stored tender plants.

Plant **water lily** rhizomes in heavy soil. The soil should be either clay or heavy garden soil or commercial aquatic planting medium to assure that particles do not float from the pot into the water. A mulch of rinsed gravel on top also helps.

1. Use a wide, relatively shallow container such as a rectangular, plastic dishpan that will comfortably accommodate the narrow, rooted rhizome set horizontally (like an **iris**). The container should be 7 to 9 inches deep.

2. Fill the dishpan about $1/3$ to $1/2$ with damp soil. Insert fertilizer tablet(s) into the soil according to package directions.

3. Orient the rhizome at a 45 degree angle, its crown where new leaves may be sprouting pointing upward. Spread its roots over the soil.

4. Add soil so there is at least an inch or two over the rhizome's cut end (if it has just been divided) and its roots.

5. Firm the soil gently over the rhizome, and water it in. Then immerse the pot in the pond or container gradually so that air bubbles have a chance to escape.

6. Set **water lily** pans on the bottom of the pond, if it is no deeper than 18 inches. Set them on bricks, overturned pots, or other supports in deeper water.

Divide and repot marginal plants as they begin to show new growth. Divisions of **iris**, **papyrus**, **pickerel rush**, **grasses**, **thalia**, and others should go into standard nursery pots in heavy soil at the same depth as they were in their previous pots. Remember to include a little granular, slow-acting fertilizer, but do not overdo, or you will be repotting again in the middle of the season. Set them on the shallow shelf at the edge of the water garden or on supports at the proper depth.

CARE

If you have not already removed the fall/winter netting over the water garden pond, do so. This is a good time to add some water-conditioning crystals to help the water quality and the fish.

As the water warms, the fish will become more active and will be interested in eating. In established water garden ponds there is vegetation for them to nibble on, so they do not need to be fed. A new pond will have very little plant life for a while, so the fish will appreciate being fed. Once the season is underway, fish can maintain themselves.

PRUNING

If submerged plants were not thinned and tamed last fall, haul out matted bunches from the pond, and throw them on the compost pile. Leave enough in the water to oxygenate it and shelter fish while other plants get established. **Anacharis**, **cabomba**, and others will regenerate enthusiastically as soon as the water temperature rises.

POTS AND PLACEMENT

Potted water garden plants, like their terrestrial cousins, grow well in lots of types of pots as long as they have drainage holes and are roomy enough for enlarging root systems. Because plants are either partly or entirely in water, it helps if the pots are substantial—clay, high-grade plastic, or poly material. Set pots securely on cinder blocks or other supports that can maintain them at the correct depth. Line those that have lots of openings with landscape fabric or white polyspun garden fleece to prevent dirt from leaking out, while allowing water to flow in and out.

PROBLEMS

Water quality will be less than ideal as the water temperature rises and biological interactions adjust accordingly. In new ponds, the helpful, furry brown algae will develop to cover liner surfaces. It promotes desirable bacterial activity.

Overfeeding fish fouls the water. Do not offer more than they can eat in three minutes. A filter attached to a pump that circulates the water in the pond helps establish and maintain water clarity. A submersed filter lies at the bottom of the pond and needs frequent cleaning. A biological filter stands nearby outside the pond; it requires less-frequent cleaning.

Position potted water plants at the proper depths using blocks or built-in shelfs.

MAY

WATER & BOG PLANTS

 PLANNING

A water garden pond cleaned or built last fall is ready to go as soon as new plants arrive from the store or those from last season are repotted. Take advantage of the wide variety of foliage colors, textures, and shapes to coordinate a pleasing design. Locate the vertical plants to form a backdrop for the flowers of specimen **water lilies**.

Consult your notes or photos for reminders of how you placed the immersed and marginal plants last year. Do not crowd the plants.

If you are interested in having a bog garden and do not have a naturally boggy spot in the yard, create one just beyond the edge of the water garden pond.

1. Excavate a shallow hole or trench in the soil about 2 feet deep and as wide as you want the bog to be. Slope the sides.

2. Lay a piece of flexible pond liner or heavy-duty plastic over the hole, conforming to the hole's bottom and reaching up its sides. Anchor its corners to keep it in place.

3. Cover the liner with soil to within a few inches of the level of the surrounding ground, gradually reducing its depth as it reaches and covers the liner edges.

Cattail

4. Soak the soil with a hose if there is no rain, and let the moisture saturate the soil for a day or two. Then plant.

Shopping List: long-handled net, fish, fish food, water dechlorinator, more plants

 PLANTING

It is time to plant the water garden.

1. Position the specimens (**water lilies**) in the water first, allowing generous space between them to allow for their foliage spread over the water surface.

(Gently nudge away floating stems of submerged plants from last year as you sink the pots of **water lilies** and set them on supports or the bottom of the pond.) Leave a prominent place for the **lotus**, if you intend to have one. Leave space for tender **water lilies** to go in when it is warm enough.

2. Set the potted, new submerged plants such as **anacharis** on the bottom of the pond between the pots of **water lilies**.

3. Put floating plants such as **water clover** or **snowflake** in next to serve as "ground cover" and to provide foliage color and

texture contrast. **Water hyacinths** will probably not be available for another month, unless you wintered some over from last season. Add them when you acquire them.

4. Arrange marginal plants in groups at their preferred depths in the shallow water on the pond shelf. Factor in their various heights and foliage shapes, colors, and textures (**canna**, **iris**, **taro**, **grasses**, **cattails**, and others) as you place them.

5. Add fish to new water garden pond after the plants are set up and the chlorine in the water has dissipated.

CARE

Hardy **water lily** foliage will open and spread over the water surface. Adjust the position of the pots slightly to prevent crowding.

Check to see that pots have not shifted or fallen over in the water garden. Sometimes fish or water currents from a pump or waterfall disturb things.

If it has not rained, check to see if the bog plants in the soil at the edge of the garden have enough moisture. If they are in a garden area that depends on pond overflow, you may have to water it until the next rain. Check the marginal plants on the shelf in the water garden pond to be

WATER LILIES

Hardy/Perennial water lilies are tougher, requiring less care.

Foliage: leaves from April to October, have smooth edges, some may have purple markings.

Flowers: appear earlier, more abundantly than Tenders/Tropicals, bloom June through early fall, bloom in sun—mid-morning to 5 p.m. Blossoms are white, and shades of pink, red, and yellow; last about 5 days; sit on the water surface; don't open on cloudy days; some are scented.

Site: can be immersed to 18 inches or more; needs still water.

Tender/Tropical water lilies must be stored indoors over the winter.

Foliage: sharp serrations on leaf edges; variegated with purple.

Flowers: pinks, reds, white, blues, lilacs—intense flower color; flowers tend to be larger-sized (up to 12 inches diameter), bloom almost twice as often as hardies; day bloomers 10 till 5; flowers last about three days; some are night bloomers, sunset to 9 a.m.; fragrance much sweeter, stronger than Hardies; rise above water on stems.

Site: needs water 68 degrees Fahrenheit or above, needs 10 to 12 inches of still water over soil surface in pot.

sure the water level is correct for them.

PRUNING

No pruning is necessary this month.

PROBLEMS

Chemicals in treated municipal water will kill fish. If you use municipal water to fill the pond or to top it off when water levels

drop, wait until the chlorine dissipates (a day) before adding fish. Add drops of a dechlorinating product as directed on its package label if fish are already resident in the water garden.

Cloudy water may persist for a few weeks because biological activity in the pond accelerates as the water warms up. Do not worry about the presence of brown, furry algae on pot and liner surfaces. That is a good sign.

JUNE
WATER & BOG PLANTS

PLANNING

Whether they are in an inground pond or aboveground ornamental containers, aquatic plants respond to the warm weather. Submerged plants and little floating plants may show tiny pale flowers in late spring.

Think about installing a pump and filter in the pond, if you have not already done so. While neither is necessary if you do not have fish, they are essential if you originally stocked the recommended 1 inch of goldfish per 5 gallons of water. Eventually, even these few little fish will grow and generate nutrient-dense waste that compromises water clarity.

For attachment to a submersible filter, choose a pump powerful enough to move up to half the total volume of water in your pond each hour. If coupled with a biological filter, which is outside the pond, the pump needs to move from one-sixth to one-fourth the total volume of the pond per hour.

Besides powering the filter, a pump will power a fountain or waterfall and circulate the water throughout the garden to keep oxygen levels high. Like a fan does with air, the pump creates a more uniform temperature by blending cool deep water with warmer shallow water. In half-barrels, kettles, and other large water garden containers, use a bubbler to circulate the water and make a soothing, soft trickling sound that attracts birds.

Shopping List: fertilizer tabs, mosquito dunks, film for camera

PLANTING

It's time to pot up tender **water lilies**. "Tropicals" need water to be over 70 degrees Fahrenheit before they really start to grow. (They are moved into the pond about the same time that young **tomato** plants are transplanted into the vegetable garden.) Keep the tubers (that have arrived mail-order or that were stored dormant all winter in the garage or cellar) moist until potting time.

1. Select wide dishpan-type pots, about 5-gallon capacity, similar to those suitable for **hardy water lilies**. Drill drainage holes if they do not have them. Fill each pot one-third full with moist, heavy garden soil, and insert fertilizer tabs in the soil according to instructions on the label.

2. Add a bit more soil, then lay the horizontal tuber on its surface, its roots distributed over the soil and its growing tip aimed upward. Cover it with soil up to its crown where some greenish buds might be visible at the growing tip.

3. Gravel mulch is an excellent additive. It helps prevent soil from entering the water as you lower the plant into the water garden.

CARE

Fertilize both types of **water lilies** with tabs once a month when the water temperature rises above 70 degrees Fahrenheit. Lean over the pond's edge, and poke them into the soil in each **water lily's** pot, then pinch soil back over the hole to assure the tab does not float out.

Remove, rinse, and replace the pad from a submersed filter every few days. As the weather gets warmer and the water gets warmer, you will have to do it more often.

Tall bog plants in soil on the edge of the water garden pond or tall marginal plants in the shallow water occasionally get floppy. Stake these plants as you would plants in a regular garden to improve their appearance.

PRUNING

Prune off injured or dying **water lily** foliage and spent blossoms. A pole pruner is useful for reaching and pruning leaves out in the center of the water garden pond. Do not let the prunings fall down in the water. Prune off dried or bent stems from marginal plants to keep them attractive.

Hardy water lily blooms are wonderful to enjoy indoors. Cut one, and float it in a crystal bowl of water on the dining room table.

PROBLEMS

Algae bloom should be receding now as the water settles after the plants are positioned. Their foliage will shade the water surface by the end of the month, inhibiting algae growth. In new ponds, the new submerged plants are slower to take over their sheltering and oxygenating duties.

Predator birds will find it more difficult to go after fish which now have some hiding places. If foliage is slow to cover the water garden pond, tip a plastic milk crate upside down on the bottom to shelter fish. They can swim through the open sides and hide. Set pots of water plants on the crate.

Large koi fish are capable of disturbing plants and causing them to come out of their pots. Cover plants with netting until they are well established.

LOTUS PLANTS

• **Sacred (Asian) Lotus** (*Nelumbo nucifera*) Not reliably hardy in Ohio, needs deep water, heights vary from 2 to 7 feet out of the water, needs large pond for scale and room. Large leaves 2 feet across, stems up to 6 feet tall. Aerial leaves unfurl after initial floating ones. Large blooms in white, pink, yellow, rose; heady fragrance; blooms six to eight weeks in midsummer. Funnel-shaped seedpods. Dwarf type is 'Momo Botan'; Miniature is 'Mrs. Perry D. Slocum'.

• **American (Native) Lotus/Water Chinquapin** (*Nelumbo lutea*) Hardy in Ohio. Plants usually 5 feet tall. 2-foot-wide bowl-shaped leaves on 2-foot-tall stems above water. Large creamy-yellow flowers; single, 5 to 7 inches across. Round seeds rather than oval Asian ones.

Lotus pods are interesting in arrangements.

JULY
WATER & BOG PLANTS

PLANNING

As the summer heat intensifies, the water garden becomes an oasis for your family and the resident wildlife in the yard. The sound of fresh water attracts birds and insects as well as local pets, squirrels, and other visitors. The new ecological niche you have created now supports less-visible residents as well—dragonflies, toads, frogs, tadpoles, spiders, and possibly a snake! The aquatic plants provide greater plant diversity in the yard, which makes a healthier environment for all.

Consider installing night lights and in-pond lights which can greatly extend and enhance the enjoyment of your water garden.

Shopping List: statuary for the water garden area, a fountain, more plants

PLANTING

Add plants to the water garden pond or ornamental containers anytime during the season. If over 60 percent of the pond's water surface is not yet covered by foliage, add more—this will prevent algae problems. Conversely, if the garden is overcrowded now that the plants are growing vigorously,

remove some of them, and put them in barrels or pots filled with water.

The small delicate foliage of many floating plants provides nice texture, size, and color contrast to the large, broad leaves of **water lilies** and **lotus**. The foliage provides shade and takes up nutrients to discourage algae. Some floaters are hardy and can stay in the pond over the winter.

The tender types such as **water hyacinths** behave like annuals in a regular garden. They grow quickly with the advent of warm weather and perform well all season.

Lotus will start blooming three to four weeks after air temperatures are consistently above 80 degrees Fahrenheit, usually this month in Ohio. They may not

bloom their first season after transplanting, but their foliage is great.

CARE

If plants are growing too fast or stems are weak and floppy, cut back on fertilization. Plants receive some nutrients from the water, especially if you have fish in the water garden pond.

Do not let the water level in the pond or container drop more than an inch or two. The liner should not be exposed to sunshine. If it does not rain and water is evaporating, top-off the garden with a hose. Check the bog garden to be sure the soil is wet just below the surface. Wet it down with the hose if there is any doubt.

For inspiration, visit botanical gardens.

The water will be clear now, indicating that all elements are in balance. There are several things you can do if stringy green (filamentous) algae appears, or the water begins to look like pea soup because it is too rich with nutrients:

- Limit food for fish.
- Reduce the number of fish in the pond.
- Stop fertilizing plants.
- Add more submerged plants.
- Shade more of the water surface from the sun.

 PRUNING

Hardy water lily blossoms will last five days or so, then begin to deteriorate. Clip them off before they get soggy and disintegrate in the water; this will keep the water cleaner and encourage new blossoms.

Prune off excess or unsightly foliage of plants both in and around the water garden.

Thin **parrot's feather** and other submerged plants that become really thick.

AMAZING WATER HYACINTHS

Research continues to reveal the virtues of plants—even those that sometimes act as pests. Although **water hyacinths** are a problem in the South, where they survive winters to choke lakes and streams, they are redeeming themselves in freshwater research laboratories.

So effective are their roots at filtering water that they have been demonstrated to convert black (not just gray) water into potable water. This has enormous implications for the future.

In your own water garden, a single **water hyacinth** plant does the job of about six bunches of submerged plants. Its bizarre feathery roots dangle underwater as deep as 12 to 14 inches, drawing nutrients and impurities out of the water as they flow by the tiny root filaments. On the surface of the water, these plants bob along with the current. They rapidly develop offshoots at the ends of horizontal stems. After midsummer they begin to produce showy, upright, pale lilac-blue flowers that open with light and close end of day. They bloom best when plants are crowded in water that contains lots of nutrients.

 PROBLEMS

Invasive plants are a problem in water gardens and bogs, just as in regular garden beds. Certain marginal and bog plants such as **horsetails** and **lotus** send out root runners and rapidly overstep their bounds. Make sure they are in sturdy pots to control their spread. **Duckweed**, a floater, is less easy to restrict. Scoop it out in sections of the water garden as it threatens to cover the water surface completely. **Water hyacinths** will choke any open water if they are not thinned periodically.

Mosquitoes can be a problem in water gardens if there is neither moving water nor fish. To avoid breeding them, kill larvae with Bt (*Bacillus thuringiensis*) in the form of a floating donut called Mosquito Dunks™. Follow package directions for use and storage.

Aphids and other pest insects might appear when plants are stressed by heat and crowding. Dip mildly affected leaves into the water, or rinse them with a hose to wash off the pests.

AUGUST

WATER & BOG PLANTS

PLANNING

If you plan to have your water garden pond cleaned by landscape contractors or pond specialists this fall, make a date before the month is over. October is a good time to schedule this project. Most plants are ready for dormancy, and tender plants need to be taken indoors for winter storage. The service should include the installation of netting to prevent falling leaves from decomposing in the fresh water. Have them service your pump and check the tubing.

Make sure your water garden pond is filled to the maximum with water before you go away on vacation. There will be some evaporation in the heat, and rain is likely to be scarce this month. If there are small children in your neighborhood, consider covering the pond with temporary netting or screening, or surround it with fencing while you are gone to prevent a possible accident.

Shopping List: leaf netting, another ornamental container for aboveground water gardening

PLANTING

It is okay to divide and repot potbound plants in midseason. Some plants may have outgrown their containers to the point where their flowering and health is compromised. Sometimes bulging tubers and restricted matted roots actually split thin plastic nursery liner-type pots.

1. Remove the plant from its pot, and lay it on a rock or other hard surface.

2. Use a sharp knife or a spade to slice through the crown and stems to make rooted chunks.

3. Trim excessively long roots from each chunk, and plant each one in heavy garden soil in its own pot.

4. Return one newly potted division to the water garden. The other(s) can go into an aboveground auxiliary water garden or become a gift.

CARE

Continue to check water levels in the bog areas as well as in the water garden pond itself. A certain amount of evaporation takes place from fountains and waterfalls, so check water level often. Protect the fish by adding the water gradually.

This is the last month to fertilize **water lilies**. As the number of daylight hours begins to shrink noticeably, the plants will reduce flowering somewhat, and there are probably enough nutrients in the water to keep them going. If the water garden has become overcrowded with **water lily** foliage and floating plants, remove a pot or two of plants and set them in a separate ornamental container of water for the rest of the season.

Pull out some of the trailing stems of submerged plants and some of the floaters to open up space in the overgrown garden. Submerged oxygenating plants should take up only about one-third the total volume of water in the pond.

PRUNING

If **hardy water lily** blossoms and foliage are rising out of the water, they are too crowded. If there is no room to correct the problem by repositioning their pots, prune off some foliage to thin it and prevent disease.

To improve their appearance and maintain good air circulation, prune off yellowed, dried, or torn foliage promptly from bog and marginal plants. Do not let stems flop into the water garden.

Do not deadhead **lotus** pods, because they are part of the ornamental appeal of this plant.

PROBLEMS

Pots of plants tipped over can be caused by several things. Often excessive growth of plant roots squeezes through the drainage holes and develops matted clumps. They can disturb the balance of pots positioned on overturned pots or bricks and cause them to fall over. Trim back roots, or repot into a larger pot. Visiting wildlife that come to drink at the water garden pond will occasionally knock over pots.

Weeds are a problem both in pots of marginal plants in the water and in the boggy soil areas. Pull them before they set and sow their seeds.

Raccoons are a problem in water gardens in some areas. Signs of their visits are disturbed edges of ponds. There may be loosened stones and/or a wet, slippery slope in the soil from the edge into the water in natural ponds where they access the water.

Woodchucks may feed on bulbs and tubers of plants such as **iris** and **thalia** at the edge of water garden ponds. The plants will suddenly disappear. A single woodchuck can do a tremendous amount of damage there, just as in vegetable gardens. Trapping or fencing might be necessary.

OUT OF CONTROL

In both land and water gardening, certain plants prove to be less favorable. While they may be attractive, they are too undisciplined to fit in the garden design, and their rampant growth requires too much maintenance. Even though they are in pots in or at the edge of a water garden, these plants grow so fast that they are constantly needing dividing or larger pots. If you grow any of these plants, give them a container of their own aboveground. When discarding divisions or prunings from these plants, take care not to let them escape into the wild in local streams or lakes. Throw them into the trash rather than onto a compost pile. Some invasive water plants:

- **Bamboo** ("running" varieties)
- **Duckweed** (*Lemna minor*)
- **Horsetail** (*Equisetum hyemale*)
- **Purple Loosestrife** (*Lythrum salicaria*)
- Certain varieties of **Milfoil**

Horsetail

SEPTEMBER

WATER & BOG PLANTS

PLANNING

Although the weather may still be warm, the daylight hours are shrinking, and water plants react to this just as all the other plants in the yard do. Now is a good time to photograph this year's pond at its peak, because foliage will begin to brown soon, and flowering will slow down. Make some notes in your garden notebook or journal about the season.

It is time to confront the big decision—whether to try to overwinter the **tropical water lilies** and other tender water plants, or to treat them as annuals and allow them to die when frost arrives. You can always buy new ones next year. Because they are literally tropical, they cannot survive the winter cold outdoors, even in the deepest part of the pond. They will require storage space such as a cellar or garage that is unheated but in no danger of freezing. Any water plants (hardy or tender) growing in large, decorative containers in aboveground water gardens will eventually need to be stored as well.

Shopping List: water thermometer, pond de-icer or heater

Ferns, Japanese primroses, and astilbe are good additions to pond edges.

PLANTING

Dividing and repotting overgrown water garden plants is normally done in the spring when they are about to emerge from dormancy—but it may be more convenient to do it in the fall after they enter dormancy, prior to storing them for the winter. If this is not a year for a major pond-cleaning project, there may be time to divide some and give them away to save storage space. Follow the directions for repotting water plants (see April). Do not fertilize them, because they will not be growing for several months. Add fertilizer tabs next spring when you get them out of storage.

Fall presents an opportunity to plant up the outside edge of the water garden with ground cover plants and hardy bulbs that will bloom attractively early in the spring. Most hardy bulbs like good drainage, so do not try to plant **narcissus** and **tulips** if the area around the pond's edge is a bog.

Delay this planting if pond cleaning is on the agenda. The sides of the pond may be trampled a bit. Good additions to a damp area at pond's edge are:

- **Japanese Primrose** (*Primula japonica*)
- **Marsh Marigold** (*Caltha* sp.)

- **Ornamental Skunk Cabbage** (*Lysichiton* sp.)
- **Sedges** and **rushes**
- **Ferns**

 CARE

Allow plants to begin to die back. The perennials will behave just like those in garden beds. Marginals on the pond shelf and bog plants along the edge will start to form seedpods, and their stems will dry and bleach to straw color. Some, especially **ornamental grasses**, may be decorative enough to remain over the next several months. Let them soften the edge of the winter pond. Eventually they will need cutting back.

Do not fertilize any water garden plants until next spring.

Feed the fish. While the weather is still mild, they feed voraciously. Limit the amount of food to what can be devoured within five minutes.

If frost is due in your region of Ohio before the month ends, begin to dismantle ornamental containers that hold water plants. Lift the plants and cut them back for storage at the bottom of a water garden pond or in the unheated area where you will store tender water plants. Drain the water from the large contain-

HELPFUL HINTS

Flexible pond liners occasionally develop leaks. A drop in the water level for no reason is usually a clue, although the water loss might be caused by other things. First rule out other causes of the water loss. Checklist:

___1. Has a fountain device tipped against the edge of the pond so it is spraying the water outside the pond?

___2. When the pump is disconnected from the fountain or waterfall, does the water level stop dropping? The leak must be in the re-circulating system somewhere.

___3. Are the edges of the liner properly secured under the edging?

___4. Has some of the edging material come loose so there is a low spot?

___5. Are all tube connections to devices outside of the pond, such as a waterfall or biofilter, tight?

If the water level has fallen and remained at a certain point even after a rain, this suggests the leak is in the liner. There are kits to patch liners.

ers, and bring indoors those pots that may crack in the cold.

 PRUNING

In expectation of first frost and plant dormancy, prune off dead and dying stems from marginal and bog plants to prevent their falling into the water. Treat them as you would any perennial, and cut them all the way back after frost.

In anticipation of leaf fall from deciduous trees, cover the water garden pond with leaf netting. If this is the year for a major cleaning, there is no need to set up netting until that job is done.

 PROBLEMS

Insect and disease problems can be reduced next year by cutting back plants as they go dormant. This will reduce pest eggs and disease spores.

Predator birds will be able to get at the fish when plant foliage no longer covers the water surface to provide shelter. Set up leaf netting early to reduce invasions from predator birds.

OCTOBER
WATER & BOG PLANTS

 PLANNING

This is water garden pond cleaning month in most regions of Ohio. Do this project either before or during leaf fall time, but schedule it as plants are going dormant and can be cut back. Whether you are doing it yourself or hiring someone to do it, clean the pond at least every year or two before the ground freezes. In alternate years, it is usually sufficient to gently scoop out accumulated organic matter from the bottom of the pond with a net.

Fall is also a good time to make improvements in the water garden:

• Install a waterfall to help aerate the water throughout the year.

• Add a pump or a filter.

• Add low-voltage lighting around the pond to softly reflect the water surface.

Empty aboveground water gardens in jars and barrels, and store the plants, because they will freeze aboveground.

Shopping List: landscape lighting kit, hardy bulbs, mulch

 PLANTING

Pull any remaining plants out of the water garden, if they have not already been removed because of cleaning. Store tender ones in their pots of wet soil in plastic bags with air holes punched in them. Tubers of **lotus** or **water lily** can be stored wrapped in damp newspaper in the plastic bags. Make sure they are in a place that does not freeze during the winter.

 CARE

Water garden ponds that have preformed or flexible liners rather than natural soil bottoms need cleaning so the decaying organic matter that accumulates at the bottom does not utilize all the oxygen in the water. This will degrade the water quality and possibly kill the fish. It is not difficult to clean a pond, but it does take time.

1. Drain most of the water by disconnecting the tube that pumps water to the waterfall or fountain and directing it to pump water out of the pond instead.

2. Remove all potted marginal plants from the shelf. Inspect them to be sure that tiny fish are not caught in them. Set them aside.

3. Net the fish, and temporarily put them in one of the pails filled with pond water. Pull up the trailing stems of submerged plants and floating plants, and save cuttings from them in other pails.

4. Lift the pots of **hardy water lilies**, and place them in the shade. If it is a sunny, warm day, cover them with wet newspaper.

5. Restart the pump, and drain the pond completely so that the layer of mud is exposed. With a plastic shovel, scrape up the mud, and put it in a garden cart or pail.

6. Rinse the sides of the pond with the hose, gently dislodging any dirt with a soft broom. It is not necessary to get every bit of matter from the sides and bottom. Pump the rinse water from the bottom where it collects.

7. Stop and inspect the liner for tears or cracks, and repair if necessary. Return to the bottom of the pond a small amount of the mud you removed to provide the microbial life necessary to promote healthy water.

8. Prune back the stems and foliage of **hardy water lilies** and other plants that will be overwintering deep in the water. Set these pots on the bottom at the pond's deepest point.

GETTING THEIR FEET WET

There are *water plants* and there are plants that will *grow in water*. Those in the first group, true aquatic plants, require a water environment to grow and thrive. Those in the second group are plants typically grown in soil, but also grow well in a water environment. Among these are **hostas** such as 'Gold Standard' and 'Frances Williams', certain **ornamental grasses**, **canna**, **creeping jenny** (*Lysimachia nummularia* 'Aurea'), **sedges**, and some **hibiscus**.

Hosta 'Gold Standard'

9. Begin to refill the pond with fresh water from the hose. Add dechlorinating and fish conditioning treatment crystals to the water as it fills.

10. Return the fish to the pond if the temperature of the water in the fish-holding pail is not much different from that of the new water in the pond. If the new water is very cold, allow it to stand for a while before returning fish.

11. When the pond is full, lay narrow-gauge netting over it. It will prevent falling leaves and debris from trees from falling into the clean water, yet it will let light through.

PRUNING

As they go dormant, cut back withered plants in the boggy garden area. Leave **ornamental grasses** to enhance the winter landscape.

PROBLEMS

Frogs and toads need to burrow in the mud for the winter. In ponds with preformed or flexible liners, they do it in the soil near the edge. When fastening the leaf netting over the water, leave a can that is open at both ends or a piece of pipe under one edge to allow frogs and toads to move from the soil to the water and back. Also leave a place for birds and other wildlife to access the water to drink when unfrozen fresh water is at a premium during the winter.

Delay spreading a fresh layer of mulch on soil beds until after the ground freezes to prevent rodents from nesting near the pond.

NOVEMBER
WATER & BOG PLANTS

PLANNING

If your water garden pond is over 2 feet deep, it is possible to overwinter the fish as well as the hardy plants in it in most areas of Ohio. (The typical preformed, molded water garden ponds are not deep enough to assure that some of the water will be below the frost line.) As long as it is not frozen solid, the water can supply necessary oxygen for the fish. Some gardeners install a water heater or de-icer device to prevent the water surface from freezing at all. Others keep their pump running to keep the water moving. A waterfall may freeze over periodically, but underneath the ice crust the water may keep moving which will aerate the pond.

Think about expanding your water garden next year with the installation of a preformed pool or setting up several decorative jars or half-barrels at different sites on the property.

Shopping List: ornamental jars or pans for growing and displaying water plants indoors

PLANTING

An alternative to overwintering **tender water lilies** in their dormant state in a cool place is to bring them into the warm house

and grow them as houseplants. Use dwarf or miniature **water lily** varieties for this.

Lift them from the outdoor water garden before they go completely dormant. Cut back dead foliage, and trim excessive matting roots. Divide overgrown tubers by cutting them into pieces with growing points on each. Repot one piece of tuber (or more) in soil in a pot. Set the pot in an attractive cache pot that holds water and place it in a sunny window. Store as dormant or discard the rest of the tuber pieces.

CARE

As hard frost threatens this month, be sure all tender water plants are properly stored in an unheated area that will not freeze. An old refrigerator in the basement set at 45 degrees Fahrenheit or a cool cellar is suitable. Last call for winterizing water gardens:

- After removing all plants, drain, clean, and cover shallow preformed ponds so they will not collect debris and water over the winter.
- Cut back and set hardy plants at the deepest part of a deep pond with a flexible liner. The filter will not be necessary during the winter. Optional: Install a heater or de-icer.

- Cover the pond with netting to keep the water clean and protect the fish from predators.
- Remove and store plants, then drain, rinse out, and overturn wooden half-barrels and other ornamental containers that will winter outdoors.
- Bring terra cotta, plastic, and ceramic jars indoors to prevent them from cracking in the cold.
- Spread a 2- to 3-inch layer of organic material over bog and soil beds as a winter mulch to buffer extreme fluctuations in soil temperature.

PROBLEMS

Blowing leaves and falling twigs from trees are a problem all winter. Stretch netting with a UV inhibitor across the pond, and fasten it securely to keep leaves from landing in the water. By doing this, light will be better able to enter the pond for the fish.

Desiccation of stored water plants can be a problem if there is low humidity. Make sure those in pots of wet soil are covered with plastic with air holes. Wrap divisions or cuttings from tubers and roots in layers of wet newspaper in a similar plastic bag.

DECEMBER
WATER & BOG PLANTS

PLANNING

It's never too soon to start your list of New Year's resolutions. Put "keep a garden journal" at the top, and resolve to try at least one new kind of water plant next year. Year's end is the perfect time to reflect on the past season of water gardening:

- Take a few minutes to catch up on this year's journal or notebook, and record the triumphs and the defeats in the water garden over the past months.
- Try to find all the labels from the plants you acquired this past season, and store them in an envelope in the back of the journal.
- Take some photographs before and after the first snow to remind you of how the water garden looks off-season.

Enjoy the glow of the holiday lights shimmering on the water garden surface this month.

Shopping List/Christmas List: a book on aquatic plants, membership in a water garden society, subscription to a water gardening magazine, an aquarium set up for overwintering tender aquatic plants

PLANTING

No planting is necessary this month.

CARE

If it has been a dry fall and early winter, it may be necessary to raise the water level of the water garden pond. Maximum depth protects the liner and the plants at the bottom. Add dechlorinating drops if there are fish in the pond.

PRUNING

Pots of hardy plants should be at least 2 feet deep in the water at the bottom of the pond.

No plant stems or foliage of overwintering hardy water plants should protrude above the water surface. If some have started to send up shoots because of a mild fall, cut them back to the soil level in their pots.

PROBLEMS

Unsatisfactory plants are invasive and/or obviously out of scale with the garden area, surrounding plants, or your yard. This is often true of varieties of **lotus**, **cattails**, and certain marginal plants such as **petasites**. Remove them from your water garden, and plant other plants instead. **Lotus** and **cattails** come in dwarf versions that may be more suitable.

A frozen pond surface is not a problem as long as there is oxygen in the water. Sometimes portions of the ice will thaw when the sun comes out later in the day or the next day. Use a de-icer, or run the pump to circulate the water in the pond and aerate it.

HELPFUL HINTS

A celebrity in any bog garden is the **pitcher plant**, and the **common pitcher plant** (*Sarracenia purpurea*) will grow in Ohio. These exotic plants, with their thick, hollow green or purple veined stems topped with hoods to trap insects, are interesting throughout the year. In the spring they send up narrow stems topped with nodding purplish flowers containing five petals. Try growing one!

Annuals & Biennials

Common Name (Botanical Name)	Bloom Time Height x Spread	Light Needs	Start Seeds Indoors (or Direct-Sow) Degree of Difficulty
Alyssum (*Lobularia maritima*)	May to frost 2 to 6 in. x 10 to 12 in.	Sun to part shade	Mid-May Easy
Asparagus Fern (*Asparagus* spp.)	Summer foliage 1 to 2 ft. x 1 to 2 ft.	Sun to part shade to full shade	Propagated by plant division Easy
Begonia, Wax/Fibrous (*Begonia* spp.)	Later spring to early fall 6 to 12 inches	Sun to shade	8 to 12 weeks before last frost Difficult
Blanket Flower (*Gaillardia pulchella*)	Summer 24 to 30 inches	Sun	4 to 6 weeks (or direct-sow fall/spring); Moderately easy
Blue Salvia (*Salvia farinacea*)	June until hard fall freeze 16 to 20 in. x 10 to 12 in.	Sun to part shade	Mid-May Medium
Browallia (*Browallia speciosa*)	Summer 9 to 10 inches	Sun to part shade	8 to 10 weeks before last frost Easy—may self seed
Cobbitty Daisies (*Argyranthemum frutescens*)	Mid-May to frost 8 to 14 in. x 8 to 10 in.	Sun to part shade	Mid-May Medium
Cockscomb (*Celosia* spp.)	June to frost 6 to 40 in. x 8 to 12 in.	Sun to part shade	Mid-May Easy
Coleus (*Solenostemon scutellarioides*)	Late spring to early fall 8 to 20 inches	Shade, sun for cultivars	6 to 8 weeks before last frost Moderately easy
Cosmos (*Cosmos bipinnatus*)	June to fall 1 to 4 ft. x 1 to 2 ft.	Sun to part shade	Mid-May Easy
Dianthus (*Dianthus* hybrids)	Mid-April to frost 6 to 10 in. x 8 to 12 in.	Sun to part shade	Mid-May Medium
Flowering Tobacco (*Nicotiana alata*)	Late May to frost 1 to 2 ft. x 1 ft.	Sun to part shade	Mid-May Easy
Geranium (*Pelargonium x hortorum*)	May to October 1 to 2 ft. x 1 to 1 ft.	Sun to part shade	Mid-May Difficult
Gloriosa Daisy (*Rudbeckia hirta*)	Summer 24 to 30 inches	Sun	6 to 8 weeks before last frost Easy—may self seed
Impatiens (*Impatiens walleriana*)	May to frost To 3 ft. x 1 to 2 ft. or more	Best in part shade	Mid-May Easy
Love-in-a-mist (*Nigella damascena*)	Spring 12 to 18 inches	Sun	(Direct-sow into garden) Moderately easy—self seeds
Marigold (*Tagetes* spp.)	May to frost 6 to 36 in. (by variety) x 8 to 18 in.	Sun to part shade	Mid-May Very Easy—self seeds
Melampodium (*Melampodium paludosum*)	June to hard frost 8 to 36 in. (depending on variety and spacing) x 18 to 24 in.	Sun to part shade	Mid-May Very Easy—self seeds

PLANTING CHARTS

Annuals & Biennials

Common Name (Botanical Name)	Bloom Time Height x Spread	Light Needs	Start Seeds Indoors (or Direct-Sow) Degree of Difficulty
Mexican Sunflower (*Tithonia rotundifolia*)	Summer to fall 36 to 60 inches	Sun	4 to 6 weeks before last frost Easy
Million Bells® (*Calibrachoa* hybrids)	May to frost 3 to 12 in. x 12 to 24 in.	Sun to part shade	Seed not available Very High—since you can't find seed to plant
Moss Rose (*Portulaca grandiflora*)	Late May to frost 4 to 6 in. x 6 to 8 in.	Sun to part shade	Mid-May Very Easy—self seeds
Nemesia (*Nemesia* cultivars)	June to frost 10 to 14 in. x 8 to 10 in.	Sun to part shade	Mid-May Medium
Ornamental Cabbage and **Kale** Brassica oleracea)	September through late fall 1 foot	Sun	Mid-May Easy
Pansy (*Viola* x *wittrockiana*)	March to June and September to winter 6 to 10 in. x 6 to 8 in.	Sun to part shade	Mid-May Easy
Petunia (*Petunia* x *hybrida*)	Early May to late fall 6 to 16 in. x 12 to 36 in.	Sun to part shade	Mid-May Easy
Polka-Dot Plant (*Hypoestes phyllostachya*)	Summer 12 inches	Sun to part shade	6 to 8 weeks before last frost Moderate
Red Salvia (*Salvia splendens*)	Summer 7 to 24 inches	Sun	8 to 10 weeks before last frost Moderate
Scaevola 'New Wonder' (*Scaevola aemula* 'New Wonder')	Late May to frost 1 ft. x 1 to 2 ft. (or more)	Sun to part shade	Mid-May Medium
Snapdragon (*Antirrhinum majus*)	Mid-May to killing frost 6 to 36 in. x 8 to 12 in.	Sun to part shade	Mid-May Easy
Spider Plant (*Cleome hassleriana*)	June to killing frost 3 to 4 ft. x 1 to 2 ft.	Sun to part shade	Mid-May Easy
Sweet William (*Dianthus barbatus*)	Late summer 6 to 12 inches	Sun	10 weeks before last frost Moderately easy
Tobacco Flower (*Nicotiana alata*)	Summer To 5 feet	Sun to part shade	6 to 8 weeks before last frost Moderately easy
Treasure Flower (*Gazania* series)	Summer 8 to 11 inches	Sun	4 to 6 weeks before last frost Moderately easy
Verbena (*Verbena* x *hybrida*)	Summer 10 to 20 inches	Sun	8 to 10 weeks before last frost Moderately easy
Wishbone Flower (*Torenia fournieri*)	Summer through fall 8 inches	Part sun to shade	8 to 10 weeks before last frost Easy
Zinnia, Tall (*Zinnia elegans*)	Summer to fall To 36 inches	Sun	5 to 7 weeks before last frost Easy

PLANTING CHARTS

Bulbs, Corms, Rhizomes, & Tubers

Common Name (Botanical Name)	Planting Hardiness	Time	Depth	Bloom Time
Allium (*Allium* spp.)	Hardy	Fall	4 to 8 inches	Late spring to mid summer
Amaryllis (*Hippeastrum* spp.)	Tender	Fall—in pot	2/3 soil covered	Force for indoor winter bloom
Autumn Crocus (*Crocus speciosus*)	Hardy	Mid to late October	4 to 6 inches	Mid to late October
Autumn Daffodil (*Sternbergia lutea*)	Hardy	Late summer	4 to 6 inches	Late September to October; wintergreen foliage
Bearded Iris (*Iris germanica*)	Hardy	Late summer Fall	At soil surface partly exposed	Flowers late May, early June; foliage all summer
Common Caladium (*Caladium bicolor*)	Tender	Spring - after last frost	3 to 4 inches	Grown for foliage; multicolored foliage all summer
Common Hyacinth (*Hyacinthus orientalis*)	Hardy	Fall	6 inches	April (strongly fragrant)
Common Tulip (*Tulipa* x hybrids)	Hardy	Fall	6 to 8 inches	April or May
Crown Imperial (*Fritillaria*)	Hardy	Fall	8 inches	Mid April to Mid May
Daffodil (*Narcissus* spp.)	Hardy	Early fall	6 to 8 inches	Late March through April (naturalizes easily)
Gladiola (*Gladiolus* x *hortulanus*)	Tender	Spring	2 to 3 inches	Mid to late summer if planted at 2-week intervals (stake)
Grape Hyacinth (*Muscari armeniacum*)	Hardy	Fall	4 inches	Leaves in fall; flowers April to May
Resurrection Lily (*Lycoris squamigera*)	Hardy	Fall	6 inches	Leafs out in spring and dies back; flowers in August
Siberian Squill (*Scilla sibirica*)	Hardy	Fall	4 inches	March and April (naturalizes easily)
Snowdrop (*Galanthus nivalis*)	Hardy	Fall	4 to 6 inches	Late February to March
Summer Snowflake (*Leucojum aestivum*)	Hardy	Fall	6 inches	April; tolerates wet soil
Winter Aconite (*Eranthis* spp.)	Hardy	Fall	3 inches	February to March (likes deciduous shade)
Wood Hyacinth (*Hyacinthoides* spp.)	Hardy	Fall	4 to 6 inches	May

PLANTING CHARTS

Culinary Herbs

Plant Name (Botanical Name)	Plant Seeds in Garden	Comments
Chives (*Allium schoenoprasum*)	March 15 – April 15	Sun. Onion substitute. Nice flowers, but flowers change the flavor. Can be brought inside in fall.
Cilantro-Coriander (*Coriandrum sativum*)	March 15 – April 15	Same plant produces foliage (called cilantro) and seeds (called coriander). Used in Chinese stir-fry and Mexican dishes.
Dill (*Anethum graveolens*)	March 15 – April 15	Needs sun and rich soil. Plant in succession for a supply all season.
Fennel (*Fueniculum vulgare*)	March 15 – April 15	Sun, well-limed soil. Grow away from other herbs. Use green version; bronze type is more ornamental than food crop.
Horseradish (*Aronoracia rusticana*)	March – April	Buy divisions the first time. You will cry when you grind this.
Mint (*Mentha spicata*)	March 15 – April 15	Sun. Easier to buy plants; many kinds available. Grow in containers to prevent invasive spreading.
Oregano (*Origanum* spp.)	March 15 – April 15	Sun. Easier to buy plants. There are several kinds.
Parsley (*Petroselinum crispum*)	April 15 – May 15	Sun to part sun. Easy to start from seed; grows better in compost enriched soil.
Peppermint (*Mentha piperita*)	March 15 – April 15	Sun. Strong mint flavor! Very invasive! Consider growing in pots rather than in the ground.
Rosemary (*Rosmarinus officinalis*)	April 15 – May 15	Sun. Woody shrub. Buy started plants. Protect or bring inside for winter.
Sage *Salvia officinalis*)	April 1 – May 15	Ornamental foliage in gray-green or multicolor. Sun or part sun. Favorite for pork, sausage, poultry, and cheese.
Salad Burnet (*Sanguisorba minor*)	March – April	Full sun. Salad herb. Use in herb cheese, butters, and dips.
Sweet Basil *Ocimum basilicum*)	May 15 – June 15	Sun. Once it bushes out, pinch it back to keep it from flowering which allows it to produce flavorful leaves
Sweet Marjoram (*Origanum marjorama*)	May 1 – May 31	Sun. Meats, salads, eggs, soups, sauces, vinegars, vegetables.
Tarragon (*Artemisia dracunculus*)	March 15 – April 15	Buy started plants. Sun to part sun. Licorice flavor.
Thyme (*Thymus vulgaris*)	March 15 – April 15	Sun to part sun. Over 400 varieties. Great groundcover.

Vegetables—A Few Favorites

Plant	Variety/ Maturity in Days	Sow Seeds Indoors	Plant Seeds/ Plants Outdoors	Spacing between plants (inches)
Beans, Snap	Bush Blue Lake/56		May 15 to July 15	3
Beets	Detroit Dark Red/63		April 15 to July 10	1 to 3
Broccoli	Packman/48	March 1 to 31	April 10 to May 15 (plants)	24
Cabbage	Stonehead/70	March 1 to 31	April 10 to May 15 (plants)	12
Corn, White	Silver Queen/92		April 20 to May 15	10
Cucumbers, Slicing	Marketmore/70	March 20 to April 20	May 15 to June 15	30
Eggplant	Dusky/68	March 15 to 31	May 15 to June 15	24
Garlic	Elephant/127		Plant in late September	4
Lettuce, Butterhead	Buttercrunch/64	March 1	April 1 and August 1	12
Onion Sets	Early Yellow Globe/96	February 1	April 1 to 30	2 to 3
Parsnips	All American/110		April 1 to 30	3 to 4
Peas, Garden	Green Arrow/70		April 1 to May 15	3
Peppers, Bell	Staddons Select/72	March 15 to 31	May 15 to June 1	18
Pumpkins	Atlantic Giant/120	April 20	June 1 to 15	6
Squash, Winter	Early Butternut/85	April 15	May 15 to June 15	36
Squash, Yellow	Sundance/50	April 15	May 15 to June 15	24
Squash, Zucchini	Zucchini Elite/48	April 15	May 15 to June 15	24
Tomatoes , Cherry	Sweet Chelsea/64	April 7 to 20	May 15 to June 1	18
Tomatoes, Early to mid	Better Boy VFN/72	April 7 to 20	May 15 to June 1	24 (staked)
Turnips, Roots	Purple Top White Globe/58		July 25 to August 25	3

PLANTING CHARTS

Turfgrasses

Name	Characteristics	Start As	Uses	Problems
Fine Fescues (Chewings, Fine, Hard, Creeping, Red, Sheep)	Very thin blades for fine texture. Tolerates shade best. Tolerates poor soils.	Seed—fall	Use in mixtures with other turfgrasses. Good for shade and/or dry areas.	Does not recover quickly from damage. Tends to lie flat and cause uneven mowing.
Kentucky Bluegrass	Fine, uniform texture. Excellent color. Repairs itself well under normal use. Full sun best.	Seed—fall. Sod—spring or fall.	Areas on display.	Heavy feeder, needs lots of water. Vulnerable to powdery mildew, other fungal diseases, chinch bugs, grubs, sod webworms.
Perennial Ryegrass	Nice texture and color. Germinates quickly.	Seed—fall. Sod— spring or fall.	Use as "nurse" grass in mixtures. Patch bare spots in summer.	Suffers in extreme heat—may get pythium. Vulnerable to brown patch, red thread, rust, snow mold, dollar spot.
Turf-Type Tall Fescue	Durable, withstands foot traffic. Relatively drought-tolerant. Needs less fertilizer.	Seed—fall. Sod—spring	Ideal alone or in mixture for lawns with heavy use, athletic fields, public areas.	Can be vulnerable to pythium, brown patch, sod webworms, billbugs.

Perennials

Common Name (Botanical Name)	Bloom Time Height x Spread	Cultural Requirements	Comments
Autumn Joy Sedum Showy Stonecrop (*Sedum 'Autumn Joy'*)	August to Frost 1 to 2 feet x 2 feet	Full sun to part shade.	Plant in well-drained soil. Very drought tolerant.
Beebalm (*Monarda* spp.)	Late June through July 2 to 4 feet x 4 to 5 feet	Sun to part shade. Moist soil.	Attracts butterflies and bees. Aromatic foliage. Red and pink mophead flowers. Plant mildew-resistant cultivars.
Black-eyed Susan (*Rudbeckia fulgida* 'Goldsturm')	July through September 2 to 3 feet x 2 feet	Sun. Moist, well-drained soil. Established plants tolerate drought.	Yellow daisy flower. Spreads quickly; self-seeds readily. Attracts butterflies and goldfinches. Disease resistant.
Blazing Star Spike Gayfeather (*Liatris spicata*)	July and August 2 to 3 feet x 2 feet	Sun. Moist, well-drained soil. Tolerates drought.	Purple or white flower spikes, grassy foliage. Long-lived native. No pests or significant disease.
Candytuft (*Iberis sempervirens*)	Late May 8 inches x 10 inches	Sun; well-drained soil.	Neat, low-growing, ever-green foliage; white flowers. May rebloom if sheared after early flowering. For edging, filler.

PLANTING CHARTS

Perennials

Common Name (Botanical Name)	Bloom Time Height x Spread	Cultural Requirements	Comments
Columbine (*Aquilegia* spp.)	May 1 to 3 feet x 1 foot	Sun, part shade. Moist, well-drained soil.	Flowers are spurred cups in red, blue, white, and yellow. Leafminer problems. Cut back midsummer for new foliage.
Coral Bells (*Heuchera* spp.)	May and June 1 to 2 feet x 1 to 2 feet	Part shade, shade. Moist soil	Semievergreen and many fascinating leaf patters. Sprays of tiny bell flowers on long stems.
Coreopsis, Tickseed (*Coreopsis* spp.)	June through September 1 to 2 feet	Sun. Moist, well-drained soil; can handle drought.	Yellow flowers rebloom if deadheaded. Some have threadleaf foliage; others, lanceleaf. Easy care.
Daylily (*Hemerocallis* hybrids)	June through September 1 to 4 feet x 2 to 4 feet	Sun for best bloom. Moist, well-drained soil.	Trumpet flowers in shades of yellow, red, orange, lilac, and cream grow on stems among strappy green foliage. Deer favorites.
English Lavender (*Lavandula angustifolia* 'Hidcote')	June until October 1 to 3 feet x 2 to 3 feet	Full sun to part shade. Needs good drainage.	Very drought tolerant. Do not fertilize this plant. Semievergreen.
Garden Mum (*Chrysanthemum x morifolium*)	August to late October 1 to 3 feet x 2 feet	Full sun to part shade. Average to moist soil.	Keep them pinched back to 12 inches. No bugs or disease problems.
Goldenrod (*Solidago* spp.)	Midsummer to fall 2 to 4 feet x 2 to 4 feet	Sun, part shde. Moist, well-drained soil. Drought resistant when established.	Sprays of tiny yellow florets on feathery spikes. Attracts butterflies and beneficial insects. Good as cut flowers, fresh or dried.
Hellebore Lenten Rose (*Helleborus orientalis*)	March to April 15 to 20 inches	Part shade, shade. Moist, well-drained soil.	Cream, maroon, speckled open-cupped flowers. Winter interest plus early flowering.
Hosta Plantain Lily (*Hosta* spp.)	July or August 6 to 24 inches x 1 to 3 feet	Part shade, shade. Moist, slightly acidic soil.	Variegated, ruffled, or rippled foliage in greens, blue-green, and yellow. Deer and slug favorites.
Lamb's Ear (*Stachys byzantina*)	July and August Insignificant blooms. 8 to 10 inches x 24 to 36 inches	Full sun to part shade. Average, well-drained soil.	Silvery foliage. Very drought tolerant. Fertilize once in spring with a time-release fertilizer.

PLANTING CHARTS

Perennials

Common Name (Botanical Name)	Bloom Time Height x Spread	Cultural Requirements	Comments
Lobelia (*Lobelia* spp.)	Summer and fall 2 to 4 feet x 1 foot	Part shade. Moist soil.	Tall flower spikes bring reds, blues, white, and pastels to late-season shade gardens.
Phlox, Garden (*Phlox paniculata*)	July and August 1 to 3 feet	Full sun. Moist, well-drained soil.	Domed flower clusters in reds, pinks, white on straight stems. Look for mildew-resistant cultivars.
Purple Coneflower (*Echinacea purpurea*)	July to August 2 to 4 feet	Sun. Ordinary soil. Drought tolerant.	Purple-petaled daisy with orange center. Attracts butterflies, goldfinches, and beneficial insects.
Shasta Daisy (*Leucanthemum* x *superbum*)	June and July 1 to 3 feet x 2 feet	Sun, part shade. Moist, well-drained soil.	White daisy attracts butterflies and beneficial insects. Easy care in flower border.
Virginia Bluebells (*Mertensia virginica*)	April to May 1 foot x 1 foot	Morning sun to all shade. Moist soil.	Use acid-loving plant food. Keep soil moist; woodland plant.
Yarrow Milfoil (*Achillea* spp.)	June to August 1 to 4 feet x 3 feet	Full sun. Well-drained soil.	Flat clusters of florets in shades of red, pink, yellow, gold. Deer resistant. Basically pest-free.

Ornamental Grasses

Common Name (Botanical Name)	Size	Ornamental Qualities	Comments
Blue Fescue (*Festuca glauca*)	6 to 12 inches x 12 inches	Wiry, blue-gray foliage; thick clumps resemble mopheads.	Good for ground cover duty, edging, and between stones in walkways
Feather Reed Grass (*Calamagrostis acutiflora*)	4 to 5 feet x 4 to 5 feet	Upright habit. Deep-green foliage. Flowers appear early summer, then turn beige; attractive through fall.	'Karl Foerster' is 2001 PPA winner. Usually massed for vertical accent.
Fountain Grass (*Pennisetum alopecuroides*)	3 feet	Glossy, narrow foliage forms a shimmering clump topped by lovely, foxtail flowers.	Great looking plant year-round. Even heavy winter snow cannot disfigure this plant.
Japanese Blood Grass (*Imperata cylindrical*)	2 feet	Red tips give this plant a colorful look all growing season.	Don't be disappointed if you see no flowers. Sometimes it flowers, sometimes it does not. It's colorful regardless.

PLANTING CHARTS

Ornamental Grasses

Common Name (Botanical Name)	Size	Ornamental Qualities	Comments
Little Blue Stem (*Schizachyrium scoparium*)	24 to 36 inches	Very narrow, strong blue foliage. Turns copper-orange in fall. Late summer blooms.	'The Blues' has startling blue foliage.
Maiden Grass (*Miscanthus sinensis*)	3 to 12 feet x spread as permitted	Widely arching leaves. Blooms August to October.	'Strictus' has yellow-banded, upright leaves. Less likely to fall.
Ravenna Grass Hardy Pampas Grass (*Saccharum ravennae*)	To 12 feet tall	Upright, gray-green leaves. September plumes "bloom" at 14-feet plus.	Drought tolerant. One of the tallest hardy grasses.
Purple Fountain Grass (*Pennisetum setaceum* 'Rubrum')	2 feet	Although not hardy, this fast-growing annual adds color to any planting bed.	Rose-red flower spikes in mid- to late-summer.
Ribbon Grass (*Phalaris arundinacea* 'Picta')	2 feet	Green and white striped foliage. Fast growing does well in sun or shade.	Moonlight will illuminate this grass, giving a beautiful glow to the garden.

Roses

Common Name (Botanical Name)	Uses	Bloom	Comments
'Betty Prior'	Specimen or accent.	Single pink flower.	Floribunda. Tall, bushy. Generous blooms. Slightly fragrant.
'Bonica'	Mass, hedge, screen, specimen.	Pastel-pink, double flowers all season.	Landscape. AARS. Orange-red hips in fall.
'Carefree Delight'	Mass, hedge, screen, foundation.	Single, deep-pinkflowers.	Landscape. Consistent color. Generous blooms.
'Carefree Sunshine'	Border, foundation, hedge, massing.	Single, bright-yellow flowers.	Landscape. Introduced for 2001.
Flower Carpet™	Ground cover, slopes, screen.	Magenta, white, apple blossom, yellow.	Landscape. Low, arching stems. Tough, pest-resistant.
'Knock Out'	Medium height. Border and mass planting.	Single, red, light-pink, or pink flowers.	Landscape. AARS. Incredible disease resistance.
'New Dawn'	Medium-sized. Train on fences and walls.	Spring. Double, shell-pink flowers.	Climber. Vigorous. Rebloomer. Great disease resistance.
'Peter Mayle'™	Large upright specimen. Great for cutting.	Double, deep-fuchsia flowers, 4 inches or more.	Hybrid Tea. Wonderful long-lasting rose fragrance. Tolerates heat and humidity.

PLANTING CHARTS

Roses

Common Name (Botanical Name)	Uses	Bloom	Comments
'Queen Elizabeth'	Large upright specimen. Great for cutting.	Large, flat, pink flowers.	Grandiflora. AARS. Some fragrance. An all-time favorite.
'Regatta'	Specimen, cutting.	Medium, double, soft peach-pink flowers.	Hybrid Tea. Fruity fragrance.
Rosa Rugosa hybrids	Border, screen, windbreak hedge.	White, or various shades of red, pink. Textured foliage.	Landscape. Handles drought and sandy or compacted soil. Disease resistant.
'The Fairy'	Mass for ground cover, low hedge. Specimen for container planting.	Continual production of small, pink, double flowers in large sprays.	Landscape. Compact 2-foot shrub. Versatile. Blooms until frost.
'Traviata'	Good for cutting.	Clear-red 4-inch flowers.	Hybrid Tea. Disease-tolerant foliage. Turns burgundy in fall.

Shrubs

Common Name (Botanical Name)	Ornamental Qualities	Uses	Comments
Azalea, Evergreen (Rhododendron spp.)	Flowers early May in pink, white, red. Bronze or maroon fall foliage color.	Foundation, hedge, border, woodland.	Funnel-shaped flowers attract butterflies. Likes acid soil. Deer may eat.
Bayberry (Myrica pensylvanica)	Hardy shrub that can withstand urban stress. Grows well in poor soil in sun or shade.	Makes a great hedge/ screen. Plant where other plants have a hard time adapting.	Females produce fragrant gray berries. Grows 6 to 9 feet high and wide. Trim to desired size.
Bottlebrush Buckeye (Aesculus parviflora)	Showy white flowers appear in late May and last for a month. Great golden-yellow fall leaf color.	Use in full sun to all hade. A great shrub for screening. Grows 8 to 12 feet high and wide.	No bugs or disease problems. If it gets leggy, cut back to the ground to rejuvenate it.
Crimson Pygmy Barberry (Berberis thunbergii 'Crimson Pygmy')	Very dwarf growing, 1 to 2 feet high and wide. Prune to desired size. Great red foliage color.	Small hedge or as underplanting around larger-growing trees and shrubs.	Red leaves turn orange in fall. Plant where it receives one-half to full day sun.
Dwarf Burning Bush (Euonymus alatus 'Compactus')	Great red fall leaf color. Does well in sun or shade.	Mix in a shrub border. Great plant for hedging.	No bugs or disease problems.
Dwarf Spirea (Spirea x bumalda)	Great, low-growing flowering shrub. Will repeat bloom throughout the summer.	Sun to half-day sun. Use as specimen or for l ow hedging.	Grows 2 to 3 feet high by 3 to 5 feet wide. Trim to desired size.

PLANTING CHARTS

Shrubs

Common Name (Botanical Name)	Ornamental Qualities	Uses	Comments
Forsythia (*Forsythia x intermedia*)	Yellow flowers in April, followed by medium-green leaves.	Specimen, foundation, hedge border.	Tough. Tolerates poor soil. No disease or insect problems. Long lived.
Fothergilla (*Fothergilla gardenii*)	Scented, white bottlebrush-type flowers in spring.	Group as accent, specimen, anchor flower bed.	Sturdy, decorate. Fall foliage color.
Juniper (*Juniperus* cultivars)	This plant family includes ground covers, some that grow 3 to 4 fet high and wide, and upright types.	Many uses for junipers. Great foundation plant. Uprights make a good evergreen screen.	Junipers do best where they receive a half-day of sun or more.
Korean Boxwood (*Buxus microphylla* var. *koreana*	Broadleaf evergreen with spreading and upright varieties. Hardy in sun to shade.	Hedging, foundation planting, great in a formal garden.	Very slow growing. Can be pruned to desired height and spread. Very insect resistant. Deer proof.
Lilac (*Syringa vulgaris*)	Cone-shaped clusters of fragrant tubular florets in late April to May.	Shrub border.	Old-fashioned favorite. Long-lived. Foliage tends to get mildew.
Oakleaf Hydrangea (*Hydrangea quercifolia*)	Upright cones of cream-petaled florets in late spring. Deep-red fall foliage, peeling bark.	Woodland, specimen, hedge, foundation.	Stunning all year. Flowers dry beautifully; great for floral crafts.
St. Johnswort (*Hypericum patulum* 'Sungold')	Yellow flowers bloom mid-June to August. Grows 3 feet high and wide.	Hedging. Mixed in a perennial bed. Underplanting around large trees and shrubs.	Beautiful gray-green foliage. Leaves persist well into winter. Full to half day sun.
Viburnum 'Allegheny' (*Viburnum x rhytidophylloides* 'Alleghany')	Broadleaf evergreen shrub twice a growing season. Reddish summer fruits turn black in fall.	Sun or shade. Great for hedging and screening.	May drop leaves during winter in Zone 5. Does not have any twig die-back or pest or disease problems. Trim to desired size.
Viburnum, Doublefile (*Viburnum plicatum tomentosum*)	White flowers in May; red, then black, fruit in fall. Purplish-red fall foliage.	Specimen, shrub border, fenceline.	Japanese snowball version has sterile white, ball-shaped flowers.
Virginia Sweetspire (*Itea virginica*)	Dripping strands of white florets in May. Purple fall foliage color.	Specimen, foundation, woodland.	Spreads by rooted suckers. Likes wet soil.
Weigela (*Weigela florida*)	Tubular white, pin, or rose flowers in late May and June.	Shrub border, anchor flower bed.	Attracts hummingbirds. Newer cultivars are more compact, colorful.
Winterberry Holly (*Ilex verticillata*)	Tiny white flowers in June. Red or orange berries on females.	Accent, focal point, shrub border, property line.	Likes moist soil. Needs a male pollinator to guarantee fruiting.

PLANTING CHARTS

Shrubs

Common Name (Botanical Name)	Ornamental Qualities	Uses	Comments
Witchhazel (*Hamamelis* spp.)	Fragrant yellow flowers in late winter; fall color.	Streetside, specimen.	Force branches indoors for winter bloom.
Yew (*Taxus x media*)	Deep-green, flat, round-tipped needles. Red berries on female yews.	Foundation, hedge, screen, container, topiary.	Accepts radical pruning to renew. Lots of cultivars with different habits. Deer favorite.

Trees

Common Name (Botanical Name)	Ornamental Qualities	Uses	Comments
Baldcypress (*Taxodium distichum*)	Green, soft-needled foliage is deciduous; turns russet in fall.	Accent, screen.	Likes wet soil but does fine in regular. The "knees" are a novelty; stately.
Carolina Silverbell (*Halesia tetraptera*)	White, bell-shaped flowers in April to early May. Good yellow fall leaf color.	Great tree for a small yard.	Grows 15 to 30 feet high by 20 to 35 feet wide. May be hard to find a source.
Eastern Redbud (*Cercis canadensis*)	Deep-pink flowers bloom on bare stems in spring; pods develop in fall. Heart-shaped leaves turn yellow in fall.	Specimen, accent, shade.	Older plants dislike being moved. Susceptible to canker. 'Forest Pansy' has purple foliage.
Flowering Crabapple (*Malus* cultivars)	April blooms in white or pink. Small red or yellow fruits in fall.	Specimen, fenceline, shrub border.	Choose cultivars carefully for disease resistance.
Goldenrain Tree (*Koelreuteria paniculata*)	Yellow flowers in July; interesting dried capsules follow.	Small yards, patios, streetside.	Handles urban conditions.
Hawthorn (*Crataegus viridis* 'Winter King')	White flowers in May, red fall foliage and orange-red fruits. Interesting bark.	Specimen, hedge, streetside, shade.	'Winter King' is disease-resistant, smaller, has fewer thorns.
Holly, American (*Ilex opaca* spp.)	Glossy leaves with spines. Pyramidal shape. Red or yellow berries on females.	Specimen	Tolerates coastal conditions; a deer favorite.
Japanese Lilac Tree (*Syringa reticulata*)	White lilac-shaped flowers in early summer. Glossy, cherrylike bark when young.	Specimen, shade tree.	Neat, conical habit. Disease resistant.
Japanese Zelkova (*Zelkova serrata*)	Pleasing vase shape, great fall foliage color.	Specimen, streetside, shade.	Tough, nearly pest-free. Substitute for elms.

PLANTING CHARTS

Trees

Common Name (Botanical Name)	Ornamental Qualities	Uses	Comments
Katsura Tree (*Cercidiphyllum japonicum*)	Small, reddish flowers in March. Blue-green foliage.	Specimen, shade.	Drought-sensitive. Fall foliage smells like chocolate.
Kousa Dogwood (*Cornus kousa*)	White flowers in June, rich fall color, red dangling fruits. Patchy bark visible in winter.	Specimen, property line, shade woodland.	Blooms later than flowering dogwood. More disease resistant.
Lacebark Elm (*Ulmus parvifolia*)	Blooms in late June. Glossy leaves. Yellow fall foliage.	Streetside, shade.	Peeling bark creates colorful mottled effect.
Linden, Littleleaf (*Tilia cordata*)	Fragrant creamy flowers in late June. Yellow fall foliage.	Specimen, streetside, shade.	Tolerates urban conditions. Flowers attract bees.
Maple, Sugar (*Acer saccharum*)	Rich red, orange, yellow fall foliage.	Shade.	Source of maple syrup.
Maple, Red (*Acer rubrum*)	Blooms in March. Rich red and fold fall foliage color.	Specimen, shade.	Fast grower. Likes moist soil. Copious spring seeds feed wildlife.
Norway Spruce (*Picea abies*)	Dark green evergreen needles. Produces cones as it matures. Grows large over time.	Sun to part shade. Screening, accent.	Deer resistant. Other great spruces include Colorado and Serbian.
Planetree (*Platanus x acerifolia*)	Large leaves. Colorful, peeling, patchy bark. Fuzzy seed capsules in pairs.	Shade.	Less prone to anthracnose; handles urban sites. Moist soils are best.
Sweet Gum (*Liquidambar styraciflua*)	Prickly seed capsules. Red or yellow fall foliage.	Specimen, shade.	Fast growing; likes moisture. Fruitless cultivars available.
Sweetbay Magnolia (*Magnolia virginiana*)	Creamy flowers in June. Semievergreen.	Specimen, flower border.	Takes wet soils. Fragrant flowers.
Tuliptree (*Liriodendron tulipifera*)	Tulip-shaped flowers in May, yellow fall foliage. Straight, stately trunks.	Specimen.	Attracts honeybees, hummingbirds, butterfly larvae. Drought indicator.
Yellowwood (*Cladrastis kentukea*)	Fragrant June flowers, yellow fall foliage, smooth gray bark.	Specimen, shade.	Blooms heavily every other year.

PLANTING CHARTS

Vines

Common Name (Botanical Name)	Habit/ Size	Ornamental Qualities	Comments
Boston Ivy (*Parthenocissus tricuspidata*)	Clinger/50 feet plus	Three-lobed shiny leaves turn scarlet in fall.	Woody perennial. Attracts birds. Mid-June flowers become blue-black berries.
Climbing Hydrangea (*Hydrangea anomala* ssp. *petiolaris*)	Clinger/60 feet plus	Deciduous, textured dark-green leaves. Flat clusters of scented white florets in May.	Woody perennial. Hosts beneficial insects. Attractive rough bark. Slow to establish.
English Ivy (*Hedera helix*)	Clinger/to 90 feet	Glossy, dark-green foliage with three lobes. Mature foliage is rounder.	Woody perennial. Many interesting variegated cultivars. Also used as ground cover.
Hyacinth Bean (*Dolichos lablab*)	Twiner/to 10 feet	Dark-green leaves on purple stems, pink pealike flowers.	Herbaceous annual. Loves heat. Interesting black seeds with a white line. Great.
Hybrid Clematis (*Clematis* hybrids)	Twiner/to 15 feet	May or June blooms, intermittent after primary bloom season. Purple, pinks, white bloom colors. Deciduous.	Woody perennial. Hybrids have large flowers. Prune hard in spring, then agan after major bloom period.
Sweet Pea (*Lathyrus odoratus*)	Clinger/to 6 feet	Charming pea-shaped flowers in pinks. Fragant.	Herbeceous annual. Cool-season; plant early.

Perennial Ground Covers

Common Name (Botanical Name)	Size	Ornamental Qualities	Comments
Allegheny Spurge Pachysandra (*Pachysandra terminalis*)	6 to 10 inches	Evergreen foliage; terminal whorls are medium-green color and smooth.	Versatile, neat, and tough. Prefers shade. Scented white flowers in April.
Bearberry Cotoneaster (*Cotoneaster dammeri*)	8 to 12 inches	Evergreen foliage, tiny white flowers, red berries.	Trailing stems may root when they touch soil.
Creeping Juniper (*Juniperus horizontalis*)	1 to 2 feet	Dense horizontal stems of blue-gree, scalelike foliage.	Tolerates urban sites including heat, drought, and salt conditions. Attracts songbirds. Native
Creeping Phlox (*Phlox stolonifera*)	2 inches	Smooth, tidy, dark-green evergreen foliage hugs the ground. Blue, pink, or white flowers on 10-inch spikes in May.	Likes partial shade, sun-to-shade transition. No mildew problems. Native

PLANTING CHARTS

Perennial Ground Covers

Common Name (Botanical Name)	Size	Ornamental Qualities	Comments
Japanese Painted Fern (*Anthyrium nipponicum* 'Pictum')	12 to 18 inches	Handsome fronds are multicolored reddish, silver, and silvery green.	Slow-growing clumps brighten shade. Likes dappled light.
Lily-of-the-Valley (*Convallaria majalis*)	6 to 8 inches	Deep-green narrow foliage; stems of fragrant, tiny white nodding "bells" in May.	**Caution:** all plant parts are poisonous. Foliage dies back in late summer.
Lilyturf (*Liriope* sp.)	8 to 12 inches	Semievergreen, narrow, green grasslike foliage. Spikes of lavender florets in August, late winter.	Some have leaves of yellow or silver variegation. Cut back in spring for new growth.
Sweet Woodruff (*Galium ordoratum*)	6 to 8 inches	Deeply cut, fine-textured, pale green foliage whorls. Flat clusters of tiny white florets in May.	Shallow, fibrous roots spread rapidly. Likes woodsy soil. Deer leave it alone.
Vinca Periwinkle (*Vinca minor*)	6 to 8 inches	Lustrous, dark-green, oval foliage along wiry stems. Lilac, purple, or white flowers April into May.	Low arching stems root as plants spread. Some have variegated foliage.
Wintercreeper (*Euonymus fortunei*)	8 to 12 inches	Evergreen foliage is all green or variegated with silver or yellow.	Tough and versatile. Also used as a vine. Long lived.

Water and Bog Plants

Common Name (Botanical Name)	Type Hardiness	Size	Comments
Anacharis (*Egeria densa*)	Submerged Hardy	To 3 feet tall	Oxygenator. Floating, evergreen , branched stems bear male white flowers in summer.
Arrowhead (*Sagittaria latifolia*)	Marginal Hardy	1 to 1½ feet tall	Ornamental. Spikes of white flowers over arrow-shaped leaves in summer.
Canna (*Canna glauca*)	Marginal Tender	To 6 feet tall; dwarf, 3 to 4 feet tall	Ornamental. Blooms all summer in many colors. Some are variegated.
Cardinal Flower (*Lobelia cardinalis*)	Bog Hardy	30 to 36 inches tall	Ornamental; transitional plant. Bright-red flowers attract hummingbirds.
Cattail (*Typha* sp.)	Marginal Hardy	To 7 feet tall	Four-season interest. Beige floral spikes in summer.

Water and Bog Plants

Common Name (Botanical Name)	Type Hardiness	Size	Comments
Duckweed (*Lemna minor*)	Floater Hardy	Indefinite spread	Water cover. Multiplies rapidly. Difficult to eradicate. Fish eat it.
Lotus, American (*Nelumbo lutea*)	Immersed Hardy	2 to 3 feet tall	Specimen. Blue-green foliage; yellow flowers bloom in summer. Native.
Lotus, Sacred (*Nelumbo nucifera*)	Immersed Hardy	1 to 7 feet tall	Specimen and accent. Needs warm weather to bloom. Grow in container to control spread.
Parrot's Feather (*Myriophyllum aquaticum*)	Submerged Tender	6-foot long trailing stems	Oxygenator and water cover. Sparse foliage on stems; soft foliate tips show above water.
Snowflake (*Nymphoides indica*)	Floater Tender	Indefinite spread	Water cover. Heart-shaped leaves; small white or yellow summer flowers.
Taro (*Colocasia esculenta*)	Marginal Tender	To 2 to 4 feet tall	Specimen. Dramatic leaves in green, purple, or both. Likes some shade
Water Hyacinth (*Eichhornia crassipes*)	Floater Tender	To 10 to 12 inches	Cleans water. Blue flowers in late summer. Unique root system. Multiples rapidly.
Water Lettuce (*Pistia stratiotes*)	Floater Tender	To 8 inches tall; indefinite spread	Cleans water. Rosettes of wedge-shaped, ribbed leaves. Troubled by aphids.
Water Lily, Hardy (*Nymphea* sp.)	Immersed Hardy	Spreads 2 to 5 feet	Specimen and accent. Summer blooms in many colors; blossoms close at night. Good cut flower.
Water Lily, Tropical (*Nymphea* sp.)	Immersed Tender	Sperads 2 to 5 feet or more	Specimen and accent. Fragrant. Some bloom at night. Blooms held above foliage.
Yellow Flag (*Iris pseudacorus*)	Marginal Hardy	To 1 foot tall	Ornamental. Gray-green strap leaves. Produces 4 to 10 yellow flowers in summer.

Marginal = potted, feet in water at edge of water feature; **Bog** = planted directly in wet soil (with or without water feature); **Immersed** = in pot with roots, crown, and stems completely in water, foliage above; **Submerged** = covered completely with water; ***Floater*** = bobs on surface; **Transition** = essentially a land plant but likes moist soil at water feature's edge

SOURCES

INFORMATION RESOURCES

All America Selections
1311 Butterfield Rd., Suite 310
Downers Grove, IL 60515
(603) 963-0770
www.all-americaselections.org

American Nusery and Landscape Association
1000 Vermont Avenue, NW,
Suite 300, Washington, D.C.
20005-4914
(202) 789-2900
www.anla.org

American Rose Society
P.O. Box 30,000
8877 Jefferson Paige Road
Shreveport, LA 71119
Phone: (318) 938-5402
www.ars.org

Ball Horticultural Company
622 Town Road
West Chicago, IL 60185
(630) 231-3600
www.ballhort.com

International Society of Arboriculture
P.O. Box 3129
Champaign, IL 61826
1400 W. Anthony Drive
Champaign, IL 61821
(217) 355-9411
www.isa-arbor.com

National Audubon Society
700 Broadway
New York, NY 10003
(212) 979-3000
www.audubon.org

National Wildlife Federation Backyard Wildlife Habitat Program
11100 Wildlife Center Drive
Reston, VA 20190-5362
(800) 822-9919
www.nwf.org/backyard wildlife habitat

Netherlands Flower Bulb Information Center
30 Midwood Street
Brooklyn, NY 11225
(718) 693-5400
www.bulb.com

Ohio Department of Agriculture
8995 E. Main Street
Reynoldsburg, OH 43068-3399
(800) 282-1955
www.ohioagriculture.gov

Ohio Nursery & Landscape Association
72 Dorchester Square
Westerville, OH 43081-3350
(614) 899-1195
www.onla.org

PGMS Professional Grounds Management Society
720 Light Street
Baltimore, MD 21230-3816
(800) 609-P?GMS
www.pgms.org

Proven Winners Color Choice
12601 120th Avenue
Grand Haven, MI
49417-9621
(877) 865-5818
www.ColorChoicePlants.com

Turfgrass Producers International
2 E. Main Street
East Dundee, IL 60118
(847) 649-5555
www.turfgrasssod.org

MAIL-ORDER & RETAIL SOURCES

A.M. Leonard
241 Fox Drive
Piqua, OH 45356-0816
(800) 543-8955
www.amleo.com
tools, supplies

Ball Seed Company
622 Town Road
West Chicago, IL 60185
(630) 231-3600
www.ballseed.com
seeds

Ben Meadows Company
P.O. Box 5277
Janesville, WI 53547-5277
(800) 241-6401
www.benmeadows.com
tools, supplies

Brent & Becky's Bulbs
7900 Daffodil Lane
Gloucester, VA 23601
(877) 661-2852
www.brentandbeckysbulbs.com
bulbs

Burpee Seed Company
300 Park Avenue
Warminster, PA 18974
(800) 888-1447
www.burpee.com
seeds, flowering plants

The Conard-Pyle Company
372 Rose Hill Road
West Grove, PA 19390-0904
(800) 458-6559
www.conard-pyle.com
roses, shrubs, perennials, ground covers

SOURCES

Duncraft
102 Fisherville Road
Concord, NH 03303
(888) 879-5095
www.duncraft.com
bird supplies

Forestfarm
990 Tetherow Road
Williams OR 97544-9599
(541) 846-7269
www.forestfarm.com
trees, shrubs, perennials

Gardener's Supply Company
128 Intervale Road
Burlington, VT 05401
(800) 833-1412
www.gardeners.com
tools and supplies

Jackson & Perkins
1 Rose Lane
Medford, OR 97501
(877) 322-2300
www.jacksonandperkins.com
roses, perennials, bulbs

The Lily Garden
4902 NE 147th Avenue
Vancouver, WA 98682-6067
(360) 253-6273
www.thelilygarden.com
lilies

Lilypons Water Gardens
6800 Lily Pons Road
P.O. Box 10
Buckeystown, MD 21717-0010
(800) 999-5459
www.lilypons.com
water lilies, bog plants

**Meadowbrook Nursery/
We-Du Natives**
2055 Polly Spout Road
Marion, NC 28752
(828) 728-8300
www.we-du.com
*perennials, wildflowers,
ferns, azaleas*

Musser Forest
1880 Rt.119 Hwy. N
Indiana, PA 15701
(724) 465-5685
www.musserforests.com
trees, shrubs, ground covers

Park Seed Company
1 Parkton Avenue
Greenwood, SC 29647
(800) 845-3369
www.parkseed.com
seeds, perennials

Plow & Hearth
7021 Wolftown-Hood Road
Madison, VA 22727
(800) 627-1712
www.plowhearth.com
tools, supplies

Proven Winners Color Choice
12601 120th Avenue
Grand Haven, MI 49417-9621
(877) 865-5818
www.ColorChoicePlants.com
flowering plants

Renee's Garden
7389 W. Zayante Road
Felton, CA 95018
(888) 880-7228
www.reneesgarden.com
*gourmet vegetables, kitchen herbs,
cottage garden flowers*

Seeds of Change
1 Sunset Way
Henderson, NV 89014
(888) 762-7333
www.seedsofchange.com
*organically grown vegetable and
flower seeds*

Swallowtail Garden Seeds
122 Calistoga Road, #178
Santa Rosa, CA 95409
(707) 538-3585
www.swallowtailgardenseeds.com
*annuals, perennials,
vines, vegetables*

Wayside Gardens
1 Garden Lane
Hodges, SC 29695-0001
(800) 213-0379
www.waysidegardens.com
perennials, shrubs, roses, bulbs

White Flower Farm
P.O. Box 50
Litchfield, CT 06759-0050
(800) 503-9624
www.whiteflowerfarm.com
perennials, shrubs, roses, bulbs

TROUBLESHOOTING PESTS & DISEASES

Pest Name	Common Target	Appearance	Damage	Some Control Methods
Aphids (aka **Plant Lice**)	Houseplants; trees; shrubs; flowers; vegetables; water plants.	Soft, pear-shaped spindly legs. May be green, yellow, pink, black, or white.	Clusters on stems and foliage of tender new growth cause wilted, curling foliage and sap plant vigor.	Pinch infested tips and discard. Wash with water spray, insecticidal soap, or neem spray. Green lacewings and ladybugs eat.
Bagworms	Needled evergreens.	Bags of fine twigs dangle from branches.	Larvae feed on foliage, then retreat to protective bag.	Pick off reachable bags. Spray Bt on foliage while worms feed.
Bean Beetles, Mexican	Green beans, limas, summer and winter squash.	Round, copper-colored beetle, rows of black dots on its back. Yellow eggs under leaves. Striped small beetle adult.	They chew on leaves, skeletonize them.	Handpick beetles and larvae. Use neem, pyrethrum spray on beetles.
Borers	Shrubs, (especially roses, lilac); trees (especially fruit trees); squash.	Larvae of beetles and moths; small worms burrow into plant stems.	Leaves wilt; holes in woody stems, sawdust nearby.	Prune off affected stems below holes. Predatory nematodes. Spray Bt on stem surfaces.
Cabbage Worm	Cabbage, broccoli, cauliflower, kale, brussel sprouts, radishes, turnip.	Larvae of small white butterfly.	They rasp large holes in leaves.	Spray Bt on foliage.
Caterpillars (Parsleyworm, Tomato Hornworm, et. al.)	Trees, shrubs, vegetable flowers.	Worm larvae of moths, butterflies.	They chew holes in edges of foliage; may leave only veins.	Handpick. Spray Bt on foliage. Trichogramma wasps.
Chlorosis	Acid-loving trees and shrubs, such as holly, azalea, mountain laurel.	Foliage becomes yellowish, green veins stand out.	Disease may indicate iron not available in soil for plant.	Acidify soil by sprinkling garden sulfur over root zone.
Damping-off	Seedlings.	Black streaks on lower stem.	Young seedlings fall over and die.	Use sterile seed-starting medium; water from below.

TROUBLESHOOTING PESTS & DISEASES

Pest Name	Common Target	Appearance	Damage	Some Control Methods
Fall Webworms, Tent Caterpillars, Gypsy Moth, Caterpillars	Trees, especially oak; trees and shrubs at roadsides and other stressful sites.	Nests resemble webbed tents in twigs.	Caterpillars feed on tree foliage, chewing large holes, possibly skeletozing it.	Prune out nests. Poke open unreachable nests with a stick. Spray foliage with Bt when worms hatch and begin to eat. Parasitic wasps will prey on some.
Fungal Disease	Turfgrasses.	Blackish or gray coating on foliage, spots, circles of mold or fungi.	Gray or dark streaks on foliage. Tattered or matted blades. Dead patches.	Mow grass dry. Do not walk on wet or frosty grass. Water early in day. Spray fungicide on healthy grass.
Japanese Beetles	Roses, annuals, perennials, shrubs and trees, some vegetables.	Metallic green-and-copper beetle.	They leave ragged holes in buds and leaves; will skeletonize rose foliage.	Handpick. Spray neem or pyrethrum as directed.
Lacebugs	Broadleaf shrubs, such as azalea, rhododendron, pieris that are stressed by too much sun.	Tiny squarish dots with netted wings; leave specks of excrement under leaves.	They suck leaf juices until leaves are pale and stippled. Leaves become dry and bleached-out.	Move plant to shadier location. Spray with insecticidal soap.
Powdery Mildew	Roses, annuals, perennials, vegetables, houseplants.	Grayish blotching or coating on foliage.	Lower leaves dry, curl, and drop. Unsightly but not fatal to mature plants.	Improve air circulation. Spray garden (sulfur) fungicide on healthy and new foliage to prevent infection.
Scale	Trees, shrubs, perennials, houseplants, asparagus.	Raised waxy bumps on leaf undersides and stems.	Insects feed on juices of plant tissues; foliage looks pale.	Scrape off gently with fingernail. Spray horticultural oil to smother.
Slugs, Snails	Plants in moist acidic soil in shade (ex., hosta)	Soft-bodied, 1 to 4 inches long; leave a trail of mucous as they travel.	At night, they chew large ragged holes in leaves.	Handpick from under debris. Trap with yeast/beer bait. Sprinkle DE on soil around plants.
Spider Mites	Ivy, houseplants; foliage of stressed plants in dry conditions.	Resemble tiny spiders; they suck juices from foliage.	Pale stippling on leaves; fine webbing on stems. Leaves curl, turn brown.	Wash with forceful water spray; repeat. Insecticidal soap. Spray horticultural oil or miticide.

Pest Name	Common Target	Appearance	Damage	Some Control Methods
Thrips	Roses (especially red, white, yellow); citrus; dahlias; foxgloves; daylily; iris; gladioli; mums; privet.	Tiny yellowish-brown insects with narrow feathery wings; they burrow into buds, suck juices.	Flowers distorted, droop. Buds fail to open, dry out.	Clip off infested flowers. Use Merit insecticide. Encourage beneficial insects.
Whiteflies	Tomatoes and some other vegetables; houseplants.	Tiny white specks fly off when disturbed. Note black dots of excrement under foliage.	They suck juices from foliage, which turns pale. Not life-threatening to most mature healthy plants.	Insecticidal soap; green lacewing larvae.
White Grubs	Turfgrass roots.	Japanese beetle larvae; fat, curled worms with brown heads; they overwinter in soil.	Grass dies; sod lifts easily because roots are destroyed.	Starliings, skunks, moles prey on grubs. Cut grass tall to discourage beetles from laying eggs. Spray with predatory nematodes.

TROUBLESHOOTING PESTS AND DISEASES
- Maintain a diversity of plants to encourage natural controls by beneficials.
- Purchase pest- and disease-resistant plant varieties.
- Keep plants happy and as stress-free as possible with good care.
- Observe plants regularly to catch a problem at its earliest stage.
- Identify the problem accurately before starting control measures.
- Use the least-toxic control measure first.
- Read product labels carefully and follow instructions exactly.
- Treat only the particular plant or lawn area that exhibits the problem.
- After treating the problem, consider the underlying cause and address it.
- Store and dispose of all pesticides safely.

AUTHORS' CAUTION
From time to time in this book, we recommend the use of pesticides. The use of such pest controls, however, must remain the choice of each individual gardener. It may not always be necessary to use pesticides to control insects or diseases. A particular pest or disease may not be harmful to your particular plants.

If pest control does become a problem, you should consider the use of alternative means. These include the use of resistant varieties, the use of botanical and microbial insecticides or soaps, encouraging predators and parasites, mechanical means such as screening, hand picking, and improving horticultural practices.

If you do find it necessary to use traditional chemical pest controls, first consult your local authorities such as your extension office for correct pest identification and control recommendations. Once you have decided to use a specific pest control product, you must read and follow label directions carefully.

GLOSSARY

acclimate. To become accustomed to a different environment.

aerate (aeration). To introduce (introducing) oxygen into the soil to improve it. This is commonly done by digging into the soil in gardens or using equipment to pull up cores of soil and open holes in turf. Air in the soil supports the microbial life that makes it fertile.

alkaline soil. Soil that has a pH greater than 7.0. It lacks acidity, often because it has limestone in it. Certain plants prefer soil that is somewhat alkaline.

all-purpose fertilizer. Either powdered, liquid, or granular, it contains a balanced proportion of the three key nutrients—nitrogen (N), phosphorus (P), potassium K)—and it is suitable for maintenance nutrition for most plants. It is also called balanced or general-purpose fertilizer.

annual. A plant that lives its entire life in one season. It is genetically determined to germinate, grow, flower, set seed, and die the same year.

antitranspirant/antidesiccant. A product that reduces a plant's moisture loss through its foli-age (transpiration) by coating the foliage with a thin film.

arborist. A person who is trained to care for trees.

***Bacillus thuringiensis* (Bt).** A bacterium that kills larval worms or caterpillars by attacking the digestive system. Available as a dust or a powder to be mixed in water and sprayed on plant foliage when the caterpillars are actively eating.

balled-and-burlapped. Describes trees and shrub grown in the field whose roots are wrapped with protective burlap and twine when they are dug up to be sold or transplanted.

bare-root. Describes the packaging of certain plants sold without any soil around their roots. Often young shrubs and trees purchased through the mail arrive with their exposed roots covered with moist peat or sphagnum moss, sawdust, or similar material and wrapped in plastic.

barrier plant. A plant that has intimidating thorns or spines and is sited purposely to block foot traffic or other access to the home or yard.

basal. At the base, growing closest to its point of origin. Basal leaves are those that grow at the base of the stem, at the crown of the plant.

beneficial insects. Insects or their larvae that prey on pest organisms and their eggs. They may be flying insects such as ladybugs, parasitic wasps, praying mantids, and soldier bugs; or soil dwellers such as predatory nematodes, spiders, and ants.

biennial. A plant that is genetically programmed to grow over two seasons before setting seed and dying.

bolting. The tendency of a leafy plant such as lettuce or spinach to to to seed prematurely. Often in response to very hot weather, such a plant sends up tall stalks that bear flowers, then seeds; this usually affects the quality and flavor of the foliage crop.

bract. A petal-like modified leaf structure on a plant stem near its flower. Often it is more colorful and visible than the actual flower, as in dogwood.

broadcasting. Sowing seed by casting out handfuls or using a hand-held spreader over a prepared seedbed. This method is used to sow turfgrass or wildflower seed.

Bt. *See Bacillus thuringiensis.*

bud union. *See* graft.

canopy. The overhead branching area of a tree, usually referring to its extent, including foliage.

chlorosis. A nutritional deficiency in plants indicated by yellowed foliage with green veins. Most common in plants that require acidic soil (such as holly and azalea), it signals that they are not able to take up sufficient iron or other micronutrient from the soil.

climber. A plant that grows vertically by means of elongating stems. It may twist, cling, or use holdfasts to climb vertical surfaces or supports.

cold hardiness. The ability of a perennial plant to survive the winter cold in a particular area.

composite. A flower that is actually composed of many tiny flowers. Typically they are flat clusters of tiny, tight florets, sometimes surrounded by wider-petaled florets like a daisy or sunflower. Composite flowers are highly attractive to bees and beneficial insects.

compost. Organic matter that has undergone progressive decomposition by microbial and macrobial activity until it is reduced to a spongy, fluffy texture. Added to soil of any type, it improves its ability to hold air and water and to drain well.

corm. The swollen, energy-storing structure, analogous to a bulb, under the soil at the base of the stem of plants such as crocus or gladiolus.

GLOSSARY

county agent/extension agent. An employee of the state university who is trained to provide information and assistance to farmers and homeowners about agricultural and horticultural techniques, soil analysis, and pest control. Usually, there is an office in every county.

crown. The base of a plant at, or just beneath, the surface of the soil where its roots meet its stems. This term is also used sometimes to describe the branching area of a tree.

cultivar. A CULTIvated VARiety. A naturally occurring form of a plant that has been identified as special or superior and is specifically selected for propagation and production.

damping off. A fungal disease that targets young seedlings. Spores in the soil cause their stems to blacken and collapse. Using sterile potting medium helps prevent this problem.

deadhead. To remove faded flowerheads from plants to improve their appearance, abort seed production, and stimulate further flowering.

deciduous. The opposite of evergreen; describes trees and shrubs that lose their leaves in the fall.

desiccation. Drying out of foliage tissues, usually due to drought or wind.

diatomaceous earth (DE). Finely ground shells of a tiny algae. This natural pesticide is an effective barrier against slugs; when sprinkled on the soil around vulnerable plants, the sharp edges of the powder cut their bodies.

direct-sow. To sow seeds directly into the garden rather than starting them in small pots for later transplanting.

division. Splitting apart perennial plants to create several smaller rooted segments. Useful for controlling a plant's size and for acquiring more plants, it is also essential to the health and continued flowering of certain species.

dormancy (dormant). The period, usually winter, when perennial plants temporarily cease active growth, and rest. Some plants, such as spring-blooming bulbs, go dormant in the summer.

drip irrigation. An efficient water delivery system through special lines, or hoses, laid through planted beds. Water either soaks through the hoses or leaks through special emitters inserted in them to go directly to plant roots.

dripline. (a) The outer reaches of a tree's branching canopy where rainfall drips from branch tips. (b) A line, or hose, that is part of a drip irrigation system.

establishment. The time at which a newly planted tree, shrub, or flower begins to produce new growth, either foliage or stems. This is an indication that the roots have recovered from transplant shock and have begun to grow and spread.

evergreen. Perennial plants that do not lose their foliage annually with the onset of winter. Describes needled or broadleaf foliage that persists and continues to function on a plant through one or more winters, aging and dropping unobtrusively in varying cycles.

fertilizer. Any material that, when added to the soil, contributes one or more nutrients required by plants. Fertilizers called "complete" or "balanced" offer the major nutrients nitrogen, potassium, and phosphorus plus an assortment of minor nutrients.

foliar. Of or about foliage. Usually refers to the practice of spraying foliage, as in fertilizing or treating with insecticide. With a foliar spray, leaf tissues absorb liquid directly for much faster results, and the soil is not affected.

flexible liner. A waterproof barrier made from PVC, butyl, or other flexible material in a pond, bog, or pool dug into the ground.

floret. A tiny flower, usually one of many forming a cluster that comprises a single blossom such as a lilac or spider flower.

fungicide, garden. Any product that acts to prevent, control, or eradicate plant diseases caused by fungi.

germinate. To sprout; to enter a fertile seed's first stage of development.

girdling roots. Roots that circle around the root flare at the base of a tree or shrub rather than growing outward into the soil.

graft (union). The point on the stem of a sturdy-rooted woody plant to which a stem from a highly ornamental plant is joined. Roses are commonly grafted.

habitat. The natural environment of a plant. A plant removed from its habitat and brought into cultivation in a residential landscape does best when the new conditions are similar to those of its native habitat.

handpick. To eliminate pest insects or slugs and caterpillars by removing them from plant foliage or knocking them into a plastic bag or jar of soapy water to kill them.

hardening-off. The process of gradually acclimating indoor plants or seedlings raised indoors to outdoor weather conditions.

hardiness. *See* cold hardiness.

hardscape. The permanent, structural, nonplant part of a landscape such as walls, sheds, pools, patios, arbors, and walkways.

herbaceous. Describes plants that have fleshy or soft stems that die back with frost; the opposite of woody.

herbicide. Any product or chemical agent that kills plants. Some act on foliage and stem tissues, some act on seeds.

hills. Raised mounds of soil created for planting seeds of certain crops such as corn or squash. There are several seeds in each hill.

GLOSSARY

hybrid. A plant that is the result of either intentional or natural cross-pollination between two or more plants of the same species or genus. This pedigree is expressed by the multiplication symbol in between the two words in its botanical (scientific) name.

insecticide. Any product, compound, or garden aid formulated specifically to kill insects.

intensive planting. The practice of planting food crops closer together than recommended to utilize garden space most efficiently and maximize production. This technique is most successful in raised beds where the soil is exceptionally fertile and aerated.

irrigation. See drip irrigation.

larva(e). An insect in its immature stage, after it hatches from an egg. Typically a worm or caterpillar form of a butterfly, moth, or beetle, larvae are voraciously hungry; this is the stage at which insects are most destructive to plants.

lime. Limestone processed as granules, pellets, or powder for use in adding calcium to soils. Spread on lawns and growing beds, it raises the pH of the soil (reduces its acidity) and provides calcium to plants. Dolomite limestone also contributes magnesium.

liner, pond. Either a molded fiberglass form or a flexible butyl or poly fabric that creates an artificial pond for the purpose of water gardening.

low water demand. Describes the moisture needs of plants that tolerate dry soil for varying periods of time. Typically they have succulent, hairy, or silvery-gray foliage and tuberous or taproots. Xeriscape plants have low water demand.

melting out. The tendency of certain plants to die out in midseason; they collapse, wither, or rot for no apparent reason.

mulch. A layer of material over bare soil that protects the soil from erosion and compaction by rain, and also discourages weeds. It may be inorganic (gravel, fabric) or organic (wood chips, bark, pine needles, chopped leaves).

native. (indigenous.) Native plants are those determined to have been growing in their wild habitat in a particular region or state before the arrival of European settlers.

naturalize. (a) To plant seeds, bulbs, or plants in a random, informal pattern as they would appear in their natural habitat. (b) The tendency of some non-native plants to adapt to and spread throughout their adopted habitats.

nectar. The sweet fluid produced by glands on flowers that attracts pollinators such as hummingbirds and honeybees, for whom the fluid is a source of energy.

organic material, matter. Any material or debris that is derived from plants. Carbon-based material that is capable of undergoing decomposition and decay.

peat moss. Organic matter from peat sedges (United States) or sphagnum mosses (Canada), often used to improve soil texture. The acidity of sphagnum peat moss makes it ideal for boosting or maintaining soil acidity while also improving its drainage.

perennial. A flowering plant that lives over three or more seasons. Many die back with frost, but their roots survive the winter and generate new shoots in spring.

pesticide. Any product, compound, or device that kills pest insects, disease pathogens, pest animals, or weeds.

pH. A measurement of the relative acidity (low pH) or alkalinity (high pH) of soil or water based on a scale of 1 to 14, with 7 being neutral. Individual plants require soil within a certain pH range in order for nutrients to dissolve in moisture and become available to plant roots.

pinch. To remove tender stems and/or leaves by pressing them between thumb and forefinger. This is a pruning technique that is used to encourage branching, compactness, and flowering in plants or to remove aphids clustered at growing tips.

photosynthesis. The process by which plants, collecting energy from the sun by means of the chlorophyll in their foliage, transform carbon dioxide in the air and water from the soil into carbohydrates that fuel their growth.

pollen. The yellow, powdery grains in the center of a flower. A plant's male sex cells, they are transferred to the female plant parts by means of wind, insects or animal pollinators, to fertilize them and create seeds.

potbound. See rootbound.

preemergent. Acting prior to the germination of a seed. A product, compound, or chemical that inhibits the sprouting of a fertile seed (as in pre-emergent herbicide).

preformed liner. A mold available in many sizes and shapes for setting into the ground to make a water garden pond; usually made of molded fiberglass or a similar material.

reversion. The appearance on a cultivar of a tree or shrub of one or more branches with foliage that is characteristic of the species.

rhizome. A swollen energy-storing stem structure, similar to a bulb, that lies horizontally in the soil, with roots emerging from its lower surface and growth shoots from a growing point at or near its tip (as in bearded iris).

rootbound (or potbound). The condition of a plant that has been confined to a container too long, its roots having been forced to wrap around themselves and even swell out of the container. Successful transplanting or repotting requires untangling and trimming away some of the matted roots.

root flare. The transition at the base of a tree trunk where bark and stem tissue begin to differentiate and roots form. This area should not be covered with soil when planting a tree.

GLOSSARY

rootstock. *See* understock.

root zone. The area that the roots of a given plant currently occupy or can be expected to spread to when mature. Water, fertilizer, and mulch are most effectively applied to the soil surface over the root zone.

scion. The ornamental, desirable part of a grafted plant. Usually refers to a cutting, shoot, or bud that is to be grafted onto the understock, which supplies the root system.

self-seeding. Describes the tendency of some plants to sow their seeds freely around the yard. This creates many seedlings the following season, which may or may not be welcome.

shearing. The pruning technique whereby plant stems and branches are cut uniformly with long-bladed pruning shears (hedge shears) or powered hedge trimmers. Used in creating and maintaining hedges and topiary.

slow-acting fertilizer. Fertilizer that is water-insoluble and therefore releases its nutrients gradually as a function of soil temperature, moisture, and related microbial activity. Typically granular, it may be either naturally organic or synthetically organic.

sod. Pieces of soil in which turfgrass plants are already growing.

soil test. Chemical analysis of soil to determine its fertility, pH, and nutrients. This is usually done by private laboratories or state university facilities. Less sophisticated tests can be done by gardeners using inexpensive kits available at garden centers.

sooty mold. A gray or black fungus on the foliage of plants infested with pest insects. It is fostered by the sticky, sweet juices that leak from plant tissues as insects suck on them. Its presence signals that a plant has an insect problem.

succession planting. The practice of promptly replacing food crops that have passed peak production with new transplants of another crop. Most effective in raised beds where the soil is rich enough to support several crops over a season, it maximizes production in a limited space.

sucker. A new growing shoot. Underground plant roots produce suckers to form new stems and spread by means of these suckering roots to form large plantings, or colonies. Some plants produce root suckers or branch suckers as a result of pruning or wounding. Some plants such as crabapples produce crown suckers that should be removed when noticed.

sulfur. An element and nutrient that is useful in the garden. Sprinkled on the soil, it lowers the pH to make it more acid. Mixed with water, it is used as a fungicide.

thinning. The process of removing selected sprouts from a crowded row of newly germinated seedlings to create sufficient space for the remaining ones to grow and mature.

transplant. A young plant that is mature enough to be planted outdoors in a garden bed or decorative container.

true leaves. The second set of leaves that appear on a young seedling. They resemble the leaves of the species.

tuber. A type of underground storage structure in a plant stem, analogous to a bulb. It generates roots below and stems aboveground (examples: dahlias, taro, potatoes).

understock (also rootstock). The plant that provides a sturdy root system onto which a desirable species is grafted to create an ornamental plant (examples: hybrid tea rose, cherry tree).

variegated. Having various colors or color patterns. Usually refers to plant foliage that is streaked, edged, blotched, or mottled with a contrasting color, often green with cream or white.

water sprout (also sucker). A tender branch shoot growing vertically from a tree limb. While some trees tend to produce water sprouts routinely, it is often a sign of tree stress.

white grubs. Fat, off-white, wormlike larvae of Japanese beetles or other species. They reside in the soil and feed on plant (especially grass) roots until summer, when they emerge as beetles to feed on plant foliage.

wings. (a) The corky tissue that forms edges along the twigs of some woody plants such as winged euonymus. (b) The flat, dried extensions of tissue on some seeds, such as maple, that catch the wind and aid seed dissemination.

witches' broom. A mass of small sprouts that bristle from a tree or shrub branch bearing otherwise normal-sized leaves and twigs. Often a response to an injury or infection of some sort, witches' brooms may provide a source for the propagation of new and unusual versions of a species.

xeriscape. Describes plants that tolerate dry soil for varying periods of time. *See* low water demand.

BIBLIOGRAPHY

American Horticultural Society. *A-Z Encyclopedia of Garden Plants*. Ed. Christopher Brickell. New York: Dorling Kindersley, 1997.

Bagust, Harold. *The Gardener's Dictionary of Horticultural Terms*. Strand, London: Cassell Publishers, 1992.

Ball, Jeffrey N. and Liz Ball. *Smart Yard: 60 Minute Lawn Care*. Golden, CO: Fulcrum Publishing, 1994.

Ball, Jeffrey N. *The 60 Minute Vegetable Garden*. New York: Macmillan, 1985.

Ball, Jeffrey N. with Liz Ball. *Yardening*. New York: Macmillan, 1991.

Barash, Cathy Wilkinson. *Edible Flowers from Garden to Palate*. Golden, CO: Fulcrum, 1993.

——. *Evening Gardens*. Shelburne, VT: Chapters Publishing, 1993.

Brady, Nyle C., Ray R. Weil. *Elements of the Nature and Properties of Soils*. Upper Saddle River, NJ: Prentice-Hall, 2000.

Coggiatti, Selvio. *Simon and Schuster's Guide to Roses*. New York: Simon & Schuster, 1986.

Cresson, Charles O. *Charles Cresson on the American Flower Garden*. New York: Prentice Hall, 1993.

Darke, Rick. *The Color Encyclopedia of Ornamental Grasses*. Portland, OR: Timber Press, 1999.

Dennis, John V. and Mathew Tekulsky. *How to Attract Hummingbirds and Butterflies*. San Ramon, CA: Ortho Books, 1991.

Dirr, Michael A. *Dirr's Hardy Trees and Shrubs*. Portland, OR: Timber Press, 1997.

Dirr, Michael A. *A Manual of Woody Landscape Plants*. Champaign, IL: Stipes Publishing, 1998.

DiSabato-Aust, Tracy. *The Well-Tended Perennial Garden*. Portland, OR: Timber Press, 1998.

Greenlee, John. *The Encyclopedia of Ornamental Grasses*. New York: Michael Friedman Publishing Group, 1992.

Fizzell, James A. *Month-by-Month Gardening in Michigan*. Franklin, TN: Cool Springs Press, 1999.

Hart, Ronda Massingham. *Deer-Proofing Your Yard and Garden*. Pownal, VT: Storey Communications, 1997.

Hedrick, U. P. *A History of Horticulture in America to 1860*. Portland, OR: Timber Press, 1988.

Heriteau, Jacqueline and Charles Thomas. *Water Gardens*. New York: Houghton-Mifflin, 1994.

Herwig, Rob. *Growing Beautiful Houseplants*. New York: Facts on File, 1987.

Janick, Jules. *Horticultural Science*. Fourth Edition. New York: W.H. Freeman and Company. 1986.

Johnson, Warren T., Howard H. Lyon. *Insects That Feed on Trees and Shrubs*. Ithaca, NY: Cornell University Press, 1991.

Lammers, Susan M. *All About Houseplants*. California: Ortho Books, 1982.

McKeon, Judith C. *The Encyclopedia of Roses*. Michael Friedman Publishing Group, Inc., Emmaus, PA: Rodale Press, 1995.

M'Mahon, Bernard. *The American Gardener's Calendar*, 11th edition. Philadelphia: J.P. Lippincott and Company, 1857.

Polomski, Bob. *Month-by-Month Gardening in the Carolinas*. Franklin, TN: Cool Springs Press, 2000.

Ray, Richard and Michael MacCaskey. *Roses: How to Select, Grow, and Enjoy*. Horticultural Publishing Company, Inc. Tucson, AZ: H.P. Books, Inc., 1985.

Shaudys, Phyllis. *The Pleasure of Herbs*. Pownel, VT: Storey Communications, 1986.

Smith, Edward C. *Vegetable Gardener's Bible*. Pownel, VT: Storey Communications, 2000.

Solit, Karen with Jim Solit. *Keeping Your Gift Plants Thriving: A Complete Guide to Plant Survival*. Pownel, VT: Storey Communications, 1985.

Still, Steven M. *Manual of Herbaceous Ornamental Plants*. Fourth Edition. Champaign, Illinois: Stipes Publishing Company. 1994.

Sunset editors. *How to Grow Herbs*. Menlo Park, CA: Sunset Books, 1984.

Tomlinson, Timothy R. and Barbara Klaczynska. *Paradise Presented*. Philadelphia: The Morris Arboretum of the University of Pennsylvania. 1996.

Uva, Richard H., Joseph C. Neal, Joseph M. DiTomaso. *Weeds of the Northeast*. Ithaca, NY: Cornell University Press, 1997.

PLANT INDEX

PLANT INDEX

PLANT INDEX

PLANT INDEX

PLANT INDEX

PLANT INDEX

PLANT INDEX

MEET DENNY McKEOWN & THOMAS L. SMITH

Denny McKeown is a respected, popular, and highly regarded gardening expert who has been in the nursery business for more than 40 years, many of them spent as an executive with Natorp's. In the early 1990s, McKeown founded the Bloomin' Garden Centre, a year-round retail garden business that he operates with his son, Chris. Another business, Denny McKeown Landscape, is a full-service landscape design company featuring design and installation for residential and commercial properties.

McKeown reaches gardeners via radio, television, and print. He is the long-time host of the popular radio call-in program, "The Denny McKeown Gardening Show," heard across Ohio on WGRR-FM every Saturday, which is also broadcast on WHOK 95.5 in Columbus. McKeown also appears regularly on the locally broadcast Scripps-Howard WCPO-TV in Cincinnati doing garden vignettes on the news.

In addition, McKeown authored *The Gardening Book for Ohio* (original and revised editions), and the original edition of *Month-by-Month Gardening in Ohio*, all for Cool Springs Press. McKeown has received numerous awards and honors. The author served as the President of The Garden Centers of America and was awarded its highest honor, the Jack Schneider Award. The American Nursery and Landscape Association presented McKeown with the Garden Communicator Award, which is given to the person who has done the most to promote gardening and planting across America.

McKeown lives in Cincinnati with his wife, Pat, and where he enjoys his three children—Molly, Christopher, and Jenny—and grandchildren.

Thomas L. Smith is Executive Vice President of Spring Grove Cemetery and Arboretum, which he joined in 1972. Smith is active in many professional organizations in the Cincinnati community, including a position on the Civic Garden Center of Greater Cincinnati Board of Directors. For more than twenty years, Smith has volunteered as an advisor to the Ohio State Cooperative Extension Service. Currently, Smith is a member of the Greater Cincinnati Professional Grounds Management Society, the Ohio Forestry Association, and The Ohio Nursery and Landscape Association, Inc.

Since 1973, Smith has taught horticulture courses at the University of Cincinnati, Northern Kentucky University, and Cincinnati State Technical and Community College.

Smith holds a Masters degree from Yale University in Forest Science, and a Bachelor of Science in Botany from the University of Cincinnati.

In addition to many other honors, Smith was awarded the National Professional Grounds Management Society's highest honor, the Gold Medal Award, in 1999. He is listed in the "Who's Who in Frontier Science and Technology," with specialties in plant growth and urban forest resource management. Smith lives in Cincinnati with his wife, Sue. Their three children—David, Lisa and Kathleen—are raising their families in Cincinnati, Lexington, and Portland.

ENJOY THESE OTHER HELPFUL BOOKS FROM COOL SPRINGS PRESS

Cool Springs Press is devoted to state and regional gardening and offers a selection of books to help you enjoy gardening and bird watching where you live. Choose Cool Springs Press books with confidence.

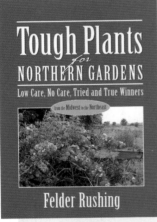

Tough Plants for Northern Gardens
ISBN# 1-59186-063-6 • $24.99

The Gardening Book for Ohio
ISBN# 1-59186-047-4 • $24.99

Can't Miss Water Gardening for the Midwest
ISBN# 1-59186-154-3 • $18.99

Ohio Bird Watching
ISBN# 1-59186-168-3 • $16.99

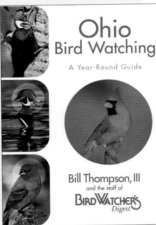

COOL SPRINGS PRESS
A Division of Thomas Nelson Publishers
Since 1798

www.coolspringspress.net

See your garden center, bookseller, or home improvement center for these Cool Springs Press titles. Also, be sure to visit www.coolspringspress.net for more great titles from Cool Springs Press.